Natural

Metaphor

Natural

Metaphor

The Intelligent Evolution of Consciousness

Karen Seymour

Copyright © 2018 Karen Seymour

All rights reserved.

9781728629063

Table of Contents

Introduction..1

1. The Primacy of Metaphor......................................19

2. Animal Intelligence..55

3. Intelligent Evolution..98

4. Coming to Life...133

5. Chaotic Evolution...167

6. Interface...204

7. Universal Origins...236

8. The Conscious Cornerstone.................................271

9. The Journey of Consciousness.............................303

10. The Road to Crucifixion.......................................342

11. Unfolding Evolution...375

    End Notes..418

    Bibliography..465

Introduction

"God of love, show us our place in this world,
as channels of your love
for all the creatures of this earth,
for not one of them is forgotten in your sight."
—Pope Francis

When life arose 3.5 billion years ago on the face of the young Earth, the words that would one day enable sentient minds to describe that momentous awakening were inconceivably remote from the basic biological processes that would eventually support them. Over the intervening ages, evolution patiently pursued its vivifying craft without any ostensible goal, performing its discriminating and diversifying ministrations on life's formal offerings through the blind and insensate forces of natural selection. Reprising themselves at progressively higher levels of organization, the processes that coated the earth in microbial biofilms adapted to the newfound complexities, challenges, and opportunities of multicellularity, which represented a whole new landscape of potential for life to mine and explore. Creatively engaging with environmentally imposed limitations, each of the multitudinous forms that vied in its turn for a place in the genetic scripts of biological history, did so from a subjective viewpoint that enabled niches to be established and bequeathed to posterity. Each organizational ascent and diversifying experiment heralded a radiation into new ecological possibilities in which life was free to reinvent itself again and again.

Throughout its vast, ongoing history of formal permutations, life has simultaneously unfolded a corresponding diversity of minds. Ranging from the relative rudiments embodied in life's first representatives to the elaborate heights of human genius, cognitive ability shows the same heterogeneous tendency as does its bodily corollary. Variously shading inner perceptual worlds, a wide range of sensory and cognitive adaptations tailor organisms to their environments, allowing the expansion and creation of new niches as burgeoning intelligence devises new interactional possibilities within its surroundings. As a result, an astounding array and degree of cognitive specializations and refinements are represented among animals, such as the memories of seed-caching birds, with their ability to retain tens of thousands of cache sites every winter; or the cultivation of aesthetics in some species like bower birds; or the sophisticated use of tools among too many species to enumerate; or highly refined systems of communication in a number of animal families, including rodents, canids, corvids, psittacines, cetaceans, and primates, among others. All of these feats of semantic specialization are significant factors in shaping social structures, local ecologies, and the branching trajectories of evolution itself. However, one particular cognitive specialization has proven uniquely transformative, not only to the semantic landscape, but the entire earth.

When cognition established a new frontier of potential within the human lineage, evolution was loosed into an entirely novel niche, ripe for its diversifying reach: a realm wherein logical objects supersede biological ones as higher-level loci of selection. The most consequential product of evolution's incursion into the cognitive domain was language. With its ability to link minds into structured, meaning-mediated correlations, language accesses a higher conceptual level than is available to the bodily bound purview of its animal precursors, whose referents tend to be immediate stimuli. Through the abstracting power of language, humankind has distinguished itself from its animal origins, using words to invoke images and understanding in other minds, even when referring to conditions not immediately observable or states not currently being experienced.

As profound a break as language represents for humans from their organic roots, it is from those very roots that the capacity for language arose. Although the fresh field of evolutionary cultivation was cognitive, it retained strong connections to its somatic origins by not only by acceding to the biological imperatives of its bodily bound carriers, but also by operating according to the same basic principles of evolution at this higher level of expression. With the pillars of its abstruse structure deeply embedded in the billions of years of evolution that brought symbol-mediated intelligibility to minds capable of wielding its higher-order levels of operation, language models its tenets of construction on the very principles that actively facilitated its unfoldment.

Systems

While language is singular in its far-reaching effects, it falls under a category of description that is essentially universal in its coverage; that of systems. Pioneered by biologist Ludwig von Bertalanffy, systems theory provided such a robust general description of the structure, inner dynamics, and development of systems in relation to their environments that it was quickly adapted to many fields, including mathematics, psychology, and social networks. Many physical and biological applications of systems theory are grounded in Iliya Prigogine's pivotal work on thermodynamically open, dissipative systems that function far from equilibrium, which became the basis for the study of self-organization. One of the defining features of a self-organizing system is that it generates emergent properties: novel arrangements and faculties that arise at a particular threshold of criticality, and which are wholly unpredictable based only on an analysis of their constituent components. Such a model of spontaneous emergence is implicative of evolution's pattern, which, although advanced contiguously through unbroken successions of generations, at the same time proceeds leap by critical leap in proffering novelty, leaving untraceable gaps in its nonlinear path. With self-organization understood as an expedient means of dissipating the entropy that naturally accrues during any interactions between entities, as demanded by the second law of thermodynamics, systems-based evolutionary models proliferated, ranging from theories of autogenic particles as the raw materials for a self-creating universe (Paul La Violette), to membrane-bound, autopoetic entities as the individualized cornerstones of the self-driven process of life (Francisco Varela and Humberto Maturana) upon a self-regulating planet (James Lovelock), to the entire self-unfolding universe (Erich Jantsch and Ervin Laszlo, among many others).

As one exemplar of the more general phenomenon of systems, language preserves the pattern of emergence which avails all systems, and evolution, to unpredictable innovation. An assemblage of words can convey a meaning that is not predictable from their mere sum, but arises through their arrangement, or their reference to different concepts or larger systems of ideas. This hierarchical structure, which concentrates so much referential power into a disproportionately small set of words, is described by linguist Roman Jakobson, and perfectly illustrates the evolution of complex systems from simpler, lower-level components wherein each increase to a new level of integration releases degrees of freedom from lower levels to the leading edge of the system. Says Jakobson,

"In the combination of distinctive features into phonemes, the freedom of the speaker is zero: the code has already established all the possibilities which may be utilized in the given language. Freedom to combine phonemes into words is circumscribed; it is limited to the marginal situation of word coinage. Informing sentences with words, the speaker is less constrained. And finally, in the combination of sentences into utterances, the action of compulsory syntactical rules ceases, and the freedom of any individual speaker to create novel contexts increases substantially."[i]

Building into its signature arrangement of a nested hierarchy that amplifies lower levels of construction into a higher level of description and capacity, complexity lends itself not only to internal diversity among the subsystems that comprise it, but also to the progressive addition of higher levels of emergence. In its linguistic aspect, complexity grows through the arrangement of letters into words, words into phrases, and phrases into sentences. When formed into paragraphs that can be built upon each other, any ceiling on the potential for expression is essentially eliminated.

Amplifying and modifying various components of non-linguistic reference systems to derive its distinctive capabilities, language is an extension of prior evolutionary attainments that opens its users to new levels of autonomy in the semantic realm. In the critical leap from indication to explication is a discontinuity, free of clear, linear, traceable gradations between a fully lingual lexicon and its less derived precursors. This leap is a turning point between the ecologies and social orders established among animals, and the societies, civilizations, and creative and rational endeavors of humanity. As axes around which evolution revolves to vault itself into new domains, the discontinuities that break evolution's succession into discreet and nonlinear patterns provide a subtle clue as to the nature of the linkage between predecessor and successor.

Turning Points

Like the leading edge of any complex system, language is only relatively uncoupled from its formative antecedents. Beneath the discontinuous turning point between foundational and emergent levels is a subtle continuity, rooted in the deep homology between begetting dynamics and their higher-order arrangement with its innovative properties. Because it is not superficially apparent, the relational congruence between establishment and emergence is partially concealed by our own rationally based prejudices against what is not directly traceable to an observable cause. Fostered by a philosophical tradition that vociferously rejects what it deems to be non-literal, this prejudice disdainfully dismisses the "tropes" that appear throughout language, particularly metaphors and metonyms, along with their various derivatives, as mere figures of speech. However, these non-literal devices do more than lend colorful flourishes to language—they actually construct it: "From the metonymic branch of linguistic structure arises contiguity, while from the metaphorical branch arises similarity."[ii] Both principles function concurrently to structure language, manifesting in relation to each other to varying degrees: "The development of a discourse may take place along two different semantic lines: one topic may lead to another either through their similarity or through their contiguity...In normal verbal behavior both processes are continually operative."[iii]

Reflecting respectively the properties of contiguity and similarity, the metonymic and metaphorical structural primitives of language are reflections of the deeper, more general trends that guide evolution as principles. In accord with the metonymic characteristic of contiguity, the unbroken succession of generations since life's advent unfurls continuously, like a single tree with countless stems and branches. At the same time, the principle of similarity operates implicitly throughout all evolutionary changes in form and capacity, which spread horizontally to saturate every conceivable niche with diversity, and vertically to secure new niche spaces through higher-level complexity. Proceeding through saltatory leaps, evolution recapitulates the same general organizational and ecological themes at new levels of complexity and autonomy as organisms couple into relational systems based on some level of complementarity that can either underlie or arise from their interactions, or both. The regularity that emerges beneath the guise of diversity led Ludwig Boltzmann to wonderingly notice, "It seemed that nature had built the most various things on exactly the same pattern."[iv]

In language, the feature that arises from the metaphor-affiliated principle of similarity is "poeticity," which "is present when the word is felt as a word and not a mere representation of the object being named or an outburst of emotion, when words and their composition, their meaning, their external and inner form, acquire a weight and value of their own instead of referring indifferently to reality."[v] Appropriately, Aldous Huxley likened "living nature" not to "a mechanism but a poem whose foundations are laid in strict, safe mechanistic principles, but whose superstructure is manifestation of highest, subtlest art."[vi] Like a trope, which indicates a turn, every iteration of biological diversity is a turning point which redirects flows of energy, material, and information. At the same time, each expression of the selfsame phenomenon of manifestation is bound to all others by a deep principle of similarity that underlies the tremendous outward variances in complexity, capacity, and form.

Living Metaphors

Like language, life is a complex and not fully definable amalgamation of structure and information. From lowly to spectacular, the self-organized systems that animate the face of the planet are, in a sense, metaphors themselves, representing a point of interchange between the two distinct domains of form and meaning that bind together in a living compromise. Like the syntax that arranges words into cogent sentences, highly organized structure supports the processes and specializations of life. It is also the conduit of the subjective, meaningful experiences and activities that transpire within its constraining, enabling frame. It is according to meaning that any living organism orders its development and, over evolutionary time, its phylogenetic legacy.

In addition to foreshadowing the broad constitutive themes of language construction throughout its contiguous and self-similar evolution, life also predicts the more localized features of sentence construction in its individualized forms. "The constituents of any message are necessarily linked with the code by an internal relation and with the message by an external relation," says Jakobson.[vii] Just as the internal logic of grammar which gives a sentence its structure collaborates with an external, objective reference to confer meaning to a statement, every living agent is a coherent agreement of interactive internal subsystems, while at the same time intimately connected to its surroundings through the adaptations that mold it into a niche and allow it to flourish under a certain range of conditions.

In meeting the demands of an ever-shifting environment, the organism is pushed toward optimizing its autonomy, which according

Erich Jantsch, "means openness to novelty; it does not suspend relations with environment, but accentuates them."[viii] As an emergent product of extrinsic reference coupled to internal coherence, autonomy draws the agent's scope of awareness outward, allowing organismal parameters to align with environmental ones and so incorporate individual agents into a larger, many-tiered ecology of relations in which, according to Jantsch, "wholeness…interacts autonomously with other wholeness."[ix] This ecology depends crucially not only on the tendency of organisms to interact with each other and the environment in patterned, predictable ways, but also to perceive these regularities and create systems of meaning around them. Meaning shared among interacting agents acts like the connective fibers of an internal logic that correlates them into a higher-level system.

The oppositional tension between the twin poles of internal and external reference resolves semantically within the individual when meaning is ascertained and responded to. Indexing its perceptual appraisal of the environment to an internal frame of reference, the organism infers conditions about its external environment through the experiential filters of sensation and perception. Such a mode of interpretation, which translates an external stimulus in terms of an embodied source domain, is essentially metaphorical. Binding all entities with a universal thread of similarity, the condition of embodiment is the foundation of individuated experience. Because the existence of a body in any form is coeval with subjective experience of it, Husserl could make the broad claim that, "The study of subjectivity is unconditionally required for a full clarification of the sense and structure of physical nature."[x]

Grounded in the physical and perceptual constraints that accompany a situated perspective, the most primary metaphors arise from the most primary experience: that of having a body with a boundary, an orientation, and a distinctive form of movement. This utterly basic ontological condition led George Lakoff and Mark Johnson to the conclusion that "no metaphor can ever be comprehended or adequately represented independently of its experiential basis."[xi] Indelibly tied to the sensorimotor immediacy of somatic experience, metaphorical understanding structures not only language, but every cognitive and conceptual edifice enabled by language. With the ability of agents to interact with their worlds metaphorically conditioned— rendering a version of the world based on similarity without conveying its totality— all organisms, including humans, are compelled to rely on perceptual "devices for understanding [that] have little to do with objective reality."[xii] The metaphorical nature of embodied cognition is a trope: a turning point and gateway between experiential sensation and intelligible expression.

One of the most powerful capacities that metaphor has imbued language with is the ability to describe itself. The referential terms utilized in a language can be turned inward to describe its own properties. "Similarity in meaning connects the symbols of a metalanguage with the symbols of the language referred to. Similarity connects a metaphorical term for which it is substituted."[xiii] In the escalating hierarchy of increasing degrees of freedom, the recursive twist of self-reference that allows a language to describe itself also allows, at a higher level, the human agents who utilize that language to describe themselves. At its global level of organization, the whole of living nature which supports the evolution of its cognitive leading edge in humanity can coil around to see and perceive itself through individualized and collective human agency.

Epistemology and Signs

The structures of meaning which mediate organisms' interactions with their environments fall roughly under the category of "conceptions," insofar as they fulfill the role of that term as described by philosopher Charles Sanders Peirce: "The function of conceptions is to reduce manifold of sensuous impressions to unity." The necessity of such an aid, he contends, "consists in the impossibility of reducing the content of consciousness to unity without the introduction of [conception]." He further describes a "gradation among those conceptions which are universal. For one such conception may unite the manifold of sense and yet another may be required to unite the conception and the manifold to which it applied; and so on."[xiv] By applying a specialized semantic framework to the stimulus it receives from the environment, an organism efficiently gleans from a world that is rife with potential information only the aspects most relevant to promoting its own interests of survival and fitness. In the organism's purposeful response to that information, the manifolds of sensation and action converge on the non-physical, subjective locus of meaning, which is an intelligent confluence of qualitative experience and interpretation.

Because all subjective understanding of the world is metaphorically and interpretively constructed, the epistemic structures which grow out of these inferential foundations are malleable to the evolutionary—and to various degrees, the individual—histories of their hosts. Born of necessity, crafted by meaningful experiences, and sustained through some form of memory, epistemic framework through which an organism encounters its environment prescribes its likely range of interactions within that context. While curbing the organism's scope of expressive potential, these semantic boundaries are at the same time an opening that allows the individual to expand beyond its own physical parameters and actively engage with its world. "To be a knower," contends William Wallace, "an organism must be able to, or have the power to, transcend the distinction between itself and another entity in the natural world and so become one in the natural world."[xv] Such a unifying power of transcendence is expressed when a self-organizing system "reaches beyond the boundaries of its identity" to become creative, according to Jantsch[xvi]—or rather, expresses the creativity that is a spontaneous byproduct of the alchemical merger between subjective, experiential feeling and the reflective prism of form through which it manifests. By providing a guiding track to direct the expression of the organism's motivations, perceptions, and behaviors, even the most implicit epistemology[1] is an internally sourced force of causal efficiency which,

---

[1] Epistemology is here given broadened scope that includes any form of subjective knowledge that is about something and thereby compels the subject to make some sort of attribution to an object. That even rudimentary epistemology can exist at the very foundations of knowledge creation is suggested by the assertion of Maxine Sheets-Johnstone (1993, p 371), that "to the degree an animal has to learn to move itself, it is self-aware." (Italics omitted).

through the actions it impels its host to, has a measurable and even predictable impact on the surrounding environment.

In addition to its causal functionality, epistemology also serves in a declarative role by guiding perceptions and behaviors in ways that reflect their origins within the intrinsic semantic spaces of the agents that enact them. In their declarative roles, epistemologies reveal their patterns through semiosis; "the semiotic," or sign processes as described by Peirce. The semiotic hierarchy scales from the most basic level of iconic resemblance, to the more indirect indexical indication, to the open-ended symbol, which augers an elaborate system of signification. Like any system, the expressive degrees of freedom from lower levels escalate with every hierarchic advance of semiotic complexity, until a whole network of self-supported relationships springs up at the symbol level. Whereas icon, founded in similarity, draws from the metaphorical pole of construction, index is based on contiguity; the metonymic branch of the conceptual binary. Emerging from the complex interactions of both, symbol is "imputed" (Peirce) and "conventional" (Jakobson); it is constructed out of associations, held in place by habits that highlight certain associations over others, and is therefore a complex and emergent composite of structural primitives at a higher level of complexity, conveying properties that are beyond the reach of the iconic and indexical components that comprise it. Since symbol is less an object than an ordering principle—it "denotes a kind of thing," but "it is itself a kind and not a single thing"—it is a "general rule" that sets the parameters of an interpretive system. [xvii] With every sign amenable to translation into "an infinite series of other signs" which share some degree of equivalence, drawing as they do from the structural principle of similarity, there is always a discontinuity, an incomplete overlap between any given sign and its referent. Rather than being a liability, this incompleteness is a source of efficacy within a semiotic system, as attested to by Jakobson, "Without contradiction [between sign and object] there is no mobility of concepts, no mobility of signs, and the relationship between concept and sign becomes automatized. Activity comes to a halt, and the awareness of reality dies out."[xviii]

Conscious Systems

Living agents are amenable to arrangement into systems of complexity because of their intrinsically sourced ability to be affected not only physically but semantically; in terms of meaning. Coming into being only when made presentable to some form of awareness with the capacity to interpret it as such, information enacts the most indescribable translation in nature as it transmutes between its physical manifestations of symbol and activity, and its mental manifestation as meaning, whose apprehension is the function of consciousness. Founded on subjective awareness, "all real unities are 'unities of sense,'" according to Husserl. "Unities of sense presuppose a sense-bestowing consciousness which, for its part, exists absolutely and not by virtue of another sense-bestowal."[xix] He adds, "The constituted unity is inseparable from the original constitution itself."[xx]

Growing out of the fundamental qualitative capacity that supports the unfoldment of sign processes, epistemology expands over the course of evolution in referential depth and scope until it ripens into human rationality. Like the nested hierarchies through which physical and dynamical complexity accrue from simplicity, sematic systems likewise grow into resplendence from elementary rudiments, with unpredictable properties emerging at higher levels of integration and degrees of freedom. However novel its form and unpredictable its effects, though, higher-level emergence is founded on and sustained by the critical merger of many semi-autonomous lower levels. In order to emerge in highly elaborated forms, then, consciousness and sentience must be present at the very lowest, founding levels of natural hierarchies. Harboring some degree of the foundational "sense-bestowing consciousness," every "constituted unity" of situated, form-clad consciousness engages to some extent—however hidden from our view—the properties of mind. Teilhard de Chardin explains, "Nothing could ever burst forth as final across the different thresholds successively traversed by evolution which has not already existed in an obscure and primordial way."[xxi]

Through a sprawling evolutionary meander that tends toward increasing explicit consciousness and volition, the singular foundation of all awareness radiates into a diversity of forms and capacities that are interconnected through systems of "shared meanings" (Peirce). Guided by the active expression of consciousness, which is intelligence, complex, ecological systems nucleate around semantic granules or order. According to Jantsch, "It is mind, rather than dynamic causal efficiency that reaches beyond the bounds of autopoeitic structure to embrace interactions with other systems and generally the environment."[xxii] And Thomas Nagel reasons, "If mind is a product of evolution, then biology can't be a purely physical science."[xxiii] The self-organization that yields systems therefore is not solely a physical feat, but has a semantic counterpart as well in the form of the epistemic structures that guide agents' perceptions and interactions. As physicist Amit Goswami declares, "There is only one subject-consciousness, and we are that consciousness."[xxiv]

Singularity and Multiplicity

Setting the grand, cosmic stage for the unfoldment of life and rational awareness on a seemingly insignificant planet, the universe itself foreshadowed the radiation of life out of a tiny swath of concentrated potential when it erupted into existence. The pattern of enormous diversity arising and unfolding again and again from very simple and deceptively diminutive origins is one that can be traced throughout cosmic evolution, biological evolution, and within the realm of ideas. The self-similarity of the unfoldment process bespeaks an underlying unity common to the evolution of all unities at all levels. The universe is populated by the many-formed microcosms of a singular, indelible truth—what Fr. Thomas Merton refers to as "the Real within all that is real."[xxv] Beneath the diverse panoply of forms, perspectives, and capacities that evolve to fill the world, the singular, conscious origin of manifestation—awakened by life and to its own objective existence by self-awareness—mandates that all evolutionary processes, and their products, proceed along a self-similar pattern.

Drawing from the patterns that first established themselves into life as biochemical activity crossed the threshold to metabolism, life in all its diversity deeply retains many properties and processes established at its dawning. By replicating itself according to a basic pattern that is amenable to variation and specialization, and retaining through a tractable memory a synopsis of its ancestral annals, the underlying Singularity is continuously and newly reborn through the experiences of its embodied reflections. Every action therefore becomes a tensor of the paradox of creation, which is the manifestation of the never-changing through the ever-changing as unitary presence reconstructs its self-similar experiential essence through countless forms and levels of complexity.

Jacob Boehme describes nature's pattern of unfolding orderly multiplicity out of pluripotent singularity, "The birth of the eternal nature is like the thoughts or senses in man, as when a thought is generated by somewhat, and afterwards propagateth itself into infinite many thoughts, or as a root of a tree generateth a stock and many buds and branches, as also many roots, buds, and branches from one root, and all of them from that one first root."[xxvi] All forms of expression descend from a singular origin, a universal consciousness, which unfolds its infinite potential for expression through them, guided by semantic channels of perception and interpretation.

Chaos and Cosmos

Beyond physical description, manifestation's conscious foundation eludes quantification, maintaining its property-free substance transcendent of the measurable attributes that define the universe it generates. Although inestimable to the empirical and even theoretical devices of science, the realm of consciousness that every situated entity partakes in to its own degree is accessible to deeper investigation, as attested to by the many visionary accounts of that metaphysical dimension. Returning from their forays into the unmeasurable "country whose center is everywhere, circumference nowhere,"[xxvii] mystical seekers describe customs native to that immaterial realm that are very different from those demanded by the material boundedness of physicality and the rational constraints of modernity. Nonetheless, unity between the two realities beckons.

The religious calling to unite spirit with situated experience is a call to bring an insubstantial ideation into physical and dynamical expression. Not just the vocation of religion, the achievement of this mystical union is the foundational project of manifestation itself. Organizing into complex systems that unite semantics with physics, agents and even their more elemental precursors signify and support the unfoldment of unpredictable capacities with unforeseeable effects. Enabling this most basic act of self-transcendence, which is the dynamical cornerstone of evolution, is semiosis. The intelligence which supports that network-creating process of semantic self-organization is what elevates interactions above the level describable by their physical properties and brings them into the realm of meaning. As points of union between the disparate domains of physical expression and intangible meaning, all incarnate entities function like metaphors in a universe whose meaning they help construct. Within humanity, the region of overlap between the measurable and the ineffable takes on a sublime dimension of potency: "God is in heaven, and the *heaven is in man*; and if man desireth to be in heaven, then must heaven be manifest, and revealed in him."[xxviii]

In a world such as our own, guided by meaning in each form and at every level of integration, all agents must chart their own courses according to their own capacities. While an open door to novelty and creativity, the subjective and self-guided autonomy that organizes itself into the living fabric of universal experience also allows the possibility for catastrophic error among its most highly cultivated constituents, with their unique responsibility of free will. Explains Romano Guardini, "Man is a person possessed of a marvelous yet frightful freedom, that he is capable of conserving or destroying the world, that he is capable of fulfilling or of surrendering and destroying himself in his very substance."[xxix] Absent a deterministic path along which to blindly set our feet, humanity is forced to turn, like the rest of nature, to guidance from within and without, each expressed in terms of the other. Thoroughly foundational within a semiotically structured universe, the tasks of interpretation and enactment rise to an unprecedented level of freedom and choice contingency when illuminated by the discerning light of rational understanding. The interpretations that guide our decisions—often below the threshold of awareness—and project onto the world through our behavior reflect back onto us, their individual and collective originators, as palpable effects of internally, semantically instantiated causes.

Externally, evidence mounts that human activities have become an epicenter of disarray, which emanates outward to envelop all levels of nature in its suffering. Socially, environmentally, politically, and economically, unrest presents itself as an inflammatory symptom of deep systemic imbalances which, practiced on a large scale, solidify into injustice. Underpinning these external cues as to the wayward nature of our present chosen path are internal signs of distress. Perhaps the deepest stratum of unease comes from the modern disconnect between humankind and our natural environment. "Modern anxiety," opines Guardini, "...arises from man's deep-seated consciousness that he lacks either a 'real' or a symbolic place in reality."[xxx] Such anxiety-begetting rootlessness is far from humanity's natural estate. Rather, until relatively recently in our history, the human condition was one of deep, vital, and integral connection with the rest of the world.

Despite their anthropomorphic stylizations, which reflected their makers' richly inhabited source domains, the earliest symbolic, ritualistic, and mythological methods humans had devised for conceptually integrating themselves into a wondrous and sometimes terrifying world served the crucial purpose of allaying any insecurity that might arise from inadequate integration with the world in all its phenomenal and numinous dimensions. In doing so, these natural responses to the awe that early humans encountered as a fundamental aspect of their experience lifted from their fragile identities the potential burdens of egocentrism and anthropocentrism by setting their makers within a context that was vastly larger, grander, and more spectacular than their own individual and even collective selves. Today, many people generally lack a worldview—a "cosmology," per theologian Matthew Fox—like those of our forebears, which bred a natural form of humility by incorporating reverence for the grandeur as well as the simplicity of life within its wider setting, embedding people fully into their environments locally, but perhaps even more crucially, cosmically and spiritually as well. Absent such a vital connection to the foundations and supports of life, modern humanity has become "less capable of attaining nature, of representing it and experiencing it."[xxxi]

    Psychological and spiritual disseverment from the rest of nature is a rejection of the most foundational premise of embodiment, which thrives only within an intensely interconnected context. From this rift issues the disarray of imbalance and injustice, which threaten to abort the age-old project of evolution in ourselves. To perceive the world through a hostile, defensive lens is to willfully squander a priceless opportunity to fulfill the heavenly potential that Boehme perceived within humanity. Jill Purce offers the insight, "It is Cosmos to those who know the way and Chaos to those who lose it." In order to "know the way," humanity must forgo attachment to surface-level distinctions and distractions to the extent that they hinder the deeply ontological duty to embody the promise instantiated in manifestation from the beginning and fulfilled evolutionarily within a living universe that cultivates the capacity to perceive itself. The choice to respond to that universal summons is grounded in profound wisdom, conscious presence, and intuitive openness to the infinite dimensions and variations of expression taken on by the singular and absolute truth condition. Deviation from the delicate balance that constitutes "the way" is to put ourselves at odds with natural rhythms, and thereby create an unsustainable polarity which invites the disruptive agitations of chaos out of stability. Today's pressing choice for humanity is whether to create a world of divisions—the very habitat of chaos—or one that embraces the totality of creation, whose concerted fullness was seen by Thomas Aquinas as the highest manifestation of holiness. Wielding the power of intentionality, humanity is uniquely equipped to purposefully and willfully choose what kind of reality to create; one that aligns with our ideals and interpretations. Capable of bringing the inner world of experience and perception into external manifestation through the channels of explicit awareness and volition, humankind represents the transformative nature of the turning point at the highest conscious level; the creative power of the trope.

1

The Primacy of Metaphor

"You don't see something until you have the right metaphor the perceive it."
—Robert Stetson Shaw

"To turn mere coexistence into mutual pertinence…is the constant result of associative functioning…That one thing points to another, in definite arrangement and connection, is itself apparent to us."
–Edmund Husserl

"In the Beginning was the Word…Through him all things were made." The opening hymn of the Book of John is not unique in imbuing a Word with supernatural potency. Just as the Christian Word, or Logos, is intimately proximate with the original creative impulse from the Beginning, the creative power of the Vedic scriptures likewise flows outward from its generative source on the vibrations of the sacred sound "Aum." In their more pedestrian role as tokens of communication, words seem far removed from the exalted potency of the procreant scriptural syllables. However, hidden beneath the ubiquity of freely exchanged words is a causal power in which echoes of the primordial utterance resound.

Prior to taking on the lofty implications of the divine reason underlying universal generativity, *logos* originally meant to gather, collect, or lay together the best of something. As time and usage reworked its meaning, the activity it originally indicated remained implicit throughout the gradual permutations of definition that led to its more widely known meaning, "word." In a metaphorical sense, words "lay together" or "collect" by not only affixing meanings to themselves, but by creating a higher level of communicability by lending themselves to endless possibilities of rearrangement. By uniting the sender and receiver of a message on the basis of mutual understanding, the meaning-based collecting power of words reaches beyond their simple outward forms to become a primary source of organization within human relations. Although one of the most fundamental activities that we partake in, the generation, perception, description, transfer, and comprehension of meaning is also one of the most intangible. Free of any physical value or measureable property, meaning is not constrained to any particular form or definition. Yet it is central to the configuration of the language which conveys it, as well as the minds which generate and act in terms of it.

Information

In performing their function as discreet carriers of particular definitions, words draw from a pool of potential meaning which is essentially infinite and, prior to expression, unformed. Assuming semblance only in an eliciting context, meaning becomes associated with words whose forms are always to some degree arbitrary, and therefore open to modification. Although individual words only express minute increments of meaning out of limitless potential, their power of conveyance is unleashed when they conjoin into sentences, which conduct volumes of meaning far greater than what would be predicted from the sum of their constituent words. A mere agglomeration of words, however, is insufficient to effectively transmit meaning. Outside of the rule-based parameters of grammar that structure sentences, the potential for random arrangements of words is enormous, although the majority of those combinations are spurious. As noted by pioneering linguist Hughlings Jackson: "It is not enough to say that speech consists of words. It consists of words referring to one another in a particular manner; and, without proper interrelation of its parts, a verbal utterance would be a mere succession of names embodying no proposition." [xxxii] Only through the sturdy regularities of structure do words become conduits of meaningful messages.

The question of message transmission is considered by information theory, which, with its focus on factors that can physically impact the conductance of a message, such as channel capacity, internal entropy, and external noise, points to the essential importance of channel structure in maintaining the integrity of a message. Dismissing for its practical purposes the message's actual meaning, the theory links information more closely to the potential structure of a message than its actual configuration. Culled possibilities implicitly attend the selected message, propagating the flow of transmission like an unformed cloud whose disorder represents an intrinsic source of entropy within the communication system, and whose range of potential supplies its degrees of freedom. For language, with its vast store of latent referential and combinatorial potential relative to what is actually expressed in a given statement, both the entropy and degrees of freedom are extremely high, demanding a channel that is sufficiently robust to support a huge variety of meaningful messages.

The essentially boundless entropic potential that is both made available to and drawn from by a language system harbors uncertainty within its constitutive degrees of freedom, which menaces that very system with incoherence. One inherent side effect of regularity-inducing linguistic conventions that naturally defrays this internal threat is redundancy. A measure of how much of a message's structural freedom is curbed, redundancy effectively reduces the amount of information a message can convey.[2] In a seeming paradox, it is through the reduction of information that meaning comes into focus at a critical point between the confusion of randomness and the monotonous rigidity of excessive order.[xxxiii] Redundancy also helps buffer the message against the corrosive effects of noise, which is an extrinsic source of entropy that can

---

[2] The measure of redundancy is 1-relative entropy of the source. The redundancy of English is 50% (Weaver 1953).

impact the integrity of the message, either by reducing its intelligibility or by causing it to resemble a different signal.[xxxiv]

Structuring Meaning

With only words as material from which to construct its channels, language infuses its very structure with meaning to create the two axes of verbal construction—word combination and word choice—recognized by linguist Roman Jakobson. Before they are summoned to intelligibility, all words have an equally low probability of being selected out of the dormancy of random potential. Application of the two distinct yet intertwined axes of construction orders words into arrangements that simultaneously conform to the strictures of grammar, and are compatible with the speaker's intended meaning. The axis of word combination guides the architecture of the message into a form predicted by the rules of syntax. By probabilistically restricting the order in which certain letters, different types of words, and their groupings into phrases and clauses appear in relation to each other, this axis arranges the components of a message into hierarchical levels of organization that are each guided by their own set of statistical regularities. Because the governing authority of syntactical rules is statistical, each message component influences the probability of its successor's selection.[3] For example, the probability of a letter *e* versus a letter *z* being selected is significantly altered according to whether the preceding letter is a *j* or an *a*; likewise for the ordering of word types such as adjectives relative others such as nouns or prepositions.[xxxv] Situated on the axis of word combination, the constraints of grammar provide a primary tier of organization that stabilizes randomness into meaning by curbing its freedom into predictable patterns.

From the perspective of the receiver, the syntactical axis of construction is of primary importance in deciphering the message's content. Grammar's conventionalized patterns, which delimit

---

[3] This is a Markov chain, wherein future probabilities are determined by the current state of the system.

combinatorial possibilities, provide a probability-based template that a listener applies to a message in order to decode it. By ensuring that every correctly produced message expresses the predictable properties that are typical of the system as a whole,[4] the rule-based form of syntax correlates with meaning.[xxxvi] However, even amid the rugged statistical terrain that grammar imposes upon linguistic entropy in its transition to communicability, correctly formulated but meaningless monsters such as Chomsky's "Colorless green ideas sleep furiously" still loom large, demonstrating that the combinatorial constraints so vital to a message's lucence are necessary but not sufficient to compress potential into meaning.

In complementary contrast to the receiver's probability-based route to interpretation, the speaker's starting point is the meaning that guides selection along the choice axis. Unlike its structural correlate, semantically driven word choice does not rely on ergodic probability distributions in order to impose its bias on word selection, but rather draws from the indefinable realm of meaning. Although its logic is not statistically determined, however, semantic meaning is still compelled to express itself within the prescriptive parameters of regularly ordered syntax. With neither axis of verbal construction sufficient on its own to support intelligibility, meaning arises at their confluence through the intentional application of choice within the constraining combinatorial rules which convey it. Layering another tier of selectivity upon random potential, word choice weaves into the reliability of syntax an unpredictable component of subjective value.

From the play of nondeterministic logic within sturdy, yet malleable, grammatical boundaries arises not only meaning, but a fertile landscape of creative potential. The patterned regularity of linguistic structure, drawn from the combinatorial axis, affords a pliable template that is amenable to variation not only in form, but also in accommodating the

---

[4] The tendency of a system to generate samples that are reflective of its overall properties is one expression of ergodicity. Another, referenced later, is the tendency of a system to pass through all of its possible states with equal probability if given enough time.

open-ended supply of signifiers available to a language. Conversely, the message's semantic pole—unconfined by statistical predictability—probes the edges of the very parameters that give it form in a continual exploration of novel expressive possibilities. Although the selective logic of each reciprocal constraint of verbal construction is irreconcilable to that of the other, they function compatibly to "collect" out of vast, latent potential the elements of a message and cogently "lay them together" in a statistically proscribed format that conducts the flow of information—a flow assisted by the entropic silence of unspoken potential that frames the selected words. With its every construct negatively contingent on what remains unexpressed, language is a perennially unfinished product of mutable relationships among words and their meanings. This permanent state of partiality allows language to be infinitely adaptive in its exploration of the measureless terrain of meaning to which it gives expression.

A Higher Level of Structure

Because formless meaning is never reducible to, nor fully contained by, the structure of the sentences that convey it, words and phrases can take on new implications according to context and even intent. By availing itself to description, the semantic pole of a message crosses over into the structural one to foment the fundamental alchemy of language, which represents the abstract and intangible in terms of structure and order. With ineffable meaning rendered in terms of transmissible structure, language reveals its profoundly metaphorical character. Although long dismissed as merely a superfluous figure of speech, metaphor reflects the unitive principle of language which fuses semantics and syntax, but at a higher level of organization by bridging disparate domains of meaning on the basis of some level of perceived similarity. Starting from a relatively well-known source domain that is often physical, metaphor reaches across to a target domain that is less clearly defined, such as an emotional experience, and joins the two domains into unity through identical language. Certain conceptual states, for instance, are described spatially by what Lakoff and Johnson term "orientational metaphors." Happiness, health, or other desirable conditions metaphorically tend upward, while sadness or sickness point down.[xxxvii] Open-ended in potential just like the language it structures, metaphor flexibly models the interpretation of its target on the source domain exemplar. For example, the metaphor "language is a conduit" makes it possible to apply the insights of information theory—with its interest in the physical properties of messages and channels—to the more abstruse endeavor of conveying meaning through a non-literal syntactical channel.

As a highly capable structural device, metaphor readily builds multiple layers of information and interactional relations by exerting its attractive power on whole systems of thought, or gestalts, which can be linked together into larger, more complex systems by similarities at various levels.[xxxviii] By highlighting similarities between ideas or even systems of ideas, a metaphor draws together and develops salient threads of information from different domains into a complex, internally coherent system of maximal outward simplicity. Bound by the sometimes abstract similarities construed by metaphor, entire systems of otherwise disparate concepts are drawn into a common orbit of emergent meaning that is irreducible to its constituent parts. The point of overlap that a metaphor designates between domains is a semantic turning point, which compels the words passing through to shed their literal meanings but retain their implications. The label of "trope," which literally indicates a turn, is therefore aptly applied to linguistic devices such as metaphor and metonymy, which shift and alter the course of meaning across a cognitive landscape through non-literal channels.

Metaphor's versatility in domain selection frees it from the heavy and predictable hand of determinism, allowing it to bring creativity to even the most mundane speech. Accordingly, Emerson likened metaphor to the "fertile soil from which all language is born."[xxxix] While its more obvious function is to create novel connections and channels of meaning throughout different domains, the persistent use of a metaphor can solidify or "lexicalize" it into common language with universally understood referents, such as the "leg" of chair, or "face" of mountain. The incorporation of such "dead metaphors" into common speech obscures any "sharp division between metaphorical and literal language," which, according to David Leary, constitute "opposite ends of a single continuum."[xl] Far from being static and categorical, with each component firmly in its place, the distinction between literal and metaphorical language is graded, and "there is continual commerce between these two poles as metaphorical concepts become more common (i.e., literal) through use and as literal concepts are used in unexpected (i.e. metaphorical) ways." Even as individual metaphors, per Emerson, "go to die" in the "graveyard" of literal language, they stand as subtle reminders of the subjective and emergent origins of language and belie any notion that words have fixed and inherent meanings.

Although metaphor is such an innate aspect of language that it is often deployed unobserved, even the most unobtrusive metaphor is invisibly surrounded by the network of unstated entailments that it implies. Drawing its power from what is not made explicit, metaphor is facilitated by an attendant host of associations from deeper relational levels that function like the entropy that silently flows a message through a channel. These unspoken assumptions are the interactive, causally effective aspects of metaphor that impart upon it the capacity to structure both thought and language. With a focal point of similarity between two domains held fast by a non-literal association, source-domain entailments pass through the transformative prism of metaphor to freely expand their implications into the less-known target region like templates for hypotheses. As logical corollaries of the source domain, entailments surreptitiously shape the inferences and the understanding fostered by the mapping from the source by establishing a pattern of familiarity within the target. Such deep and far-reaching associations magnify the ability of metaphor to convey meaning far beyond the capacity of literal language alone. This is why, according to Halyoak and Thagard, "for any interesting metaphor, it is impossible to find a precise literal equivalent that captures all of its nuances."[xli]

Although predicated on a very simple, dyadic movement, metaphor's scope of versatility in accentuating convergent aspects across virtually any set of domains is immense. The interactive quality of entailments enlivens metaphor into a dynamical interface between subjective experience and practical description, building these otherwise irreconcilable opposites into a communicable framework that is open-ended in its capacity for growth. Activating that framework into adaptability is the reflection of the fundamental source-to-target movement back to the source, with understanding altered by its cross-domain interlude. When considered in terms of the target it informs, the source is opened up to unexpected revisions that reverberate into other domains. Through this single, self-reflective movement, established knowledge interacts with known information in the formulaic pattern of domain crossing to produce an emergent and altogether unpredictable result.[xlii] Source and target fluctuate in relation to each other in a mutually adjusting association that generates, amplifies, diversifies, and transforms meaning. Former target domains become integrated into the semantic structure as potential source domains in a process that unfolds a complex hierarchy of understanding supported by the scaffolding of cross-domain connections. The semantic structure that evolves from countless replications of this most foundational of dynamics reflects its recursive origins by becoming closed in the sense that it is bounded by self-reference; every condition it encounters is assessed in terms of its internal structure. At the same time, it is also free to endlessly expand within the boundaries woven by those self-referencing coils. From the simple reverberation between source to target and back again with modification, a contingent, tunable dynamic resonates throughout the whole network of associations that comprise the subjective system of understanding.

Metaphor effectively contracts the semantic space between divergent domains, drawing them together into a single unit through its power to divine the non-apparent relational similarities that underlie externally diverse contents.[xliii] In highlighting the deep-seated and even abstract similarities between domains, metaphor creates information by offering a variety of perspectives on the same condition. Acting as nodes of order that connect and redirect meanings and associations throughout an intricately branching, many-leveled hierarchy of understanding, metaphors are points of stability that create coherence within a conceptual system. As microcosmic epicenters of order, metaphors are well described by Arthur Koestler's concept of a holon: an autonomous, self-reliant unit within a natural system that is simultaneously whole in and of itself, but also inextricably part of a larger system. Although the concepts and gestalts that constitute the system are varied and distinct, they are bound together by the larger sense of meaning, akin to an identity, to which they collectively contribute and which provides them with a common cause toward which to orient their interpretive outcomes. It is the task of metaphor to access this often hidden, deeper-level commonality, which functions like the redundancy of language, to impart cohesion and robustness on the integrated system.

How Do We Know?

Framed by a halo of unexpressed potential at every level of construction, language draws meaning from inchoate origins into expression through a process that leaves much latent at every step. Founded on incompleteness, language is necessarily limited in what it can express, which implies limits to what can be conceptually known. While language can provide a description about a particular referent, the actual object, the "thing in itself," cannot be wholly conveyed by words. The limits of expressible meaning have long challenged philosophy at its roots by begging the fundamental question of ontology versus epistemology and the attendant uncertainty of how we know what we know. This fundamental question quietly underlies any scrutiny of understanding itself, including the nebulous study of how we glean meaning from messages, which is not wholly answered by analyses of selections, combinations, root words, or structural devices.

For the classical Greek thinkers, reason was the tool that provided access to complete knowing. The Platonic universe was filled with multitudes of roughly transcribed forms striving toward manifestation of the perfect Ideas which they imperfectly instantiated. Whereas the inferior outer forms were accessible to the senses, their causal essence was attainable only by reason. Since Plato held that we could know our thoughts directly, once an object was apprehended by reason, its essence was presentable to our knowing in a rational, complete, and objectively true act.[xliv] Confounding the purity of knowing, though, was the transcendent nature of the true essential Ideal, far beyond the cognitive reach of ordinary people. The best guides available to those seeking that sublime pinnacle were "likely stories" which were, like the rest of nature, mere strivings for unattainably high perfection.

Just as for his predecessor, knowing for Aristotle came by virtue of the mind's capacity for perfect access to the underlying essence of an object via the faculty of reason. A mental object was indivisible from its material counterpart because they shared the same nature, making the object completely knowable when its intentional representation reflected its true nature.[xlv] In sourcing causal efficacy in the properties and interactions of the object itself rather than in a supra-material realm of ideas, Aristotle's more organic metaphysics created a hierarchy of attributes ranging from particular, outward manifestations, to more general and causal aspects or principles. Knowing became a process of unfolding, with reason's function to infer from the more readily observable aspects of objects to their less known underlying cause, or nature.

Because of the high premium he placed on the ability to reason from the more known to the less known in the quest for true knowledge, Aristotle was able to proclaim that "the greatest thing by far is to be a master of metaphor."[xlvi] Although he praised it as a means by which "we can best get hold of something fresh"[xlvii] by transcending the limits of "ordinary words," which can "convey only what we know already," he, like Plato, rejected a role for metaphor in his route to objective, immutable knowing. Lakoff and Johnson explain the source of this ambivalence:

> "The logic of an idea, for Aristotle, is part of the structure of the external world. Because a domain is in the world, not just in the mind, a cross-domain mapping would have to be part of the world. But that is impossible. In the world, things exist as distinct kinds, as part of distinct categories. Each essence has its own inherent logic and not that of another kind of thing. The idea that the essential form

of a thing could be that of another kind of thing makes no sense in the Aristotelian world-view."[xlviii]

Knowledge was not a relationship and could not be created, only grasped as it already existed through reason, which, when polished to its purest pitch, mirrored the outer world perfectly. Because of its suggestions of an order of knowledge other than immutable and objective, metaphor—despite its usefulness in their teachings—was regarded by mentor and protégé alike as a "deviant" use of language, altogether aberrant to the objective and truthful fruits of infallible reason. Along with the likewise subjective, and therefore suspiciously viewed disciplines of poetry and rhetoric, metaphor was on the brink of a centuries-long banishment from a central place in human understanding, while rationality and reason claimed ascendency to truth.

The Age of Reason

The deep distrust of metaphor and its subjective, emotional, and nonliteral kin—which Leary dubs "tropophobia"—is traceable throughout the philosophical lineage leading to the empiricist tradition, which believes that words ought to have "'proper senses' in terms of which truths can be expressed."[xlix] St. Augustine confessed as one of his greatest sins his pre-conversion proclivity for the subjective art of rhetoric; John Locke likewise disdained rhetoric and metaphor as low tools deployed for the purpose of misleading the judgment. One of metaphor's bitterest foes, Thomas Hobbes, decreed metaphors to be "contention, sedition, contempt." Reasoning upon these misleading tropes was to "wander amongst innumerable absurdities."[l] Pierre Duhem scathingly—and metaphorically—decried as "parasitic growths" the metaphors and models that accompanied physical theories.[li] The wayward and spontaneous attributes of metaphor could not be reconciled with a "building-block" conception of language—which enjoyed favor throughout even the 20th century in certain objectivist theories—that understands the world to be made up of objects with well-defined, inherent properties that are free of subjectivity and lend themselves to being represented by sentences that directly correspond, in a one-to-one fashion, to any situation in world.[lii]

Joining the ranks of influential philosophers in setting a framework to direct future directions of thought, Renee Descartes pursued his passion to be "wholly freed from doubt about that which we understand"[liii] through work based on the conviction that our own thoughts were uniquely knowable and potential sources of unerring, reason-based truth. The zenith of this faith crystalized into "*Cogito, ergo sum*," the wedge that he famously drove between the human mind and all "extended things" of material and bodily nature. With the internal "thinking thing" newly dissevered from nature's "extended," external aspect, reason could no longer form a unifying bridge between the two previously undivided realms. In its search for objective reality, the "light of reason" now had only one direction in which to shine: back onto itself, where mental objects could be interrogated free from the "fluctuating testimony of the senses" to yield true knowledge without any need for empirical investigation.

Although some degree of separation between subjective observer and known object—referred to as the "epistemic cut" by Howard Pattee—is presupposed by other philosophies, the Cartesian rift created two unbridgeable poles, with one extreme containing the human mind as the singular outpost of reason, able to "know the idea as it really is;"[liv] while all things bodily, nonhuman, and inanimate were swept together under the single rubric of mechanistic senselessness. Ensuing schools of thought—which Charles Sanders Peirce skeptically opined had "partly originated in an attempt to escape the inconveniences of Cartesian dualism"[lv]—sought starting points to knowledge in places other than reason. For Hume and Locke, it was "sensation." For Kant, with echoes of Platonic forms mingling with Cartesian division, the source of knowledge was "experience" rooted in a world whose outer, phenomenal aspects avail themselves to the senses, but whose numinous substance debars itself from direct investigation. Again, it is the saving grace of Reason that nobly imparts "consistence and objective reality"[lvi] to the otherwise unknowable, "captur[ing] a reality existing prior to its operations"[lvii] through the *a priori* nature shared by both noumenon and Reason.

For 20th century philosophers carrying on in the long shadows of the Cartesian and Kantian traditions that strictly tethered knowledge, cleanly husked of material trappings, to reason, lines of inquiry followed three guiding tracks, according to William Wallace.[lviii] Recalling Descartes, the first stipulated that "the clear and distinct idea is the criterion of truth." The second regarded with agnosticism the human ability to understand reality in more than a superficial way, and the third, with a certain irony regarding the Cartesian attempt to liberate mind from flesh, contained the scope of human knowledge within the sensible. Mathematical advances and shifting scientific paradigms—particularly those brought about by relativity—stirred the rise of empirically driven schools of philosophy, notably logical positivism. According to positivism's narrative, the verifiable truth of a mind-independent reality was to be sought through the objective, incorporeal reality of mathematics—which it deemed synonymous with pure reason—along with empirical science, with its view of nature's workings as essentially mechanistic. While logical positivism unreservedly placed "the glories of number, in the service of science" (Quine) as synonymous with truth, philosophy was allotted precedence over reason, with the caveat that meaning and the language that conveyed it were restricted to logically or empirically verifiable statements.

Analytic philosophy likewise favored the use of words intractably bound to fixed, objective referents, as summed up by Quine's axiom, "To be is to be the value of a variable." Mathematics, the height of pure, practical reason, and refreshingly free of the taint of subjectivity, was the preferred tool for bringing abstractions within the orbit of their more empirical brethren. However, once abstraction and empiricism found themselves inhabiting the same continuum, the latter was condemned to the same purgatory of theoretical existence as the former. The seat of reality then shifted to the structure of discourse, still confined to the strictures of a theory of one-to-one correspondence between signifier and referent. Linguistically "deviant" tropes rendered language unequal to meaning's demands of precision for its conveyance, according to formalism, which saw a need for a structural shift in language toward mirroring mathematical formulae.

A tacit element silently at work in the backdrop behind these evolutions of thought was a shift in the metaphors applied to the sciences. The long-preferred anthropomorphic source domain fell out of favor in late 1800s, to be replaced with metaphors sourced in buildings, structures, and mechanical objects.[lix] While unintended— metaphors were frowned upon in science, especially by the logical positivists—they stealthily framed the architecture of thought as it grew and developed during rapidly modernizing times. Finally, the creeds of mechanization and localized motion—another Cartesian inheritance—penetrated to the final frontier: the workings of the mind itself. Psychology of the 1920s and 30s seized upon the conditioning experiments of Ivan Pavlov to extend the metaphor of "biological machine" into the previously inviolable realm of human consciousness and behavior. Steeped in Hobbsian metaphors of mechanism and prompted by a desire to produce a theory of knowledge that did not rely on abstract processes, disembodied entities, and homunculi, the school of behaviorism effectively eliminated consciousness from behavior in favor of a machine-like stimulus-response model in which conditioned response replaced knowledge.[lx]

Throughout the course of more than two millennia of testing the separating, dividing, and distinguishing capacities of rationality, Western philosophy effectively exalted reason to the highest status of the ultimate diviner of truth. As truth became synonymous with an abstract but objectively extant rationality, metaphor fell into disgrace as a belonging to the realm of the subjective. In a strictly rational world-order, explain Lakoff and Johnson, subjectivity encompasses the emotional and non-rational, becoming not only a dead end in the quest for pure knowing, but even a slippery slope toward losing touch with objective reality.[lxi] In the Cartesian eschewal of the bodily and subjective, metaphor, with its deeply somatic roots, was naturally numbered among the rejected lot.

Although much of western philosophy has anchored its faith in reason as the guardian of cognitive coherence and the source of knowledge about the world, a closer examination of how we perceive our world and express that perception through language generates a much more complex picture, with far fewer assurances of an absolute, extra-mental truth condition that sufficiently honed reason can subdue into a precise, complete, and objective presentation. While reason is an invaluable tool in constructing a bridge between domains that are more familiar and those that are less, it is bound to its source domain as subjectively understood, rather than issuing unconstrained from an unequivocal fount of pure knowledge. [lxii] Like metaphor, reason is a means of structuring knowledge and adjusting understanding within that structure. Metaphor, however, is not confined to the surface of language, where rationality is tethered by correspondence theories. Rather, its reach penetrates into the very structure of the concepts and even perceptions through which we understand, define, and relate to our world.

Knowing From Within

In agreement with post-Cartesian philosophers such as Locke, Berkeley, Hume, and Kant, who located the starting point of knowledge with sensation rather than rationality, theories of grounded cognition trace their roots to the perception of sensation. For Husserl, sensation is absolutely foundational: "[The Body] becomes a Body only by incorporating tactile sensations…in short, by the localization of the sensations as sensations."[lxiii] At once recursive and constructive, the basic cognitive action of recognizing the new in terms of the known arises from the condition of embodiment, whose basic parameters of boundedness and orientation provide experiential grounding from which all other mental capabilities arise.[lxiv] Rough and unpolished, sensation is a foundational source domain that furthers the development of psychological representation by sampling what Peirce describes as the "chaotic manifold" of potential experience that "must be brought into the unity of one thought," or rendered decipherable to judgement.[lxv] The metaphors arising from immediate experiences are fundamental ones that erupt spontaneously and unconsciously as a means of differentiating aspects of the environment in terms that already have intimate, experienced connotations.[lxvi] "All knowing is action by a knower, depending on the structure of the knower," conclude Maturena and Varela.[lxvii] Or, as Maxine Sheets-Johnstone explains it, "mental aboutness arose from bodily aboutness."[lxviii] Metaphor is a primary tool of perception.

In a model of understanding that is sourced in bodily sensation, metaphor is neither deviant nor superfluous, but simply a natural expression of the sensorimotor activity that underpins linguistic meaning. Metaphor's function as a bridge between experience and expression is revealed by how the brain processes the metaphors woven into everyday language. Even the "dead" metaphors that are so familiar as to be unrecognizable to the casual speaker as tropes still invoke the associative mapping between a source domain corresponding to a particular brain region, such as one related to planning or sensory reception, and the more dedicated language centers. For example, the textural metaphor in the phrase "I had a rough day," although not being presented in a tactile sense, incurs activity in the parietal operculum, a brain region receptive to many surface neurons and activated in response to sensory stimulation. In contrast, the more literal phrasing "I had a difficult day" elicits no such correlation.[lxix] Because even lexicalized metaphors compel complex relational processes throughout the brain, metaphors don't truly "die," but rather become implicit, below the level of perceptual awareness. In the unexpected and involuntary cognitive activities incited by metaphor lies a hidden source of structured, logical unpredictability.

Deeply informed by the sensible experiences born of interaction with the surrounding world, structures of understanding grow and develop into a hierarchical order organized by concepts, which translate sensations into logically presentable and interpretable ideas. Prior to offering itself for capture by a verbal label, however, a concept is corporeally, rather than linguistically, understood.[lxx] Supported by the same neural structures that register the bodily mediated experiences of orientation, spatial relations, sensation, proprioception, and boundedness, concept is a secondary response to the condition of embodiment.[lxxi] The intimate proximity of sensation, movement, communication, and concept lend support to Jesper Hoffmeyer's conclusion that "cognition... is as much connected to registration of movements... as it is to the brain and symbolic reflection."[lxxii] It is integrated somatic experience—the "original bodily logos"[lxxiii]—which prepares brains for conceptual experiences.

Although concept is a progeny of sensation, it is not necessarily a simple, linear addition to its sensorimotor precursor. The path to creating a concept first entails the integration of multiple types of sensory impressions into a percept, or an understanding based on the particular observed properties of a considered object. As the basic unit of intelligibility, a percept is the basis for comparison between sensations.[lxxiv] Much like metaphor, concept creation requires the detection of similarities across different domains—initially sensory ones—which are drawn like relevant threads into a new union based on perceived correspondences. By projecting a refined sampling of the information delivered by the senses from the domain of observable particulars into the more obscure realm of generalization, a concept is formed. Recruiting support from other cognitive faculties, such as memory and imagination, conceptual systems carry out the important work of evaluating and incorporating new percepts into their informational structures by calling up analogous percepts and their respective conceptual schemes through imaginative "re-presentation."[lxxv] Jose Ortega y Gasset highlights the distinction between abstract concept and its roots in specific immediate experiences, "Now we should note that if the impression of a thing conveys to us its matter, its body, the concept contains all that the thing is in relation with other things, all that superior treasure with which the object is enriched when it becomes part of a structure."[lxxvi]

From its higher level of organization and semantic integration, a concept's power to construct meaning is hugely amplified over that of mere perception. Relative to its perceptual predecessor, concept is a far more globally organized, complex system that is not reducible to, or describable in terms of, its sensory constituents because it incorporates not only representational properties, but also non-observable causal constructs imputed by the subject.[lxxvii] Open to conditioning from not only sensations, but also perceptions, which are in turn influenced by associations or even other concepts, the process of conceptualization is a compounded admixture of experiencing, sorting, and inferring. "To perceive," notes Sheets-Johnstone, "is not to just extract meaning, but also to transfer meaning, this is the root of concepts."[lxxviii]

With their enhanced degrees of semantic freedom, concepts engage in a multi-layered play of selective domain transfer based on different forms and levels of similarity, making inferential relations the constructors of subjective meaning. Supported by the domain-crossing girders installed by metaphor and elevated by concepts, comprehension "bootstraps"[lxxix] itself to greater scope and complexity, as demonstrated by the increased flexibility, depth, and outward-reaching span that conceptual understanding layers upon perception. Growing in sophistication through layers of emergence, the simple lateral movement of metaphor, extending outward from familiarity toward a less known target, resounds at a higher level in concepts. When this same simple movement across domains establishes itself among the higher, logical entities of the mind, it has entered the realm of reason.

Metaphors and concepts not only arise from what we perceive, but also affect how we perceive. As Lakoff and Johnson explain, "the very systematicity that allows us to comprehend one aspect of a concept in terms of another…will necessarily hide other aspects of the concept."[lxxx] Even as metaphor conditions conceptual development by simultaneously highlighting and obscuring different aspects of the same considered object, it also constitutes the generative base upon which entirely new systems of understanding can be constructed. As the very foundation of comprehension, metaphor can be said to construct our inner world, which is a subjective understanding of the outer. The partial, conditioned, and essentially relative nature of perception compels new knowledge to be extrapolated, entailments intact, from what is previously understood—effectively leaving each individual with an embodied analogy of the world.[lxxxi] In turn, we base our behaviors and decisions on this understanding, and so directly create an outer world in terms of our bodily grounded apprehension of it. In this way mind can, as envisaged by William James, metaphorically extend into space to transform its surroundings on the basis of its understanding of them.[lxxxii]

That the expansive, creative potential for learning, exploring and understanding facilitated by metaphor primarily plays out in the brain's sensorimotor regions rather than in the higher-level cortices helps illuminate the source of antipathy that many body-disdaining philosophies express for tropes. However, the deep entanglement between somatic experience and cognitive capacity makes any conceptual boundaries between the "extended thing" versus the "thinking thing," or the Kantian faculties of Sensibility versus Understanding, indistinct, since concepts arise from the selfsame neural base as sensation and proprioception. Far surpassing a mere category of speech in its formative significance to processes of understanding, metaphor is both foundational to and a dynamical extension of conceptual systems. It is an interface between domains—most fundamentally the domains of experience and expression—which is mediated by interpretation. Although it is the tool we rely on to construct systems of knowledge about the world, metaphor is not predictable, algorithmic, or systematically quantifiable in its workings. Instead, it draws our minds into constructive informational relationships with objects of interest through the union of reason and imagination.[lxxxiii] Free of preset outcomes or correct answers, it hovers creatively, even playfully, at the edge of intelligibility, relying on certain conventions in order to skillfully circumvent others.[lxxxiv] Metaphor occupies a space between what is strictly necessary to communicate and the expressive edge that makes language flexible, evolvable, and open to interpretation. It is this insistent invitation to non-determinism that condemned metaphor to the outer fringes of linguistic respectability by much of western philosophy, until its relatively recent exoneration.

The Process of Analogy

While providing a foundation for higher-level types of cognitive organization like concepts and reasoning, metaphor retains its neotenic form of complete identification with its source, which bespeaks its bounded, bodily origin. In its foray across domains, metaphor projects the entirety of its source onto its target, rather than only the highlighted aspect, speaking with the unequivocal certitude of being ("hope is the thing with feathers...") that is at odds with its more tepid cousin simile ("hope is like a thing with feathers..."). Such immediacy that lacks explicit awareness of its own internal differentiation is the voice of the sensorimotor mind that identifies itself entirely with the inputs of the body.

In the emergent realm of mental construction which grows out of a vigorous ecology of interacting conceptual capabilities, the domain-crossing activity epitomized by metaphor is a primary mode of creating structure and expanding contextual frontiers. However, the shift in semantic locus from sensorimotor immediacy to higher-order logical relations ushered in by reason demands a more refined vehicle of domain crossing. Fulfilling this role among entities of the mind and their second-order relations is analogy. Sensory perception and analogy find themselves on opposite sides of the bodily divide that is traversed by metaphor: while metaphor is embedded in the experience of the body, analogy completely bypasses the "bodily route."[lxxxv] Unlike the sensorimotor sourcing of metaphor, analogy's activities recruit heavily from various portions of the prefrontal cortex, utilizing their sophisticated capacities of retrieval, integration, and selection. Additionally, the inhibitory capacities unique to this highly derived control center of the brain allow a distinction from bodily consciousness that frees analogy from the need to perceive a stimulus either directly or through an internally generated simulation, as in metaphor.[lxxxvi]

Although analogy is an evolutionary branch stemming from metaphor, its ability to transcend sensory experience firmly establishes it with other modes of high-level perception, where it acts as a cognitive guide by continually refocusing the lens through which it views challenges.[lxxxvii] Just as its more corporeal antecedent opens new regions of understanding by mapping a testable structure from a physically relatable source domain onto a more nebulous target, so analogy creates new contexts of inquiry by linking previously unconnected concepts. As an ongoing background process, analogy subtly shapes a worldview in a fluid, dynamic tangle that weaves between source and target domains, ultimately changing the understanding of both.[lxxxviii] It is the constructive agent in the "'higher' spheres of consciousness in which a number of noeses are built up on one another."[lxxxix]

While most analogy transpires as a silent backdrop to more explicitly conscious perceptions, implicitly structuring our perceptual frameworks according to what we have drawn and interpreted from prior experience, analogy can also be a much more intentional process. When confronted with the challenge of explicating a less-known concept, analogy mobilizes a vast pool of associated information to compare with the problem that acts as a source domain during the "pre-mapping" phase. Transforming an amorphous swell of possibility into a single, well-fitted mapping requires sturdy constraints that, like redundancy in the structure of a message, filter out any noisy irrelevancies that may threaten the integrity of the analogy and therefore its fitness as a solution to the problem. Like the structure provided by syntax, the selected parameters must also provide a rule-based template to guide the arrangement of the mapping without being so rigid as to restrict the nondeterministic upwelling of "serendipitous insights."[xc]

The distinct but interrelated constraints of similarity and structure interact with the context surrounding the problem to direct and limit the possible range of the analogy's application. Such contextual dependency acts as a source of flexibility to endow a single analogy with the potential for multiple distinct mappings—depending on the goal of the problem, which acts as yet another source of constraint against the inclusion of less relevant possibilities.[xci] Throughout the phases of analogy creation, which involve choosing a source analog, followed by its mapping onto the target, the various constraints selectively reduce and guide the broad, plastic potentiality of pre-mapping into a narrowed basin of pragmatically proscribed goal relevance. Problem parameters guide the identification of correspondences between different elements of source and target, with the pertinence of possible inferences depending on how easily they can be modified to fit the target.

As the mapping process draws source and target into alignment at a level of focus that depends on the objective of the analogy, further similarities can be highlighted or even created, until the target is increasingly understood as an exemplar of the category the source is understood to represent at a structural, rather than surficial, level of correspondence.[xcii] At this point, inferences can be generated, even taking into account some goal-irrelevant information as a source of interpretive flexibility, and the whole process culminates in evaluation and learning.[xciii] When channeled together by the common goal introduced by the parameters of an analogical challenge, information from different domains is bound into a variegated unity of semantic coherence.

A flexible, discerning tool that is dynamic in its ability to affect perceptions and open-ended in its applications, analogy freely crosses domains to modify target and source alike in terms of the conceptual system's constructed understanding of each. Its responsiveness to new information is crucial to building and adaptively adjusting a subject's interpretive inclinations, which reflect a cognitive structure founded on metaphor. The higher-order mental realm occupied by reason, analogy, and inference is constructed by a self-crossing web of domain transfers that sifts, selects, winnows, presents, and re-presents available information to a pitch of refinement according to the individualized "habits of mind" (Peirce) that constrain and condition each act of cognition. Contrary to the concept of reason held by Plato and Aristotle, the intricate mental construction that supports high-level cognition is not a faithful yet passive representation of an external order. It is a self-creating, complex structure that explores mental terrain with internal degrees of freedom that belie its foundational constraints of physical boundedness. Contrary to the Pure Reason of Kant in the Cartesian tradition, rationality is not a conduit to the pristine knowledge of a non-contingent truth condition "found prior to experience in the mind." Knowledge—even that based on reason—is only a partial reflection of a complete truth because, as Peirce points out, "Carried to the highest point, [resemblance] would destroy itself by becoming identity. All real resemblance, therefore, has a limit."[xciv] Instead, our understanding of truth is a highly subjective, bodily grounded and mediated process, malleable to conditionings and biases.

Like his predecessors, Peirce paid his respects to the faculty of reason, declaring that the "power of drawing inferences is the last of all our faculties, for it is not so much a natural gift as a long and difficult art."[xcv] Despite its stature as the most sophisticated of cognitive capacities, the reasoning that underlies inference is based on much simpler forms of thought, amplifying echoes of the conceptually primitive precursor even to metaphor, metonymy. In particular, the metonymic form of synecdoche signifies a whole idea by a single part, as in the phrase "a familiar face." The observable, selected feature is only tangentially related to the whole, complex idea that it invokes. Similarly, a cohesive system of concepts is not reducible to any of the correlated observables that comprise its basis. When called upon to represent a concept, these surficial features take on meaning beyond their apparent presentations, symbolizing the entire causally efficient, abstract structure—the "superior treasure"—they are being associated with. Together, metonym and its primary descendent, metaphor, supply language with the two foundational ingredients for its functionality: the metonymically afforded contiguity of linear progression is complemented by the penchant of metaphor to unpredictably invoke distant-seeming domains based on what Jakobson refers to as "equivalence," or similarity.

In exalting the faculty of reason as the proper and authentic route to understanding absolute universal truth conditions, its champions were extolling its transcendent aspects while failing to recognize its deep embeddedness in humbler organismal processes. The concepts that support rationality are grounded in metaphor, which provides a bridge from sensorimotor source domain to conceptual target through a complex series of abstractions, associations, and inferences. At its higher level of logical order, conceptual reasoning replays the actions of metaphor by abstracting salient similarities and largely discounting irrelevancies in its encounters with circumstance. By moving from the source domain of localized and particular instances of events to their generalized implications, concepts emphasize a vertical aspect of domain crossing, much like an inductive reasoning process. Inductions assess stochastic probabilities and project them into concepts, which firmly fix their premises into a system that can in turn guide deduction from generality back to the particular. Along with the lateral reach of analogy, the vertical movements of induction and deduction, which recall metonymy's vacillations between aspect and idea, are all the higher-level tools by which reason achieves inferences. Drawing from the same principle of associability as metaphor, induction and deduction are its derivatives, rather than primary structures. They operate within the contexts that metaphor and its higher-level offspring, analogy, open up in lesser-known target domains, expanding into inductions and concepts, contracting into deductions, and transforming through inferences based on all of these higher-level aids to interpretation. It is reason's higher-level extrapolation of these processes—which build into conceptualizations and reveal themselves in the structure of their communicable extension, language—that makes it "the last of all our faculties."

Knowing is a systemic, hierarchical process, with the same essential movements of vertical and lateral domain transfer repeating at the various levels of semantic integration. Woven together into an ascending complex wherein each subsequent level is entirely dependent upon—without being reducible to—those that support it, the system as a whole is not amenable to dualistic fragmentation that segregates mind from body. Such a distorted partitioning would undercut the delicate structure from its very foundation, rather than yielding two fully functional wholes. The "thinking thing" is indissolubly enmeshed with the "extended thing" in a balanced cohesion that fosters autonomy only through the growth of the rational regime from within its somatic context. The system grows from the bottom up in complexity, scope, and sophistication, rooted in very fundamental sources that we all share in common, yet experience individually. It is integrated from the top down by differentiated understandings and interpretations that guide decision-making, behavior, and future amenability to new information. With its causal efficiency tied to semantic integration, the rational mind, grounded in physicality, is a system of embodied meaning.[xcvi]

The Semiotic

Conditioned by selection at the various levels of cognitive activity that judiciously reduces potential information into a refined, actionable interpretation, knowledge is inherently subjective. "The brain," says Jesper Hoffmeyer, "is there to give us a track to act upon, it is not there to give us the truth."[xcvii] Absent the reliability of an absolute knowledge accessible through infallible Reason, the "track to act upon" is one that we interactively create as an approximation of the world we navigate. The concepts that organize this interpretively cultivated understanding are based on constituent ingredients expounded upon by Peirce in his philosophy of "the semiotic."

When he simultaneously denied the reliability of Cartesian introspection while embracing Kant's detection of inference in every cognition, Peirce recast thought, not as an experience of pure self-knowing, but rather as a system of interpretive relations between the products of a mind that is itself relative. The token of currency exchanged among participants in this system is "an object which stands for another to some mind," or a sign that prompts an inference.[xcviii] Far from a static entity, a sign, like a metaphor, is a "border-crossing process"[xcix] that stirs within the mind of the receiver a causally creative process that begins, like an analogy, by summoning a pool of associations, from which resolves an intentional representation, or "interpretant," of the referent indicated by the sign. Semiosis entails the experience of a sensation which correlates with the condition, internal or external, that summons it.

Peirce identifies three levels of signs, each dependent on the prior one for its existence, and each respectively correlated with properties he dubbed "firstness," "secondness," and "thirdness." Through firstness, Peirce roots his theory of knowledge in perception, asserting that "there is no feeling which is not also a representation." The private, interior experience that is unique to firstness is what makes this "fundamental requirement" for knowledge the causal, or "real" connection in the triad linking referent to signifier to signified "representamen." The foundational premise of firstness, "whose being is simply in itself," is "that which is common to [all] objects: undifferentiated being."[c] Incarnate as a sign, firstness takes the form of an icon. Although in its expressed forms icon is marked by resemblance between referent and sign,[5] it takes on an internal invocation as well which links the mental world of meaning with the presentable world of signification; a visceral level of subjective awareness described by Merleau-Ponty: "Things have an internal equivalent in me; they arouse in me a carnal formula of their presence."

As an immanently felt yet unnamed response to some aspect of the environment, whether internal or external, an icon is a bridge between the referent and the subject's understanding of it. Experiential icon bespeaks Husserl's "primary intuitive space…sensuously given"[ci] that is the beginning of all awareness. Like all signs, an icon is indicative of but not identical to its referent, and so possesses attributes apart from its representative function.[cii] This differentiability, however slight, opens an icon to the interpretive process that is semiosis. Before the selective sifting and sorting of interpretation can transform an icon into presentable meaning, however, the icon must first be rendered in terms of something else.

Whereas Peirce describes firstness as the unanalyzed, self-contained "tender thing" of experience, secondness is an unfelt but interactional "dead thing" that signifies the first.[ciii] Accordingly, the index, which names—but is not itself—feeling, exists dependently and in dyadic relation to its perceptual counterpart, constituting the "passing from being

---

[5] Peirce grouped icon into the two subclasses of images and diagrams, including equations. Instead of focusing on these presentable examples of iconic signs, this interpretation of semiotic processes concentrates on the internal manifestation of firstness as the sensational experience of qualia that lays the foundation of sign processes. James Hoopes (1990, p 160), explains Peirce's thinking, "All thought is in visceral signs requiring inferential interpretation."

to substance."[civ] An index essentially interprets iconic sensation and "represents" it in an expressed form, such as a shriek or a laugh. By pointing to its iconic correlate, index distinguishes and expresses outwardly otherwise private, unshareable experience. In communication, it elicits in the receiver an inference to the initial condition—the referent of the icon, as well as the iconic experience of the sender—while generating a platform for inferential predictions. It is the first intelligible expression of meaning.

From the deceptive simplicity of the dyadic union between icon and index propagates a many-layered referential system. A network of indices is bound together by the icons whose meaning they both impart and fix into relation with each other through representation.[cv] As in metaphor and analogy, this gestalt of fixed relations can act as a source domain in terms of which new experiences and stimuli can be evaluated, interpreted, and incorporated into new meaning. The primary perception of icon is the experiential embodiment of the source domain, while the referential capacity of index extends, or projects, that primary awareness through communication to the domains of other minds. The indexical messenger stimulates iconic sensation, carried through bodily indices—such as biochemicals and action potentials—which translate into understanding that correlates the experience of the receiver to that of the sender through mutually corresponding cycles of meaning creation. Domain crossing therefore acts as a structural fundament not only in the internal mappings that build the framework of cognition, but also in the intersubjective arena of communication through sign relations.

The stable self-sufficiency of the icon-index coupling prompted Pierce to label it "absolute,"[cvi] with each aspect complimenting the other to perfection: the existence of the index is predicated on the icon, which in turn gains transmissibility from its expressive but unfeeling progeny. The ability of the recursive flux between iconic identification and indexical representation to blossom from a simple dyad into a complex yet stable hierarchy of informational contingencies depends on the tractability of these relations to allowing new iconic correspondences, along with their indexical attendants, to emerge at new levels and from various relational configurations among the existing structure of signs and meanings. The significations of individual indices are shaded and nuanced through contextual conditions, with circumstances biasing the scope of inferences likely to be drawn from a given signal. All of this potential variation within the system can give rise to internal differentiation into parts, levels, and even subsystems of indexical signification.

While such a rich matrix of interrelationships is sufficient in itself as a communication system, it is also a necessary precondition for the emergence of a wholly new and transformative level of semiotic capacity. Peirce describes this unfolding: "First and Second, Agent and Patient, Yes and No, are categories that enable us to roughly describe the facts of experience, and they satisfy the mind for a very long time. But at last they are found inadequate, and the Third is the conception which is then called for."[cvii] Thirdness is the quality of "mentality," which "brings into relationship" the first two levels from whose complex, systemic relations it is born and which it contains completely within itself. It is subtly present in any sign interaction as the property of "Mediation," but it "reaches its fullness in Representation."[cviii] Silently guiding the continuous creation of meaning below the level of linguistic expression, and even conscious perception, interpretation aligns sign processes according to a receiver's semantic structure. At the apex of the hierarchy of signs, interpretation is at once embedded in and the culmination of the dynamic cycle of semiosis. In the form of a sign, thirdness manifests as a symbol.

Just as index functions by everting the inward orientation of icon toward public accessibility, symbol changes the arrangement of established relations by forgoing the direct correspondence of the icon-index relationship in favor of a loosely affiliated, multiply realizable entanglement of mapping potentials that draws on relations among indices at different levels as its referential substrate.[cix] Because the shift from indexical to symbolic communication is a transition away from the more solid relational properties of the icon-index dyad, it requires a new learning strategy that "recogniz[es] a higher-order regularity" between indexical relations.[cx] According to Terrence Deacon, these relationships are essentially "recoded" by place-holding tokens, or symbols such as words, which highlight particular aspects of indexical interrelationships. The many-to-one mapping potential between symbol and referent effectively streamlines the mnemonic burden that a brain must store and process by stripping away the "redundant details" of an indexical system, wherein each signifier is associated with only one referent. With its heightened capacity for complexity drawing from the fertile ground of indexical relationships from which it springs, a symbolic system arranges itself in a complex and self-referencing form, with the value of any given symbol arising from its relationship to all others in the system.[cxi]

With the expansion of referential capacity beyond individual associations, indexically secured relationships become available to analysis by the abstracting power of symbols. This more encompassing way of communicating, based on learning relational patterns, opens up the realms of potential that language has afforded to humans in a cognitive landscape that is partially unmoored from contextual contingency, replete with high-order perception, and supportive of illimitable meaning construction. Symbols function in this rich cognitive environment as placeholders whose meanings can shift, change, grow, or fade away as the processes that create them forge new mappings between previously separate systems of representation.

Although language affects a "certain coded isomorphism with relationships between objects and events in the world," [cxii] it is not capable of limiting its scope to simple one-to-one reporting of truth conditions aligned with an absolute extrinsic reality as demanded by correspondence theories. Rather, as an irreducible outcome of innumerable interacting biases and interpretations wending their way through the cognitive labyrinth that yields conceptual understanding, the symbolically enabled capacity for linguistic expression is a mode of insight whose basis is informational redundancy—an act of recognition. Rather than relying on rote association, symbolic understanding "must instead be discovered or perceived…by reflecting on what is already known."[cxiii]

As a means of expanding into cognitive realms inaccessible to nonlinguistic minds, language is a vehicle of transcendence. Within those realms, it is a force of convergence. Based on a complex but logical tangle of relations, the processes leading to language summon vast amounts of formless potential to order based on relevance. Through active selection, meaning is congealed into a syntactic structure that both reflects and helps shape our understanding of the world, while connecting us to each other through the shared meanings by which "two minds in communication are...'at one.'"[cxiv] The triad of sign relations, unified into a single unit of causal connectivity that conjoins the known object and the process of knowing within the mind of the knower, allows communicators to—in the words of William James—"trade each other's truth."[cxv]

Semiotic Construction

As not only the culmination, but also an integral aspect of a many-step, multi-level process, interpretation tacitly validates signification at every level. It directs and constrains behavior and belief through countless normative assessments ranging from apparently automatic to carefully measured, creating meaning that is dependent on, but not reducible to its parts. Each level of emergence leading toward the explicit self-awareness that is the highest capacity augured by thirdness entails a judicative process of abstraction, distinction, comparison, and integration which informs the uniquely combined content that will comprise the next, emergent level of semantic and semiotic expression.

With each transformation in the process of construing meaning from signs, much is left behind. Icon, a self-contained whole of potential meaning, only embodies the aspects of the referent that are most relevant to the observer. In turn, index only highlights a particular aspect of icon, leaving the rest unexpressed, and so unformed. The potential left implicit by these two levels of signification—and which increases with every interpretive act of thirdness at every hierarchical level—is the entropy that is key to their transmissibility.[6] Each compression of pluripotent possibility into a specific token of signification amplifies the creation of potential meaning, along with the overall uncertainty of the system. Although unacknowledged, each dormant well of untapped potential at every respective level silently and indirectly informs higher-level interactions: "What each [name for a thought] knows is the thing it is named for, with dimly perhaps a thousand other things."[cxvi] Each Amplification of meaning, along with its attendant entropy, impels some degree of uncoupling between emergent layer and embedding structure, creating flexibility through increasing degrees of freedom at the leading hierarchical edge of the system. Potential at a lower level, which remains latent unless summoned to form by a sufficiently corresponding challenge, is sacrificed for usefulness, or work, by which the system as a whole gains greater pliability at a higher level of expression. With enough complexity and flexibility, the twin features of explicit understanding and implicit associations ultimately unite to allow the system to investigate itself. This is why a complex system like language, unlike an indexical system, can become the "subject and object of its own investigation."[cxvii]

As the pinnacle of a system of mental processes that transmutes inceptive sensation into coherent presentation, the symbol level conjures out of indeterminate totipotency a malleable form of meaning, clothing it through a series of abstractions and associations in the pragmatic intelligibility of expression. Husserl captures the curious blend of arbitrariness—embodied by the signal—with nebulous indeterminacy, which somehow conspire to impart comprehensibility and transferability to internal experience:

> "Words function as signs…everywhere they can be said to point to something. But if we reflect on the relation of expression to meaning…the word comes before us as intrinsically indifferent, whereas the sense seems the thing aimed at by the verbal sign and

---

[6] According to Weaver (1953, p 269), the best transmitter maximizes signal entropy to make it equal to capacity of channel.

meant by its means: the expression seems to direct interest away from itself towards its sense, and point to the latter."[cxviii]

Thirdness, or interpretation, represents a source of uncertainty within a system already largely influenced by subjectivity and entropy. All possibilities, from creativity to insight to error, arise from the interpretive component of the semiotic triad. The interpretive contingency of information renders meaning a dynamic and evolvable process rather than a static reflection of an absolute precondition. Its predication on the perception of similarities makes thirdness, particularly in the form of symbolic language, uniquely equipped to face what Peirce saw as the great challenge of living within this "universe of signs," with its potential to besiege us with overwhelming volumes of information: to bring "into unity of one thought" the chaotic "manifold of impressions" by "searching out whatever elementary conceptions there may be between the manifold of substance and unity of being."[cxix] Language represents just such a confluence, acting as an interpretive plane upon the "chaotic manifold." As such, it expresses some of that chaos in the concourse of the undefinable logic of word choice with rule-based combinatorial possibility. These "manifolds of [semantic] substance" all resolve into the "unity of being" that expresses itself primarily as experiential icon.

A Universe of Signs

Silently underlying all sign processes and responding to them experientially is the undefinable awareness that precedes even the qualitative "firstness" of sensation. While this ineffable witness—the "insider of all sign processes"[cxx]—responds semiotically to conditions within an environment by registering them as information and building them into epistemic systems, it holds itself aloof from precise definition. Philosophical constructs from the Cartesian "I Am" to Universal Reason depict this enigmatic quality as a uniquely human attribute responsive only to logical verity. From within Peirce's "universe of signs," however, the relationship between logic, rationality, and consciousness shifts. Even while rejecting the particular dualisms of his philosophical forebears, Peirce continues to hold logic firmly in its symbiotic orbit with conscious mind. However, he expands its scope to envelope all of nature. After deducing the applicability of logic to all thoughts by virtue of their status as signs, he extrapolates that logic must therefore apply to all signs, mental or otherwise. Logic, he concludes, is the science of sign relations, rather than the sole province of human thought processes. As a system governed by logic, the entire "universe of signs" must be contingent upon the property of thirdness, the interpretive union of experiential sensation and its representation as information, which serves as the coin of the semiotic realm.[cxxi] The ubiquitous entanglement of subjectivity, logic, and interpretation permeates all organic relations. That participation is the only mode of being in a "universe of signs" undercuts the trap of dualism by understanding the inner experiential and outer interactive aspects of embodiment as one indecomposable whole: "Viewing a thing from the outside…it appears as matter. Viewing it from the inside…it appears as consciousness…[I]f habit be a primary property of mind, it must be equally so of matter, as a kind of mind."[cxxii] Guided by the "induction" that is habit, all semiotic dynamics shelter under the umbrella of logic in its many forms.

The "corporeally constituted and absolutely basic experiential category"[cxxiii] of "insideness" is the basis of the subjective experience that differentiates into sensation. Speaking to this immediacy, Husserl explains, "Apperception is not inference, not a thinking act….every apperception…points back to a 'primal instituting,' in which an object with a similar sense became constituted for the first time."[cxxiv] This intimate subjectivity is the fundamental substrate, the primary source domain, which supplies the context of awareness for the logical play of sign processes. Only through the indefinable perception of consciousness do signs instigate the experience and process necessary to take on meaning. Ethereal consciousness registers sign processes and represents them as measurable tokens by which it signifies meaning, which is an indirect and contextually conditioned reflection of that deepest of constituting layers. Beneath all of the modifications that activate it into sensation, reaction, and epistemology, consciousness is the quiescent basin of all potential which, when stirred to activity, embraces structure as a means to convey its essence as the ultimate source domain in meaningful, nondeterministic form.

Differentiated into the experience of bodily sensation, consciousness is the primitive, evolvable bastion of understanding. Conveyed in terms of physical form, the meaning that contextually adapted consciousness takes on becomes the incarnate locus of directed action. Every living body, therefore, is "as much symbol as substance"[cxxv]—a condition noted by Peirce, who describes the "living symbol, realizing the full idea of a symbol."[cxxvi] Like any other sign, the "man-sign" must develop into expressive fullness, and only through this development "[come] to mean more than he did before."[cxxvii] The level at which an individual interacts with the world, then, is the symbol level. Like a sign or a metaphor, the full meaning of each "living symbol" can never be conveyed, but its expressive potential continually compounds through each interaction—always a sign process, and always consummated and potentially elevated by each act of interpretation.

Although the complexity and potency of language are reflective of operations that are of a higher order than the more immediate, pre-inferential, body-centric modes of intelligence, the faculties that support language and reason are connected in the most intimate way to their very organic metaphorical roots. Predicated on semantic structures which develop through domain crossing, the compass of potential understanding extends above, below, and beyond the knowledge afforded by rationality, penetrating deeply beneath even the level of language. "No language can be spoken for which the body is unprepared," Sheets-Johnstone reminds us. "To understand the origin and evolution of a language is to understand a sensory-kinetic lifeworld."[cxxviii] Metaphor is a span that connects body with mind, reaching all the way down to the level sensation, at which the external environment is contextualized within the individual's semantic structure through qualitative experience. As the neural conjunct of the body, the brain's sensorimotor system has been just as responsive to the sculpting of natural selection as the body itself. Metaphor and, to lesser degrees, its emergent scions—concept, analogy, and, indirectly, reason—therefore reflect the nature of the body as a "semantic template."[cxxix] This embodied understanding is an encoding that is first understood in nonlinguistic terms that mediate between organisms and their surroundings to develop mental structures that are attentive to the most pertinent aspects of their context. From the most basic level, metaphors act as filters that attenuate the reception and perception of information. The roots of human intelligence therefore necessarily reach below the linguistic constructions that convey it, threading deeply into a corporeal form of understanding common to all embodied beings.

2

Animal Intelligence

"For nature has given to everything its language according to its essence and form...Everything has its mouth to manifestation; and thus is the language of nature, whence everything speaks out of its property, and continually manifests, declares, and sets forth itself for what is good and profitable; for each thing manifests its mother, which thus gives the essence and the will to the form."
—Jacob Boehme

"The senses delight in things duly proportioned as in something akin to them; for, the sense, too is a kind of reason as is every cognitive power."
—Thomas Aquinas

Although the organizing powers of metaphor are readily discernible in language, their roots are deeply prelinguistic. Arising from conditions of embodiment such as orientation, proprioception, and self-propulsion, the capacity of domain crossing to generate and structure knowledge and meaning reaches beyond the scope of human ontogeny and becomes a question of phylogeny. Because learning mechanisms among vertebrates appear very conservative,[cxxx] the metaphor-enabled cognitive scaffolding that develops in the human mind must have analogs in the minds of nonhumans as well. Gregory Bateson explains, "In order to make syllogisms...you must have *identified classes*," which are carved out by the rules of syntax. This is "so that subjects and predicates can be differentiated." As he goes on to point out, however, "apart from language, there are no named classes and no subject-predicate relations. Therefore syllogisms in grass [i.e., metaphor] must be the dominant mode of communicating interconnection of ideas in all preverbal forms."[cxxxi]

The cognition that evolved to support symbolic language in humans—and allows certain nonhuman species, including some apes, cetaceans, corvids, and psittacines access to simpler symbolic and rule-based systems of communication[cxxxii]—manifests itself variously throughout Animalia, commensurate with the spectacular radiation of forms within which it explores many of the same potentialities that we observe in ourselves from a viewpoint elevated by rationality and explicit self-awareness. The clear prevalence of intelligence throughout the animal kingdom prompted Darwin's famous surmise that the difference between human and animal intelligence is one of "degree and not kind," based on the naturalistic understanding of human brains and intelligence as having evolved from those of animals. Dissenters to that claim offer the counterargument that the very clear biological continuity passing from animal to human masks a profound functional discontinuity, citing in particular human capacities for language, high-level relational inferences, and a propensity to interpret the world in terms of unobservable entities such as mental states and causal forces.[cxxxiii] These attributes are evolvable features of a semantic landscape, which is the domain in which humanity has so markedly distinguished itself.

Just as the leap from percept to concept opens up a realm of ideational potential that is utterly alien and inaccessible to the more foundational level, the cognitive tools available to humans give us unique access to a higher-level and more abstract mental plane from which to understand our world than is available to nonlinguistic species. And just as concept is separated from the perceptual level that gives rise to it by a discontinuity that obscures direct causality, human intellect is likewise derived from, while not reducible to its animal precursors. While the animal-to-human discontinuity is an obvious example of emergence in evolution, it is far from singular. In fact, from some angles evolution appears less continuous than saltatory—characterized by leaps with no clear path between origin and outcome. Conversely, with so many overlapping shades characterizing evolved bodies and minds, it is very difficult to draw a clear line at the boundary of one capability and its higher-level expression. Despite the confusion that the overlap of distinction and continuity can present to analytical attempts, both of these aspects have an important role to play in tracing the roots of intelligence.

Creating Language

Perhaps the most distinguishing aspect of human intelligence which is at least interdependent with, if not a primary causal factor in the development of other cognitive distinctions, is language. Representing one highly specialized and cultivated branch of semiotic evolution, symbolic language requires a particular kind of brain with specializations that can uncouple mental processes from sensory perceptions. In contrast, icon and index are universal ingredients among all communication systems supported by nervous systems.[cxxxiv] Anchored firmly in sensorimotor perception, these semiotic fundaments yield communication systems that are based on spontaneously formed behavioral analogs of referents that are expressed in gestures, postures, and vocalizations.[cxxxv] These signs, such as the physically elevated position of a dominant individual over the vulnerable posture of a subordinate, are indexical in that they signify a particular referent. Unlike symbolic language, an indexical meaning-token is not arbitrarily structured. Rather, it correlates in a direct way to its referent. For example, alarm vocalizations tend to be short, with abrupt onsets and broadband noisy spectra—features well suited to capturing receiver attention, and piquing physiological responses through arousal to flight-oriented behaviors.[cxxxvi] An indexical message's semantic component can be amplified through modulations of its physical properties such as frequency or amplitude, conveying information that is referential regarding both the nature of the situation and the motivational state of the sender.[cxxxvii] For nonlinguistic animals, whose epistemologies are bodily bound, information transmission depends crucially on behavior transmission.[cxxxviii]

Peirce noted that the indexical level of secondness would "satisfy" communicative imperatives for a "long time." Ultimately, though, the growing force of cognitive power demanded a new realm of expression that could only be supported by thirdness, with language serving as a high-level vehicle of creative exploration. Although the meaning of an index can be contextually conditioned, enhancing its referencing potential, its referent is always a whole, undifferentiated event. In contrast, a syntactically constructed statement is textured with layers of distinction through its role-based structural support of various classes of potential referents—actors, actions, and magnitudes[cxxxix]—which allows the incorporation of pragmatics.[cxl] While this third universe of experience burst into full flower in human cognition, it is very probable that, just as concepts precede linguistic labels, syntactically structured and functionally compositional understanding occurs in at least some animals, particularly species with more complex brains.[cxli]

One source of complexity in highly elaborated brains arises from the need to process information from multiple sensory domains—an inbuilt evolutionary drive that is universal. A multimodal brain, although energetically expensive to maintain, is still a considerable asset to its bearer because it enhances the robustness of collected data by allowing cross-checking across sensory domains based on informational redundancies. Even at the level of sensory perception, then, domain crossing is instrumental in condensing available information into a relevant structure of meaning. By converging on a single meaning iterated through different forms of information, domain crossing spurs the evolution of complexity within the unifying context of the whole organism.

The very redundancy that facilitates semantic convergence from among different sensory domains simultaneously fosters its divergence. One of evolution's favorite devices is that of exaptation, in which a structure devoted to one function is recruited to a novel context or purpose. It is because "everything was once an exaptation"[cxlii] that apparently disparate processes—such as registering movement and forming a concept—are deeply intertwined. The logic of exaptation demands that the precursors of language arose as cognitive rather than linguistic entities.[cxliii] What it does not demand, however, is that there is a traceable, linear connection between the nonlinguistic and linguistic. Seemingly small organizational changes can have disproportionate functional consequences in a manner reminiscent of the outsized effects of power laws.[cxliv] This view, representing an update from classical neurolinguistic attempts to locate a precise brain region dedicated solely to processing language, allows a model of language as a capacity dependent upon extensive multimodal coordination throughout many regions of a brain that is biased toward its acquisition.[cxlv] One such biasing mechanism is the sheer size of the human brain, as expressed by its very high encephalization quotient[cxlvi] of 7.4-7.8, compared with the mean for mammals, which is about 1.[7]

The rough correlation between brain size and intelligence predicts an increased processing capacity to be associated with a large brain—a capacity that could potentially facilitate lexical signaling rather than a more limited one-to-one system of correspondences.[cxlvii] While the former greatly expands the potential scope of what can be communicated, it also bears a high cost. Because neural tissue is expensive to maintain, and the enhanced flexibility that increases expressive potential also increases the risk of error at any step in the communication and interpretation processes, most species attain maximal fitness by limiting their repertoires to a smaller numbers of objects, with their concordantly lower error limits.[cxlviii]

Along with its larger overall size, the human brain comes equipped with a relatively large prefrontal cortex (PFC), a uniquely mammalian structure[8] that, like the highly interconnected central nervous system itself, is notable for reentrant pathways and back projections.[cxlix] It is the

---

[7] The encephalization quotient is a ratio between actual brain mass and predicted brain mass for an animal of given size. For comparison, the EQ of bottlenose dolphins is 4.14, and that of chimpanzees is 2.2-2.5.

[8] The functional analog of the PFC in birds is the nidopallium, which is similarly extensively connected to other forebrain regions and generally operates as a freely associated, distributed network shaped by learning experiences; it is notable for its lack of modularity, and is not linearly organized (VP Bingman in Animal Thinking: Contemporary Issues in Comparative Cognition).

widespread connectivity that the PFC propagates throughout the cerebral cortex which allows the coordination and integration of the various cortical modalities that are believed to facilitate symbolic representation. In a self-amplifying evolutionary feedback loop, symbolic language, so dependent on the PFC, may have played the recursive role of itself being a "prime mover in prefrontalization," according to Deacon.[cl]

Just as certain capacities of the sensorimotor faculties that enable self-guided locomotion foreshadow those that are essential in communication, including automatic prediction and preparation and purposive awareness,[cli] some of the functions assumed by the PFC in nonhumans foreshadow and support the more recent applications that play a role in symbolic language. Expressing the exquisite economy of exaptation, the PFC's integrative functioning gives it an executive role in goal planning, decision-making, behavioral modulation and, for highly prefrontalized species such as monkeys, the flexibility to filter and juggle sensory priorities by focusing attention on one stimulus by holding it in short-term memory, while simultaneously engaging in a different behavior.[clii] The inhibitory capacities of the PFC enhance learning and behavioral plasticity by not only allowing for conscious direction of attention, but also by possibly enabling learning through imitation.[cliii] Thanks to the selectivity enabled by a well-developed PFC, it is hypothesized that individuals are able to select which behaviors they imitate while inhibiting imitation of non-target ones.[9] Unlike nonlinguistic vocalizations—with the large exception of vocal mimicry in birds—language is unique in relying on imitation to be learned. This highlights another crucial distinction between brains that support language and those that do not: whereas nonlinguistic communicative signals, likely derived from a common ancestral source, arise from the subcortical sensorimotor regions—those areas once categorized as the limbic system, the midbrain, and the brainstem—temporal and frontal-lobe cortical structures play a large role in human language production

---

[9] The hypothesis is just that: it is difficult to distinguish imitation from other forms of social learning like emulation.

and processing, likely because of the large role learning plays in language acquisition.[cliv]

The features that allowed humans to open up an entirely new cognitive niche seem to arise from brains that represent a compilation of changes in degree which, when collectively interactive, support a transition to something completely new and unpredictable—emergence separated from its constituents by a causal discontinuity. Underlying that leap, however, certain continuities are preserved, to be transformed and released at the higher level. These homologies maintain the link between the aspects of human intelligence that are indeed a change in kind, and the qualities that converged to precipitate that change.

Behaviorism

The observable differences between the brains of humans and closely related nonhumans do display a strong mark of continuity, as Darwinian evolution predicts. However, the implications for the distinctions between minds is more uncertain, especially in light of the long history of hesitation, solidified into dogmatic rejection with the rise of behaviorism, of attributing the faculty of mind to animals at all. Just like physical and biological phenomena, the question of animal awareness was subjected to the wringer of a scientific rationalism that was conceived in terms of a yawning chasm between the conscious experience of "insideness" within the human mind as the "thinking thing," and everything else. This split, along with the attendant conception of local cause-and-effect determinism that held sway over much scientific thought well into the 20th century, enabled the behaviorist charge, led by J.B. Watson, to eschew any role for consciousness in animal—and eventually even human—responsiveness. Bolstered by the work of Pavlov, behaviorists championed a mechanistic model of conditioning-dependent, stimulus-response causality as an explanation for behavior that precluded mind, consciousness, or purpose. Watson himself carried this ideology to its logical extreme when, responding to data on differences in vocal structures that are relaxed versus those that are reading aloud, is reported to have concluded that thinking is a "laryngeal behavior."[clv]

An early voice of dissent against the behavioristic trend was found in the work of E.C. Tolman. His embrace of William James' very counter-Cartesian metaphor of mind as an entity extended into space prepared Tolman to accept the insights he extruded from years of poring over rats in mazes as evidence of behavior as purposive, and organisms as active participants in information processing rather than passive subjects of conditioning.[clvi] However, Tolman's perspective on behavior remained largely an outlier until the latter portion of the 20th century, when human psychology rekindled its curiosity in "the distinctions between conscious and unconscious processes in everyday cognition,"[clvii] and even animal consciousness was declared a field ripe for study.[clviii]

Enjoying cautious freedom from the strictly mechanistic constraints of behaviorism, modern ethology still finds itself wrestling with the quandary raised by Darwin's radical suggestion that links human intelligence with that of animals in kind. Historically, the response has spanned an interpretive spectrum ranging from rampant anthropomorphism to its polar opposite as formalized by Morgan's Canon, which forbade attributing to a "higher psychical faculty" that which could be explained in terms "of one which stands lower in the psychological scale," and was foundational to behaviorism.[clix] The lure of the latter view, which encouraged mechanical metaphors as a frame of interpretation for cognitive processes, was lauded by Clark Hull as a "prophylaxis against anthropomorphic subjectivism." The limitations of this view are summed up by David Leary when he wryly ponders on "what will provide a safeguard against the excesses of 'mechanopomorphic objectivism.'"[clx]

Through the metaphor of mechanism, behaviorism sought to eliminate any trace of subjectivity from cognition. Reflectiveness was replaced with reflexiveness by the presumption that mental activity at every level was essentially Pavlovian according to the prevailing interpretation of conditioning: circuits constructed via association between stimulus and response directing behavior, free of any intelligent mediation. As useful as the metaphor of mechanism has proven in facilitating insights into certain aspects of biological and psychological workings, its entailment that eliminates conscious subjectivity from living entities has hindered understanding in other aspects—thus providing a cautionary tale regarding the traps of false understanding that come from conflating a metaphor, inherently incomplete, with the totality of truth conditions in a target domain.

Umwelt

Reawakening from the mindless torpor of lawful regularity through the "insider" approach of semiosis, life's milieu is freed to display sentience at every level of activity through "organisms' capacity to do self-preservative work."[clxi] Cognition—which we will define as the acquisition, processing, storage, and response to information[clxii]—is implicated in the activity of survival in its most primordial, fundamental form: the ability to discriminate self from non-self. Arising inseparably with life as a necessary condition of the differentiated body, incipient intelligence manifests as a felt distinction: an iconic, experientially primitive apperception inherent in all life forms as "insiders of sign processes."[clxiii] Perception is an experience which only arises in the context of a distinctly experienced self.

Much like a developing seed, the conditions needed to prod the germinal spark of proto-cognition to development are supplied in the life form itself, within the context of a supportive environment. As discreet agents whose existences are marked by variability, each organism faces the basic challenge of integrating the multiple domains traversed by life processes into a single experiential framework. The most fundamental cross-domain coupling is between the primitive stirrings of intentionality—the appetitive motivations that originate within the organism—and outer behavioral expressions, such as motility. "The distinction between the world as sensed and the world as acted upon defines the basic condition for the survival of adaptive organisms," observes Herbert Simon.[clxiv] The disparities between sensation, motivation, and action demand that the organism establish correlations between the experiential domains and their physiological responses.

Offering rapprochement between these divergent domains is the "unitary"—and unifying—experience of perception, which "arises essentially out of the playing together of two correlatively related functions."[clxv]

The tight coupling between inner impetus and behavioral expression in even the simplest forms of life is the outcome of sign processes carried out in terms of the organism's structural and biochemical organization. The iconic experience of stimulation unleashes orderly cascades of chemical activity, with chemical messengers acting indexically to impel thirdness, or interpretation, often in the form of movement rather than explicit awareness. Throughout the various echelons of complexity and responsive potential to be found in the living world, the unchanging factor is the "corporeal consciousness"[clxvi] bounded by the particular capacities of a given animate body, which serves as a primary reference frame to create a dynamic balance between organism and environment. As the sentient locus of coordination between the interlinked domains of sensation, motivation, and action, the living body serves as the original "semantic template," or source domain from which meaning can be construed regarding the external environment. Since this meaning is only fructified to the extent that it shapes the organism's interactions with its environment to the creature's advantage, its creation should entail changes within the organism's experiential domain that guides its perceptions and consequent behaviors toward the end of promoting survival and fitness. Such changes, when established as regularities by heredity, become arbiters of which potential stimuli are perceived by the organism as information, and which as mere noise.

Peering into the meaning-mediated perceptual constructs of animals, Jakob von Uexkull developed the notion of Umwelt. Variously interpreted as the "cognitive" or "conceptual lifeworld," "cognitive niche," or "semiotic niche," Umwelt is the "subjective reality" that is the basis of individual organismal activities.[clxvii] Salient environmental regularities become "carriers of perception marks," or signs, which the organism responds to as information.[clxviii] "Governed in all its parts by meaning for subject," an Umwelt is an active cognitive dynamic playing across the perceptual interface that integrates the organism into its environment through sign processes. All life forms, rather than just humans, become "living symbols" through semiosis and Umwelt, each indelibly embedded in an environment whose congruent aspects it relates to as carriers of meaning. To such an active participant in semantic construction, the difference between relevant information, or a sign, and irrelevant noise depends largely on the creature's motivations,[clxix] but even more fundamentally, on the structure of the creature itself: what and how it is capable of perceiving. Umwelt is essentially "a template of perceptual readiness that allows an organism to experience the world within its own frame of understanding."[clxx]

Husserl sums up the receiver-dependent nature of perception marks: "While what constitutes the object's appearing remains unchanged, the intentional character of the experience alters."[clxxi] The highly subjective nature of perception marks and the responses they elicit particularly captivated Uexkull, as he considered, for instance, the different meanings a single oak tree could have within the various Umwelten of its many denizens: the fox denned at its roots; the owls, squirrels and small birds respectively nesting, springing, or flitting among its branches; the ant foraging amid the grooves of its bark; the bark beetle seeking food and a place for its eggs below the bark; the woodpecker and ichneumon wasp seeking the larvae of this same beetle within the trunk's fibrous tissues; the little girl playing in the woods; and the forester carrying out his work.[clxxii]

Guiding the perceptual capacities and interpretive proclivities of the subject, Umwelt acts as a prototype of the world, providing a "lead track" that guides a creature's assessments of and responses to the various stimuli that it encounters.[clxxiii] Such perceptual contingency represents a vast source of potential for the diversifying operations of evolution to act upon, sculpting organisms to select, filter, order, and interpret different, yet overlapping aspects of their environments into a meaning-world informed by actionable information—a job so endless in possible variations that neural mechanisms evolved to augment sensory systems in the task of processing the information they are receptive to.

Presenting to the Umwelt like mental artefacts of its evolutionary history, the perception marks that an organism is sensitive to tailor it to its environment so finely that the closest analog conjured for Uexkull was the musical glory of contrapuntal harmony.[clxxiv] Drawing meaning like a thread of melody from its surroundings, the organism adaptively structures its behaviors relative to the multitudinous conditions of a complex environment in a symphonic, creative dynamic. Perceptual adaptiveness traces its origins, then, to conditions reminiscent of the incipience of a metaphor or analogy: the scope of perceptual possibility that confronts any single organism far surpasses actual sensory capacity. Any resulting perception is therefore going to necessarily highlight certain aspects of environmental input and occlude others. Just as the largely unconscious pre-mapping phase of analogy selectively hones the range of possible source domains to those that lead to the most valid inferences for a given problem, perceptions are likewise contextually biased to attend to the most pertinent signs. And just as cross-domain mapping highlights certain aspects from its selected source domain while obscuring others, only the most relevant aspects of the information collected from the environment are presented to explicit perception for interpretation.

The primary perceptual filter is the bodily boundary itself, which encounters environmental stimuli as indexical signs that are conducted inwardly to be experienced and interpreted. Bodily structures bias the information registered toward relevance to the organism. A sense-poor creature like Uexkull's iconic tick admits only three perception marks into its tiny Umwelt for the greater part of its life cycle: light, in a general, directional way, the smell of butyric acid, and the warmth of a mammalian body. For more expansive Umwelten, there is a greater difference between what can be perceived relative to what is perceived, leading to the tendency of sense organs to monitor cues rather than to precisely relay the totality of external conditions.[clxxv] With multiple sensory modalities contributing to overall perception, information from each must be sifted, refined, and integrated with complementary threads of information from every other. Rendered through specialized sensory—and, for those creatures so endowed, neural—biases, information presents conditions most probably relevant to the organism for fulfilling the most basic fitness imperatives of self-preservation and reproduction. As a cohesive confluence of the biological fundaments of metabolism, growth, reproduction, motility, and at least an implicit self-frame of reference, subjective agency unites the different internal domains by responding to information from the environment, including from other organisms.[clxxvi] The limitations of embodiment, which constrain perception and oblige an organism to acquire energy and materials from outside of itself, are the basic drivers of intelligence and meaning creation, even in the most basic biological systems.

The Eye of the Beholder

Spanning the spectrum of complexity, Darwin's innumerable "wedges in the economy of nature" collectively explore every nuance of perceptual possibility in a synergistic complex of niche creation and exploitation, carried out among myriads of autonomous, interacting organisms like a highly choreographed dance. The formal and perceptual variety that is foundational to a self-sustaining landscape of such intricate complexity is dependent on sensory systems that are infinitely amenable to evolutionary fine-tuning. This is well illustrated in the modality of vision, whose Precambrian advent was so gravid with possibility that some speculate on its possible role in fueling the Cambrian explosion.[clxxvii]

An animal's view of its world is conditioned by factors including its size, diet, mobility, circadian patterns, and habitat. About ten different eye types accommodate these and other variables, and are malleable to countless specializations, such as in placement; cornea shape; lens shape; fovea placement; the distribution, type, and relative abundance of photoreceptive cells; and pigment distribution. The resultant variations between acuity, sensitivity, color and depth perception, light sensitivity, field of vision, temporal resolution, and UV detection among terrestrial, aquatic, and amphibious creatures alike reflect the enormous ingenuity latent in open-ended adaptive systems.

Selection from this ambit of potential is generally predicated on the animal's niche. Many predatory species, for example, enjoy the depth perception afforded by binocular vision, whereas most prey species largely forego this benefit in favor of lateral eye placement with its panoramic radius, and only a small swath of binocular vision in front. Some non-predatory birds supplement their frontal vision with a fovea in the binocular region in addition to the lateral one. Owls also notably display specialized fovea placement, with the greatest concentration of photoreceptors in the lower portion of the eye, which sweeps the ground in search of prey.[clxxviii]

Another adjustable variable in vision is color perception.[clxxix] Nocturnal, deep-water, or cave-dwelling species, with only a single photopigment type, see a drab, grey world. Many mammals, nocturnal insects, marine fish, crustaceans and spiders are dichromats whose grey surroundings are tinged with shades of yellow, green, and blue. Trichromats like humans, apes, Old World monkeys, and some insects, spiders, freshwater fish, reptiles, and amphibians, experience a world rich in hue and saturation, while the ancestral condition of tetrachromatism is preserved in birds, diurnal reptiles, as well as in certain fish and amphibians. Although some species of butterflies boast even more photopigment types, the most distinctive specialization for color vision is claimed by the mantis shrimp, 12 of whose 16 types of photoreceptors are modified for color vision.[10]

The photopigments that enable color vision are malleable not only in variety, but also in distribution. For example, when a guppy looks up, it does so with green receptors, but when looking to the side for food or conspecifics, it does so with red.[clxxx] Lycaenid butterflies also

---

[10] As extraordinary as its specializations for color vision are, the mantis shrimp does not actually discriminate color better than a human with only ¼ the number of photopigments. While a heavy burden of data processing is carried by the human brain, the shrimp eye accommodates much of the processing necessary to turn stimulation into an image by separating the information leaving the retina into multiple parallel data streams. (Cronin and Marshall 2001)

demonstrate remarkable specificity in photopigment variety and distribution. In *L. heteronea*, the visual-pigment spectra are closely matched to the wing-reflectance spectra of the male; however, the dorsal region of the female eye has an additional color pigment that allows her to spot the red coloration of the food plants that she will spend most of her 2-week adult life seeking out for oviposition.[clxxxi]

In the evolutionary quest to taper the scope of sensory inputs to the most salient, the many fine-tuned adaptations of the eye only represent the first tier of filtration which biases how light is received. The next level of selective culling comes from the retina, which must reduce its informational load before sending a signal to the brain.[11] Acting as an interface between icon and index, the stimulated retina transforms its encounter with photons into a bioelectrical excitation that travels along the optical nerve and will ultimately present as a signal to the neurons at the axons' termini. Following the branching byways of the optic nerve, the action potential is redirected toward different brain regions, each of which, like its own distinct Umwelt, will construe unique meaning from a single light-induced signal. Whereas a superchiasmatic termination stimulates an interpretation related to circadian rhythms, signals bound for the pretectal nucleus are relevant in terms of eye reflexes. A signal that propagates through the lateral geniculate nucleus—where it encounters another layer of informational amendment as it interacts with inputs both related and unrelated to vision—to the visual cortex, is even further spliced into modular pathways that separately interpret the signal as features like space and motion, or color and shape, before binding them into a coherent visual percept.[clxxxii]

In addition to the selective rarefication a stimulus undergoes in its passage to percept, it must further run the gamut of central-processing-level refinements before becoming consciously presentable. Vastly more plastic than sensory filters, neural filtering mechanisms pre-attentively highlight salient features of the ripening percept, even tailoring them to suit the organism's very specific and often-changing needs through the

---

[11] The human brain is being referenced here.

various stages of its life cycle.[clxxxiii] Spatial perception in rodents provides an example of this fine-tuned specificity. In two monogamous rodent species, the pine and the prairie voles, members of both sexes range equally over their territories and display no detectable difference in spatial cognitive abilities. However, among their polygynous meadow-dwelling cousins and, more distantly, kangaroo rats, a marked sexual dimorphism exists in navigational ability and object location memory in favor of the male, whose home range is 4 to 5 times larger than that of the female.[clxxxiv] While the reproductive benefits of such cognitive enhancements may justify extra energetic investment during the summertime breeding season, the same talents become liabilities during the rest of the year, as the high costs of maintaining neural tissues and the increased risk of predation that accompanies roaming exact their toll. Accordingly, spatial cognition in males—along with its physical correlates of increased cranial volume, brain mass, and neural density within the hippocampus— peaks during the summer months, ebbing low during the winter. Demonstrating a variation not of degree, but of kind, females of these polygynous species display greater sensitivity than males to fine-grained spatial details like landmarks—a kind of familiarity that helps them efficiently navigate their smaller home ranges.

With an untold array of preconscious processes continuously refashioning received information according to a particular corporeally informed understanding, vision can be described as an act of "interrogating the environment" that entails "continuously noting and inserting one's cognitive framework."[clxxxv] Of its subjectively constructed nature, Merlau-Ponty explains, "Vision is not the metamorphosis of things in themselves into the sight of them…It is a thinking that unequivocally decodes signs within the body. Resemblance is the result of perception, not is basis." The same is true of any sensory experience that an organism's intelligence functions in relation to. Out of all of the possible information available, a small amount registers as relevant perception marks, whose presentation is molded according to the needs and niche of the organism. Within this "universe of signs," life is a dynamical locus of thirdness, guided in its interactions with the world by particular viewpoints and interpretations that structure how the environment is perceived and acted upon. In this way, "the individual mind is immanent but not only in the body. It is immanent also in pathways and messages outside the body."[clxxxvi]

The Organization of Intelligence

A traditional anthropocentric view of intelligence depicts a stepwise ascent of cognition as a global property along the continuum of a *scala natura* whose triumphant culmination at the human apex is particularly characterized by reason and language. Framed in this way, comparative psychology becomes a quest for "what appears to be missing"[clxxxvii] in animal intellect relative to human. The question of intelligence affords a more nuanced answer, however, when considered in terms of an animal's ability to solve ecologically or socially relevant problems.[clxxxviii] This more modular approach allows the possibility of probing the constituents of particular forms of intelligence by predicting the universality of certain cognitive fundaments, whose open-ended flexibility avail them to specializations within and across domains.[clxxxix] For example, models of different types of recognition learning, including habituation, imprinting, and kin discrimination, predict essentially identical cognitive processes.[cxc]

A modular approach to the mind reverses simplistic correspondence-based ideas about learning. For example, while conditioning was long held to be merely reliant on the temporal pairing of stimuli, it is now more fully understood to be a complex confluence of many factors related to the subject's perception of stimuli and events. Unlike a linear hierarchy with its uncomplicated structure of subordination between levels, the organization of behaviors and their cognitive sources is more aptly compared to the nested hierarchy characteristic of nearly decomposable systems, which are comprised of multi-level interactions between self-contained, partially independent components much like Koestler's holons. The interacting cognitive modules that form a nested semantic hierarchy are the proximate causal factors that underlie the similarly hierarchical organizations of the stereotyped motor patterns that behaviorally express cognition.[cxci]

Despite their complexity, nearly decomposable systems usually only consist of a few different kinds of subsystems in various combinations and arrangements.[cxcii] The substructures diverge formally through the differential coupling strength of their semiotic interactions, which are closely correlated within modules, but approximately independent in the short term from other modules.[cxciii] Evolutionarily, this points to highly conserved learning mechanisms, with behavioral differences arising less from selective pressures on the behavior itself, but more from non-learning processes like sensory or motor systems that shift the spectrum of inputs that register as perception marks, or the nature of the organism's physical response to them.[cxciv]

Specializations are codetermined within the top-down integrating context of the organism whose features they, in a circular twist of causality, help determine from the bottom up. Differential responsiveness to various informational inputs based on different goals and routes of processing results in specialization within modules that render them "functionally incompatible" with non-target applications.[cxcv] From the global perspective of the whole organism, however, the multiplicity in form and application of different modules is united by their underlying redundancies, the broadest of which is their common orientation toward supporting optimal fitness outcomes.

On this modular view, cognition as a non-differentiable monolith dissolves into localized components that can respond with some independence to selective forces. Such quasi-independence imparts a unique evolutionary history, not only on the organism, but on each and every cognitive attribute it harbors.[cxcvi] Plasticity should therefore be able to coexist with species-specificity to yield a flexible, subtly tunable range of cognitive adaptability to ambient selective pressures within a single species. Into this predictive framework enters the ubiquitous chickadee to offer a supportive example. Birds hailing from the northernmost reaches of their range are inured to limited, unpredictable food supplies, and correspondingly display superior spatial memory to conspecifics from more temperate climes with less variable conditions. This cognitive adaptation is a response to environmental pressures on the birds to remember locations of food sources and caches.[cxcvii] The malleability of intelligence brings the capabilities of its hosts into alignment with the particular challenges they face in their given environment.

The Ingredients of Cognition

As with any feature that affects animal behavior, cognition can be viewed through the four-fold lens of ethologist Nikolaas Tinbergen's classic "whys" of causation—proximate cause, adaptive value, and phylogenetic and ontogenetic histories. While cognition itself may be an answer to the question of proximate cause, it is also subject to the other three.[cxcviii] Cognition and its expression, then, is the result of the confluence of multiple factors, one of which is itself.

The formative strands out of which cognitive complexity is woven are universal. Although sensory and cognitive modules are characterized by what distinguishes them from each other, the redundancy underlying the different aspects of a complex system ensures some generalities across domains. Like the modules they beget, the cognitive fundaments can themselves function as semi-independent units, each of whose properties are applicable to various degrees under different circumstances. Their relative independence arises from the irreducibility of each to any other, as well as the distinct operation each performs on information as supplied by sensation and construed by perception. Operating in concert, they constitute a complete act of cognition whose universality precludes a strict view of cognitive processes as psychological capacities, which are absent throughout much of the biosphere. Before it establishes itself as a mental competency, cognition is a bodily activity.

Agency/subjectivity

Cognition is, most fundamentally, the creation of meaning. While meaning transpires through interpretation, the third level of sign processes, it is dependent upon both indexical conveyance of information and raw, iconic sensation. The "unities of sense" that Husserl speaks of are all rooted in "a sense-bestowing consciousness which, for its part, exists absolutely and not by virtue of another sense-bestowal."[cxcix] Independent of any experience or perception is an irreducible consciousness that provides a context in which all sign processes unfold their meaning according to the evolutionary conditionings of the subject perceiving them. This experiential foundation of semiosis enables perception, information, and meaning to exist as such, thereby distinguishing directed action from mechanical reaction.

Arising from the most basic imperative to distinguish "self" as the fundamental experiential template from "non-self" as the domain to be explored in subjective terms, subjectivity within bodily confines is unavoidably self-referencing. This recursive tendency affects what Teilhard de Chardin describes as a centering; a spatial, perceptual, as well as cognitive condition: "[The observer is] obliged to carry with him everywhere the center of the landscape he is crossing."[cc] For mobile organisms, self-referencing is intimately tied with the act of movement itself—Husserl's kineses or "I cans"—and makes navigation possible through a perceived localization of the self that allows for the understanding of where one is going relative to where one is.[cci] In many mammals, the self-frame of reference relative to spatial cognition is anchored to the eye, head, and limbs, and integrated into coordinated actions in the parietal cortex. The internal orientation of self-reference is offset by the "aboutness" of external objects of meaning as conveyed through sign processes, which draw the focus of the subject away from itself—albeit in terms of itself.[ccii] Continuously perceiving and classifying presentable aspects of its environment in accordance with its own structure and imperatives, the agent's sensitive inner dynamics are ever responsive to changing outer conditions.[cciii]

Subjectively generating information and behaviorally implementing its entailments for fitness-promoting ends is a function of agency, which, circularly, is prerequisite for meaning creation. For many forms of life, inputs admitted as information are highly specified by restrictive sensory gatekeepers, ranging from glucose receptors in bacteria to pheromone receptors on moth antennae. Such tiny glimpses of information constitute the objects of meaning within Umwelten that elicit responses and so become loci of behavioral organization. With the increasingly autonomous agency that unfolds through more elaborate systems of perception and cognition, sensory filtration is supplemented by cognitive means of information selection, such as attention. Without conscious direction, attention is a bottom-up quality bound to sensory input. In more behaviorally complex animals, the job of filtering information for relevance shifts from a strictly sensory function to a choice-contingent one as well. Supported by an extensive neural network, the descending feedback signals governed by the PFC in particular are implicated in enabling flexible manipulation of top-down attentional control.[cciv] Aided by short term memory, intentionally directed attention becomes a potent arbiter of focus and meaning. Perceptually, it relates separable environmental features into unitary objects much more coherently than preconscious perception alone.[ccv] Cognitively and behaviorally, it can enable task complexity, or even simultaneity, such as in an animal that can feed and maintain vigilance at the same time.

While thirdness, or interpretive capacity, provides an active expression of subjectivity by supporting interaction with the environment, subjectivity itself does not depend on objects of meaning—these merely comprise its contents and invite its focus. Rather, subjective agency is the substrate upon which the strands that weave themselves into cognition create meaning about the objects they reflect. Over the course of evolution, the nature of this subjectivity shifts and expands, eventually giving rise to a unique form of self-referencing when it becomes, through humans, aware of itself.

Memory

Continuously informing the experience of a perceiving subject like a "thread of melody running through the succession of our sensations,"[ccvi] the creation of meaning becomes capable of refinement into learning when it builds upon its own past. Predicated on the continuity afforded by retention, meaning is the aspect of experience that creates a change—whether significant or imperceptible—within the cognitive structure of the subject. Providing a stable platform that is the basis for the directed, interpretational modifications of learning, the preservative power of memory functions somewhat paradoxically by facilitating changes in how organisms relate to their environments. As a summary of the organism's past experience, memory provides a source domain, replete with entailments, from which to enact a temporal cross-domain mapping onto new experiences.

That memory is a fundamental capacity is attested to by the humble, unicellular paramecium, which is able to retain the learned effects of classical conditioning for at least 24 of its approximately 96-hour life span.[ccvii] Neural complexity, with its enhanced opportunities for specialization, allows for diversification within the function of memory. As the process of exaptation gradually coaxes new functions from preexisting ones, adaptive specializations cordon off certain applications of memory into module-like systems which, while selfsame in mechanism, operate according to rules that are specifically suited to particular environmental demands.[ccviii] With unique rules governing the timing of plasticity and the conditions for closure; input sensitivity; and the duration that the memories are retained without decay, certain memory systems become dedicated, such as to imprinting, and exclusive of other types of learning.

While a window of plasticity is a significant feature of memory specializations like imprinting and avian song learning, it is by no means unique to them. Many brain regions, including sensory systems, begin life in a very plastic state, ready to integrate experiential inputs into the developing neural architecture. These exposure-based "sensitive periods" roughly correspond with age, but depend on an adequate statistical sampling of environmental conditions for closure.[ccix] After the initial period of plasticity, the system enters the more stable adult phase, which, while not open to functional reorganization through passive exposure to stimuli, can be induced to reinforcement-based plasticity by behaviorally relevant experiences, such as an associative pairing or—for sensory systems—cross-modal stimulation.[ccx]

In addition to differential life cycle-based receptivity, memory also falls into distinct categories operationally: declarative, which is representational and includes episodic memory, and non-declarative, or procedural memory.[ccxi] While episodic memory secures particular details of certain events—especially unusual ones, tending to highlight contextual variances—procedural memory allows skill development by eschewing details and instead retaining invariances across episodes.[ccxii] These two types of memory, while drawing on the same experiences for their formation, appear to engage different brain structures, which may reflect different strategies of learning, and allow for different aspects of the same experience to be highlighted.[ccxiii]

By itself, memory does not create meaning. Rather, the temporal integrity it affords is the basis of modification through learning. Functioning closely in tandem with the subjective and interpretive facets of intelligence to preserve the meaning they generate, memory unites past with present through the durational coherence it lends to the essence of acquired experience.

Classification

As players in an economy of energetic trade-offs, organisms must optimize their fitness outcomes by utilizing available information as efficiently as possible. Often, this means basing decisions on classification-based heuristics rather than on highly precise representations.[ccxiv] Based on the partial information afforded by perception, the highly subjective endeavor of classification offers the advantage of simplifying—thereby expediting and lowering the energetic costs of—decision-making and learning.[ccxv]

One well-known model of classification, proposed by Richard Herrnstein, offers a 5-tiered hierarchy, whose first level is discrimination; second is rote memorization; third is open-ended categories; fourth is concepts; and fifth, abstract relations.[ccxvi] Similar to the selective bias of sensory inputs toward the most relevant aspects of stimuli, categories likewise prioritize particular pertinent aspects of an animal's typical experiences. Primarily based on object similarity, categories display central tendencies that can be represented as prototypes, with fluid overlap rather than clear demarcation along their boundaries.[ccxvii]

Discrimination, the first level of categorization, is a qualitative distinction demonstrable even in paramecia, which can distinguish between different gradations of perceptual stimuli such as vibrational frequency or illumination.[ccxviii] Based on dissimilarity, discrimination creates discreet reference frames according to which an organism may catalog its various experiences. As the foundation for all subsequent levels of categorization, discrimination, like an icon, is self-contained and can exist independently of the others levels. However, it is the preservative intervention of the second level of categorization, rote memory, which bestows longer-term utility upon categorization. Like an index affixing communicability to an icon, memory structurally stabilizes categories, fixing their members into place.

While useful for a small number of inputs, memorization can quickly become limiting and burdensome. Just as the shift from index to symbol demands relinquishing individual associations in favor of the more fluid many-to-one potential of relational associations with their expanded referencing power, the third level of classification, the creation of open-ended categories, reorganizes informational relations in a way that enables an animal to discriminate at a higher level; not just between individual stimuli, but between categories that are established in terms of interactional rather than inherent properties. Pigeons display this ability when asked to discriminate between perceptual features in photographs of items in different categories. While some of this work is carried out by rote memorization—pigeons have the astonishing ability to memorize over 800 photos—the birds are able to generalize from their memorized store of perceptual features to open-ended categories.[ccxix]

In the same way that an index can affect how an icon is understood, the way an animal categorizes affects how it remembers, which in turn affects both associative and recognition learning.[ccxx] Again, pigeons can create not only perceptual categories, but also superordinate, or functional categories for the same items.[ccxxi] That these are genuine categories to the pigeons is demonstrated by their reliable transfer of novel exemplars to correct categories at both levels. Such discriminative transfer is one of the hallmarks of conceptual behavior and demonstrates the natural flow from the level of classification to the creation of concepts.

Categorical learning ripens into causal understanding as a consequence of the nature of concepts, which rise above the level of mere sorting or descriptive capacities by incorporating inference.[ccxxii] Far from a simple process of meaning extraction, conceptualization is an inductive transfer of meaning among members of a category. Inference within a conceptual domain raises the possibility of inference across conceptual domains, which is the foundation of the fifth level of categorization, the creation and apprehension of abstract relations. This is the lofty realm of second-order analogical reasoning—the ability to appreciate relations between relations—and is generally deemed solely the province of human intelligence, although some behavioral evidence with symbol-trained chimps presses at the edge of this boundary and raises intriguing questions regarding the relationship between symbol use and high-level perception.[ccxxiii]

The ability to distinguish among different grades and classes of stimuli is essential for organisms that must orient their responses within a heterogeneous environment. By decomposing an otherwise intransigent whole into salient frames of understanding, categorization is an active, intelligent engagement with sensation as information. Its divisive nature, which segregates according to differences, simultaneously amplifies similarities by allocating category members according to some level of affinity. Semantically constructed themselves, categories are foundational to the creation of more complex meaning. With their members acting as source domains, categories supply the entailments that transfer into new contexts when domains are crossed.

Doman Crossing

While the metaphorical understanding of a target domain in terms of a source has been explored as foundational to meaning creation, domain crossing also functions in a less holistic way by uniting domains through association. While the capacity for association is universal among animals, the neural and molecular details that underlie it can differ widely across and even within species.[ccxxiv] With its unitive properties operating closely in tandem with the distinction-making faculty of categorization, association integrates information across domains based on what William James describes as the "keel and backbone of our thinking: sameness."[ccxxv] Like all of the other cognitive structural basics, association creates the scaffolding for its own higher levels of functioning, and so is operative at all levels. Demonstrable even among unicellular organisms, association in the form of conditioning illustrates a universal mechanism of learning.

One of the most thoroughly researched branches of psychology, classical conditioning effectively couples a perceptual, or conditioned stimulus (CS), to an unconditioned stimulus (US) capable of releasing a particular behavior. In Pavlov's famous experiments, the ringing bell—the CS—came to evoke the same response as the US—the presentation of food—even in the absence of the latter. The behavioristic interpretation prevalent at the time saw a simple conflation of temporally correspondent stimuli within a reflexive neural circuit. The intervening decades, however, have revealed a vastly more complex phenomenon wherein subjects act, not as circuit boards passively awaiting rewiring, but as learners actively construing logical and perceptual relations between context-sensitive events whose temporal dependence matters less than their informational contingency.[ccxxvi]

This more enlivened description of conditioning suggests room for a modulatory, rather than a solely eliciting role for association.[ccxxvii] Tolman believed that what a subject acquired in a learning experiment was expectation, which casts the CS into the role of a cue that can enhance an animal's preparedness for certain situations, rather than the trigger of a reflex.^{ccxxviii} Studies with gourami fish lend some support to this viewpoint by demonstrating that males conditioned to the flash of a red light preceding an aggressive encounter are prepared in a way that unconditioned males are not, as indicated by the increased number of bites, tail-beating responses, and victories displayed by the conditioned males over the control males.[ccxxix]

Because association calls for the representation not only of events, but relations among events, the potential complexity of associative relations is much greater than predicted by the mechanistic circuit model of conditioning.[ccxxx] With an image of the US replacing the actual perception, associations can form a propagative hierarchy, with new associations arising from prior ones.[ccxxxi] Among rats trained to pull a lever to receive sucrose, for example, the lever as CS invokes an image of the sucrose. When that rewarding US is replaced by an episode of sickening, the rats relate that event to the *image* of the previously conditioned US. The image, rather than the actual experience, is what enters into the new associative relation, and the rats have learned to avoid sucrose, rather than the lever.[ccxxxii] By uniting events on the basis of shared relational properties, association affects a semantic coupling between the perceptual features of a CS and the entailments of a US.

The possible evocation of intentional representations may elevate instrumental conditioning, once the basis for a mechanized view of consciousness, to the level of candidacy for a goal-directed behavior. The psychological definition of such intent-driven activity requires it to be mediated by a representation of a causal relationship between an action and outcome, as well as by a representation of the value of the outcome.[ccxxxiii] Viewed in these terms, even the most elemental domain-crossing between intention and behavioral implementation appears laden with assiduous, animating intelligence. The gulf between the internal representation and external expression would have to be navigated by inferences that evoke internal representations of possible routes to goal achievement in the context of emotive responses to motivationally significant events.[ccxxxiv] The interface at which affect meets action is conscious intentionality.

Far from being solely the province of cognitive learning and behavior, the corporeally instantiated faculty of domain crossing fundamentally shapes the meaning-value an organism imparts onto various aspects of its lifeworld, as sensory events are collated into perceptual units of experience. Information accrued in the semi-isolation of a sensory module arguably only takes on meaning when it is relieved of solitude through integration with information from other modalities.[ccxxxv] Some brain regions, like the superior colliculus—in which converge visual, auditory, and somatosensory inputs utilized in directed movements—or the posterior parietal cortex—where multiple sensory modalities conjoin with representations of motor actions—are considered associative because they host concentrated populations of neurons responsive to two or more sensory modalities.[ccxxxvi] Many other brain regions once believed to be unimodal are also revealing more inclusive proclivities. Activity in the auditory cortex, for instance, is strongly modulated by visual and tactile inputs.[ccxxxvii] Even such a simple act of perception as registering the turning of its head summons from within a rat's brain collaboration from vestibular, proprioceptive, motor efferent, and visual modalities.[ccxxxviii] The active and continuous integration of multiple modes of input into the process of information construction prompts organismal responses vastly different from those invoked either by single-modality stimulation, or even by consecutive stimulation of different modalities.[ccxxxix] Such supramodal representation entails a "transposition of meanings"[ccxl] across the different sensory domains, highlighting complementary aspects of different forms of information into an integrative, immersive experience.

From the progressively complex interlinking of semantic domains unfold many-dimensional, inter-level networks of meaning joined at nodes of correspondence. Mutually interdependent and catalytic of each other's activities, divisive categorization and synthesizing domain crossing fuse their respective powers of discriminative awareness and relational perceptiveness to craft an experientially, semantically causal framework that supports emergent levels of perception and cognitive organization. Enabled by subjectivity and sustained by memory, the activity and substance of meaning creation is in the complement of categorization and association. Interpretation, or thirdness, dynamically binds all of cognition's activities into a coherent unity.

Interpretation

Because of the fundamental subjectivity of all cognition, every aspect of it is implicitly guided by thirdness. Attention interprets relevance; memory reflects priority; categorization ascertains distinctions; and domain crossing affects associations. Conversely, when interpretation is examined as a cognitive fundament in its own right, each of the other four strands is inextricably interwoven into it. At its most basic, interpretation is a bodily function expressed behaviorally. A cascade of sensation-stirred signals propagates within the organism to generate the subjective prehension that underlies purposive behavior. Even unicellular organisms have a suite of bodily expressed "interpretations" including kineses, taxes, and tropisms. The evolution of a nervous system significantly expanded the scope of interpretive and responsive latitude by both facilitating a broadened behavioral repertoire, and supplying an avenue to increasing judicative discretion in more highly articulated forms of cognition.

While malleable in varying degrees to the instructive offerings of experience, an animal's interpretive capacity, which links directly to its learning ability, is constrained by intrinsic factors—a tension pondered by William James: "Are [the mind's] contents arranged from the start, or is the arrangement they may possess simply due to the shuffling of them by experience in an absolutely plastic bed?"[ccxli] The first option of "arranged" mental contents suggests a unidirectional arc tracing from genes through neurons and emerging behaviorally, fully formed and unbidden by functional experience.[ccxlii] The almost uncanny fit between spontaneous adaptive behavior and organismal niche inspired Uexkull to wax mysterious on the timeless "supersensory knowledge" of the spider, which weaves its web in conformity to the ghostly dimensions of the fly's "primordial image."[ccxliii] While such Uexkullian favorites as the spider and the pea weevil do benefit from the tightly scripted regime of prefunctional adaptive modularity,[ccxliv] which binds behaviors to the anticipatory purview of the genetic code, this model fails to encompass the full spectrum of animal responsiveness to environmental exigencies. However, the second option of complete plasticity fails to account for cognitive and behavioral biases that stipulate how an animal is most likely to encounter its environment and be affected by experience.[ccxlv] Spanning the poles of rigid structure and *tabula rasa*, a probabilistic interpretation of the "developmental manifold" predicts a two-way flow of reciprocal interactions between internal and external environments wherein an organism "interprets" its evolutionary history anew each generation in the context of current environmental conditions.[ccxlvi] In this multi-leveled "co-actional construction," learning serves as a necessary complement to biological information by expanding complexity and diversity beyond what genomic changes alone could support.[ccxlvii]

Phylogenetically etched into cognitive and behavioral mechanisms, the bounds of possible learning are selectively narrowed through experience—broadly defined as function or activity, including endogenous neural activity and proprioception[ccxlviii]— into the limited range of probability that shapes and is shaped by the animal's ontogenetic trajectory. So formative are early perceptual encounters that visual experience with one's own toes—if one happens to be a baby chick—can be a decisive factor in the future success of one's encounters with possible food sources.[ccxlix] For bobwhite quail chicks denied exposure to species-typical exemplars of audio-spatial congruency, intersensory integration is disrupted and perception is impaired.[ccl] Independent motor components of a behavior, such as the pecking of a chick, await the experience of actual ingestion in order to integrate into the complex behavioral system of functional foraging.[ccli] The interplay between an organism's internal directives; its perceptual, cognitive, and behavioral capacities; and the environmental promptings that cue them, coalesce in the acquisition of species-appropriate behaviors through what Gilbert Gottlieb refers to as "experiential canalization."[cclii] At the neural level, this canalization is apparent in the relative pliancy of motorsensory neurons to the formative potential of experience, which shifts and reduces as the life cycle proceeds into maturity. The receptive fields of young neurons are large, but are unable to integrate multi-sensory inputs, whereas more mature stages of development show much less openness, even as they become more refined and integrative.[ccliii]

While learning opens up avenues of complexity that could not be achieved by genetic encoding alone, in many species it requires highly constrained parameters to optimally bias probabilities toward particular outcomes. Imprinting, which resembles classical conditioning in some ways, restricts both the range of inputs that cognitive mechanisms are responsive to and the time frame of responsiveness, which typically terminates with the establishment of object preference.[ccliv] This specificity allows the greater spotted cuckoo, a brood parasite that parts ways with its "foster family" at fledging, to flock with members of its own kind—if it has had the appropriate imprinting experience. Accordingly, adult cuckoos visit parasitized nests during the chicks' sensitive period within a few days of fledging.[cclv] Without this fortuitous exposure, young cuckoos fail to aggregate either with conspecifics or with their host species, upon which they are apparently not susceptible to imprinting. The restrictive bounds on this crucial act of interpretation guide it toward an optimally fitness-producing conclusion.

In addition to the non-cognitive biasing factors of imprinting, pre-existing cognitive biases can also steer animals toward species-relevant stimuli. The specificity of these biases is demonstrated by two similar and closely related species, the swamp and the song sparrow, which each learn their own correct song even if exposed to those of both species when young.[12,cclvi] Predispositions to specific phobias can be inherited in many animals as "expectancy biases," and easily be affirmed through experience.[cclvii] Naïve monkeys, for example, readily acquire the species-relevant fear of snakes by merely observing a fearful reaction in other monkeys. In contrast, an irrelevant fear, such as of flowers, does not

---

[12] The song sparrows will produce some of the simpler swamp sparrow song in adulthood, as well as their own. Preference may come from how the song is learned: in the swamp sparrow, the key unit is the syllable, but in the more complex melodies of the song sparrow, both syllable and syntax are important learning components. For both species, when the conspecific song is withheld, the heterospecific song will be learned.

transfer to the neophytes in the same indirect way and is more difficult to instill directly.[cclviii]

The inclination to be affected in a specific way by experience bespeaks a "preparedness" for a particular kind of relationship with the environment.[cclix] Expressed through the selectively focused lens of Umwelt, the organism's relationship with its environment develops and crystalizes through its particular ability to extract, interpret, and respond to information in a way that allows it to dynamically reach out and manipulate the world, "act[ing] on [its] own behalf."[cclx] Thirdness, which negotiates the organism's ongoing relation with highlighted aspects of its environment, is both creator of subjective value and mediator of behavioral expression. It is an essential guide for an organism that lives in a world wherein "however disorderly the chaos, the *number* of regularities must be infinite."[cclxi] The detection of these regularities and the meaning they carry requires the subject to compare competing options in parallel and assesses them in terms of what it has inferred from previously established patterns in an attempt to optimize the outcome of its selected option. An affirming outcome reinforces the organism's tendency to perceive the target stimulus as part of a pattern. Those patterns that a creature detects or composes can be parlayed into heuristics that provide a basis for the predictive function of interpretation, such as where to find a food source or how to evade a predator. Just as with all other cognitive fundaments, the interpretive power of prediction is not strictly a psychological one. Animals express "predictions" through physiological changes, such as voles that slow their growth rates in advance of a water shortage, or carp that deepen their body design—reducing swimming efficiency—in the probable future presence of predators.[cclxii]

In contrast to the profusion of behavioral "interpretations" possible throughout the countless forms constituting the biosphere, a silent, expressively passive option is universally available to living organisms. Habituation, which is marked by its *lack* of responsiveness to selected stimuli, is deceptively active—cognitively and sometimes physically—in its establishment. Complex interactions between the subject and stimulus are often necessary in order for the subject to categorically assess its target, and then associatively integrate it into a context, at which point the subject has become habituated. Juvenile brown trout illustrate this two-part process when establishing a school. Through frequently aggressive interactions, individuals learn to recognize each other within the framework of a social hierarchy.[cclxiii] Once these relations are established, the habituated young fish largely ignore each other and allocate their attention to other pursuits, such as feeding and predator detection. That the addition of a new fish elicits intense focus and social activity within the otherwise desensitized school indicates that the target of habituation is not merely a stimulus, but rather a whole class of information.[cclxiv]

The biphasic behavioral outcomes of habituation—with sensitization, or enhanced responsiveness to the stimulus followed by desensitization—are mirrored by neuronal activity.[cclxv] The frequently-probed siphons of *Aplysia* sea slugs, which the animals defensively withdraw in response to aversive stimuli, show an increase in neuronal varicosities in sensitized animals, whereas those of habituated slugs show a reduction.[cclxvi] Similarly in mammals, synapse formation increases in response to environmental manipulations or learning tasks, and neural activity relative to a new task is widely distributed in a pre-habituated brain. After habituation, the same stimulus evokes neural activity along a specific, functionally isolated pathway that reduces energetic costs to the organism by selectively compressing the scope of stimuli that elicit responsiveness, albeit at the expense of context-sensitivity and flexibility.[cclxvii] From the open, unintegrated plasticity of the sensitization phase, a neural pathway is etched toward a particular cognitive outcome, along with its corresponding behaviors. This is the formation of a habit, which does not require significant cognitive input to be maintained; rather, it routes cognitive activity through the channel-like "chreodes" envisioned by biologist C.H. Waddington, which guide it like water along a riverbed. "The whole function of thought," opines Peirce, "is to produce habits of action."[cclxviii] Both "primordial" and "inductive"—pointing to the logic that Pierce deemed to be omnipresent in nature—the tendency to form habits produces a "semantic template" that predicts how experiences will be encountered, "for what a thing means is simply what habits it involves."[cclxix]

By inductively rendering noisy possibility into the increasingly ordered levels of felt sensation, intelligible perception, structured concept, and the learning that these support, subjective intelligence at all levels within the organism selectively compresses the range of eliciting stimuli it is susceptible to. Interpretation contextually aligns resulting behaviors by rendering outer conditions in terms of internal semantic constraints. In this way, interpretation is vitally active at all levels of cognition, integrating the internal, subjective environment with the objective outer one by contracting potential into canalized channels of habit whose function is to create behavioral regularities out of perceived environmental regularities. These habits are etched into an animal's neural circuitry as a current synopsis of both its phylogenetic and individual histories. They are the structures of an organism's intelligence; an active backdrop against which the leading edge of intelligence perceives, records, categorizes, associates, and infers as its wends its way from intention toward expression.

Binding the irreducibly interactive elements of intelligence like a seam, interpretation presides over the expansion of interactional possibilities that constitutes learning. Contra to this expansion is a simultaneous compression, or resolution, of noisy potential into a preferred form of understanding that provides the scaffolding to support the outgoing probes of intelligence. Interpretation is a simplification—the "reduction of the manifold to unity"—that serves to guide future interpretations and, in a top-down manner, the steps leading to those interpretations. The elements that make agency viable patiently explore the "universe of experience" in ever-new combinations and proportions, sampling and accruing evolutionary innovations over time and according to circumstance. Selectively expressed through the channels of embodiment and enactment, potential condenses into realization at each level of organismal activity through the continuous generation of meaning. At once the process of potential's creation and the context of its expression, thirdness subjectively coheres multitudes of cycles of meaning creation into organismal form. With each cycle culminating at the cusp of a new one, every product of intelligent action informs the protean potential from which future acts of cognition will unfold.

Like a brief and emergent summary of all of the intricacies that contribute to its development, interpretation channels the complexities of intelligence toward a particular goal that is generally related to advancing an organism's fitness; it is a fundamentally end-directed process. Originating in internally generated motivations and their subjective, species-specific routes to fulfillment, interpretation drives animals' abilities to relate to their surroundings in discerning and goal-directed ways. For example, in navigation, many animals plan routes based on what they know about relative efficiencies or opportunities for rewards along the way.[cclxx] Animals like homing pigeons that travel great distances may do so with the explicit, neurally encoded intention of reaching a specific destination.[cclxxi] Although often performed in the service of current motivational states, end-directed behaviors can be uncoupled from the present through planning for future potential motivational states. Rather than being directed to the reduction of an immediate gradient, such as a state of hunger in the presence of food, future-oriented behaviors like food caching relieve an intertemporal gradient between current abundance and eventual scarcity.[cclxxii] The complex process of planning links memory and attention with perception and anticipation in order to guide action.[cclxxiii]

The end-directedness of cognitive processes pervades biological activity and suffuses it with meaningful purposiveness. Flowing vectorally outward from an intentional source, motor processes coordinate into an Uexkullian "carillon made of living bells," whose every "self-tone would induce the next" in anticipation of the end condition they are enacting.[cclxxiv] Although independent of each other outside of the context of the global aim of the current action, the neural circuits underlying the "kinetic melody" of motor activity that expresses as a behavior link to each other in seemingly prewired intentional chains, in which each motor act is facilitated by the previous one.[cclxxv] Similar to the Markov chain of continually adjusting probability distributions out of which flows language at its various structural levels, motor processes are likewise orchestrated into a flow that can be assessed probabilistically, and whose enactment is directed to the external expression of an intentional meaning.

Although corporeally grounded like each of the other cognitive primitives, interpretation reaches its greatest heights of flexibility and possibility when loosed from the sensory immediacy of the body.[cclxxvi] With the ability to shift points of input away from direct sensory stimulation, brains capable of integrating multiple modalities with reentrant pathways allow the "kinetic melody" of neural activity to "loop" through a pathway that does not entail a somatic response.[13] Freed from real-world time constraints, the activity of motor imagery can occur at a much higher speed and with greater flexibility than in motor or visual tasks and internally generate information for interpretation to act upon.[cclxxvii] Agency blossoms into phenomenal consciousness and even self-awareness; memory comes to support a coherent concept of "I" as an experiencing subject; categorization and domain crossing discriminate and connect over many scales of resolution, even reaching into abstract domains and, with the aid of the entailments of crossed domains, ripen into reason.

Symbol-Level Presentation

Intelligence, according to Peter Godfrey-Smith, "is made incarnate in overt action, using things as means to affect other things."[cclxxviii] The internal model of knowledge that an organism harbors in its genes and expresses through perceptual and behavioral biases is the culmination of a history of leading-edge intelligence interacting with the challenges of survival. Built up over many ancestral rounds of contention with evolutionary forces, this store of knowledge is bequeathed upon the young of a species as an *a priori* guide to its interactions within its

---

[13] In humans, such a pathway engages the ventral and medial PFCs, which receive inputs directly or indirectly from all sensory modalities, and contain convergence zones which hold a record of temporal conjunctions of activity in other neural units from internal and external stimuli (Damasio 1996).

environment—although for the species as a whole, this body of knowledge is hard-won and *a posteriori*.[cclxxix] In its active engagement with the environment, an organism is enacting its particular meaning paradigm by symbolically externalizing its Umwelt into interactional properties. The surface-level division between the perceptual and the expressional, which is the symbol level at which all interactions transpire, is a turning point that compels actors within the "universe of signs" to engage with each other as living symbols.

With the very body of an organism presenting as a symbol to other subjects, the intelligence that shapes the contents of the creature's consciousness reaches beyond its individual boundaries to create new forms of intersubjective enactment. Like the integration of sensory modules that creates an immersive, meaningful perceptual experience within an organism, so also do organisms themselves function, not in isolation, but in a richly textured fabric of social interaction. So vital is the intersubjective aspect of animal lives that most animals devote a disproportionate share of cognitive effort to social activity.[cclxxx] Husserl believed that, just as the concept of "I" arises from bodily conditions such as boundedness and proprioception, individual experience is just as ineluctably the generative center of communities. Indeed, the thread of communication that knits them together is fundamentally rooted in the experiential primacy of icon, carried by an indexical "seed" to sprout anew as interpreted meaning within the subjective ground of receiving participants.

Social knowledge, like that of the physical world, is based on predictive relationships between events, which can allow for inference to similar events, with the ideal goal of reducing uncertainty about potential decisions while maximizing the utility of acquired information.[cclxxxi] Intentionally or not, animals unavoidably secrete information about themselves into all of their behaviors and signals.[cclxxxii] Attending to behavioral cues is the most indirect way of gleaning information about other individuals, because they can be very general, with a high potential for misinterpretation.[cclxxxiii] With the metaphorical and probabilistic tools that discerning agents are equipped with, one creature attempts to predictively deduce one thing—intentions—in terms of something else—the cues embedded in behavior.^{cclxxxiv} Of the cues that can be monitored, only a few correlate precisely with the condition of interest, a situation of partial information that is the inevitable outcome of the tradeoffs between perceptual limitations, energetic economics, and the multiple objectives that an animal must balance. "Mutual understanding demands a certain correlation among the mental acts mutually unfolded in intimation and in the receipt of such intimation, but not at all their exact resemblance," observes Husserl.^{cclxxxv}

While evolution rarely favors the provision of perfect information, animals have developed ways to derive and impart information via signals, which are much more highly correlated with referent conditions than cues.^{cclxxxvi} For some songbirds, an effective strategy is to exaggerate features of the species' stereotypical song,[14] which can lead to higher mating success.^{cclxxxvii} This underscores the distinct roles, and even diverging interests, between signalers and receivers in communication.^{cclxxxviii} While the function of a signal is to influence the behavior of the receiver, the receiver is intent on ascertaining reliable information, particularly about the sender, putting the two at different points within a communication system that generally entails asymmetries not observed in formal systems like language.^{cclxxxix} Despite their differing interests, the sender and receiver are also closely linked by their system of correspondence, for example by usually utilizing the same neural pathways for encrypting and decoding messages. The result is an unstable symbiosis, with receiver bias driving differentiation in signals between closely related species and even populations.^{ccxc} While they carry the advantage of reducing receiver-end interpretive uncertainty, signals bring with them a new level of uncertainty through possibilities of mistaken deployment or outright dishonesty. Despite the risk of abuse, however, the high costs of producing signals tend to skew stable systems of communication toward an honest average, resulting in a flow of information that is roughly intermediate between random signaling and perfect coding.^{ccxci}

---

[14] The exaggeration of certain signal features is known as "peak shift."

Since relatively limited lexical systems tend to be evolutionarily favored, messages may be buttressed with "pragmatics" such as contextual contingencies or even physical modifiers, like skin, feather, fur, or carapace color, to augment their meaning content.^{ccxcii} Multimodality increases the semantic robustness of a signal, such as when a territorial red-wing blackbird flashes his brightly colored wing epaulets as he calls out his auditory display. Through the "principle of robust overdesign," the impact of the message is intensified as the potential for meaning creation is magnified by the informational redundancies, along with the disparities inherent in utilizing multiple sensory modalities, which elicit different, but overlapping responses within the receiver.^{ccxciii} The non-redundant aspects of the signal affect the receiver's discriminative capacity, which usually coevolves with the form of the signal, and also leaves open the potential on the part of the receiver to add new responses or refine existing ones.^{ccxciv} The redundancy that imparts robustness also enables the potential for subsequent specialization of redundant components into novel signals.^{ccxcv} A complex associative response is induced in the receiver as the compound stimuli, with their similarities and differences sorted out in terms of each other, resolve into a new meaning that a single modality alone could not convey, while the cognitive cost of processing the signal is simultaneously lowered.

At the outer, interactive symbol level of bodily expression, interpretation is both expressed and invited. The external level of bodily presentation is not only a physical and dynamical interface with the environment, but also a semiotic one in that it both receives and signifies meaning. Just like Peirce saw the "man-sign" as the global-level carrier of an individualized system of sign processes, any interacting organism acts as a "living symbol" whose bounding surface receives perception marks through sensation while transmitting them through form, feature, or behavior. The "living symbol" expresses itself outwardly by what zoologist Adolf Portmann referred to as "phenomenon proper"—the observable features of an organism that may play a representational role by conveying sensory information to a potential observer.^{ccxcvi} The "semantic organs" Portman argues for, such as the vividly aposematic warning painted on the eyes of a red-eyed tree frog, or the exaggerated features that some species display to attract mates or challenge rivals, are definable based on their meaning, not just functionality. The "representations of selfhood" (Portman) that organisms produce as signs identify them as members of certain class of individuals, while being malleable enough to allow individuals to distinguish themselves, such as in competition.[ccxcvii] By facilitating meaningful interaction between the self-expression embedded in perceptible traits and the observer's perception of these, the body acts as a juncture of symbolic reference between semiotic participants.

Ritual

The tendency to express one thing—such as social status, reproductive viability, or a motivational state—in terms of another, such as a signal, is tied to the nature of sign processes, with their indexical representations of subjective, internal, source-domain experiences. The non-syntactic, whole-event modes of expression that prevail among non-symbolic forms of communication closely couple the semantic locus of both subjective awareness and signification to contextual immediacy.[ccxcviii] The highest expression of thirdness, symbolism, offers some degree of emancipation from this tight coupling, as demonstrated by language. Among animals, however, symbolism is generally not a lexical feat, but rather a bodily expressed ritual, whereby the "objective expression of motivated states, often involving conflict,"[ccxcix] becomes modified to enhance communicative function. Behaviors that become ritualized derive from preexisting behaviors, such as preening, allogrooming, and food sharing, which often do not serve a signaling function in their originating contexts.[ccc] As these behaviors are gradually exapted to their new status as signal, they undergo revisions to increase conspicuousness and redundancy by reducing and exaggerating their components until, through repetition, they rarify into an unambiguous, highly recognizable stereotype.[ccci] Uncoupled from its original form and function, the signal can attain new levels of referencing power by associating with new and distinct types of information.

One of the greatest benefits of the "psychological monism," (Huxley) or "shared meaning" (Peirce) that such a stylized form of communication imparts upon semiotic participants is to reduce intraspecific damage in otherwise aggressive encounters. Loosed from their operational contexts, threatening behaviors no longer have to be carried out to their literal conclusions, allowing conflicts to be settled through displays, ritualized "tournaments" of combat, or bluffs.[cccii] Ritualization not only provides animals with a means to symbolize their intentions and motivational states, but also a means of assessing each other's probable strength without physical damage. Animal "weapons" such as horns and antlers tell the evolutionary tale of co-option from operational to symbolic function, with the sharp, dangerous ancestral condition yielding to the larger, more elaborate ornaments of more derived species that act both as a handicap signal of physical condition, and also facilitate the ritualized fighting that the species bearing them often rely on for strength assessment.[ccciii] Some caterpillar species exemplify this evolution, with the crawling function of their anal prolegs having yielded to symbolism over time, becoming "oars" that the territorial larvae use to create vibratory signals through a motion derived from an aggressive advance toward an opponent. The caterpillars accompany their vibratory display with mandibular signaling that recalls its origin as a means of pushing, hitting and biting the opponent.[ccciv]

Ritualized signals help forge and buffer social interactions in non-aggressive contexts as well, such as maximizing efficiencies and reducing conflicts among parents engaged in cooperatively rearing offspring.[cccv] Many courtship displays are highly elaborated and ritualized, such as the extremely stereotyped, synchronized "weed ceremony" ritual of the Western Grebe. Another courtship ceremony that reveals the power of symbolic behavior to uncouple the communicative function from its sensorimotor underpinnings is found in salamander species in which the male deposits his spermatophore before courting the female. In a ritual involving the intense coordination of behavioral and pheremonal signals, the vigorously tail-waving male leads the female to the spermatophore, which she collects in her cloaca.[cccvi] The male's reward is not sensory stimulation, but the successful consummation of a symbolic act of communication. The adaptive alchemy that turns a behavioral idiosyncrasy into a fully ritualized display is the bodily-instantiated domain-crossing characteristic of metaphor—in this case nonlinguistic—that renders the body "as much a symbol as substance."

Coursing through the evolutionarily wrought sluices of intelligence, consciousness is constrained in its reach by the parameters of category; funneled into convergence through association; and propelled along its course by memory. While passing along well-worn channels, intelligence continually carves out new exploratory meanders through interpretation. Orchestrating organismal perception and behavior, intelligence stabilizes incoming stimuli into regularities, forming over evolutionary time the behavioral "chreodes," or habits, which guide responsiveness into the reflexes and instincts that were once assumed to constitute the totality of animal cognition. In addition to crafting the interior landscape of sentience, the activities of intelligence reach far beyond the bodily boundaries of the individual to structure interactions with others in a meaning-based way. According to Husserl, "To turn mere coexistence into mutual pertinence…is the constant result of associative functioning…That one thing points to another, in definite arrangement and connection, is itself apparent to us."[cccvii] From the tiny source domains of individual Umwelten intermingling—distinguishing themselves, crossing through various levels of interaction, and being ever ready to adapt—intelligence shapes and sculpts organisms' relationships with other subjects and with the environment in a reciprocal way. Evolution, then, expands from the tale of an arms race between competing interests to include the much richer textures unfolding from the equally foundational, coeval imperative to engage in processes of shared meanings. Reflecting the ever-expanding potential of intelligence, the growth of individual as well as intersubjective complexity requires agents that are at least sufficiently unitary to be dynamically distinct from their environments, so as to serve as their own source domain; an evolvable form of memory that enables experiences to become meaningfully embodied; the ability to distinguish between relevant domains of experience and then creatively but judiciously cross those domains, and the capacity to interpret the entailments of domain-crossing in new contexts. Agents of such activities have spent ages diversifying and populating the biosphere, as the slowly turning kaleidoscope of forms reveal that the condition basic to life is the stability offset by change that is evolution. The condition of evolution, in turn, is intelligence.

3

Intelligent Evolution

"Life is always under pressure everywhere; and that where it has succeeded in breaking through in an appreciable degree, nothing will be able to stop it carrying to the uttermost limit the process from which it has sprung."
—Teilhard de Chardin

The way animals perceive their environments and each other is a complex function of phylogenetic and experiential conditionings, accented by the inherent spontaneity that subjectivity expresses to various degrees in its assorted forms. Constructing not only the scope of meaning for an individual, the various influences that condition perception also reverberate through intersubjective interactions and even guide the temporal march that populations, existing within their parameters of limited resources and differential reproductive success, evolve through. Buffeted by forces beyond their control, biotic entities from individual to species levels and beyond are subject to principles that are descriptively similar to the construction of logical entities such as analogies: from an externally constrained, internally abundant pool of varied potential, a relatively small, probabilistically well-fitted contingent suggests itself for manifestation. Triumphant contestants wrest from natural selection its highest token of favor in furthering the persistence of their genetic legacy.

Natural Selection

Goalless and passive, natural selection is more of a description than a force. Along with the corresponding idea of fitness, it embraces numerous factors that sway the course of evolution, including environmental influences; genetic makeup; population heterogeneity; plasticity on many levels; and reproductive capacity and relative success. A major contributor to the diversity that evolution plays upon is environmental randomness. Short-term irregularities layered on top of more predictable long-term trends ensure that no single phenotype can precisely express optimal fitness. The scope of phenotypic possibility is set genetically, with heredity's inbuilt randomization features of recombination and mutation introducing an internal source of variation and uncertainty. The organisms which sample the immense range of genetic possibility fare forth into a precarious world whose impersonal, exacting parameters further cull this subset of genetic potential into one that, on average, embodies an optimal "interpretation" of the various selective pressures that influence it. Underscoring the important role of externally imposed constraints in promoting biological creativity, shifting environmental parameters open up space for many possible phenotypical expressions, while compelling individuals and populations to continually adapt and innovate. The resultant heterogeneity provides numerous starting points for generating novel forms of potential responsiveness.

While many factors coalesce to drive evolution, none are strictly causal. Natural selection, while often given a starring role in explanations of evolution, can also operate on populations without producing evolution. Conversely, the random fluctuation of allele frequency, known as genetic drift, is a nonselective process that under some circumstances can be on par with, even indistinguishable from, natural selection in its ability to impel evolution.[cccviii] Particularly in small populations which lack a central tendency, the effects of drift become more pronounced, and a previously coherent population can fracture into subpopulations or even new species.[cccix]

Natural selection hovers at the indistinct boundaries between the individual and the population, and between the individual and its discriminable traits—which, even if favorable, can't be selected independently of the whole, phenotypically integrated organism.[cccx] Each trait, in turn, represents a point of convergence between two distinct systems of variable, and only loosely correlated dynamics: while the environment has a range of alternative possible states, the organism does, too.[cccxi] The lack of a clear, one-to-one correspondence between environmental conditions and evolutionary outcomes tempers the explanatory capacity of natural selection and makes the exact locus of selection difficult to ascertain. However, the outcomes of selection can be assessed at the population level, but only indirectly, by examining the portion of the population that hasn't been eliminated and their successful descendants. A statistical record accrues at the population level of successful, discriminate interactions of a trait with the environment that is not available at the individual level due to the sheer stochasticity of events: sometimes bad luck befalls even carriers of well-fitted traits.[cccxii]

The complex interplay of the primary evolutionary factors of genetic and reproductive variability is often modeled with fitness landscapes. The highest, most difficult-to-ascend peaks correspond to the genotypes that beget the highest levels of fitness.[cccxiii] These elevated peaks are generally correlated with nearby peaks, sometimes through epistatic interactions that interlink different fitness contributions between multiple genes. The result is a range of compromise solutions to the problem of fitness, which can be expressed as multiple low-altitude ridges of well-fit genetic combinations that are not mutually compatible.[cccxiv] Between the ridges are "holes," or genotypes that fall between the well-fit clusters. These holes, along with the continuous expansion of population variation by genetic drift, and local demands of adaptation, all can conspire to push populations apart and thereby promote reproductive isolation. The result of distinct genotypic clustering, along with drift's action of spreading genetic potential throughout a species while reducing the individual's load, is a cloud-like "smearing" of genetic potential. Amid this haze, certain fitness-related alleles become fixed, tearing apart the genotypic cloud along fracture lines of differential, locally consolidated mutations and leading to speciation.[cccxv]

Contrary to "survival of the fittest" scenarios, environments are capable of supporting many expression of fitness, even within the same species. Phenotypic expression is a multiply realizable property, with different genetic combinations potentially yielding similar outward expressions while harboring completely different suites of potential responses to the same environmental pressures. Although belied by a population's phenotypic conformity, this hidden reserve of genetic plasticity patiently awaits conducive conditions to invite its expression as a possible route to new phenotypes.[cccxvi] Epistatic and pleiotropic interactions among genes at different locations can give rise to different phenotypic traits, which makes genomes abundantly available to exaptations—even complex ones that require correlated changes in different systems to arise together.[cccxvii] The result is variable plasticity of evolvability itself.

Despite the latitude of phenotypic expression made possible by a population's genetic diversity, actual expression tends to cluster around an average mean, compressed toward this optimum by common environmental pressures. The stressors that drive phenotypes to convergence are simultaneously local—in that they interact with each agent individually—and nonlocal, in being widespread so that their average impact is statistically measurable at the population level.[cccxviii] Each phenotype is like a trajectory which originates arbitrarily close in phase space to other starting points, all of which will encounter variations on the same general theme in their individually waged contests of survival. The details of the each life trajectory are unpredictably unique, but are washed away in the view from a higher statistical level.

Even as they suffer the slings and arrows of environmental uncertainty, organisms are simultaneously beset by stochastic flux from within, as demonstrated by genetic drift. Genotypes, like phenotypes, often cluster around a central tendency, but are also prone to spontaneous fluctuations that spread out their distribution. Despite this tendency to randomness, the gene frequencies of a population indirectly reflect environmental vagaries by constantly shifting as a function of population size in response to selection, mutation, and recombination. Therefore, genes are not precisely targets of environmental selection in complex organisms, although to the approximate degree that they correlate with the phenotypic traits that do run selection's stringent gauntlet, they represent the phenotype's heritability.[cccxix]

While natural selection guides genetic outcomes by constantly sieving the genes expressed from a population's pool, changes spread gradually at best through populations. Phenotypic expression is interpretively extruded from its deeply internalized genotypic encryption, which embeds the organism in real time within an environment whose vagaries of stasis and flux play out across a nesting of scales, both spatial and temporal. The behavioral and cognitive lability that such conditions can call forth spans the gap between the relatively stable internal realm of genetic encoding, and the mutable external realm of environmental contact, allowing the more rapidly responsive behavioral changes to precede genetic ones. One counterintuitive example is in the advancing encephalization of primates—presumably corresponding to higher intelligence—that appears to have followed, rather than prompted, an expansion into new environmental niches.[cccxx]

Just as many non-sensory factors support a relevant sampling of perceptible environmental features to create a semantic structure within an organism, a phenotypic expression of the genome that maximizes its reflection of the environment likewise engages many non-genetic factors, particularly developmental experiences, to kindle activity from different sets of genes through various routes to enactment.[cccxxi] In this way, the environment is instrumental in guiding individual development, as well as species evolution. This is primarily because the environment is the context in which a relationship is established between the individual and its fitness, or the average influence that the individual could be expected to have on the gene pool. Also, environmental conditions inform the development of the phenotype, which mediates between individual fitness and the environment within its bounds of plasticity, tending toward a probabilistic expressional outcome known as the reaction norm.^{cccxxii} Since reaction norms are modifiable and to some degree heritable, they promote the evolution of phenotypic plasticity, through which small genetic changes amplify into large phenotypic ones.^{cccxxiii}

One arena that sees a radiation of expressed reaction norms is that of behavior, which can vary according to factors including an individual's encounters with its environment, or its compilation of "behavioral syndromes," or personality, which defines the quality of its interactional behavior in terms of boldness or shyness.^{cccxxiv} Another source of behavioral plasticity is cognitive ability, a trait that appears as amenable to selective sculpting as any other biological character.^{cccxxv} Cognitive flexibility is one of the most potent methods of addressing the challenges of a selective environment by enabling complex, novel, situation-specific behaviors that alter an organism's causal relationship to its environment by reordering the meanings of, and therefore the relations between, the objects that surround it.^{cccxxvi} The very forces of environmental unpredictability that help summon this plasticity into being can come under its sway to some degree as the organism exerts its cognitive capabilities to alter the immediate environment in its favor, thereby adjusting selection's focus and modifying the adaptive context of future generations.^{cccxxvii} The effects that organisms have on their environments are directly linked to their perceptions of those environments.

World Creators

In navigating noisy contexts within and without, organisms are abetted by a nonrandom element pointed to by Uexkull, who saw "nothing left to chance, but rather, that the animal and its medium are everywhere connected by an intimate meaning rule which binds the two in a duet in which the properties of both partners are composed contrapuntally to one another."^{cccxxviii} The tight coupling that effectively unites the organism and its environment into a single system casts the latter in the role of ongoing selector of changes that the individual organism undergoes ontogenetically, as well as a member of an evolving species. At the same time, the organism acts just as fully as a selector of structural changes within its environment.[cccxxix]

In the very course of daily activities, all organisms affect to some degree the flow of matter and energy through the ecosystem by altering their environments in regular ways. While conducting itself according to the predictable aspects of the environment that it perceives as meaningful, an organism is at the same time a source of regularity to which its surroundings adapt. Thus the organism not only seeks regularities in its environment, but is also organized at every level to generate them.[cccxxx] The typical way a species alters its environment is reciprocated in how environmental pressures direct the evolution of the species. From this balance of "mutual perturbations,"[cccxxxi] congruencies arise between species and environment that result in a unique history carried in both genome and biome, which are both inherited by the next generation. The organism's niche, the aspect of its ecology which meaningfully reflects back on it, is an outwardly constructed corollary of the intentional structure of its Umwelt.

Crucially, the changes that an organism visits upon its surroundings are not simply matters of energetic and material redistributions, but also reflect a semiotic flow that affects each creature individually and evolutionarily according to the parameters of its meaning-world. Unlike the more conventional ecological measures of energy and material flow, semiotic flow is less directional, meandering among individuals and even against the flow of trophic cascades, such as when potential prey animals send signals to their predators.[cccxxxii] With every action guided by meaning and interpretation, subjectivity is a primary causal factor in structuring the relationship between an organism and its environment. The adaptive "structural congruencies"[cccxxxiii] that arise between them epitomize the confluence of the blind forces of selection with an animal's perception-mediated awareness. By accruing information that it integrates with prior knowledge, whether phylogenetic or learned, the animal can adjust its understanding and responses within its range of plasticity. In this way an organism "import[s] the environment into [its] dynamics by reorganizing"[cccxxxiv] them all levels, from the epigenetic tempering of genetic expression to the sculpting of fitness landscapes that inform a species' evolutionary trajectory. The "mutual specification"[cccxxxv] that characterizes the interplay between organism and environment means that the minimum unit of analysis of either development or evolution is the entire environment that the organism interacts with biologically and socially.[cccxxxvi]

Rather than being an objective process that visits upon passive populations, evolution arises from within the members of a species when their traits, abilities, choices, and predispositions collectively interact with external forces and with each other in a complex, overlapping entanglement of multi-level embeddedness. As Teihard de Chardin came to believe, "Adaptation is an effect not of external forces but of psychology."[cccxxxvii] In mustering its own self-referencing and anticipatory resources to meet the demands of a complex environment by creating opportunities within it, an agent is exerting a bottom-up countercurrent in creative opposition to the generalized, top-down directives issued by impersonal selective forces in favor of particular phenotypic traits. Far from being confined to the level of the individual, evolution unfolds at many different loci, from alleles within genomes, to changes at the level of the population and even beyond, affecting entire species and even ecosystems. At the individual level, the trajectory of evolution is directed from within the subjective interiority of the organism by its intelligence-guided activities. These local interactions translate into large-scale changes that give intelligence a temporal extension through its proactive effects on the course of evolution.

Intelligence in Evolution

The niches that species create and individuals occupy are internally sourced as probable potentials; they are genetically scripted and behaviorally enacted through perspective-dependent acts of intelligence that are both internally and externally conditioned. In their transition from inner potential to outer manifestation, these essentially mental entities draw aspects of their environment's dynamics into alignment with their own internal ordering. At the same, the environment informs the potential that is expressed, thereby embedding organisms in a recursive relationship that is never static or at equilibrium, but rather engages "rules that change themselves, directly or indirectly."[cccxxxviii] This is Douglas Hofstadter's definition of a "strange loop," wherein a system entangles itself into a self-referencing loop of causality and is, he believes, at the core of intelligence.

Representing a unique sliver of the potential available to a species to express itself anew in current environmental and social contexts within each generation, the individual organism acts as an evolutionary source domain that projects its entailments onto the environment by crafting the niche that relationally integrates it with its environment.[15] While evolution is analyzable in terms of the ongoing metamorphoses of life forms at various scales over time in relation to environmental pressures, the conscious interiors of organisms likewise undergo changes commensurate with their physical adaptations. These interiors, which are not available to direct empirical measurement, and so not entirely predictable or conveyable, are actively engaged in conversation with evolutionary processes. Individual perceptions, motivations, and even preferences can texture the strokes of evolution at local levels and, when amplified across a population, potentially produce species-level effects. Viewed from the inside, evolution is a process closely entwined with intelligence. While memory, categorization, domain crossing, and interpretation are active processes, the context of awareness whose space they structure, fill, and grow does not directly express itself. Its primary observable effect is in its role as source domain, which renders each action of intelligence ultimately self-referencing.

---

[15] "Individual" is used to denote a more or less individuated organism that generally corresponds with our idea of an animal. The majority of actual organisms—protists, fungi, plants, and 19 phyla of animals—skirt Weismann's doctrine of germ line segregation. Competition and selection play out differently within those loosened parameters than for the vertebrate-type genetic processes referred to here.

The Self-Referencing Subject

Key to the fitness, if not survival, of most organisms is the ability to interact with members of its own kind. Semiotic interchange is a vital mediator of all intraspecific interactions that impact individual fitness. Like metaphor, semiosis and the processes that support it are contingent upon self-referencing, and grow in complexity through increasingly higher-level recursions of that constitutive pattern of recognizing other in terms of self. Different species demonstrate in countless ways how foundational self-referencing is to social interaction. For many bird species, self-reference takes auditory form. Ducklings unable to hear their own call or that of their siblings prenatally are unprepared to recognize their mother's after hatching.[cccxxxix] Songbirds rely on the auditory feedback of their own voice and, to a lesser degree, the somatosensory sensation of their syrinx in order to develop and maintain their social song.[cccxl] For the female ring dove, it is not the coo of courtship from her paramour that stirs her passion, but rather her own reply that releases the endocrine response that stimulates egg-laying.[cccxli]

Some animals utilize self-referent phenotype matching to mediate interactions with their own kind.[cccxlii] The cowbird chick, a brood parasite, does not have visual access to conspecifics during development, and so likely relies on a visual self-frame of reference when selecting a mate, preferring birds most similar to itself in coloration.[cccxliii] Belding's ground squirrels, a species with multiple paternity and a nepotistic social order, awaken from hibernation each year with their memories of previously familiar animals vacated. A self-frame of reference, however, helps them to establish relations anew, distinguishing between littermates and non-littermates.[cccxliv] Females of this same species, even when raised with both full and half-sisters, behave more altruistically to the former.[cccxlv] The parasitic wasp *Copidosoma floridanum* carries self-referencing to an extreme. When it finds itself in the company of an unrelated conspecific, the wasp egg will divide clonally, producing non-reproductive soldier wasps that battle the strangers, and even their own less related haploid brothers and non-clonally produced sisters, leaving their clonal sisters free to pupate.[cccxlvi]

Rooted in the deeply individualized experience of recognizing other in terms of self, the widespread strategy of kin-based altruism influences evolution in predictable ways as well as producing some surprising outcomes. In addition to providing obvious benefits to carriers of the target genome such as group protection and shared access to food supplies, over evolutionary time it can give rise to some unexpected forms of protection, such as aposematic coloration. This vivid system of communication to predators, if accessed by other species both innocuous and harmful—Batesian and Mullerian mimics—extends its blanket of protection over them as well. Such a semiotically based method of protection underscores the "decisive role of the subject"[cccxlvii] in interactions that cumulatively impact evolution—in this case the predator who interprets the warning, thus tipping the selective scales in favor of a particular distinctive phenotype.

A self-frame of reference allows animals the option of either utilizing public information, whether in the form of signals or inadvertent social information, or drawing from their own private store of knowledge in decision-making. While public and socially transmitted information can reduce foraging costs by providing details about resources such as location and the presence or absence of particular features, as well as promoting social cohesion, animals may forgo these benefits and decide to rely on their own knowledge.[cccxlviii] The information-laden waggle dance of the honey bee—which conveys particular, graded information about the features of a food source—is exercised to recruit foragers to a profitable patch. However, when the dance diverges from the self-acquired information of a forager, that bee will often utilize her own private information, even if she follows the dance vigorously.[cccxlix]

Self-referencing is actively implicit in the all-important endeavor of mate selection, which temporarily draws two individuals into a new, higher level of selection through the combination of their genetic endowment. Particularly for species that share parental duties, like many birds, choosing a mate whose behavioral traits are compatible with one's own can be an even more decisive factor than the intrinsic quality of the chosen individual in producing a successful outcome. This is true across the whole behavioral spectrum, and becomes an even more significant factor in reproductive success among long-term perennial pairs, and during times of environmental stress.[cccl]

At higher levels of cognition, self-referencing can provide a template by which animals may understand others' behavior in terms of their own.[cccli] The cardinality of self as source domain appears to be enshrined in the very structure of mammalian cognition in the form of mirror neurons. This very fluid neural system develops as both product and process of social interaction through sensorimotor learning via both performance and observation.[ccclii] Neural pathways that integrate sensory cues associated with performed actions and their motor representations are recruited to activity not only when the subject performs an action, but also when observing its performance.[cccliii] They appear to function in both an end-directed way—the mirror neurons of monkeys fire differentially for the action of grasping a food item and eating it versus placing it in a bowl—and in a predictive way, for example by firing when a monkey watches a person reach for an object that the monkey had previously watched be hidden. In a sequence of intentional behaviors, each motor act is influenced globally by the final act, and locally by the subsequent action into which it flows. Reflecting this, the strength of firing by the majority of active neurons is likewise contingent upon the ensuing motion, linked together by an end-directed "kinetic melody" in which different brain regions, unconnected outside of the context created by an intention, fluently coordinate into a "prewired intentional chain in which each motor act is facilitated by the previously executed one."[ccccliv] This same system that allows the seamless integration of motor acts into an end-directed behavior also allows the observing animal, based on its own experiences in similar situations, to "read" intention into the actions of the demonstrator, and to predict the goal of the observed action.[ccclv]

The ability to understand the behavior of another in terms of one's own opens the door to increasingly sophisticated forms of social interaction based on "mindreading," or using behavioral regularities predictively.[ccclvi] Food-caching corvids such as scrub jays and ravens—

among many other caching species—display remarkable memory not only for locations of the food they store, but also for those of the food items that other birds store. Additionally, they even remember which individuals, if any, were looking on when they cached their own supplies, going so far as to distinguish between attentive and inattentive observers.[ccclvii] A bird may use this information to determine whether to return later to re-hide its treasure.[ccclviii] In a quirk of self-referencing, only birds that have been successful in pilfering the caches of others will re-hide their own; having been defrauded by another is not sufficient to create a template for this possible act of experience projection. [16, ccclix]

While the question of whether the predictive power of mindreading constitutes a theory of mind in nonhumans remains in debate, animals are likely applying a more visceral self-frame to those around them: what primatologist Frans De Waal argues is the phylogenetically ancient capacity of empathy. Each of the four levels in the empathetic hierarchy is characterized by emotional engagement, and each is an evolutionary elaboration of the one prior: (1) arousal state affectation, when one animal's excitement incites others; (2) emotional contagion, with animals expressing distress in the presence of distressed others—to the point that pigeons will suppress a conditioned response if it is the source of distress; (3) emotional contagion combined with appraisal of the situation and attempts to understand the cause of the emotion, as in targeted helping by apes; and (4) perspective-taking, where cognition plays a dominant role through imagination and mental state attribution, which may be limited to humans.[ccclx]

In perceiving the emotional state of another, the observer partakes in that iconic experience. Empathy, even at its most basic levels, propagates motivational correlations among subjects so rapidly that it is arguably the most efficient route to evoking a response, far beyond what passive reflexivity could achieve. For example, a hen rushing to the assistance of a chick calling out in distress is impelled to action because she shares a

---

[16] Experience projection is using one's own behaviors to predict those of others. Whether this is what prompts successfully perfidious corvids to be wary of pilferers is the subject of debate.

corresponding physiological stress response.[ccclxi] Similarly, vocal communication among songbirds, while certainly a stimulant of neural activity in conspecific receivers, derives its effectiveness from the whole-body experience it evokes in them. The increased heart rate of engaged listeners implies an emotional state on the part of the sender that, for young birds, makes the song more readily learnable. For potential partners, this state provides a basis for appraisal of the signaler's internal state.[ccclxii]

A shift in perspective accompanies the higher tiers of empathy, as the receiver becomes increasingly capable of attributing the induced emotional state to the other as its source.[ccclxiii] Such a distinction-making capacity presages the heightened self-identity that enables the mental precursors to self-awareness, including metacognition, or the ability to monitor one's own mental processes. An animal that can "think about thinking" can intentionally modify its attentional focus or behavior in a way that takes into account its own internal proclivities, which it may have difficulty controlling. For example, capuchin monkeys trained to refrain from consuming a small treat in exchange for a larger one if they wait for a certain duration of time will adopt techniques of self-distraction, like looking away from the source of temptation or holding it at arm's length.[ccclxiv] One view of metacognition is that the mindreading enabled by the mirror neurons is simply turned on oneself.[ccclxv] This would resemble metaphor's increasing complexity as it reflects back on itself from the perspective of a target that has been familiarized into a source domain. Such higher-order reflection would allow differentiation within the original source domain—a capacity that metaphor lacks—and pave the way for the higher-order domain-crossing of analogy, which can freely make distinctions in both source and target. Similarly, empathy begins as utterly undifferentiated bodily identification with the state of another, which evolves to higher levels of perceptivity through the crossing of visceral experience into the distinction-making domain of mentality.

Memory

Like ontogeny, evolution is predicated on the continuity of some form of memory. The "habits" that constrain an animal, whether individually as acquired knowledge, or phylogenetically through accumulated genomic acumen, are its memory; the template which biases its perceptions and interpretations. Biological memory is formalized into replicators, which pass on encrypted summaries of past generations' contests with selection and avail them to fresh testing each generation against current conditions.[ccclxvi] From the stability of a formal system of inheritance, cumulative selection can accrue new adaptations on top of prior ones, leading to increasing sophistication over evolutionary time.[ccclxvii]

At the opposite end of the inheritance spectrum is ecological inheritance, which is an indirect way that the activities of a species can affect evolutionary outcomes across generations. The pattern of alterations a species visits on its environment accrue over time, and can actually modify local selective pressures and generate selection for adaptations that entrench successful niches. In this way, the effects of niche construction can override external sources of selection to create new evolutionary patterns that natural selection alone could not generate.[ccclxviii] Between the biological and ecological poles of heritability lie many non-genomic mechanisms for spreading and preserving behaviors that utilize behavioral, social, and, for rare species, such as chimpanzees or dolphins, cultural transmissions, all of which can be decisive factors in contests against selection.[ccclxix]

The amenability of evolvable systems to open-ended plasticity, particularly at cognitive levels, proceeds from underlying patterns that are essentially conserved, but which diverge formally when iterated under different conditions and in different contexts. Within social groups, certain behavioral patterns likewise avail themselves for exaptation to novel applications. Social learning in many animals, for example, is most important, not for introducing new behaviors, but for spreading new adaptive uses of pre-existing behaviors, which can gradually allow new behaviors to develop without explicit innovation.[ccclxx] From behaviorally transmitted information, group properties can be established through social learning, which can stabilize the whole behavioral repertoire and life-style of the group. This lays the foundation for the evolution of complex social groups, which in turn can facilitate cultural evolution, which distinguishes groups and creates a new basis for selection between them.[ccclxxi]

Categorization and Domain Crossing

Simultaneously arising from perception and defining its parameters by delineating domains, categories that form at the individual level can amplify into impacts at the species level. One reliable route to species-appropriate categorization is imprinting, which guides the subject toward species-typical preferences. By specifying the stimulus that a young animal is receptive to, learning through imprinting promotes stability, both developmentally in an individual, and among populations of related individuals, by efficiently aligning the preferences of the emerging generation with those of its predecessors. Although such intergenerational continuity can maintain species integrity, it can also enhance species divergence by warding off hybridization, keeping the general category of "species" distinct through individual preferences. The specifications that channel a young animal's choice contingencies through particular types of imprinting—such as paternal or self-imprinting—can amplify even slight differences in mate or signal preferences. This can promote divergence not only between species, but even between local populations within the same species, leading to the genetic isolation that can foster the development of new "categories" within a species in the form of subspecies.[ccclxxii]

While categorization sets the informational boundaries that contain the contents of a category, domain crossing overcomes these stabilizing forces to yield rich potential for evolutionary exploitation through exaptation. In extending beyond established functions to explore novelty, the recruited trait—which may be either dedicated to a different function or merely be the unselected byproduct of a different trait—is loosed into a fresh selective context.^{ccclxxiii} Unlike canalization, which requires that the meaning of a stimulus stay constant through generations, exaptation is a semantic shift that arises not from a change in the form of a potential stimulus, but in the meaning it carries for a subject.

Sensory biases are examples of interpretive predispositions that become canalized into stereotypical patterns along phylogenetic lines. Reaching across domains to become exaptations, those biases, stabilized by their evolutionary value in their originating context, represent an opportunity for co-option to other applications, particularly if they influence mating success.^{ccclxxiv} Mate preferences in many animal species, for example, are frequently derived from non-mating contexts. A classic exemplar is the male water mite, which vibrates his legs in mimicry of the mites' copepod prey in the presence of females.^{ccclxxv} This ploy is more effective the more precise the mimic, and the hungrier the female is. Such sensory exploitation that conflates attractiveness across separate domains can play a role in shaping phenotypic characteristics of the presenting sex, typically the male. For guppies, with their preference for the orange color of the rare but prized cabrehash fruit, this pre-existing sensory bias is of great benefit to males with orange color in their tails, even attracting females (under laboratory conditions) from populations whose males do not express this phenotype.^{ccclxxvi}

Trophic contests are also potent battlegrounds of evolutionary arms races that can summon the domain-crossing powers of cognitive plasticity. Cryptic behaviors and morphologies that prey species employ to disappear into their surroundings can favor inferential shrewdness from predators, requiring them to deduce a fact about one domain in terms of another. Chickadees demonstrate the flexible heights they are able to take operant conditioning to when using leaf damage on broad-leaved trees to detect the presence of certain types of caterpillars. Under the downward selective pressure of predation, the delicious caterpillars in question have adapted by eating neatly or clipping off damaged leaves, while their distasteful compatriots leave tatters behind. Chickadees, in turn, respond with a suite of individually variable strategies that range from direct searches for prey to utilizing leaf damage as a cue, but all of which require them to summon their knowledge of various tree species, the preferences of palatable prey for these, and the tendencies of certain tasty unfortunates to associate with messy eaters, which can vary according to the species of tree.[ccclxxvii]

Interpretation

Driving the evolutionary unfoldment of life from the inside through a panoply of lifeworlds, with their concurrent experiential and cognitive capacities, the multitudinous radiations of Umwelt and their countless shades of meaning interact amid a wellspring of signs whose meaning is not pre-given but rather created through the interactive process of living. Representing a delicate balance between competing and shifting constraints and imperatives, Umwelten and their organismal meaning-carriers are, like any other open system, malleable to open-ended evolution. In a "universe of signs," information's transmissibility and construal are highly attenuated by the predispositions and objectives of the receivers. The semantic basis for worldview construction, and the interactions that guide its evolution, functions by expanding into new domains, linking them in a dynamic, ongoing process of creativity that is subject to continual revision and recombination as the parts of the whole continually redefine their relations to one another according to their unique forms of adaptive logic.

Constructing interactions between organisms, and between organisms and their environments, intelligence is the internally sourced, bottom-up answer to the downward pressures of natural selection. Evolution among animals, then, has an inner component that is responsive to, but not dictated by environmental conditions, but which thrives when maximally correlated with its environment. The endless possible routes to fulfilling life's mandates provide a deep well of potential, which intelligence acts on in a discriminatory way to sway probabilities in its favor. This leads to the branching, fanning spread of phylogenetic radiation, which struck Teilhard de Chardin as an optimal form to allow a phylum to sample many possibilities of form and niche in parallel. As some species' branches become more specialized, and others are sheared back by selection, the space of distinction expands between them. This divergence, along with evolution's penchant for saltatory expansions in complexity, leaves behind a biotic and cognitive landscape shaded by differences in degree and punctuated by changes in kind.

Unicellular Intelligence

While animals demonstrate a remarkable propensity to interact with their environments in flexible, intentional ways that to varying degrees free them from the implacable mercies of blind selection, simple unicellular organisms appear at first blush to be just as blind as the conditions they evolve in relation to, begging the question of whether such relatively simple organisms can generate any recourse within their tiny life-worlds. In a warm tribute to ooze, Peirce answers definitively, "Each slime in its growth preserves its distinctive characters with wonderful truth; protoplasm feels and exercises all functions of mind."[ccclxxviii] The centrality of semiosis in evolving and maintaining complex systems entails that even the most primitive agents experience certain aspects of their world as patterned information. By selectively attuning to particular contextual elements, even the least among autonomous agents can engage tiny swaths of their environments in mutually transformative experiments of evolution as they carve out livelihoods that integrate them with their surroundings.

To a much greater degree than more complex creatures, unicellular organisms are closely circumscribed in their responses to environmental conditions by their genomes. However, even within these tight confines, plasticity abounds. Genomes combine complexity with efficiency to maximize the information they carry, with alternate possible "programs" of expression layered on top of each other, capable of crossing at certain points and so acting as a flexible lexicon of potential responses. The organism's interactions with the environment modulate which of these different pathways is activated. Not only can genes be selectively engaged relative to environmental conditions, but they can apparently be selectively altered, as well. In sharp contrast to the "conspicuous fidelity" with which DNA normally replicates itself, under certain circumstances, mutations are more to the organism's advantage. For example, when faced with carbon starvation and unable to digest the lactose in their culture medium, *E. coli* bacteria will undertake a multistep mutation process that results in the ability to utilize lactose as a nutrient—mutations that fail to materialize in the absence of lactose.[17] To test the veracity of the conclusion that the mutations are directed, non-mutated bacteria were placed in a lactulose culture. The transition to lactulose digestion requires yet another mutational step (Lu+) beyond lactose digestion (Lac+) that is more difficult to achieve. Yet when placed in a lactulose medium, the bacteria undertook the necessary steps to avail themselves to this food source, with the more easily attainable stage of Class I (Lac+Lu-) bacteria failing to accumulate even as the less likely Class II (Lac+Lu+) did—strong evidence that bacteria can alter their own DNA in an intentional, directed, and adaptive manner.[ccclxxix] The agent, by adjusting the contents of its stored memory in response to a categorical interpretation it has made of environmental information, adjusts its internal source domain to align with a previously untenable target. These bacteria display every aspect of intelligence.

Just as intersubjective pursuits preoccupy many animals, so also do unicellular organisms coordinate their social interactions in complex ways. Bacteria tend to occur in genetically similar cohorts that interact extensively with one another, frequently by quorum sensing. Mediated by signals that often engage multiple chemical pathways simultaneously, quorum sensing guides adhesion, biofilm formation, and virulence. Some quorum sensing circuits allow bacteria to transition from a set of low-cell-density behaviors to a different set of high-cell-density behaviors, while others promote the transient expression of particular traits or behaviors followed by reversion, while yet others allow bacteria to alternate between distinct genome-wide programs.[ccclxxx] Large synchronized groups can "eavesdrop" on other colonies and monitor the area for potential niche competitors in an aggressively kin-selected model of organization.

---

[17] A possible mechanism for this intriguing talent is discussed in Chapter 6.

Such a preference for their own genetic likeness can even prompt some bacteria to take up the arms of chemical warfare against non-kin. In order to survive their own offensives, individuals within the group must alter their phenotype to allow both production of and immunity against particular toxins.[ccclxxxi] While this plasticity can be mediated through active signaling, random noise within the population is enough to produce a coexisting population of genetically identical, phenotypically differentiated cells—a condition that can be used to the population's advantage during times of stress.[ccclxxxii] Facing the specter of starvation, *Bacilius subtilis* bacteria will begin the high-cost process of sporulation, converting themselves into inert "seeds" capable of regrowth in favorable conditions. At the onset of sporulation, about one-third of the cells become capable of producing a cell-lysing killing factor such as would be used upon a foreign bacterial colony, along with immunity to it. The hapless remainder of the colony, having failed to develop immunity, is cannibalized and the risky process of sporulation is arrested.[ccclxxxiii]

Coordinated activity among large numbers of cells enables the species that employ the tactic of collectiveness to infiltrate niche states that would be inaccessible to any one cell individually. The collective unit is able to access resources, confront competitors and address environmental challenges as a cohesive entity whose concerted capabilities enhance the survival of individuals within the group. The price to be paid, however, is the autonomy of the individual to pursue its own self-interest. For example, when slime molds assemble into a closely related, signal-mediated group in response to environmental stress for the purpose of launching hopeful spores to more congenial climes, the aggregate "slug" possesses skills absent from the individual amoebas, such as the ability to orient toward even low levels of heat and light, which suggest fertile habitat. Even fruiting bodies are oriented away from each other in order to maximize spore dispersal.[ccclxxxiv] Although this adaptation of collective behavior preserves the genetic legacy of the group, some individuals must make the ultimate sacrifice of foregoing reproduction by transforming themselves into the stalks that support the fruiting bodies. These individuals have deferred their own interests in order to take part in a higher level of organization.

A New Level of Agency

Even the simplest biological agents prove themselves adept at deriving "meaning factors" from their environments and adjusting their own internal workings accordingly. When enacted as a unified endeavor, this coordinated effort imparts the advantages of collectivity to all group members, even while demanding that they forsake a large degree of individual autonomy in order to profit. Each time multiple agents incorporate themselves into a new level of individuality, the transition is sustained by a transfer of fitness from the lower, previously independent units to the collective, higher-level one.[ccclxxxv] As "living symbols," each individual transitioning to collective behavior changes its meaning in relation to the others, and its referential locus shifts from its own tiny, minimally individuated source domain to include the directives of the group. The benefits of group cohesion are substantial enough that it evolved into permanent multicellularity five different times: in animals, fungi, plants, red algae, and brown algae.[ccclxxxvi] New physical properties, such as size and organizational features—including threads, biofilms, and internal structures—representing novel expressions of complexity became possible as a result of these early evolutionary transitions in individuality, or ETIs.[ccclxxxvii]

During the actual transition phase of an ETI, the dominant fitness component shifts over the course of three roughly delineated stages that subsequently transcend each other. The first, least individuated phase is characterized by differential expansion, or growth, as the still quasi-autonomous agents interact closely within their local group. The second, intermediate phase is marked by the differential persistence of the stabilized group relative to the turnover of its constituents, and the third by differential reproduction, which heralds the emergence of a new Darwinian individual, with the features of fitness, heritability, indivisibility, and evolvability shifted to the level of the collective.[ccclxxxviii] The formerly autonomous agents have coalesced into a new evolutionary agent with much greater structural and hierarchical complexity. This new leading edge in selective potential extends and evolves the nature and scope of natural selection's targets; the niche space that life can colonize and explore; and the ecological complexity into which the new level of agency integrates itself.[ccclxxxix] As evolution explores its own creative potential by expanding into what Stuart Kauffman calls the "adjacent possible," it does not do so randomly or blindly, but guided by the same elements of intelligence that pervade every other aspect of life's expressions.

United by Memory

Just as multicellularity comes in two flavors—obligate, as in animals, and facultative, like the slime molds that only aggregate under certain environmental conditions—evolutionary transitions themselves come in two varieties. An egalitarian alliance allows all participants to retain reproductive rights, while a fraternal alliance composed of similar, related units, demands that some of its members forgo them.[cccxc] The former transition type may have given rise to the eukaryotic cell, with commensal prokaryotes eventually fusing into a larger cell with bounded organelles. The latter type of transition unites the members of a multicellular body through their shared genetic memory, which provides the basis for heritable fitness at the higher evolutionary level while reducing variations in fitness and reproductive competition at the lower hierarchical levels, as well as significantly restraining conflict by narrowing its potential scope.[cccxci] The harmonious, low-conflict assurance of a clonal group provides the impetus behind the establishment of the life cycle, with its unicellular genesis that ensures the genetic homogeneity of clonal divisions, and the development process which supports the establishment of "irreducible complexity" (Michod).[cccxcii]

Not only did burgeoning multicellularity demand internal genetic agreement, it also created the need for efficient transmission of epigenetic information in order to maintain appropriate states in cells; to allow systemic coherence despite turnover among lower levels; and to coordinate the activities of different types of cells.[cccxciii] New levels of complexity in early evolutionary individuals were therefore mirrored by the increasing complexity in the evolutionary process itself, which was called upon to generate novel channels of inheritance; increase the fidelity of inheritance; facilitate open-ended sources of variation; and support the development of even further complexity and specialization by enhancing developmental control, thereby allowing the increased vertical complexity and potential for adaptation afforded by cumulative selection.[cccxciv] Because of these factors, ETIs can be viewed largely as transitions in how information is transmitted. As the non-linear product of various tendencies, information is an emergent, rather than absolute property, as are its channels of transmission.[cccxcv] Evolution shifts the parameters that guide and enable the intergenerational transfer of information, and therefore the structure and channels of the evolutionary process itself. Complexity compounds through the recursive dynamic of these intricate and emergent processes, which bespeak intelligence in its apparently preferred condition: far from equilibrium. Aided by emergent forms of memory, intelligence expands its functional compass by changing not only the level at which categories can be created and domains crossed, but by deepening its vertical dimension, which is structured by the nested hierarchy typical of complex systems and representative of the system's interiority, both physically and semantically.

A Collective Source Domain

The harsh eliminative logic of limited resources, stochastic environmental conditions, and differential reproduction that begets competition, even at the level of group selection, also engenders its opposite: cooperation. Group formation furnishes its members with a degree of protection from the perils of natural selection at their level. Acting as the cornerstone of ETIs rather than an anomalous specialization peculiar to a few outlying lineages, cooperation appears to function as a primary creative force in generating new levels and forms of selection that export fitness from lower levels to higher ones.[cccxcvi] Stabilized by factors such as repeated interactions, reciprocity, and mutualisms, cooperation essentially codifies the nonrandom distribution of these behaviors, amplifies their beneficial effects, and secures them into the evolutionary repertoires of interacting agents.[cccxcvii]

When the locus of selection shifts upward from the parts to the whole, the emergent entity is internally characterized by cooperation and a relative lack of conflict, indicating that the properties governing the lower levels are subject to the global-level, top-down influences of the system.[cccxcviii] Through signal-mediated social regulation, group members are integrated into irreducibility, while the cooperative unity wards off the depredations of selfish cells unwilling to relinquish their individual evolvability through mechanisms including germ line segregation or apoptotic elimination of nonconformists.[cccxcix] The fitness at this new, integrated level is no longer the average fitness of the cells, with the lower-level, non-Darwinian components becoming individually expendable.[cd] Instead, according to Jantsch, "each new level brings new evolutionary processes that coordinate and accentuate processes of lower hierarchical levels in particular ways."[cdi]

Differentiation

The innovation of multicellularity proved effective at isolating the organismal conglomerate, with its unitive genetic structure, from the environment to a much greater degree than unicellularity could achieve. Multicellularity also buffered the process of individuation by ending the free horizontal exchange of genetic material—which widely occurs among bacteria—among the integrating cells, and allowing the group's distinctive genetic signature to ripen for transmission in relative isolation. With the unified, cooperative whole acting as a new context or environment within which its members could function, the evolutionary propensity for differentiation is still maintained. However, that tendency, which can scatter individual trajectories at lower, unintegrated levels, is harnessed by the unitary context of an organism to channel the differentiated capabilities of lower levels into a singular global aim: the fitness of the system. In the context of multicellular adaptation, this entails the division from a homogeneous type of cell into new types that represent new forms of labor.

While the most primary division of labor is between fecundity and viability, the very geometry of the emerging individual, with its shifting boundaries between inner and outer, spurs other divisions of labor, as well as the semiotic processes that coordinate them. With just a subset of cells in actual contact with the environment, the genetic expression of the interior cells is no longer responsive to the external environment, but rather to signals transduced from the surficial cells that do directly perceive it. These semiotic adaptations to the new conditions of multicellularity helped maintain functional cohesion among the cells within their larger context. Facilitated by epigenetic mechanisms, the emergent division of labor allowed the cells to remain genetically identical while expressing their genomes differently, and ultimately laying the groundwork for later specializations such as sense organs, nervous systems, and organs of digestion.[cdii] The increased efficiency that specialization brings to tasks adds depth and versatility to the ways those tasks can be accomplished.[cdiii] This increase in expanse and flexibility serves as a wellspring of redundancy—the source of robustness and raw material for exaptation.

Reinventing Selection

Even after the many coalesced into unity, with their activities placed in the service of a greater whole that became a new locus of fitness and agency, the cellular constituents of lower hierarchical levels retained the potential to be stirred by the atavistic Darwinian impulses of their bygone autonomy. While often deleterious to the organism, these inclinations are sometimes recruited by the organism as a tool for its benefit. During development, the nervous system employs Darwinesque logic in its overproduction and selective elimination of cells. Axons are only generally guided to their termini, but must compete with each other in contests of electrical excitation to claim their ultimate destination, according to the Hebbian axiom that "cells that fire together wire together," and dooming the unsuccessful contenders to self-immolation. Such nondeterministic freedom allows greater heterogeneity and potential for differentiation than is available to other organ systems.[cdiv] Similarly, the immune system relies on evolvability for its efficacy, with its rapidly mutating B-cells in competition with each other to achieve the greatest affinity for a given antigen, thereby securing their long-term survival within the bodily ecosystem. This highly nonrandom selection allows the body to rapidly adapt to threats that may surface within its ever-changing environment.[cdv]

The complexity and plasticity of nervous and immune systems alike appear to be best achieved not by strict genetic guidance, which would require vastly more information than a genome could efficiently carry; but rather through the competitive, cooperative, and adaptive intelligence of evolutionary processes. Complementing the stored, internal, nucleotide-based memory of the organism, non-encoded intelligence supplements generational wisdom with a real-time biological response to prevailing conditions and introduces a factor of spontaneity that accommodates unpredictability. By allowing the spontaneous yet selective logic of Darwinian processes to play out under limited conditions, order and stability commingle with chance and probability to produce the conditions of life and evolution.

Where Does Intelligence Begin?

In the emergence of a new level of organizational complexity is epitomized the principle of one thing in terms of another, as lower-level activities correlate at a higher level of description, under a single guiding principle that imbues them collectively with a new shared meaning. Neither reducible to nor predictable from its constituent parts, the emergent system is simultaneously maintained by, and the condition for the maintenance of, its parts.[cdvi] Selectively drawn together by the "evolutionary dialectic"[cdvii] of conflict, cooperation, and mediation, a new level of agency represents a formal and semiotic innovation. Taking its place as a leading edge of ecological evolution, the complex agent interprets its surroundings to craft a niche in ways that didn't exist prior to its emergence. As the capabilities of former, lower-level agents specialize within their unitary organismal environment, and the many become irreducibly, but "distinguishably one"[cdviii] through intersubjective couplings that obscure the any single contribution from the lower levels to the workings of the whole, the biosphere itself expands into a new realm of potential for complexity and niche construction. Meanwhile, the precise locus of agency and its intelligence has become indistinct, since it now spans multiple levels. The cells that make up the bodies of organisms are themselves the result of the radical reordering of living components that came together in the egalitarian transition to the eukaryotic cell. Attempting to trace the roots of agency to even more elemental levels only further obscures the questions of what constitutes intelligence and consciousness as the divide between the animate and inert looms, wavering and indistinct.

Some models of pre-cellular conditions envision collaborative mosaics of protocell-like structures metabolically conjoined in an intricate network of autocatalytic transactions, complemented by a free, horizontal flow of memory structures which precludes heritability-based selection and its consequent Darwinian "procession of forms." In such a quasi-biotic world, phenotypic properties would be derived more from neighbors and immediate predecessors than from ancestors.[cdix] This agent-free model would govern the internal ecology of the quasi-animate primordial stew from its incipience until at least the emergence of distinct, membrane-bound entities. With no clear demarcations within the homeostatic broth between ecology and agency, any prebiotic selection would be multilevel, with an admixture of direct and indirect effects arising from the tension between the global stability of the overall ecosystem and the degree to which individual interactions maintain their robustness against perturbation.[cdx] From the multilevel linking of interactions would arise novel strategies that simple altruism-egoism dichotomies would not predict, with global dynamics differentially impacting the evolutionary trajectories of otherwise identical microscopic entities.[cdxi]

Stirring within that fecund brew were activities so fortuitous that chemistry alone would be inadequate to explain them without the intangible, guiding framework of intelligence. Autocatalytic sets propelling their own production hint at recursive self-referencing. Their creation of the very chemical pathways, out of countless less-fit possibilities, that maximize their own long-term integrity subtly nod to incipient memory and purposiveness, harbingers of intentionality and interpretation. Dynamically distinct enough to distinguish itself from a noisy environment, distinction-making is embodied in primordial life. Simultaneously, the ability of subsystems to exist and evolve lies in their ability to advantageously couple with other systems—selective domain crossing. Yet such a self-maintaining system could presumably function ad infinitum with no further stirrings toward the Darwinian revolution that beguiled from life its multitudinous capacity of differentiation.

While the answer to the origin of life and species remains elusive, the double-origin hypothesis makes the intriguing case that the vibrant and self-maintaining stew was invaded by nature's most successful parasites: nucleic acids.[cdxii] Installing themselves and staking out their territories within the primordial metabolic distillate, the hypothetical invaders would have been able to partake with that vital, but non-individuated broth in a commensalism that fused the very competencies that in later evolutionary transitions would necessitate a division: viability, or metabolism, and fecundity, or memory-based reproduction.

Just as Peirce envisioned the relative stasis of an indexical world upended by the transformative potential of symbol, the stable harmony of a complex metasystem of autocatalytic sets may have itself experienced a revolution in agency with the advent of the symbol. Intelligence untraceably leaps from dyad to triad to create the symbol level—the level at which meaning is exchanged. The leap that begot language is foreshadowed in the deepest biological stratum wherein the "self" was no more than a syntactic arrangement of digital code that, within its context—the unarticulated, pragmatic background against which its semantics unfolded—could interact, self-replicate, and self-ligate into updated versions of itself.

Pre-Darwinian Agency and Memory

Even in its most primordial form, identity emerges from a distinction between an experiential, if not formal, "inside" with which the subject identifies and the "otherness" outside of its perceived boundaries. The "inside" aspect is the primary source domain that is the basis for all activity. Among abiotic RNA molecules, agency appears synonymous with the syntactic arrangements of the nucleotide sequences that make up their hairpin-shaped bodies, which endow them with competencies beyond those of mere chemistry, including that ability to innovate the structure of their own genetic codes and partake in social interactions.[cdxiii] Nucleotide sequences impart more than bare functionality on such proto-entities; they also endow them with identity.

According to the quasispecies theory, these primordial, interacting, and self-replicating RNA stem-loop molecules—and later viruses—assemble into consortial "clouds," or systems existing far from equilibrium, cooperating as a collective to compete with and exclude less related populations and suppress reproduction of their own members through lethal defection. The identity specified by the very form of RNA proto-agents is central to maintaining membership in such clouds, distinguishing molecules both individually and as members of particular groups, while their syntactic codes provide information storage as well as a basis for interactional signaling. The population must be large and diverse enough to support an array of behavioral motifs, incorporating that diversity into one collective "memory" comprised of many semi-autonomous strands. While fitness is distributed through an aureole of genetic variants surrounding a "master fittest type," much like the drift-induced smear of genotypic variation around a "most-fit" type in Darwinian populations, minority types are also maintained as crucial contributors to the overall fitness of a consortium by providing complementary catalytic control and a reserve of diversity.[cdxiv]

The minimalist structure of RNA stem loops makes them candidates for ancestors of agency by their ability to readily accumulate complexity, especially at a group level. RNA's low-fidelity replication and high recombination rate, along with its inherent tendency toward folding into highly conserved structural motifs such as loops, bulges, and junctions, opens up many possible variations among composition patterns, identities, immunities, and functions within a consortial cloud.[cdxv] Although the factors that promote high diversity also limit the evolutionary potential of individuals, they enhance the collective capacity of the genetic system to explore new sequence spaces and their various unpredictable impacts on individual and communal competencies and membership.[cdxvi]

Distinctions

In order to engage natural selection at the most conducive level of consortium, membership must be limited in order to promote the coordination that enables collective activity. Just as for single cells transitioning to multicellularity, the advantages of consortial collectivism come with stiff restrictions on the scope of individual autonomy. Although the capacities of individuals are conserved within their protective social context, they are redirected to the benefit of the group, with potentially lethal consequences for violators as the system imposes top-down self-regulatory controls that promote collective survival and simultaneously, group identity.[cdxvii]

One of the most notable abilities of RNA is its apparent capacity to direct its own mutations to some degree. Although a low-fidelity vehicle of hereditary transmission, RNA is likewise not simply a repository of random genetic mutations and transcription errors. Such defects act much like noise on a signal: they reduce its informational content and integrity, and so are beneficial neither to the individual nor to the collective. However, mutations are an ongoing feature of RNA, resulting in new capacities and greater complexity, and must therefore be seen to some degree as directed.[cdxviii] While such an attribute may seem to ascribe too much ability to a mere molecule, modern RNA displays some striking capacities in editorial distinction-making that would be requisite to such guided development. In particular, tRNA shows talent for precise recognition of substrates and remarkable discrimination capabilities among nearly identical substrates. It further recognizes specific points in transcript sequences for alteration, changing their syntax and therefore information content in a manner suggestive of sign-using agency.[cdxix]

Domain Convergence

A functional collective is distinguishable from a mere group of individuals by its internal communicative interactions, which determine its features. For RNA, this distinction is a turning point that transforms single strands of RNA from chemical species whose simple interactions are circumscribed by the bounds of chemical laws, into a sociologically dynamic consortium united by an identity-based common "language." It is not until they merge into groups that share historical and interactional features that RNA consortia spring to "life" and display their impressive array of complex behavioral motifs. As cooperative quasi-agents, stem-loops participate in ligation reactions to produce new forms of stability and even some limited ribozymatic, or catalytic, activity that is foundational to generating novel nucleotide sequences and for inserting, changing, or deleting such sequences into the host sequence. The resulting potential for diversity leads to a consortium with emergent, transformative properties, populated by a diversity of behavior types, some of which can be derived from identical sequences. Also, like any other agents, naturally evolved RNA sequences are never entirely specified, or closed, since they must interact with the environment, replicate, and adapt. This openness makes them vulnerable to parasitism, which they actually can utilize to increase novelty, as opposed to closed systems which must limit all parasites. In contrast to Darwinian evolution, consortium members have multiple ancestral histories, many originating from parasitic lineages that were able to penetrate the network's defenses and influence its character with genetic novelty.[cdxx]

Molecular Thirdness

While the syntactic structure of code-bearing RNA proto-agents provides an orderly guide to their range behavioral probabilities within their particular contexts, outside of those contexts, the syntax has neither meaning nor functional activity. Context, then, provides a pragmatic substrate that informs the internal evolution of the system, particularly its semiotic conventions, or rules of meaning by which individuals interpret the symbol-bodies of their consortial kin. The non-deterministic, historical, and so non-replicable worlds constructed by these molecules are governed, like Umwelt, "in all parts by [their] meaning for the subject."[cdxxi] While these posited original agents are obedient to chemical and physical laws, they also answer to a higher law that does not exist in inanimate matter and brings a new level of complexity to their interactions: a representational law structured by the syntax constituting their very bodies, pragmatically constrained and semantically laden to irrevocably bind meaning with agency.

Almost literally embodying Peirce's "living symbol" at the fringes of life, RNA proto-agents share with their animate descendants both individual and collective adaptability. As ecological actors in their own right, these astonishing molecules use their only available tools—their own bodily ingredients—to actively construct niches that create complex and evolving life-worlds truly in their own image. The DNA "habitats" occupied by modern denizens of the RNA world may have originally been the creation of their consortial forebears, which, leaving off their wild-type ways, built new structures: double-helical silos of informational storage, much like themselves, except exchanging the semi-autonomy of mutability for stability and passivity.[cdxxii] The changes they created in their environments brought about inevitable changes in the RNA species themselves as they shed their former roles of self-declaration, information storage, and self-replication and became more specialized, like eusocial ants or bees that have little individual meaning or prospect for survival outside of their ideally constructed habitat and social structure. Aided by the versatile capabilities of the protein "tools" it became proficient with, RNA became capable of constructing catalysts far more efficient than its own ribozymes, ushering in the inception of the genetic code and its translation.[cdxxiii] With this momentous evolutionary epoch, ribonucleic acid sequences became a "language," symbolically representative of amino acid referents.

RNA's early efforts at translation were rough, allowing transcription of only small proteins in imprecise sequences that were simple and general in function.[cdxxiv] Evolutionary time and selective adaptation, however, ripened these crude attempts into an expansion of complexity, functionality, and specialization among proteins, clearing a path for the emergence of modern cells.[cdxxv] Some newer, more domesticated strains of RNA abandoned coding altogether to take on regulatory functions derived from their original talents of identifying and selectively altering the syntax of their own nucleotide strands. Transferring that ability to higher-level applications, noncoding RNA has become responsible for adjusting the meaning content of DNA transcriptions, and translating that meaning into the protein products that enhance the well-being of its microscopic habitat. With the increasing sophistication of that habitat, RNA's duties expanded to include nuclear organization, gene and gene network regulation, transcription and post-transcription regulation, chromatin modification and epigenetic memory, transcript regulation, control of alternative splicing, mRNA turnover, and translation and signal transduction.[cdxxvi]

The Story of Life

Within the stygian borderland in which the quick and the dead skirt the margins of their categories, a nonrandom thread insinuates these domains together by elevating chemistry above its thermodynamic level of description into a systematic metabolism. Orderly processes emerge, diversify, couple, and adapt, coaxing vitality from somnolent matter. Formal diversity radiates, offering its variations to selection like hypotheses for testing. Those affirmed by their own persistence provide the basis for a new layer of complexity. With the onset of individuation, the directionality of interpretation vacillates across the symbol-level interface that segregates internal perspective from external presentation. From its subjective epicenter, this semantic current circulates into a positive feedback loop of complementary adjustments between the organism, which carves out the very conditions of its evolution, and the environment, which reciprocally demands organismal responses to its challenges.

While the nondeterministic responses offered by organisms to natural selection supply it with material for editing, the impulse to evolve is endogenous. In a recursive "strange loop" of causality, subjectivity and its active, intelligence-guided corollary, agency, create meaning through all levels of Aristotelian cause: material, formal, efficient, and final. Materially causal chemistry supports and is transformed into functionality by the increasing regularity of its formal causes, or relations among parts, as they congeal into a self-sustaining system. Efficient, or proximate, causes abound in the myriad interactional intricacies of autocatalysis, but are insufficient to provide a full explanation of the evolutionary process. Rather, it is final cause—the one most vehemently rejected by modern science—that is pointed to in the unification of the diverse imperatives of perception, cognition, reproduction, self-declaration, and communication into symbol-level singularity. The "logic of nature" reveals itself here, fulfilling Peirce's standard that "rationality is being governed by final causes."[cdxxvii] Both ubiquitous and infinitely specialized, the "rationality" of end-directedness, which is the province of thirdness, drives intelligence through countless routes and forms of expression while deriving its validity from the silent, subjective context it expresses and whose contents it fills. This context is the basis for plasticity in semiotic participants—plasticity regarding what constitutes a stimulus and what constitutes an optimal response.

From their minimally individuated beginnings to the innumerate iterations of increasing complexity throughout the biosphere, the agents of life have consistently used the selfsame set of tools to impel their own evolution. While intelligence is the foundation from which evolution proceeds, it is also apical, emerging continuously anew as a leading evolutionary edge. From the smallest scale of individual experience, to vastly more consequential turning points, such as the ETIs that shifted and expanded the locus and scope of individual identity while opening up new levels of possibility within the environment, evolution unfolds in the play of intelligence just as surely as intelligence, cloaked in countless forms, unfurls through evolution.

4

Coming to Life

"Each thing sees the other as a kindred with which it can unite its whole function and with which it can realize its whole purpose in actual results."
—Emmanuel Swedenborg

"The innumerably many components that constitute a kind of unity in us are distinguishably one."
—Emmanuel Swedenborg

"My world is but one in a million alike embedded, alike real to those who may abstract them."
—William James

From the diversifying biomolecular ecology that presaged life, multiformity begot more of the same. As Teilhard de Chardin observes, "Where [life] has succeeded in breaking through in an appreciable degree, nothing will be able to stop it carrying to the uttermost limit the process from which it has sprung."[cdxxviii] According to Kauffman, "The biosphere as a whole may be collectively autocatalytic and…supracritical, collectively catalyzing…exploding diversity."[cdxxix] While life's beginning was humble, its expansion has been maximal. From our current vantage point, after some 3.5 billion years of biotic radiation, the original slime and its primitive agents trace their connections to countless endpoints in the form of species that have arisen, passed, and a rare few that persist. In the exploratory expansion of formal divergence, the potential for diversity and novelty spurred by life's evolution has expanded even more exponentially than the radiations of the forms themselves. Curtailing this burgeoning propensity through the stabilizing establishment of constraining loops, self-organization at every level curbs the diffusion of potential to make evolutionary gains stable and sustainable.

Evolvable systems, from RNA consortia, to organisms, to species, to ecosystems, to language, share in common the unlikely-seeming confluence of stabilizing regularity with innovative unpredictability. Constrained from within by an internal logic that subjectively expresses outer conditions, evolvable systems innovate and hone forms that express meaning, the currency of consciousness. In language, it is the triad of syntax, pragmatics, and semantics that creates the global regularity reflected in the local, probabilistic Markov chains that are drawn from intention into expression by the final cause of purposeful, meaningful expression. In the biosphere, every life form takes on the role of "living symbol," presenting itself for interpretation on the part of other subjects. Encompassing the countless generalized and specialized expressions of evolutionary ingenuity, from the tiniest individual to the entire biosphere itself, the threads of intelligence, exuberantly impelled by the generative impulse of life, weave a fertile tapestry of forms and relationships which, like words and syntax, reflect to their own degree the method of a larger, meaning-based ordering principle within a larger context to which they all collectively refer. The orderliness of intelligence-driven evolution is rooted in an apparent paradox: although the laws of thermodynamics—in particular, the second law which predicts an increase of entropy with every physical interaction—appear prohibitive to the development of order, let alone the complexity necessary to support life, this is precisely the context in which they materialize.

Order Ascending

In its coeval emergence with life, intelligence was less an individualized quality than a diffuse dynamic of stabilization, counterbalanced by adaptiveness. Before the divisive power of differentiation summoned individuality from the potent primordial brew, life was likely a holistic, unitary phenomenon that emerged above a critical threshold of complexity.[cdxxx] Out of that fecund ooze a metabolism distilled—an orderly, homeostatically integrated system of sub-networks that flowed into each other, the product of one feeding the next in sustained, autocatalytic cycles. In contrast to sprawling, reversible entropy, this complex assemblage was characterized by directionality. From the relative torpor of equilibrium prescribed by the second law of thermodynamics, wherein various chemical reactions could emerge spontaneously but with low probability, catalysis prodded an otherwise refractory amalgam of chemistry to enterprise by altering the probability and speed of certain reactions. Catalytic agents, acting somewhat in the role of Maxwell's demon, began to impel specific reactions that promoted their own formation.[cdxxxi]

By conforming themselves to the specifications of different reactions, catalysts etched various niches into their molecular habitats, some as generalists and others as obligates to particular reactions. In constraining their scope, specialized catalytic molecules created regular chemical pathways that generated product gradients. Products accruing from one set of reactions became fodder for the subsequent set, allowing otherwise disparate processes to become coupled into networks. With the relative quiescence of chemical equilibrium replaced by a dynamic disequilibrium, the fledging system established a rudimentary, dynamic "memory" by connecting chemical processes with their own posterity in stabilizing feedback loops that closed the catalytic cycles, with the final product feeding back into the beginning of the cycle as its substrate.[cdxxxii]

Driving not only individual chemical reactions, but also the larger process of self-organization, the constraint and directionality promoted by catalysis—along with and the resulting networks that grew out of these simple beginnings—presided over a developing system whose order increased along with the interdependence of its components. When the recursive dynamics structuring the smaller cycles became the global description of the system, "catalytic closure" was achieved across multiple levels of organization and the causal efficacy of individual chemical reactions became subsumed by the collective dynamics of the system they came to comprise.[cdxxxiii] Integrated into irreducible complexity, the intricately woven dynamics of the system embarked on an emergent, unpredictable evolutionary trajectory as a cohesive unit.

The orderly channels established by the numerous interlinking cycles performed the vital function of metering and directing the flow of energy along their myriads of chemical byways in order to harvest its power to drive metabolism. The systemic redundancies that naturally arose from the recursive foundations of autocatalysis acted as a buffer against constant perturbations from the environment. These disturbances, in turn, induced the system away from an inflexible state of inordinate self-reference by forcing it to account for external conditions within its internal dynamical ordering. Recruiting the very redundancies that strengthened and reinforced its defining regularities but also supplied it with a surplus of overlapping capacities, the system availed itself to environmentally influenced adaptiveness.[cdxxxiv] Specialized variation overlaid upon redundancy is the core common to the nested hierarchy that is universal among complex systems.[cdxxxv]

The earliest adaptive systems were not physically bounded from their environments, but became dynamically and organizationally distinct as they generated conditions within and around themselves that enabled their own autonomy.[cdxxxvi] The distinct patterns of flow through which a system shuttled and harnessed energy, material, and information distinguished it from its environment with boundary-like conditions.[cdxxxvii] While a source of dynamical distinction from the environment, the chemical and energetic flows through the system's channels also exerted a "centripetal pull" on their surroundings, as they replenished their internally depleted stores of raw chemical supplies by extracting needed materials from the environment. In this way, the system selectively incorporated certain aspects of its environment into its structure and dynamics, while simultaneously exporting the entropy it inevitably accrued, in deference to the second law, through the course of its own inner workings.[cdxxxviii] When dynamical boundary-like conditions came to be punctuated by actual boundaries, the singular, amorphous living broth fractured into multiplicity at a new level of agency: autopoeisis. Reprising the circular insularity of autocatalysis within membrane-bound semi-isolation, the self-maintaining activity of autopoetic entities became more than a dynamical distinction between a system and its substrate, but an identity distinction between self and non-self.[cdxxxix]

The march toward increasing order within the prebiotic world proceeded through recursive, looping pathways that canalized into biological habits. Habit, which is the end result of all thought according to Peirce, is a circularly referential and stabilizing source of regularity. In order to become adaptive, the internal reference of habit needs to become attuned with its external environment. From this contact, the system can modify aspects of its basic pattern to reflect its context. The ongoing adaptiveness of self-organization requires the steadying hand of patterned regularity in order to stabilize and become autonomous. However, order is not enough to drive self-organization. Disorder is also required.

Entropy

The backdrop against which complexity emerges initially appears precisely contra to that very endeavor. With its blind drive to maximal uniformity and randomness, the shadowy specter of entropy forever stalks the perimeter of improbable, hard-won order. To prevail against the ubiquitous leveler, complexity must innovate and embody adaptations that offset the low-entropy state entailed by high levels of organization. The primary mechanism available to a system to abate internally generated entropy is to selectively reduce its potential range of states by introducing constraints that restrict degrees of freedom at lower levels of organization while generating entirely new dynamical behavior at higher levels.[cdxl] This concerted, spontaneous response to entropic concentration supplants the inefficient dissipative mechanisms of an uncoordinated molecular assemblage, whose movements are essentially Brownian, by creating long-range correlations that arrange constituent molecules into a larger-scale ordered state that is more conducive to the through-flow of the energy that exports local gradients of entropy.[cdxli]

Balanced against the mandates of orderly energetic and entropic dissipation is flexibility in the precise structural details of dissipative pathways.[cdxlii] These pathways exploit the vitalizing randomness of lower levels of organization by coupling spontaneous processes to non-spontaneous ones to create work cycles.[cdxliii] Although out of all possible structural configurations, those that simultaneously exploit while being constrained by considerations of entropic balance are a rare minority, these are the very ones that enliven the biosphere with seemingly illimitable diversity.[cdxliv] In contrast to the tendency of thermodynamics to favor the most probable outcomes of random interactions, self-organization accesses improbable states to create function and amplify self-referencing feedback loops into complexity. The abundantly adjustable potential arrangements of dissipative pathways represent an open-ended frontier wherein evolution can freely explore diverse avenues of formal possibility to create new channels for energetic flows. As the system samples new configurations, it automatically alters its field of future expression—Kauffman refers to this as "creating salience in the adjacent possible."[cdxlv] Like its entropic foil, evolution spreads out to reach unfilled possibilities.[cdxlvi]

While complex systems are forever bound to the treadmill of paying entropic dues, life's relationship with the second law of thermodynamics goes much deeper than simply finding loopholes to circumvent it. Its inevitable local emergence in any relational activity, and the consequent need for ordered systems to vitiate that ever-present supply, makes the dissipative mandate a thermodynamic final cause that all events mediated by energetic flows conform to.[cdxlvii] Driven by the selfsame internal imperatives of dissipative attenuation and entropic export, while contending with the countless external variables of different local environments, complex living systems have lent themselves to endless adaptive, context-dependent refinements through which they embed themselves within their niches. These specializations implicitly embody a "deep knowledge" of, or integral relationship with, their particular environments, which allows organisms to persist within their thermodynamic bounds.[cdxlviii] When passed on through heredity, this "deep knowledge" accompanies an expansion of dissipative potential, as reproduction multiplies the pathways of energy dissipation and loci of constraint generation.^{cdxlix} Endowed with the parents' degrees of freedom at the structural level, the scions carry on the circular race into which order is locked with entropy.

Despite their apparent antagonism to each other's effects at the focal level, from the higher system level, entropy and order are conjoined in a cycle of mutual obligation.^{cdl} Just as the very internally generated noise that threatens to overwhelm the meaning of a message also makes its transmission possible, the entropy that appears antithetical to organization at each level is the very pool of potential from which order arises, and against which it juxtapose its forms and dynamics. The tension generated by the recursive tangle through which order and entropy chase each other acts as an engine to drive an increase in complexity and variation in biotic forms. At the same time, it escalates the potential for disorder as entropy shadows complexity at ever-higher degrees of global systemic freedom.

Free Energy

In its constant quest to balance the tension between sustaining order and acceding to thermodynamic constraints, a complex system must attune to its environment by ascertaining and embodying salient regularities. However, because of the perceptual limitations with which organisms encounter environmental complexity, the scope of what can be perceived is framed by uncertainty, or surprisal,[18] much like the entropic shadow of order. While surprisal itself can't be measured, the free energy outside of its bounds can be assessed as a function of sensory data—and, for agents so imbued, brain states—and reduced.^{cdli} Providing the lure of the unknown outside of the bounds of surprisal toward which the system's perceptions strain, free energy is an impetus for evolution whose pervasive presence demands that life's ability to organize and adapt be open-ended. The original dilemma of complexity—how to contend with entropy—is therefore not merely a thermodynamic consideration, but extends its insidious reach into the subjective realm of perception as well.

---

[18] Surprisal is a probability distribution for prediction error in information theory.

It is the ever-presence of uncertainty at all levels that calls forth an agent's interpretive capacity.

Because free energy is always larger than surprisal, a reduction in the former necessarily yields a decline in the latter. Typical of evolution-inducing challenges with many potential solutions, the universal constraint of entropy reduction summons from evolutionary players a variety of methods for reducing free energy and therefore surprisal. The spontaneous response of a system to free energy, both within and without, is to convert it to the work of reducing uncertainty. By continuously converting the ever-generative store of free energy supplied by constrained thermodynamic randomness to its own construction and maintenance, the system deploys work to carefully modulate the internal gradient between noisy potential and order. When work is directed outward through perception, external free energy can most efficiently be reduced through the detection of environmental regularities like food sources, danger, or social cues. The bounds of surprisal are also contracted through the system's natural tendency to draw to itself energy, materials, and information from the environment and recast them in its own formal description. Niche construction is a primary means of affecting environmental regularities. A creature such as the termite, for example, manages climatic surprisal by constructing a nest that maintains regular, favorable conditions. Other species may rely more heavily on cognitive and behavioral plasticity, employing heuristically guided decision-making to explore their latitude of adaptive responsiveness.

Self-organization inherently breaks up the infinite symmetry of maximum randomness, dividing it into free energy, order, work, and entropy for export. By enfolding components into a unitary system, self-organization addresses the free energy dilemmas of lower levels, reducing their surprisal by maximizing the regularities they encounter. However, the emergence of a new hierarchical level, with its expanded degrees of system-level freedom, simultaneously unfolds new forms of indeterminacy, and the system finds itself locked in an unavoidable tangle with uncertainty at a higher level.[cdlii] The "blind spots," or perceptual discontinuities, of one domain can only be abated by generating blind spots in another.[cdliii]

Functionality to Agency

The inceptive stirrings to biochemical order within the quickening primal broth were not unique innovations on the relatively nascent planet. Its material and efficient causes were and are ubiquitous, not only on Earth, but throughout the solar system, where biochemicals assemble themselves with the same spontaneity as did those in the living cauldron. It was the complex coupling of systems that created new formal causes that could all be described by the same overarching final cause of systemic persistence through energetic flow and entropic balance. While still subject to the universal laws dictated by their chemical compositions, these advancing systems of interaction altered the local expression of those laws to create a new mode of existence that couldn't fully be described by them, generating the traits that would ultimately become definitive of life: directionality, relative stability to perturbation, and escalating order encompassed by system-level guidance.

Although the transition to life is one with nebulous boundaries, the prebiotic system, in the broadest sense, displayed through catalysis the most general effect of mind: to alter outcomes by biasing probabilities. Within the directionality that spawned and sustained the primitive metabolism and transformed inertia into agency, is the normative whisper of functionality—a directed property that carries at its margins hints of agency's corollaries: subjectivity and even incipient purposiveness. Not inherent to any biological structure but intrinsic to any biological process, function by its very definition implies purposiveness, or final cause, to the system whose interests it serves. Arising as a product of constraint, functionality manifests variously from different angles of consideration. From the system's perspective, function is measured in terms of an adaptation's contribution to the overall homeostatic balance. Relative to the environment, functionality is essentially informal fitness, which is a description of the degree to which an adaptation's interactions with the environment advance the fitness interests of its bearer. All of the diverse modes of functionality within a system are enfolded into the simplified symbol level of description, which confers on them a global identity that makes all functionality at least partially semiotic.

In primordial systems, the sum of functionality was metabolism, which achieved persistence by adjusting itself to environmental parameters. In promoting the integrity and autonomy of the systems they supported through their circular self-propagation, the autocatalytic subsystems that changed in response to environmental conditions appeared to be "act[ing] so to attain certain ends."[cdliv] While this Peircian criterion for rationality may be too generous an assessment of molecular abilities, at least discernable are the primitive glimmerings of functionality in the system's directed application of work to maintain its integrity against thermodynamic erosion even amid the continual turnover of constituent material.[cdlv] Although work is a universal feature of systems that are far from equilibrium, it is specifically focused within an integrated system to constrain and organize the kinetic behaviors of lower-level components into functional processes by establishing gradients and unstable asymmetries that are anathema to thermodynamic equilibrium, but which provide the system with an efficient means of energy storage.[cdlvi]

The inevitable outcome of the integration of structure with function is an increase in autonomy.[cdlvii] Increasing autonomy, in turn, supports the advancement of agency, which distinguishes itself by its ability to shape the very conditions involved in maintaining its integrity as a system.[cdlviii] The agent not only resists the homogenizing forces of equilibrium, but actually harnesses them to drive its evolution. Internally, it accomplishes this by exploiting thermodynamic loopholes that allow it to store and direct energy for work that is functional in maintaining the system. In relation to its surroundings, the organism co-opts the potentially erosive forces of equilibrium through the impact—both induced by and generative of regularities—that it has on its environment through the niche it constructs.

Agency develops at a critical point of tension within a paradox. While predicated on a clear distinction between the agent and its environment, it demands autonomy that is gained through adaptations that accentuate the organism's relations with the environment and help integrate it thoroughly into its niche.[cdlix] In its ascent out of the milieu of generality, individuating agency is aided through the incorporation of memory in some form.

Memory

Prior to the syntactically codified, nucleotide-based memory of cells, an implicit sort of internal heredity guided complex systems' evolution in the form of deeply preserved patterns. Similar to the spontaneous order induced by the tension between constraint and entropy, a system's temporal integrity balances between stability and mutability. Despite the adaptive range available to systems that enables the same thermodynamic outcome through different channels and under various conditions, formal relations—for example, the very ancient citric acid cycle—are highly conserved throughout evolution. Even as these highly functional constants are preserved through new levels of emergent complexity, the system allows change by shedding ancillary information regarding the initial and boundary conditions of lower levels, supplanting them with new organizational parameters.[cdlx]

The advent of digital redescription through nucleotides transformed the prevailing semiotic landscape from essentially indexical to symbolic.[cdlxi] Although radically different in both degree and kind from non-formalized means of pattern retention, genetically mediated adaptations echo and even amplify the dissipative, retentive, and innovative abilities of their dynamical adumbrations. However, the scope of potential for variation and adaptation expanded immeasurably when memory gained temporal stability through codification, allowing heredity with modification. The encryption of heritable material formalized and even ritualized the interactions between the system, its environment, and its form of memory.

Like every other adaptation, the ability to transfer a symbolically scribed template intergenerationally provided another potential avenue for tuning the dissipative balance available to and definitive of a system. It ensured that each generation would face its own renewed contest with the environment from a stable platform, anchored in the successes of prior generations. But whereas each individual would be facing a completely novel experience with unpredictable short-term environmental fluctuations, the genetic template could only estimate general, probable environmental parameters. Rather than hindering the individual as a liability, this lacuna in specificity actually proves to be to the individual's benefit as the property of thirdness is summoned to develop an "interpretive" phenotypic intermediary between genomic possibility and environmental stochasticity. A successful "interpretation" incrementally adds to the species' store of hereditary knowledge through the arduous sieving of natural selection. In the shorter term, epigenetic variations, which are more environmentally sensitive, and are both reversible and to varying degrees heritable, help phenotypic expression navigate its internal and external constraints, rapidly adapting in the short term while the highly conservative genome only slowly accepts updates to its archives.[cdlxii]

Instead of providing a deterministic blueprint to guide cellular activities, genetic expression guides how different processes are tuned to each other as a function of the state of the system. A system interprets its environment in relation to its needs by employing heuristics that strike the fine balance between energetic affordability and efficient reduction of entropy. The power of such nondeterminism, which epitomizes the flexible sensitivity of functional intelligence, is that its moment-to-moment needs inform selection.[cdlxiii] As the system adjusts its perennially incomplete stored memory—such as through epigenetic modulation—based on its interactions with the environment, it is expressing the updating capacity of a Bayesian memory. Each experience allows the system to fine-tune its store of information to model changes or greater details in its environment. Like a conclusion drawn from the premises of environmental conditions, adaptation becomes the deductive "inference" that the system embodies.[cdlxiv] By conserving stability while allowing adaptiveness to local contingencies, Bayesian updating enables the system to maintain its deftness at thermodynamic balance despite ever-changing outer conditions.

The validity of Bayesian updating rests on the second thermodynamic law that the system is forever striving against. Just as the second law biases the outcomes of situations toward typical and makes surprises outliers, anticipation based on inferential memory is generally aligned with the outcomes of highest probability.[cdlxv] The formal memory of an organism is therefore not merely a record of its history, but also an anticipatory framework—the confluence of a discriminating interpretation of the past with future predictions, continually updated by dynamical thirdness.

Like a metaphor, adaptation's simultaneously dissipative yet selectively retentive nature streamlines the "fit" between highlighted aspects of source and target, or organism and environment, as the demands in one elicit complementary responses from the other. The flexible fidelity of memory enables adaptive change, with past spilling into future by rotating around the axis of current conditions, in terms of which the agent's intelligence samples from and modifies its store of potential. As changes accrue, stabilize, and transmute, historicity insinuates itself into the system's evolutionary trajectory to condition future expressional probabilities in terms of the past.[cdlxvi]

Boundaries and Domain Crossing

From its memory, a complex, multilevel system draws the stability it needs to probe its extent of adaptive capability as it negotiates a variety of outer conditions. The interface at which these conditions encounter those of the system are the system's boundary conditions. Delineating two distinct dynamical orders, the boundary is a region of non-linear interactions and informational generation and conductance, with relevant environmental information relayed inward to be semantically received by the system, while the system's effects on the environment propagate outward. In exchange for the boundary's buffer against the environment's effects, the components it constrains into a single entity forego some degrees of freedom to the coordination that defines the system's dynamical regime.[cdlxvii]

Boundary conditions lie not only between organism and environment, but also delineate internal subsystems into a nested hierarchy of dynamical and semiotic distinctions that penetrates down to even subcellular systems. The system's ability to differentiate itself at the symbol level from its environment is an external reflection of its internal tendency to distinguish domains. Diverging from an underlying core of self-similarity, the specialized variations of that singular and unifying systemic theme distinguish themselves according to the information they are receptive to, coordinated by a system of matching signals and reinforced by the common significance of incoming stimuli. Within the complex, nearly decomposable system, intra-component linkages are much stronger, closer, and more frequent than inter-component ones.[cdlxviii] This quasi-segregation of relatively loosely interacting subsystems encourages local concentrations, reactions, and interactions that enhance recirculation and create regularities within the system—a perfect internal mirror of the system's engagement with its environment.[cdlxix] The modularity that results from the constrained, adaptive divergence of self-similar processes equips a system with a diverse suite of potential from which to engineer responses to evolutionary challenges by essentially providing different "perspectives" on the same condition, thereby maximizing the information that can be measured. The information accrued through multiple sensory channels is correlated into cogency by the semantic agreement that the interpreting system recognizes beneath the different modes of presentation. A sufficient degree of informational overlap is an essential unifying component of a delicately balanced dynamic coalition of semi-divergent domains, although too much complexity or information threatens this fragile alliance with dissolution.[cdlxx]

As parts of a larger collective whose aggregate dynamics entrain and inform those of its components, subsystems are compelled to domain transfer at two levels. The first level is the horizontal transfer of interactions within and among subsystems. Creating robustness and global coherence among components through structured correlations, interacting subsystems retain enough plasticity to learn and adapt as a result of the interactions that coordinate them into larger systems.[cdlxxi] The second form of domain transfer among interacting subunits is a vertical one wherein lower-level dynamics are parlayed into a global level of emergence, composed of but not reducible to the bottom-up actions that create it. These bottom-up dynamics inform the emergent level, while in turn being constrained themselves—in addition to the constraints of specialization—by the global dynamics of the system. At each level of hierarchical ascent within a complex system, the detailed activities at lower levels are smoothed into a statistical average that is descriptively simplified into the balance between the energy available for work, and entropy.[cdlxxii] Far simpler than the detailed motions of the elements they guide, the top-down, system-level constraints integrate all lower levels, enriching their ensemble of expressional possibilities and autonomy at the higher, collective level of integration.[cdlxxiii]

The two streams of causality that comprise a system flow in complementary opposition to each other, each deriving its explanatory power from the other.[cdlxxiv] The upward flow supports the emergence of novel properties that are not reducible to the local interactions that give rise to them. The resultant globally consolidated network issues counterbalancing top-down directives which guide lower-level dynamics to support system-level interests. Occurring simultaneously and superimposed on all levels of order, the higher level directs the lower, which constructs the higher in a loop of reciprocal causality.[cdlxxv] This dialectical loop of circularly referential dynamics provides a system with the closure necessary to distinguish itself from its surroundings, and coordinates not only ascending current with descending, but initial conditions with final cause as equally consequential drivers of systemic organization, maintenance, and evolution. The system's final cause, which is global maintenance and persistence, emerges at the critical juncture between the tension of opposites in a reciprocally causal counter-flow which amplifies complexity into autonomy.

A Larger Whole

While its particular expression is bound to the parameters and interests of a given system, from a broader stance, final cause is reflective of the self-same principle of system support and fitness, despite its countless formal guises. The closure of the reciprocally flowing circuit between upward non-determinism and downward incorporation generates an integrating, contextually conditioned logic which embeds and differentiates agents into stratified classes of relatedness, which all uniquely contribute to the functional description of the greater whole which they collectively comprise. The self-same final cause of life approached from countless perspectives links agents of differing niches into localized orbits with various degrees of interdependence.

Wending its way up the nested hierarchy of integration, complexity continuously unfurls under diverse circumstances by selectively summoning innate potential to emergence. As subsystems within the tightly coupled progenitive stew became increasingly distinct and autonomous, the measuring work of natural selection, facilitated by the organismal ability to accumulate heritable changes, drove the differentiating systems apart as they reenacted a sort of biological Big Bang of radiating biodiversity. Echoes of their ancestral unity attended emergent agents along their evolutionary travels internally through the deep conservation of biological processes and genetic mechanisms, and externally through their niche-mediated propensity to self-organize with other agents into integrally connected systems at larger scales.

In the continuously flowing transitions across the domains of energy, order, and entropy are generated the regularities that enable pattern-seeking agents to establish interactional couplings that cohere them into a system, which begins to arise with the first stabilizing hint of habit. When order converts potential energy into free energy available for work, followed by entropy for export, it does so on the basis of perceived regularities in the environment that allow it to optimize its ability to secure these as resources. The subjective perception of regularity raises ecological interactions above the level of mere stochasticity by facilitating recurrent interactions between agent and environment through the development of a history of mutual structural changes.[cdlxxvi]

Once interdependence through feedback—whether energetic, material, or semiotic—is established, the interacting agents become a coupled into a system at a new level, with exports connected back to the system's inputs at a higher hierarchical level.[cdlxxvii] The conservative recirculation of these assets is as foundational to the establishment of a system as the dissipation of entropy. Reciprocally causal feedback loops establish ecologies which nest into larger systems, effectively removing any upper limit on not only the potential hierarchical arrangements of complexity which life can attain, but also the size of the system that can be acted on by natural selection.[cdlxxviii] The Gaia hypothesis is a logical extension of the intractable tangle of upward and downward causation, positing that Earth's entire biosphere acts as a collective, complex, self-regulating system that arises from the tight coupling that adaptation brings between organisms and their environments. Developing from the local activities of organisms, the global regulatory system is nearly decomposable, and characterized by informal associations among its constituent ecosystems and species, whose diversity and autonomy supply an important source of longevity and strength to the system.[cdlxxix]

Interpretation

With their adept routes to entropy dissipation and ready application of free energy, self-organizing systems are spontaneous, energetically efficient responses to fortuitous conditions that provide the raw materials for complexity.[cdlxxx] The phenomenon of self-organization is sufficiently regular, principled, and law-like to allow generalizations that hold true from prebiotic levels of complexity to those sophisticated enough to create language. However, the broad outlines of the dynamical activities that describe these systems and their responses to natural selection fail to account for the subjective aspect of evolution: the agency that makes meaning, and thereby its expressed state of utility, possible. Whether devoted to system maintenance, resource acquisition, or signification, utility is an interactional rather than an inherent property, arising directly out of the subjective capacity to recognize one thing in terms of another. By parlaying one thing—molecular forms and relational properties—in terms of another—order, structure, and functionality—life animates its molecular substrate, converting free energy into work on the basis of potential. Such meaningful domain crossing, in turn, is a directed application of one of agency's foundational properties: the facility to be changed iconically and interpretively by experience. Iconic representation acts as the first tier of structured correlation between a subject and an object, establishing an experiential template along which to guide interpretation. Because icon is an experiential state rather than intelligible information about the circumstance that elicits it, even the most fundamental capacity for functionality requires an inference between sensation and the many-leveled hierarchy of processes that yield responsive actions.[cdlxxxi]

Through form, dynamics, and openness to adaptation, a complex system engages in a dialog with its surroundings that informs its responses to new environmental challenges. Mediated by the system's boundary, which is its symbol level of presentation, interactions transpire between the distinct, yet profoundly entangled dynamics of agent and environment. Despite their apparent differences, the interactions of the two systems are based on a deep level of isomorphism that represents a point of overlap between the ranges of potential that lie on either side of the systemic divide and allows the embedded system to intelligently cross its own boundary to engage with its embedding target domain. By marshalling its interpretive aptitude, the agent highlights conditions that are external to it in terms of those that are internal, correlating perceived regularities into patterns.

Fraught with uncertainty of its own, the process of interpretation is one of multiply realizable outcomes, each of which engenders its own measure of causal efficiency for the interpreter.[cdlxxxii] Out of the entropic disarray of equiprobability, the processes of intelligence that support interpretation and guide intentionality divide, unite, and infer to break the symmetry of possibility into well-fitted, contextually aligned probabilities. By collapsing noisy, stochastic potential into coherent percepts that can be acted on, the selective contraction of possibility draws together, in its crossing, the domains of meaning and expression to affect a particular outcome that is preferred over others because it is anticipated in an intentional state. The uncertainty that is affiliated with large amounts of potential drives not only physical systems, but semantic ones as well. From agent-less, generalized processes that roughly align with the processes of intelligence, the circular tangle between order and entropy moves a nebulous, undivided system over evolutionary time toward the clarity of individuation, and reflexive responsiveness toward the intentional, agent-dependent heights of choice capacity.

Semantic Self-Organization

Even prior to life's outset, primeval stirrings more mysterious than the material and efficient causality of mere chemistry steadily summoned order from the earth's trove of elements and molecular compounds. The dormant potentialities ensconced within inert atoms were animated through formal relations that unfolded and sustained order in apparent defiance of entropy's presumably iron-fisted rule over the physiosphere. By itself, order IS inadequate to account for the emergence of life. Low-information and unable to compute, order is actually at odds with the high-information, dynamical complexity of life.[cdlxxxiii] Another ingredient is necessary to account for the shift from equilibrated randomness to self-ordering autocatalysis, to the even higher levels of organization necessary to support life.

Although the rise of matter into dynamism and eventually autonomy are describable in terms of the material and efficient causes of chemicals and their reactions, the subtler forms of causality, formal and final, are those that bestirred chemistry to rise above the lifeless probabilities set by thermodynamic laws. The material-based efficiencies of physics are vitalized by a causal element founded on an "insideness" that is not necessarily a spatial orientation, and that is wholly outside the realm of measurement and lawful predictability. The leap from merely dynamical to living is a nonlinear one that imposes new parameters on physicochemical interactions, elevating them into a new arena of functionality that prolongs autocatalysis and thereby the duration of the system; employs feedback-based controls on biochemical and metabolic pathways; and governs itself through the lawful regularity of algorithmic rule-following.[cdlxxxiv]

Driven by expansive potential and curbed by stabilizing recursion, complexity deepens through the diversifying iterations of biological generation to unleash degrees of freedom at the leading, symbol-level edge of the intelligence which guides the formal changes of evolution. Constrained by the same principles and arising out of the same material, efficient, and—in a general way—formal and final causes as the lower levels of hierarchical complexity, the increasing influence that active, agent-centered intelligence plays in the higher echelons of systemic complexity bespeaks the unfolding of a quality which, however obscure and decentralized, is never wholly absent from the project of evolution. Instead, it is the starting point of the most fundamental domain crossing of all, even more primitive than that between self and non-self.

Coeval with physically describable and adaptive systems is an unmeasurable domain of semantic self-organization, whose impalpable presence is only discernable through the proxy of its material effects. Although the dynamical realm of time, energy, and rate of change is fully proscribed by physical laws, it is affected in its workings by the semantic domain, which operates within those parameters but whose functions of measurement, memory, selection, and interpretation are not described by them.[cdlxxxv] Instantiated in a dimension independent of temporal dynamics, the bodiless patterns of the semantic domain teleologically entrain elements of physicality into dynamical correlates of their informational structures.

Semiosis and Agency

Although dynamically expressed, a system's internal integrity is semantically ordained, with the untraceable leap between directive but discarnate intelligence and measurable physical expression negotiated semiotically. The constraints that attenuate energetic dissipation are reflections of formative mental qualities, while the work that supports the transfiguration of a chemical collation into life provides a primitive referential basis for semiosis. Even prebiotic molecules and the autocatalytic sets they form participate in the growth, development, and maintenance of their molecular world through complex interactions that are mediated by meanings not present in simple chemistry.[cdlxxxvi] With its perpetual but discontinuous transformations between sensation, representation, and interpretation, semiosis bridges the two domains of physicality and mentality by rendering meaning in terms of a symbol-vehicle, and vice versa. Qualitatively distinct but indistinguishably entwined, semantics and expression converge at the discontinuous turning point between a physical signal and its meaning. The commensalism between symbol and dynamics is a union between two disparate domains whose differences can only be reconciled through an interpretive bridge.

Intrinsically and fundamentally semiotic, agency is the locus of meaning generation and interpretation. Far more than mere physical contingencies, the actions of an agent are biased, driven, and channeled by the information that perception sifts from the environment and reconstructs according to its own template. Through the triadic process of icon experienced and re-presented as index, and interpreted as meaning, every communication impels a process of self-organization in the semantic domain as meaning is created out of the life processes of the receiver.[cdlxxxvii] The prevalence of semiosis even in systems striving toward the threshold of life implies at least a whisper of subjective agency, rooted as it is in experiential icon. "Experience," believes Husserl, "is original consciousness."[cdlxxxviii] As a primitive, homologous prefiguration of metaphorical understanding, embodied experience is the foremost link conjoining the closely coupled, but non-linearly correlated, semantic and physical evolutions of a single system. By tying an affective state to a subjectively construed category, icon underlies the semantic framework which guides perception, interpretation, and consequent activity. Passing all information through its primarily experiential intentional structure, each semiotic actor roots its understanding in its own subjectivity. Although iconic and therefore representative, that subjectivity is also to some degree objective. This is because iconic representation signifies a referent by affecting some change in the agent—a change which is efficiently causal in its actionable incarnation of interpretation. Because the "presence in the knower of something that is known constitutes knowing in its basic sense...cognition, or the knowledge act, is not doing something but becoming something."[cdlxxxix]

The rules by which an agent relates to the signs that furnish its Umwelt are informed by its evolutionarily wrought, inwardly sourced initial conditions and its perception-mediated boundary conditions. Expressed through the logic that animates matter into life-supporting systems, the subjective factors that an agent brings to its interactions are hemmed in by the universal laws governing physics, and therefore the expression of semantics. The layers of contingency that separate the tenets of physical regularity from those of mentality place severe limits on how directly a system of signals corresponds with its symbolic implications for a given agent.[cdxc] With its measurable properties conveying no hint of the symbol's significative value, "an everlasting conflict originates from this: the 'idea' or 'sense' of each thing and its 'materiality' trying to fit into each other."[cdxci] Distantly foreshadowing the vital role of conjoining "two minds...as one through signs," signals in early systems were instrumental in carving the initial inroads of biological order into chemical randomness by establishing, through informational corridors, the long-range correlations among interacting entities at the multiple hierarchic levels that are so characteristic of functional, complex systems. As the first stabilizing structures grew out of incipient directionality, stochastic reminders of the systems' thermodynamic origins asserted themselves in semantic form as well as physical.

Signals and Symbols

A signal's meaning is activated by entailments whose first application in a system is to elicit some degree of regularity from randomness. Like the open range of possible initial conditions in which a system can germinate, the signals guiding that system's construction are founded in a non-deterministic arbitrariness that is reflective of their adventitious origins. A signal is arbitrary in the sense that its role is not strictly functional, but rather representational.[cdxcii] Just like biological function, symbolic function is not an intrinsic or law-based property of the material elements that fulfill it, and so not reducible to the physical features of its carriers. Context-dependent and multiply realizable, the same sign may differ in meaning according to changing perspectives and situations. While "the reality of that [semantic] order has a value or significance different from the reality possessed by its elements,"[cdxciii] both "orders of reality" are necessary in accounting for the functionality of a complex system.

Both the domains of meaning and dynamics share the common property of presenting themselves at a unitary global level that is a simplified rendition of very complex lower-level processes.[cdxciv] Out of the indeterminate spectrum of possible meanings that an object can acquire in its representative role as a sign, those that are ascribed to it reflect a normative value for the interpreting subject. Derived from its associations and entailments, the sign's assigned meaning provides the basis for reference, pattern perception, and functionality, which are all foundational ingredients of "aboutness;" the rudiments of epistemology. Enfolded into a signal, those subjective distinctions guide the agent's perception of and response to meaning, much like the material and energetic parameters of a system meter and direct the local activities of subsystems into a concerted whole. Entangling otherwise uncoordinated activity into dynamically functional arrangements, semantic agreement is an important basis of long-range, structured correlations.

Although the activity of symbolic interpretation is subjective, its effects ripple outward to structure not only local interactions, but evolution itself. With its potential meaning malleable among interpreting agents, a signal or system of signals can differentially link groups together on the basis of shared meanings that draw the intentional structures of multiple actors into alignment even as those from outside groups are rebuffed. In this way, the use of signals serves as a selective property of populations whose members respond to them in a particular ways that structure their dynamics and affect how they utilize available resources.[cdxcv] Symbols, observes Howard Pattee, are recognized individually because they function in the propagation of a whole social system that is based on interpretation.[cdxcvi] The meaning collectively imputed to signals coheres a population into an approximation of a higher-level unity whose constituting individuals can differ in their memories both genetically and ontogenetically.[cdxcvii] Spreading out the population's range of potential in this way maximizes the diversity it can sustain and therefore its collective ability to respond to environmental contingencies, while minimizing the memory burden of each individual.

Through symbols, the nonlocal world of principles, which are evident only through their effects, is localized into the many-formed microcosms which reflect those principles through measurable regularities and subjective perspectives. The autocatalytic closure that provides a foundation for metabolism finds an analog in the self-referencing semantic closure necessary for abstract construction. With the sign's imputed meaning acting as a discontinuous point of union between the semantic and physical domains, a significative source of constraint is layered upon the system's law-determined physical dynamics that cannot be fully accounted for by them.[cdxcviii]

Under the semantically laden auspices of symbol, meaning assumes a place of primacy that is coeval with that of mechanism in supporting and impelling evolutionary unfoldment. Drawing their potency from the immaterial domain of meaning, symbols signify constraints on the fundamental laws of nature by localizing, contextualizing, and conditioning the factors that impact their interactions and expressions. Binding the enactment of general laws within limited locales via situated forms, symbols impose contingencies on the expression of those laws that beget the evolution of agent-like capabilities and the dynamical boundary conditions that are regions of information generation.[cdxcix] Like any other expression of intelligent self-organization, symbols participate in the creation of the very boundaries that their meaning must cross. From the complex interplay of universal laws with local conditions, boundaries arise as nonlinear hybrids of regularity and contingency, and so like the symbols and signals that they mediate, are arbitrary in regard to their initial conditions. Despite their inchoate origins, however, all of these order-inducing constraints provide essential supports to the system's subsequent evolution, which is eminently logical within the bounds—physical and semantic—which circumscribe its particular rendition of intelligence into a stable structure.

Degeneracy and Interpretation: Dual Aspects of Stored Memory

Arguably the most transformative union between symbolism and dynamics is the one at the very foundation of the biosphere, with the potential for all ensuing radiations of biodiversity encapsulated in its relatively compact structure. By facilitating the transfer of new levels of specification between individuals and eventually generations, the digital redescription of the system's essential components allowed the uncoupling of biochemistry from its communal forge into discreet, unitary agents; each guided by an objective frame of reference whose entailments exist prior to the individual agent's experience of them.[d] Like a metaphor, the syntactically rendered description of cellular information highlights only certain aspects of the system it represents, and depends on interpretation to integrate these into their context.

In their non-interpreted, time-independent state, the structural representations of memory are all equiprobably constrained within the same energetic parameters, and so equivalently accessible from the perspective of energetic expenditure. This is energy degeneracy, which correlates with a large informational capacity by affording a large range of variation in memory states—such as those contained in nucleic acid chains—and avails these to an external, interpretation-dependent selection process.[di] Energy degeneracy is a requisite aspect of stable biological memory that allows open-endedness in coding potential, simplicity of reading and transcribing, random access, passivity, and isolated storage.[dii] Although all nucleically archived information is equivalent in terms of the energetic costs of storage and expression, the content within each state is causally distinct from that in all other states.

While syntactic representations of the cell's possible proteins exist in the dormancy of a rate-independent symbolic form, the interpreting structures that mediate the transfer from the symbolic to the time-dependent realm of dynamical activity are unrepresented in the genetic script.[diii] The dynamics that are implied but not genetically encoded are only determined when they couple with rate-dependent laws that remove equiprobable degeneracy in favor of a decisive expression through a multistep process involving genetic transcription, translation into a polypeptide, and post-translation modifications. In its linear form, the product is in an inactive state of metastability whose syntax alone is not enough to impart meaning. The mapping from the symbolic domain of semantic possibility to that of causal efficiency is only completed when the polypeptide integrates into its context with the help of chaperone proteins, which quickly and precisely guide the chain into its functional shape. Neither process nor outcome is genetically dictated. Rather, these non-encoded constraints are emergent, and arise in a complex environment whose intricate details are washed away at the higher level of systemic description.[div]

The domain transfer that imparts effectual form upon abstract meaning is interpretation-dependent and so open-ended in its execution, which is carried out by an interworking control regime of agents ranging from different types of RNA to specialized proteins. Every interpretation they apply to a given stretch of DNA, with its overlapping superposition of potential meanings, is contextually contingent, rather than correlated with a predetermined outcome. This variability in interpretive potential allows many possible semantic closure loops to arise from the same symbol, enabling the maximal compression of information, as well as interpretive latitude.[dv]

Symbol is a turning point between a semantic construct and the material analog which conveys its meaning as though through a channel. A symbol can be at once an objective, sender-based signal and a subjective, receiver-based perception that unites these two opposing poles through a single meaning. Common to sender and receiver, but divergent in the response it compels from each, the symbol is both a boundary and a turning point whose informational potential is maximized on either side of the interpretive divide by the contingency of its signification. As a highly refined expression of symbolism, the formalized genetic code represents a point of reflective inversion in the temporal twining of reciprocal causality that an organism unravels throughout its life cycle. The objective, sender-based symbol derives from a global level that is *a priori* to the dynamics that its passive presence precipitates at the molecular level. It presents a common referent for the many agents of cellular activity, which are themselves almost essentially messages, and provides a semantic focal point on which their activities, although highly varied, can functionally converge. United by the common endeavor of interpreting through their many forms the salience relative to ambient conditions of this global-level signifier, which becomes a referent at the local level, the activities of the agents which occupy the most foundational hierarchic rungs within the organism are correlated with each other in terms of the system's overarching mandates. Lower-level subjectivity, localized into numerous interacting and complementary forms, is the basis for the bottom-up dynamical regime. End-directed and purposive, this activity creates and sustains the global level that sets the parameters for local activity at all levels by its symbolic description of itself. This feedback between global and local levels closes many fundamental semantic and autocatalytic loops that internally integrate the system by providing a description of its symbol-level agency as semiotic kindling for the activities at its lowest levels.

    The intelligence that bridges the domains of symbolism and physics is not amenable to descriptive compression because although its expression is time-dependent, the meaning it interprets is independent of temporal confines. Drawing its causal efficiency from the conscious substrate whose essential wholeness it reflects as a teleological template to guide local dynamics toward a global end, intelligence creates structures whose partiality affords both signification and interpretation. Genetic inheritance is a process of re-membering, through discreet parts and stratified levels of integration, the higher, synchronized completeness implied in its arrangement. Like branches growing from a single indivisible root, the diametric twins of symbol and dynamics vacillate together in a patterned dance between meaning, interpretation, and expression. This interwoven choreography resonates the latter to the activity of fructifying symbolically signified possibility by manifesting complete, coherent, higher-level wholeness out of the correlated interactions of many semi-independent parts.

Epistemic Cut

Directed and meaning-based, intelligence relies on the distinctions into which it perceptually measures its environment as the basis for ordering its functions. Because perception is able to sample only a small portion of available information relative to the totality, a simplified and inferential description replaces complete knowledge and condenses the redundant intricacy of possible information into discernable, predictive patterns. While the subjective measurer that creates relational distinctions, and the objects that it measures, are both describable in terms of physical laws, the product of a measurement is conceptual and abstract.[dvi] Like the symmetry-breaking selection that removes energy degeneracy from internal symbolic stores to express an interpretation, or a catalyst that drives decisive directionality from open-ended possibility, categorization judiciously constricts and arranges the potential information that the subject confronts within its environment, availing it to the ordering power of interpretation. In imposing cuts on the otherwise undivided wholeness of environmental conditions, subjective distinctions create fertile regions along the boundaries of categories where information freely propagates.

From the foundational distinction of agency between inner and outer, and thereby self and other, arises all other properties of distinction-making. As the very basis of semiosis, this primal distinction, which Pattee deems the "epistemic cut," reveals a complex system's partial transcendence of physical laws. Based on the agent's perception, the epistemic cut is, like the signals that traverse its bounds, arbitrary. Not necessarily synonymous with a physical boundary, this division is a subjective construct that integrates the agent with its environment to such a degree that the agent's tendency to alter its surroundings to reflect its own dynamics obscures precise delineation. From within those subjective confines, intelligence creates semantic structures founded on the objects it interacts with and rouses the system to normative action relative to these. By embodying the conditions in terms of which stimuli are distinguished and interpreted, complex systems implicitly embody and enact their epistemologies.

The semantic structure that unfolds from heuristically derived patterns is interpretively constructed out of the manifold articulations of meaning precipitated by the epistemic cut—a source of uncertainty that allows the possibility of error, but also provides the open-endedness essential to evolvability within and among agents.[dvii] Sealed into unity like all self-organizing systems through many-leveled closures of reciprocally causal loops, interpretation fulfills the premise of the epistemic cut by establishing semantic closure between knowing subject and known object.[dviii] By attracting the subjective flow of perception and interpretation, the object establishes an "intentional presence"[dix] within the subject as a node of organization within its Umwelt around which threads of meaning ravel. By closing interpretive loops between itself as a source domain and the objects it relates to, the "insider of sign processes" constructs a pattern of regularities within its context that reflect its inner, semantic properties in terms of the interpretively guided relations it establishes.

Intelligent Structures

Because of the intractable interconnection between measurable physicality and intangible mentality, the impulses to signify and interpret are primordial ones that share the same final cause of creating meaning. Organic, evolving systems therefore trace their origins to a dual ancestry. The metabolically capable progenitor was law-abiding, existing largely in the measurable and dynamical realms of chemistry and physics—but not entirely. The province of the other parent was largely the abstract realm of meanings, although it expressed its meaning through the physical constraints of embodiment. Within each complement was a seed of the other that enabled its existence. When they fused into an emergent union, they engendered a radiation of diversity, structured by populations that shared signals, but dynamically entrained at a higher level of description than that of local interaction. Over the evolutionary eons, countless variations of meaning, interpretation, and the embodied, agent-borne semantic structures that support them have unfolded, yielding not only endless variety, but also increasingly explicit levels of intentionality, supported by niche-appropriate intelligence. As evolution gradually accumulates layers of complexity and specialization upon its prior achievements, the gap widens between the measureable components of the system, such as its chemistry, and the meaning and intelligent activity toward which those materially and efficiently causal properties are mobilized.

Physical embodiment, from its barest expression, declares the essence of metaphor by expressing ineffable intelligence in terms of physical, measurable expression. Contracting that expansive and other-dimensional potency into the channelizing strictures of form, regularity, habits, and thermodynamic openness, which all facilitate evolution, iconic experience directs its referential frame outward toward objects whose symbol levels comprise the substance of its epistemology, and which it interprets in terms of its own situated form. As entities systematically arrange themselves into the layers, facets, and dimensions of complex order, evolution reveals its essential nature as what Bateson terms a "mental process."[dx] The key criteria he designates for such a process include circular to more complex chains of determination, and responsiveness to differences that transforms previous events into new forms. These criteria embrace the essential elements of physical self-organization, with its complementary control regimes of upward and downward causality integrated into the intelligent loop that is the cornerstone of agency; and the semantic self-organization whose cycles of closure originate in the semiotic translation that renders signs interpretable. Like Peirce, who sees inner mind and outer matter as a singular entity, Bateson rationalizes that the "relationship between mind and matter can obtain only if either mind has material characteristics or matter is endowed with mental characteristics."[dxi] Mind and matter share two facets of the selfsame existence, much like an icon and an index—an irreducible, self-contained "tender thing" conveyed by an externalized vehicle, the "dead thing."

As active agents within a "universe of signs," all "living symbols" embody the union of semantics and structure, acting as turning points which harness and redirect flows of energy, material, and information. The confluence between materiality and meaning is embodied in adaptive, life-sustaining, complex self-organization, whose physical aspect is a supportive medium for the inscrutable vitality that animates it from within, yet beyond the confines of physical law. Every aspect of intelligence, culminating in interpretation, functions in close tandem with, and expressed through, the interactions of its physical, measurable vehicles. The reciprocally causal countercurrents that cohere systems into unities behave in the teleological way they do, not only because of physical constraints, but because of semiotic ones as well. Physical feats of self-organization and cumulative evolution are analogous expressions of the evolution that is simultaneously occurring in that semantic realm whose effects are inferable, but whose substance is immeasurable. Driving the continual evolutionary unfoldment of meaning as apprehended through innumerable situated perspectives that are informed by their boundary conditions, the measureless and abstract domain of mentality is one of immaterial structure that impels system dynamics toward its given ends.[dxii]

Growing through the very complexity that it constructs, intelligence expresses itself on the largest scale over time as open-ended evolution. In the contests for fitness that drive the evolutionary modulation of constraints, it is intelligence that is being selected for, and which actively engages with the forces that test it. Endemic, foundational, definitive of, yet irreducible to life at every level, interpretive intelligence activates the indeterminate region of potential, drawing from its unformed depths the structures and forms to be expressed through channels sourced in intention. By shifting and amplifying the scope of possibility accessible to a system as it evolves from intention to enactment through a variety of possible means, proliferating potential offers the system it animates flexibility at every level in devising optimal solutions to environmental challenges. At the same time, however, that very amplification of possibility corresponds with the entropy that passively goads the system with destructive equilibrium. Like entropy, mind in its most underived form is nondescript potential; its contents degenerate and equiprobable. As mind, localized into subjectivity by physical constraints, establishes meaningful regularities of interaction with salient objects of reference, open-ended plasticity intelligently narrows into the semantic structure that guides an agent's encounters within its environment. Even as structure arises, the dictums of the second law that find an analog in the degeneracy of unattenuated mind persist by expanding into elaborations of potential at every level, enabling intelligence to reiterate its processes in ever-changing contexts and at higher levels of complexity. The resultant hierarchy of organization ascends in complexity and capacity through a process of enfoldment, with each emergent level of description encompassing those from which it derives. Fusing the semantic with the formal and the mental with the physical, the descriptions of emergent levels disclose a corresponding hierarchy of logical types that Bateson sees as immanent in the phenomena that represent them. The "patent world of mere impressions" is necessarily built in conjunction with "the latent worlds made up of structures of impressions."[dxiii]

Intelligent Evolution

Rolling forward from its humble conception in totipotent ooze in one unbroken, but highly differentiated wave, life flows through countless permutations of form and niche across scales in its supercritical pursuit of complexity, impelled to evolution by the continuous striving of intelligence to penetrate the ever-receding uncertainty beyond its bounds. Complex, contingent, and nondeterministic, the branching, weaving fibers of intelligence are discernable in the subtle yet robust scaffolding that supported the crystallization of autonomous agency from a non-individuated milieu. From that complex ecology of coupled autocatalytic processes gelled a metabolism to form the first bridge spanning the newly emerging gulf between inanimate and living. As metabolic parameters supervened upon—while being constrained by—thermodynamic ones, the edgeless boundary between the two domains fostered a turning point between degree and kind to awaken the biotic potential of a hospitable planet.

While the precise point of delineation between the matter and life, with a clear set of necessary and sufficient conditions, is evasive, the domains it segregates are qualitatively distinct. Above the critical, quickening threshold, intelligence works systematically, yet non-deterministically, to create a relational scaffolding of crossed domains whose potential becomes activated into causally efficient, end-directed vigor by the informational redundancies explicated between them. On the emanant side of the phase change between inertia and life, the all-encompassing final cause of entropy dissipation is re-expressed as a drive to reduce free energy and therefore surprisal. The boundary conditions and local rules begetting self-organization that constrain the lower levels of dynamics, while still valid, are no longer sufficient to describe the entire system. Even as it sheds these as a comprehensive description of its global character, the system retains their patterns in principle by recasting these interactional primitives as increasingly complex formal relations whose emergent capacities are not expressible at lower levels of integration. This "upward heritability"[dxiv] of the principles that pass unscathed through dynamical reordering represents the deep conservativism underlying the unpredictable novelty of evolution.

Order and entropy, light and shadow, life and death—the tension of opposites drives the criticality of evolution at every level. When intelligently contained in a system that acts in dynamical integration with its context, oppositional tendencies come together, not as mortal enemies, but as dialectical complements that create new organizational, semiotic, and even cognitive planes on which to act out the self-same principles that govern their activities at lower levels of integration. Intelligence is the creator as well as the beneficiary of structure and conditioned perception, which are the tools it utilizes to rise above equalizing randomness and evolve through the "three universes of experience." It radiates into multiplicity of form and angle of perspective to optimize the meaning it makes intelligible from its interactions. The modularity which intelligence tends toward diversifies within the context of holism, uniting multiple domains into a complete whole through the long-range correlations of intelligently interactive subsystems, which collectively achieve, based on a subtle and unifying shared meaning, the coordinated enactment of a universally common final cause.

5

Chaotic Evolution

*"I have realized that the homeland of creation lies in the future;
thence wafts wind from the gods of the word."*
—Velimir Xlebnikov

Supporting the integrity of biotic structure is a deeply embodied comprehension of environmental conditions. Expressed in terms of complexity, the self-organized tiers of dynamics that comprise an organism point to a systemic logic that is at once prior to expression, and expression's final cause. Abstract yet compelling, the final causes of survival and fitness set mandates that can be filled by many possible formal arrangements, which act as bridges between the dichotomous domains of semantics and physics. Through the specializations that they evolve, agents become increasingly adept at correlating environmental conditions into information within their own physical and intentional structures. By replicating patterns—structural, semantic, and behavioral—which have proven adaptive means of fulfilling the teleological tasks of survival and propagation, the causally active semantic template that prescribes the parameters of individual intelligence avails a system to new capacities and localized expressions of final cause as it develops and evolves.

While genetically proscribed patterns internally cohere a system into a persistent unity, the interactions that agents establish among themselves enjoin them to order at a higher level of organization. Like all patterns, the regularities established between interacting agents are perspective-dependent. Agents' abilities to perceive and adapt to these patterns elevates their interactions above the level of mere randomness. The sign processes that facilitate the establishment of interactional regularities serve as tools of higher-order self-organization. Through the information they convey, sign processes are instrumental in reducing surprisal among agents, effectively drawing them into closely coupled, regularity-based relations that can develop into complex systems.

The orderly structure that emerges from local interactions offers a statistical summary of the average interactions of its constituents. Network models that represent interactions within a system simplify agents into nodes connected by edges which represent the interactions that pass between them. Far from linear or static, these interactions propagate multi-directionally into feedback loops wherein the roles of individual agents fluctuate between sender and receiver. The nonlinear reverberations of interactive signaling increase the ratio of edges to nodes, which can promote self-organization by allowing the rapid emergence of collective choices over both short and long distances, and thereby influence outcomes of various group properties, such as the ability to efficiently utilize a resource.[dxv]

Even when functionally integrated into group dynamics by the rules of the system, which emerge from the reciprocal countercurrents of upward and downward causation, each agent is still individually responsive to information—much like the energetically identical but causally distinct states of energy degeneracy. This individual-level variation supplies the system with stochasticity which, much like free energy in thermodynamic systems, is a source of both novelty and flexibility, especially when amplified by the same nonlinear feedback processes that promote cohesion.

The balance that a system must strike between stability and novelty avails a coordinated collective to a more highly functional outcome than the uncorrelated activities of individuals could attain, through the reciprocal causality that circulates between the system's lower levels of organization and its global description. Eusocial insects such as ants demonstrate the ordering power of this fundamental dynamic of self-organization. As they forage, ants leave chemical trails that others can detect and follow. While the effect of these chemical cues is at the level of the individuals that detect them, they collectively comprise a global field that is reflective of the whole group's chemical interactions. The field, in turn, influences chemical signaling at local levels, altering the behavior of the individual ants in a self-perpetuating cycle whose lower-level dynamics inform and reflect changes at the system level.[dxvi] From this multi-level informational exchange, these insects—each individually little more than a "ganglion on legs"[dxvii]—collectively execute tasks as complex and varied as nest construction, food gathering, and coordinated care of larvae. Some species demonstrate amazing feats of specialization, such as farming other species of insects, swarming, and even hacking into other species' chemical cuing codes to become indolent, parasitic overlords.

Critical Networks

Local, simple rules of interaction among agents offer little predictive power regarding the dynamical tendencies of their complex composite. But when sufficiently coordinated, these interactions can lead the system to a critical state that heralds a phase change. The procession toward coherence begins with unsynchronized network actors randomly oscillating between two equiprobable states. Within the overarching global field of fluctuations, pockets of local influence arise that can promote coupling between near neighbors. When synchronization begins to percolate throughout the system under conducive conditions, nested hierarchies of synchronized clusters form, followed by larger communities, up to global coherence and the establishment of long-range connections that coordinate previously random dynamics.[dxviii]

Ferromagnetism provides an example of the phenomenon of synchronization in physical systems. Below a critical threshold of agreement within the system, its electrons occupy one of two possible spin states with equal probability. When enough electrons converge on the same spin state and their dipoles align, the magnetic moment emerges. Similarly, many different types of organisms self-organize in this way, with a sharp rift delineating a random, uncorrelated behavioral phase from a highly correlated, "activated" one.[dxix] Desert locusts display synchronized order when a random assemblage of individuals rouses itself to collectivity by following simple rules of interaction. When in their uncoordinated, "solitarious" phase, the insects divide their time between active and inactive states, with the former being favored in the presence of a crowd and under particular conditions of vegetation distribution and abundance. As crowd density increases, the active state becomes increasingly probable. At a critical threshold, the symmetry of the random-state aggregation of individuals breaks and lowers, shifting far from equilibrium in the form of a highly aligned collective motion, and the locally "gregarized" group moves into neighboring regions to recruit more insects. One possible outcome is a failed recruitment attempt, followed by disbandment and resumption of solitarious behavior. However, favorable conditions can abet synchronization into a full-fledged swarm capable of functioning as a coherent collective. The dynamical instability reigning over the swarm propagates information rapidly, for example allowing the collectivized horde to change direction without external perturbation, or in response to subtle environmental variations indicative of resources that would not elicit responses in isolated individuals.[dxx]

This type of synchronous behavior is achievable in the assortatively linked networks that typify the social behaviors of various species, wherein nodes with similar characteristics tend to link preferentially—such as the desert locusts, whose contagious excitation elicits the same state from others as a source of attraction. While affording the group access to abilities unavailable to individuals—the typical benefit of self-organization—the assortative system is low in complexity relative to the disassortativity of many biological and ecological systems, which favor connections between dissimilar nodes. Highly connected nodes become hubs which link preferentially to nodes with lower degrees of connectivity, while straining away from each other in mutual repulsion.[dxxi] The structure that emerges is self-similar across scales, marked by large centers of organization that only loosely interact with each other to form a nested, modular hierarchy.[dxxii] From this nearly decomposable structure, a diversified assemblage can emerge, its global order held together by structured correlations across quasi-autonomous modules within a framework that promotes robustness, even to the removal of some hubs.[dxxiii]

While the assortatively connected locust swarm maintains its short-term cohesion through sheer numeric volume and a single shared behavioral state, a disassortative network is substantially more constrained by its initial conditions in its ability to synchronize.[dxxiv] Subsystems separated by hub repulsion chart their own evolutionary paths in relation to each other within shared contextual confines. Species, and to varying degrees their members, differentiate by carving out sundry overlapping niches that enable them to maximally utilize available space and resources—essentially applying different "interpretations" to the same set of environmental constraints to find unique ways of satisfying the same internally generated fitness imperatives.

Just as the criticality of the assortative system allows collective access to new types of information and responsiveness, disassortative networks can achieve their own form of criticality that nests temporally and spatially variable cycles into a multi-tiered rhythm that contrasts with the homogenized synchrony of assortativity. Modular systems instead achieve a sort of stable coherence, not through the direct route of a unified state, but through diversity and specialization, and the regularities that establish through repeated interactions. Like the enhanced collective intelligence of a synchronized group, the formally masked synchrony of disassortativity seemingly imparts on its actors intelligence beyond their individual capacities. Consider the case of the cleaner wrasse, a small blue tropical marine fish whose humble resume consists primarily of its willingness to scavenge ectoparasites from the bodies of fellow reef dwellers. While their beneficial line of work enhances the popularity of these lowly workers, it is arduous and relatively low-paying. However, wrasses have another, more lucrative option: to "cheat" by biting the apparently preferable and more highly nutritious mucous coat of client fish. From this simple dichotomy—whether to be honest or to cheat, as a small minority of individuals do under different circumstances—a whole repertoire of highly sophisticated behaviors emerges throughout the society of fish. When a cheater takes an indiscreet nip, the indignant client may retaliate by chasing the offender, or, if other cleaning stations are nearby, withdrawing patronage.[dxxv] Seemingly mindful of such punishments, the wrasse makes apparent mental notes of each individual client, offering those which have been previously offended—even by a different wrasse at the same station—honest cleanings and even placating fin strokes. Wrasses particularly find honesty to be the best policy when in the audience of attentive potential patrons, and when other cleaning stations are nearby. These behaviors, flexibly deployed relative to context, help to offset the short-term losses of increased effort and decreased nutrition that trustworthiness can accrue, in the form of the long-term benefits of a loyal clientele.[dxxvi]

The wrasse carves out its niche in a complex sociological setting, with interactions ranging from tightly coupled to oblique and indirect. Nonlinearity arises in these interactions not only from the complexity of the network linkages, but from conditions internal to the agents themselves. The wrasse, for example, begins life as a female and is only able to switch status to a more highly fecund male after reaching a certain size. This is one of many factors that weigh on the decision of whether or not to cheat. While the physical parameters of a given habitat are shared by many denizens in a dense and varied community like a coral reef, each inhabitant functions from a unique starting point of internal constraints imposed by phylogeny, ontogeny, and its own suite of "behavioral syndromes," or individual characteristics that influence its responses to the circumstances it encounters. Variation between individuals, and even within the same individual over time, adds layers of complexity, contingency, and unpredictability to the details of the system's dynamics—even as the system as a whole gravitates toward stability. At the scale of the community, this tension between local unpredictability and global stability can generate evolutionary solutions as various as symbiosis, evolutionary convergence, specialization, and generalization. In a seeming paradox, the arrangement of agents into a coherent network capable of releasing intelligence to the leading edge transpires when the dynamics of chaos interact with those of order.

Chaos, Order, and Identity

The cohesiveness implicit in agents' ordered relations is described by Teilhard de Chardin, "We do not get what we call matter as a result of the simple aggregation and juxtaposition of atoms. For that, a mysterious identity must absorb and cement them."[dxxvii] The fabric of this "mysterious identity" is in the legion of interactive couplings that support complexity by knitting an assemblage into a hierarchy cross-stitched by varying degrees of interconnection. Its character can be summarized by a statistical account of the small range of stable states that lower-level dynamics converge on, and which promote self-organization by preferentially amplifying the probabilities of certain system configurations over others.

With the incompressible intricacies of lower-level interactions subsumed by a simplifying global description, the critical juncture of self-organization finds itself delicately wedged between the opposing tendencies of order and stochasticity. Suspended between antipodes, the system establishes its character and integrity by navigating their conflicting effects. From the ordered end of its spectrum, the system draws structure and continuity, and even identity in the form of internal regularities that adapt in relation to external regularities. In turn, the distal pole of disorder supplies the flexibility for open-ended evolution and resilience to inner and outer sources of perturbation. From the critical combination of the two, the system constitutes an orderly yet flexible channel for propagating information. In mediating a balance between these two different dynamical regimes, the system conducts itself along the edge of chaos.[dxxviii]

Instead of sheer, uncorrelated randomness, chaos is describable as "a superposition of a periodic motion and a chaotic motion in state space."[dxxix] The turbulence of chaos is distinctly punctuated by characteristic forms of order, such as the strange attractor, which draws wandering trajectories from throughout the system into its rough orbit. While fundamentally unpredictable, chaotic dynamics are deterministic rather than random. Somewhat like an autocatalytic assemblage, the system continually iterates its basic function on the products of its previous evolutions to quickly grow into a system of nonlinear trajectories that stretch and fold through their phase space in self-interacting loops.

Initial Conditions

One of the hallmarks of a chaotic system is its sensitive dependence on initial conditions (SDIC). This feature is epitomized by the emergence of two trajectories from indistinguishably close starting points that, through the deterministic course of their evolution, deviate rapidly to yield arbitrarily divergent states.[dxxx] Because subsequent states aren't derivable from previous ones, a probability measure replaces predictive rules to describe the functions' paths through phase space. As they propagate, the functions diverge not only from each other, but from their own prior history, providing an indicator of the instability within the system.[dxxxi] The information created by the function's divergence from its own probability measure is internally generated entropy that can uncouple the system from its previous states, dynamically altering the system's "memory," or self-contingency.

Although SDIC can occur in linear systems, it leads to nonlinear, chaotic dynamics when trajectories are bound into non-wandering sets contained within borders. Spatial constraint encourages the kneading, folding iterations of chaos that transform static boundaries into a fluid spectrum of interchange, passing through each point of their orbit within their confined phase space rather than unwinding toward infinity as in unbound systems.[dxxxii] The constraint of otherwise divergent trajectories within the system's parameters can lead to the self-similar folding pattern of a fractal, and the trajectories' asymptotic convergence on an attractor.[dxxxiii]

Bifurcations and Fractals

A system both enters and exits chaos through the same "windows" of intermittency and period-doubling.[dxxxiv] The journey to chaos begins when a trajectory breaks away from the steady equilibrium of a limit cycle through a Hopf bifurcation. The resulting oscillation can, through further Hopf bifurcations, devolve from periodicity to quasi-periodicity, and finally to chaos in a series of period-doubling cascades that become increasingly unstable as they multiply. Conversely, the route leading to stability resolves chaotic noise into increasingly ordered states of periodicity.

The dynamics of chaos are nonlinear functions of the system's properties, which are roughly translated into a self-similar pattern across spatial and temporal scales. In forging an unruly yet deterministic path through the tumult of chaos, the fractal propagates order by carrying a compact record of the system's iterative history. Although the antagonistic domains it traverses defy the simplifying descriptions of algorithmic compression, they are nevertheless united by the wavering, indistinct fractal boundary, which calls on subtle invariances tucked deeply within the non-differentiable details of their dynamics. By divining the underlying homologies between stability and disarray, the fractal that divides these polar opposites also deftly weaves them together along a seam within which they are indistinguishable.

Despite its simplicity at the global level, the fractal dimension gives way to strange properties at the focal level, carrying self-similarity to its logical extreme by perpetually expanding under magnification to take on infinite dimension. Even though it represents a thread of regularity within chaos, the fractal's steadying effect is counterbalanced by the new boundaries it generates at the periphery of each level it occupies, evoking chaotic dynamics throughout each phase change.

Strange Attractors

Curbed by externally imposed boundaries, nonlinear dynamical systems also generate internal constraints which establish a stable set of conditions for the system.[dxxxv] As the complex evolution of nonlinearity draws low-level, microscopic dynamics away from reversibility, the trajectories emanating from a range of starting conditions asymptotically converge on a region of attraction and begin to generate macroscopically observable statistics.[dxxxvi] Within the maelstrom that some nonlinear evolutions can generate, attractors offer havens of relative order by condensing the infinite possible configurations of lower-level dynamics into orbits confined to a few small regions of state space that unite their various constituent trajectories under a single statistical description.[dxxxvii]

When the region of convergence not a fixed point, nor periodic or even quasi-periodic, it is the topological constant of chaotic systems: a strange attractor. Clothed by an accretion of unpredictable trajectories, the basin of attraction is a center of relative stability within a volatile tangle of sporadic orbits that can best be described by their probabilities of passing through different regions on the attracting set—some of which tend to be more densely populated than the rest, like nested attractors-within-attractors.[dxxxviii] Analysis of chaos, then, turns to the statistical properties of an orbit through phase space while foregoing a close examination of particular details. In negating the details of its constitutive trajectories, an attractor becomes a leveler on par with entropy.

Like the precarious balance of criticality, the dynamics of chaos that generate the strange attractor are balanced between opposing tendencies that, if expressed in excess, would threaten their already tenuous stability. Although itself a relatively stable region of state space, an attractor is actually comprised of instability at a finer level of resolution. While its accumulating trajectories arise from the amplification of instabilities,[19] the integrity of the attractor depends on the decay of small perturbations. Its tempestuous order arises from the balanced tension between the system's ability to offset perturbations from within and without, and its reliance on the internal instability rooted in SDIC to send errant trajectories into the ambit of the attractor.

When a system parameter changes due to a bifurcation, the number, and stability, of attractors in a system can shift. An increasing number of attractors increases the overall symmetry of the system, elaborating its ability to self-organize by increasing its order. As the system rebuilds the symmetry it breaks through bifurcations with an increasing number of attractors, the geometrical description that suffices at lower levels of complexity must be replaced by descriptions in terms of constraints and the probabilities that predict them. As chaos tightens toward order, it approaches the critical line of self-organization that allows efficient transmission of information, in contrast to the minimal propagative capacity offered respectively by systems of either pure chaos or rigid order.[dxxxix]

The ingredients of self-organization are implicit in chaotic dynamics. Random distributions channel into the complex collectivity of self-organization by following simple rules. These, and the patterned regularities they establish, act as local attracting sets to pull otherwise disparate activities into concert around a small, cohering set of probabilities. For systems within or striving toward life's broad attractive basin, with its nebulous outskirts, the internal constraints that drive them far from equilibrium are supplied at chemical levels by catalysis. By removing reversibility from the nonlinear networks that they help structure, catalysts promote the conditions for dynamical convergence into closed, feedback-based autocatalytic loops of energetic, material, and informational flows. These micro-attractors of lower-level dynamics reflect the more orderly pole of complexity by imposing formal

---

[19] A system's relative stability is expressed through its Lyapunov, or characteristic, exponents. A positive Lyapunov exponent indicates SDIC and therefore the instability of a chaotic system.

arrangement, directed to the final cause of self-maintenance, on an otherwise random assemblage of probabilities. Drawn to stable-state attractors at a higher level of description, these tiny, local cycles collectively comprise homeostasis and metabolism. The recursive and interconnected cycles of autocatalysis and cross-catalysis that comprise a complex homeostatic system are stable and non-wandering, as is their final cause of self-persistence, which is described by the global level of system dynamics. Superimposed on stability and continuity are the dissipative, wandering dynamics of entropy release and adaptation. While order is an attractor of small confines, entropy is an attractor, or final cause of all activity.[dxl]

Opposite Poles

When the tumult of chaos is sufficiently stabilized by order, their union begets the organization of evolvable complexity as an emergent offspring. The system absorbs and reforms the energetic oscillations between the two poles, rendering order's stability and chaos's flexibility into a nonlinear, sustained convergence. The overall balance between the poles of rigidity and pliability is tuned within an organism by its interactions with selective environmental forces that affect how its highly nonlinear, epistatically interlinked gene networks express their potential.[dxli] The highest fitness occurs near the cusp of the phase transition from stability toward chaos—a narrow ledge of congruence that nevertheless allows abundant room for diversity to flourish.[dxlii]

From life's very outset, the bipolarity between order and chaos is evident. The high degree of homeostatic order that upholds life through purposeful tangles of biochemical activity is, by itself, too rigid and limited in scope to propagate open-ended evolution. Counterbalancing this in the double-origin model of abiogenesis is low-fidelity RNA, which, with its high error rate, is too unstable to carry the burden of life.[dxliii] Over the course of their collusion, metabolism and information—initially representative of order and instability, respectively—crossed freely over toward each other's poles. The exigencies of evolution solidified the genetic code into a low-error catalog of replicable data, while the cytoplasmic task of living took on new plasticity by interpreting its multiply realizable DNA hardware in terms of its ongoing experience like flexible software.[dxliv] With the roles of information and metabolism intertwined in a domain-crossing weave between order and chaos, the system of complementary opposites established itself as the robust foundation of the creative and evolvable biosphere.

    The commerce between the opposing poles of spontaneity and stability adjusts to accommodate the needs of an organism under different conditions, and at different points throughout its life cycle. The balanced superposition of the two contrasting regimes maintains itself as the foundation of identity, even as the organism develops through a series of bifurcating divisions en route to maturity. In particular, the de-stabilizing tendencies of entropy dissipation dominate an organism's dynamical description during times of intense order-building, such as growth or learning. Stability intervenes with maturity, reducing instability to a low-level fluctuation, anchored by the precedents established during earlier phases of expansive growth.[dxlv] All of the metamorphoses of ontogeny are threaded together by the fractal-like preservation of an underlying, constitutive identity which acts both as memory and basis for domain crossing. The eventuality toward which an individual develops, informed by the interaction of intrinsic potential with extrinsic circumstance, acts like an attractor that draws the organism's life-trajectory into its basin of possibility. As a stabilizing guide to otherwise potentially divergent trajectories, the attractor functions as a final cause; a general principle whose specifications are determined at the individual level and so is open to different "interpretations." Indeterminate of outline and contour, the substance of the attractor is created emergently through the many dimensions of thirdness that organisms are capable of expressing. Despite the unpredictable details that affect the wanderings of intentional trajectories, their many-formed convergence on a single final cause-attractor creatively explicates the underlying, self-similar potential held latent in that shapeless form.

Not just limited to the level of individuals, the precise suspension between order and chaos along which life processes balance is the same edge to which species dynamics drive ecosystems.[dxlvi] Temporally, ecosystems express a nested hierarchy through their successive stages, with short trophic chains initiating ecological succession and evolving toward a species–rich pattern of ecology.[dxlvii] As it matures, the ecosystem maintains mosaics of its prior successional states, which maximizes its biomass, productivity, diversity, and the intricacy of connection among the disassortive mix of species and stages it supports. This ever-shifting pattern of long-term richness and variability reflects the self-similarity carried in the fractal thread, which emerges at the critical accord between opposing dynamics in complex networks to impart a scale-invariant theme of replicated patterns under different conditions and at different scales of resolution.[dxlviii]

In the ascending ranks of organization, chaos and order fluctuate in dominance relative to the level of description.[dxlix] The dynamics of each lower, constituting level appear chaotic until viewed from the perspective of the higher level at which they correlate, which congeals them into a new level of meaning. Each symbol-level, leading-edge description of the system represents the self-organizing confluence of lower-level dynamics into a macroscopic final cause, or attractor, that itself becomes entrained to a more encompassing level of description as the system increases its levels of complexity. While most of these levels are concealed beneath the subsuming symbol level of the system as a whole, their properties inform and are preserved within it, comprising not only a lateral spread of modular diversity, but a vertical axis of depth as well. Between each saltation of critical expansion that separates levels of description is a causal gap that fails to reduce emergent-level properties to the dynamics form which they issue. This gap is spanned by the fractal that unites the chaotic and ordered phases of the system, forming at the point of bifurcation which presages a phase change.

Self-Similarity and Symmetry Breaking

The basis of chaos, and one of its crucial contributions to complex systems, is the spontaneity of lower-level dynamics. Once ensnared in an attractor's orbit, each trajectory occupies its phase space probabilistically, drawing uncertainty up through the system's increasingly ordered tiers. While continually, unpredictably novel, chaotic dynamics nevertheless inhabit proscribed parameters. In contrast, the qualitatively distinct, emergent properties ushered in by symmetry breaking represent a foray into unprecedented possibility.[dl] Unfolding beyond the bounds of previously established parameters, this transcendent form of non-determinism refreshes itself at the emergent level, with new formal patterns expressing conserved principles with expanded degrees of freedom to create a new level of potential.[dli]

In its abstract, mathematical form, symmetry breaking generates complexity and sometimes chaos, and establishes long-range correlations that confine the system to the recursions of the non-wandering set. Drawing from a broad range of possibility, such as would be provided by the energy degeneracy of stored memory or the interpretive scope of a symbol, symmetry breaking selects one state out of clamoring potential for manifestation. As equiprobability yields to differentiation, symmetry is lowered with the accompaniment of a large entropic release, and constraints among interrelating subsystems shift, altering the available pool of potential states that the system can access.[dlii] When amplified to the point of criticality, such as through feedback loops, broken symmetry can re-order at a higher level of complexity, instantiating a new level of hierarchy.[dliii] The fractal divide across which system metrics translate themselves acts like an obscure line of symmetry, whose subtle invariance envelopes coherence and confusion alike, in a "recoded," more highly complex form.

The basic premises of symmetry breaking and self-similarity that bring order and complexity to even thermodynamic systems are preserved and replicated at higher levels of elaboration and meaning within the organism. For example, DNA behaves like a fractal in that it is a highly compressed carrier of the code whose underlying, self-similar pattern, iterated in all nucleated cells, unites the outwardly variant subsystems it begets. The segments of DNA that are awakened for transcription vary according to cell type and location, bifurcating from the symmetrical state of unexpressed totipotency to selectivity express only small portions. Iterated throughout a body, this process of partial expression awakens a mosaic of activated stretches of genetic material that allow differentiated interpretations of the same underlying template. Further, the genome embeds in its helices superimposed, degenerate states of information whose meaning is receiver-dependent, enfolding multiple possible specialized, contextually aligned interpretations within the same series of codons. The meaning potential of DNA acts like an attractor, in relation to which the cell's incalculably, irreducibly complex interpreting dynamics arrange themselves, nested within a hierarchy of meta-attractors that culminates in organism-level imperatives.

A process not confined by form, self-similarity arises from the dynamics of trajectories that, at lower levels of integration, are temporally self-correlated, rather than correlated to each other's movements. Passing ergodically through an inexhaustible array of states, a system of ostensibly random, Brownian motion continually propagates outcomes that are strictly referenced to prior states—the study of which would never allow prediction of the next state—to create a high-entropy, high-information, system wherein each possible outcome is equally and profoundly improbable and transmission is negligible. Far from being anathema to the regularities that denote order, the random and improbable are the foundations upon which all else rests. Far from implying illogic, lawlessness, or lack of causality, the seeming randomness that begets probable and improbable alike is operating according to a very subtle logic that unites form with vitality to emanate possibility of every kind. For David Bohm, randomness is not an objective property, but rather a subjective inability to ascertain a pattern of infinitely high degree. Far from being haphazard, each state of the ever-changing system represents a summation of conditions that conceals historical trajectories and proves refractory to prediction. Such a chaotic milieu of potential information yields to intelligibility through the regularity-inducing compression of constraints, which conduct randomness to the critical edge of evolution between chaos and order.

Perception and Pattern

Interchanging roles according to the subjective level of description, chaos and order creatively coexist throughout the system they form, interpolated by the self-similar fractal thread that unites their dynamics across scales. Within its stochastic, yet invariance-preserving meander, the fractal weave is an impartial mediator between the opposing manifolds, relying on both for its existence, yet drawing no distinction between either. Ultimately, the arbiter between order and disorder—meaning and noise—is embodied, situated perspective. According to Ortega y Gasset, "The ultimate reality of the world is neither matter nor spirit, is no definite thing, but a perspective."[dliv] Leibniz seizes on the profound logic of a world ordered according to perspectives: "And this is the way of obtaining as much variety as possible, but with the greatest order possible, that is, it is the way of obtaining as much perfection as possible."[dlv] From the subjective divide between order and chaos; salience and irrelevance; information and noise, arises every form of biotic expression, internally impelled by perceptually mediated interpretation.

With its outward reach blunted by the implacable bounds of surprisal, perception folds upon itself like a fractal in self-referencing cycles that build order by establishing patterns. Order and its perception arise concurrently from the unfolding of intelligent, interpretively capable agency, which highlights a limited cross-section of environmental regularities. Umwelt takes on the role of attractor by entraining to the agent's perception salient stimuli from a span of apparently unrelated domains, analogous to the initial conditions of a chaotic system, which converge on the agent's final causes of survival and fitness. The freedom of potential is bifurcated according to the agent's criteria of intelligibility, arranging it into order as the set of source domains the agent refers to and in terms of which it seeks patterns. Stimuli representing different classes of information merge into a higher-level pattern based on their relevance to the interests of the agent. It is the perceptive pinnacle of interpretation that wrests from the unstable manifold a transition to order by setting parameters on the scope of information an agent is amenable to and how the agent is impacted by that information. For human agents, interpretation adjusts the metaphors we use, and therefore which entailments we are guided by. Uncorrelated with the agent's interests or capacities, the vast majority of potentially available information is relegated to the unincorporated realm of surprisal.

Habits

Grounded in semiosis, agents are able to attain the Peircian end of "reduc[ing] the manifold of sensuous impressions to unity" through the patterns they perceive and the relationships they establish. By heuristically evaluating environmental regularities, even the most unembellished of unities are able to engage according to their respective capacity with the "logic of nature." By correlating their internal dynamics to some degree with environmental conditions, the niches that organisms carve and inhabit are points of stability within the tumult of chaos. The ability to formalize those dynamics as heritable adaptations maximizes future probabilities of certain interactions relative to particular environmental regularities by perpetuating the conditions that favor them. In yielding to nature's "primordial habit-making tendency"[dlvi] by codifying the properties that optimize engagement with select aspects of environment, the agent that carries and propagates these traits with modification becomes a historically conditioned conduit, transmitting a cultivated suite of potential that biases semiotic outcomes through established patterns of physiology, behavior, niche, sociology, and psychology.

Habits, according to Peirce, are inductions, with the particular falling under the embracing description of generality as a result of the repetition of many instances. Establishing a habit of action, he concludes, is the function of thought, and constitutes meaning according to the "sensible effects," or interactional properties, it engenders between agent and surroundings.[dlvii] In establishing relational regularities between intersecting dynamical properties, habits prove themselves foundational to self-organization by channeling interactions toward outcomes whose probabilities they favor. Once entrenched, established patterns are easier to maintain than to alter. Like attractors, habits are central to reducing the potential scope of activity within and among agents to a limited set of constrained possibilities. Incorporated into their enactment is a summary of every leading edge of adaptive learning that contributed to their formation. Steadied by habit-born consistency is the possible trajectory of a future leading edge, whose emergent spontaneity is guided but not impinged upon by its channelized history. While some established habits avail themselves to the cross-modal utility of exaptation and radiate toward new applications, others may turn inward to amplify their own patterns into ritual-like regularities that restrain wandering consciousness into a stereotyped pattern whose empty, ordering core is an iconic state.

Within organisms, habit directs the flow of consciousness by curbing the leading edge of intelligent exploration into a channelized route from intention to enactment, until the original and underlying "fortuitous spontaneity" that established it becomes a "sensation not attended to."[dlviii] For neural organisms, James describes a habit as "a new pathway of discharge formed in the brain, by which certain incoming currents ever after tend to escape."[dlix] "The essence of belief," decided Peirce, "is the establishment of a habit," which turns the leading edge of consciousness into unconscious functionality.[dlx] As phylogenetic inheritances, habits manifest behaviorally in the "supersensory knowledge" that awed Uexkull in his contemplations of the pea weevil's unlearned adaptive behaviors. Not only instinctual arbiters of behavior, habits express themselves developmentally as well. Rupert Sheldrake envisions organismal development as directed along formative chreodes, or species-typical patterns, that guide it from a single cell to final form, inherited from the patterns established ancestrally and flowing toward an attractor whose basin lies in the future.[dlxi] From an even higher evolutionary level, Kauffman discerns a force of downward causality pulling traits cultivated in one context to a novel domain that they are fortuitously preadapted to exploit.[dlxii]

Like Peirce, James did not limit habit-formation to brains, but deemed the very laws of nature "immutable habits."[dlxiii] The collective transmission and individual development of habits can be viewed as different aspects of the same process whereby "the past becomes present on the basis of similarity."[dlxiv] For Peirce, James, and Sheldrake, habits are universal features enabled by the "plasticity of material bodies" (James). According to Sheldrake, the regularities, including the most ironclad foundations of physics, "within an evolving universe evolve."[dlxv] Habits are the structures—the syntax, the channels—that conduct the flow of spontaneity into meaning, arranging events into regularities whose forms vary but whose function of conveyance is preserved across scales. The universal habit-making tendency expresses itself as a fractal: self-similar at all magnifications, but with abundant room for interpretive variety that fills the same roles through different means, and with different levels of conscious awareness, across scales.

The evolvable conditions of thermodynamic and semiotic openness, which necessitate recurrent interactions between agents and their environments, promote the dissipative, expansive potential supported by learning, while simultaneously curtailing it through the inductive recursions of habit. Amplification of canalizing chreodes occurs through feedback loops, which simultaneously provide stability and adaptability. While an intrinsically generated condition of systems, this stability can be strengthened or adaptively altered by the external perturbations of environmental selection. Self-organization and natural selection thereby come together in a reciprocally causal dialectic, united and embodied in the synthesis of living form.

Living Attractors

Like the endlessly expressing fractals generated from the self-referencing iterations of a chaotic time evolution, a diverse array of structurally and dynamically heterogeneous entities emerged from the selfsame pool of potential to carry forward as discreet individuals the communally instantiated torch of life. In so doing, each became its own attractor by ordering its surroundings according to its internally generated parameters through the course of its typical, niche-constructing activities and drawing into its tiny orbit the informational, material, and energetic trajectories that would sustain it. As David Bohm notes, "The seed contributes little or nothing to the actual material substance of the plant or the energy needed to make it grow."[dlxvi] Rather than contributing materially to its own growth, the seed relies on the information enfolded in its chromosomes to direct the environment around it, from sunlight to carbon to water and minerals, arranging them according to the cryptic pattern carried in its core. The genetic blueprint, its epigenetic modulations, and the internal dynamics that support its development transform local environmental factors, aligning them according to the agent's intrinsic intelligence.

Replicated within countless forms, the principles of intelligence are variously expressed throughout evolution's incursions into as many niches, or angles of perspective, as possible. The open-ended quest of niche construction drives intelligence into the phase space of potential, searching for a new expression of the self-same attractor—a different perspective from which to establish regularities that enable the fulfillment of biological mandates. Teilhard de Chardin noticed a phylum's antenna-like "need to pluralise itself in order to cope with a variety of needs or possibilities."[dlxvii] Life's branching strategy of speciation allows the "limbs" to explore their ecological "phase space" by sending out variations of the same pattern to test their inner parameters against those of their environs. Over the course of evolution, the broad branches of phylogeny grow finer at their tips as experimentation gives way to success, establishment, and refinement.[dlxviii] Each fork of the phylogenetic tree represents a break in symmetry—the point at which inner variations and outer circumstances create enough pressure to isolate and amplify a subpopulation into a whole new species and a possible ground state of a whole new cycle of evolution.

In a singular, many-formed dissipative flow that readily readjusts itself to local conditions, life simultaneously sheds parameters that have become ancillary while preserving a continually amended skeleton of self-similar patterns which incite novelty as they propagate far from equilibrium. Expressed in living systems, and the systems that they in turn comprise, self-similarity is free to eschew surficial resemblance in favor of the dynamical unfoldment of a generalized principle that is shared in common among actors at every level. Drawing on different material, efficient, and formal causes to foster diversity, the underlying themes of life and fitness that are replicated among organisms offer endless modes of expression within the same encompassing final cause. In all its variations of form and relationship, life is an integrated, complex system that emerges globally from the upward currents of local interactions to envelop them in the unifying countercurrent of downward causality that draws them into coherence like an organizing attractor. All agents are therefore to some degree constrained and organized relative to each other into normative processes that support the maintenance of the whole which they collectively comprise. This normativity unites each iteration of the self-similar fractal chain with every other by the sensitive, epistatic couplings that finely tune complex networks from genomes to ecosystems to the entire biosphere itself.

Like the final cause of life, which is fundamentally ecological in its need for deep interconnection among its many-formed bearers, the abstract principle of intelligence also acts like a broad basin of attraction that has ample room to host numerous expressive variations. Hierarchically structured like their physical counterparts, semantic systems entrain the chaotic-seeming dynamics of constitutive levels into a higher-order pattern, which renders each successive tier an increasingly ordered level of chaos. Deriving its logical structure from meaningful correlations at lower levels of expression, the semantic system correlates subsystems of dynamics, which orbit their own small-scale final causes, while allowing them retain their identities even within a larger integrating context. Always looming beyond the purview of localized centers of order is the possibility of a higher-level attractor, partially tying all current expressions—made ready by adaptability to answer its call—into a basin of undetermined future possibility.

Information, Semiosis, and Attraction

Arising with the closure of reciprocal causality, the driver and final cause of self-organization is the maintenance of the system at the symbol level, and the corresponding propagation of its meaning. The entangling threads that bind randomness into the unifying, describable level of an attractor are informational, from the DNA that prescribes a particular kind of relationship with the environment and reflects the trends of a population, to the signals that pass among agents and structure their interactions into networks. Although subjective and intangible, the meaning carried by signals is a causally efficient organizer of objective conditions. Despite its amenability to changeable trappings, which lend themselves to the contingencies of circumstance, meaning can remain intact while at the same time open to formal modification. In this respect, meaning shares the essential quality of an attractor: both are abstract principles that are indicated by the alignment of the measurable phenomena that surround them. Both are conceptual entities—products, not of the material dimension, but of the semantic realm—that imply rather than cause the conditions of their own existence. Like an attractor, meaning is a description of what unites outward disparity.

Because a self-organizing system such as communication attains functionality by amplifying the stable features of chaos, inherent instabilities permeate order from its very foundations. Communication betrays this potential with its profoundly nonlinear character, which Peirce muses on when he considers the strange condition that "a sign should leave its interpreter to supply part of its meaning,"[dlxix] imbuing it with an almost agent-like autonomy. In particular, he was referring to the circuitous routes to meaning creation engendered by generalizations. Sender and receiver may fill in the implications of a generalization with different instances, and still arrive at the same sense of meaning. Conversely, the same instances of a generalization may actually lead to different inferential endpoints. Husserl explains, "If we or others repeat the same sentence with like intention, each of us has his own phenomena, his own words and his own nuances of understanding."[dlxx]

Even indexical signs can be highly conditioned by the perspectives of their receivers. For example, a lion's roar across the savannah can simultaneously incite pride members to anticipation of a hunt, nearby prey animals to caution, more distant ones to varied states of alertness, scavengers to attention, herdsmen to guard their flocks, and even some third parties like birds and monkeys to call out warnings. The meaning of the signifier is agreed upon by all affected agents. But like a dissipative wandering set layered upon a closed, self-referencing non-wandering set, the different implications of the same meaning-token among different agents scatters semantic trajectories, leaving a gaping plenum of information between them and their probabilistic paths.

Since meaning can only be approximated rather than definitively fixed, it must be constructed afresh with every communication in the context of the participants' interpretive infrastructure. The potential for interpretation to diverge from the message's intended, or most probable meaning represents a significant source of instability in the system. Counterintuitively, this is the precise condition to optimize signal propagation. As Kauffman reminds us, a signal cannot be propagated through either a chaotic system or a rigidly ordered one. However, an ordered regime at the edge of chaos is an ideal conduit.[dlxxi]

Because communication is explicitly meaning-driven, and therefore teleological, the individual details of a signal are fungible. Recalling the SDIC of chaotic evolution, the many possible interpretations of the same sign are not predictable from the properties of the sign itself. Rather, they are heavily conditioned by the interests of the individuals receiving the sign. For indexical communication, the signal's "initial conditions" are largely tied to factors in the immediate environment. Although the meaning of indices can be contextually conditioned, or deceptively manipulated by the sender, indexical communication overall has low uncertainty relative to more complex symbol-based language. This is because the index is closely aligned with both the iconic state it invokes in the receiver, and its interpretation.

For less emotionally immediate communicative forms like speech, initial conditions are more internal to the communicators and their respective frames of interpretation, compelling each party to make implicit attributions of others' mental states.[dlxxii] With uncertainty abounding, symbol-based communication particularly mobilizes the reservoirs of chaos in the mental spheres of sender and receiver alike, oscillating between the uncertainty of possibility and the stability of shared understanding. Until it is selectively compressed into syntactical expression, potential meaning is free to formlessly meander within the semantic space of the sender. The phase change that breaks the symmetry of non-articulable possibility toward presentable expression is impelled by meaning which, when it assumes an intentional form, acts like an attractor that arranges words into rule-governed channels of conveyance toward the final cause of expression. From the unformed chaos of potential, salience induces bifurcations of possibility toward the dual attractors positioned on the combinatorial and choice axes of verbal construction. The receiver reconstructs the message's meaning through a process of statistical deduction that summons an intrinsic body of knowledge relevant to the properties of the signal. A message decoded by the receiver hews to the line of criticality if its statistical properties match those at the sender's end to produce semantic alignment between communicators.[dlxxiii] Husserl points out that this alignment is not necessarily precise: "Mutual understanding demands a certain correlation among the mental acts mutually unfolded in intimation and in the receipt of such intimation, but not at all their exact resemblance."[dlxxiv] Largely below the level of conscious awareness, the instability of unresolved meaning undergoes a phase change through the self-organizing process of semiosis, to yield stable comprehension in the mind of the receiver that is, ideally, symmetrical to that of the sender. As Jantsch observes, "Information is not transferred linearly but circularly and born anew."[dlxxv]

The Ecology of Language

The primitive advent of a syntactically structured, symbolic form of molecular communication saw the agent wholly identified with the structure of its denotation, whose meaning acted as an ordering principle among message-agents. Upon the union between the autonomous symbol-string—with its prominent relationship to abstract semantics—and the stable amenities offered by the complex, orderly, but undifferentiated homeostatic broth, a new cycle of chaos began at a more highly ordered, creatively potent level. With the evolutionary leap enabled by the merger between signification and homeostasis, the symmetry between syntax and self broke, freeing agency to become a transcendent property encompassing both metabolic dynamics and the meaning structure that came to guide them.

Although still tethered to its symbolic code at the genetic level, meaning came uncoupled from syntax at higher levels of agency, freeing it to transmit through an endless array of indexical vehicles commensurate with the capabilities of increasingly complex, interacting agents. Along with form, complexity, and niche, meaning evolved and spread throughout the biosphere, commandeering the symbol level of agency as its declarative, multimodal canvas of expression. Not until the refinement of vocal communications in species including some birds and cetaceans, but most notably in humans, did semantic transmission again revisit its original syntactical mode. In contrast to the thorough percolations of non-linguistic meaning throughout every conceivable niche of the semiosphere, syntax made a tremendous leap from its position at the cornerstone of biology to the elevated evolutionary field of the mind—a domain of evolution whose selective targets are logical entities and types—which Teilhard de Chardin terms the "noosphere." Language and the second-order cognitive processes it mobilizes facilitated a phase change in the mental sphere, becoming foundational to a whole new evolutionary context by unfolding a complex and infinitely differentiable landscape of potential. Stitching together the obverse domains of expression and meaning like the superposition of periodicity upon chaos, the advent of language, layered upon the dissipative property of mind, generated high-order semantic attractors that could capture, constrain, and simultaneously liberate potential into new levels of meaningful presentation.

Like the biosphere that supports it, the noosphere is fundamentally ecological. The rules of grammar demand that an assemblage of actors of very different types come into close relation with each other, as in a disassortative network, to add their unique and essential contributions to the construction of meaning. This selectively arranged assortment of actors is summoned to coherence as a nested hierarchy of words, phrases, clauses, sentences, paragraphs and beyond, by a guiding, unifying final cause that requires all of their contributions, ordered within grammatical bounds, in order to convey its formless content. The redundancies that language imposes on the free-roaming potential of meaning to bring it into productive alignment function like autocatalytic feedback mechanisms to amplify the orderly, self-referencing aspects inherent in expressible meaning, and limit its wide-ranging potential to well-ordered, probabilistically favored regions of semantic phase space.

As it traverses, inspects, and inhabits the ideational landscape that language uniquely summons and conveys, intelligence expresses a pattern that is self-similar to its behavior at every other level of integration. It explores its conceptual habitat in a branching fractal pattern just like a phylogenetic tree, which describes a phylum's radiations from a single point—a common ancestor—into overlapping as well as diverging forms and niches. Just as in biological evolution, spaces between semantic branches open as some conceptual lineages are pared back and thinned by rejection, or separated by drift. As the structure develops, the distinctive branching form of a radiating system supports both breadth of diversity in its broad limbs, as well as refined probes of close examination in its finely forked tips.

When the well-established processes that summon the biotic domain to order are expressed anew in a mental context, they beget wholly emergent and unpredictable results. With increasing layers of complexity accruing to the semantic structures that support symbolic communication, degrees of freedom channel upward through the system's interconnected tiers to radiate at the leading cognitive edge. With sufficient flexibility supplied by high-level degrees of freedom, explicit awareness becomes capable of coiling back around itself in the recursive twist of self-reference that is foundational to complexity and intelligence itself. Balancing on a critical precipice between the bottom-up expansiveness of a holistic perspective and the fine-grained penetration of rationality, self-awareness unfolds as the leading edge of cognition.

Signifying the underlying currents that supply its meaning, the linguistic vehicle of expression likewise doubles back like the fractal folding of a nonlinear bound set, and language becomes "both the object and the subject of investigation."[dlxxvi] Reflecting the inward coil of expanding intelligence, an evolutionarily novel branch of distinction sprouted from within the kneading folds of language—the category of "I" that functions as a mirror through which consciousness can explicitly perceive itself.[dlxxvii] Teilhard explains the momentous consequences for the newly self-aware consciousness: "When for the first time in a living creature instinct perceived itself in its own mirror, the whole world took a pace forward."[dlxxviii] This novel cognitive branch uncovered, for the first time, its own foundation and that of agency: the epistemic cut. With this explication comes a symmetry break that allows the differentiation common to all agents—differences in degree—to be amplified into individuation, a change in kind.

Metaphor

While grammar and syntax act as lower-level attractors to channel randomness into semantic order, metaphor functions as a higher-level source of linguistic structure. Conducting meaning between bodily and semantic domains, metaphor's power is to create a reality that deepens when the agent acts according to it.[dlxxix] Biasing interpretations and directing decisions, metaphors alter probabilities in favor of outcomes aligned with their entailments. Like an attractor, a metaphor can gather multiple different expressions of possibility toward the same expressed outcome. Alternately, like the diverging dynamics of an unstable manifold, it can drive seemingly similar possibilities arbitrarily far apart.

Spanning the two seemingly uncorrelated domains of mind and measurability, the meaning-seeking impulse of metaphor replicates chaos when it becomes unbound from the outer foliations of its source domain to traverse phase space until drawn into orbit around a self-similar basin of attraction in a different domain. The split from source to target is a bifurcation in potential meaning, which breaks and lowers the symmetry of equiprobability into distinction and ushers the system toward a change in stability. The two manifolds, source and target, are resolved into singularity at the stabilizing point of attraction, creating a convoluted, multi-dimensional, and nonlinear phase space for semantic trajectories to explore. At the same time, metaphor curtails wandering trajectories by bringing them into a complex orbit with other domains from arbitrarily different source domains, acting as initial conditions. The relations established by domain crossing create the logical scaffolding of complexity.

Amplified through recursion when it connects with a counterpart in a fresh context, the meaning conveyed in a metaphor asserts its dissipative buoyancy when it reflects back onto its source domain. Like a bound trajectory, it folds back on itself by inviting questioning of the target in newly established terms of the source, and vice versa.[dlxxx] Source and target oscillate positions in a nonlinear, reverberating cascade of informational exchange in which each informs the other by allowing a narrowly selected, abstract aspect of the other's meaning to enliven its own. Weaving between the regions of dynamical distinction that cordon off different domains, metaphor is a non-differentiable turning point; the wavering fractal boundary that is never clearly defined and augers self-similarity across domains. Embedded within this interface, which insinuates unity between the orderly and chaotic, is intelligent perception probing for commonality beneath surface-level variances.

The trans-domain connections that metaphor establishes ultimately bring greater symmetry to the system by increasing the number of attractors, and therefore the system's order, complexity and informational capacity. Through the stochastic course of its similarity-seeking sojourn, metaphor creates information by its deviation from probability. In creating new meaning, it retains, yet transcends the descriptive parameters of its originating context, or initial conditions. By partially uncoupling meaning from form, metaphor can encounter potential targets without the literalistic burden of ancillary details. It is deterministic in its purposiveness, but unpredictable because it eludes any simple algorithmic description at the detailed level of its trajectory. Based on non-apparent layers of isometry, metaphor awakens the dormant potential of "recoded" redundancy between domains, explicating shared meanings into structured correlations across modalities.[dlxxxi]

The function of metaphor is to call forth a new form of relational understanding by activating a link that exists only *en potentia* until established in terms of the two domains which act like stabilizing poles to provide a context for emergent meaning. Summoned from formless potential to assume localized expression, meaning arises only in the context of the two poles of a semantic relationship—whether subjective and objective, or source and target—which, in the circular twist of reciprocal causality, only function in relation to each other by virtue of the meaning that conjoins them. Outside of the boundary conditions established by the selected alignment across domains hovers the larger potential of untapped knowledge beyond what is being expressed—and possibly even what can be expressed. With only embodied intelligence to infer approximate truth conditions in the form of patterns, complete ontological knowing eludes perception. "The universality of an inference from induction is only the analogue of true universality," says Peirce. However, as a fundament of perception, domain-crossing logic is itself the ultimate analog of universality—it is universal to all perceiving entities and the basis of all interaction between them.

Final Cause

Uncertainly situated on a nonlinear spectrum between randomness and order, chaos is a volatile bridge which mental structures must cross in order to instantiate physical corollaries. In its pre-expressive formlessness, potential ergodically explores its degenerate state space until stirred to responsiveness by intimations from the surrounding environment. Rousing equilibrium into chaos, the impulse to manifest bifurcates totipotency into favored probabilities based on correspondences with extrinsic parameters. While the selection of potential states is informed by environmental conditions, these only guide its outcome by exerting probabilistic sway, rather than causal power, over the system's prospects. The discriminate reduction of open possibility functions purposively to optimize the alignment of expression with its informing context. Daniel Dennett points to the nature of the attractor that so effectively orders possibilities: "The scale of compression when one adopts an intentional stance toward statistical properties of a situation—that is, perceives a pattern—is stupendous."[dlxxxii] Guided by a final cause whose expression is seeded in initial conditions, intention mobilizes the activities of the system toward its overarching mandates. This renders activities at even the lowest hierarchical levels anticipatory of the final cause which draws their activities through intention toward exposition.

Drawing from a serendipitous admixture of randomness and irreversibility,[dlxxxiii] final cause arises with the directionality of far-from-equilibrium evolution. Separated from its intentional initial condition by the ceaseless industry of spatiotemporal dynamics, this active abstraction is both prior to and emergent from the directional processes that parlay asomatous ideation into substantial expression. Wresting meaning from the depths of chaos through purposiveness, order and complexity divide the roiling currents and constructively harness their power to express an "internal teleology, whereby finality is brought about by the internal logic of the system."[dlxxxiv] Like an attractor, final cause draws from pluripotency the material, efficient, and formal means to its enactment. Through these flexible channels and the formal variety that they support, arbitrary initial conditions project themselves into a concerted outcome which they anticipate, even as they fulfill it without foregoing the spontaneity and self-correlation of the intervening trajectories.

Fording the unstable and immeasurable space of potential that is neither intention nor expression, but contains both, final cause is suspended at a discontinuous juncture between interior and exterior constraints. In reconciling these, intention agitates equilibrium by deploying local symmetry breaks to highlight pertinent aspects of potential into an expressed pattern as it graduates from mentality into physicality.[dlxxxv] Dissipating unexpressed potential in its energetic path toward manifestation, fluid plasticity narrows into a directional arc as possibility closes toward finality.[dlxxxvi] The moment of actualization is a critical point which breaks the metastable symmetry of the potential that had delineated the seeds of intention from the fruits of expression. When completed, this domain crossing melds the manifolds of semantics and physics into a meaning-mediated unity conjoined at a stable point of deep homology, which resolves the complexity of constitutive details into a simplified global description. Like a homoclinic orbit cycling through instability only to reconnect with its own steady center, the meaning underlying both intention and expression locates itself firmly and self-similarly in both initial conditions and final outcome. Husserl expounds on the interpenetrability of this relationship: "Since in the unity of fulfillment the act of intention coincides with the fulfilling act, and fuses with it in the most intimate fashion...it readily seems as if the expression first got its meaning here, as if it drew meaning from the act of fulfillment."[dlxxxvii] As inner and outer forms of the self-same meaning, the twin poles of initial, intentional conditions and their measureable, expressed counterparts are connected like a heteroclinic orbit, which joins equilibrium points within a manifold of instability, to yield a result which is "simply a purpose in its final form."[dlxxxviii]

Founded in the semantic space that comprises the internal initial conditions of an agent, final cause informs every aspect of potential's journey to expression—an "effect...which participates in its own production."[dlxxxix] Final cause not only draws the trajectories of a system's activities toward itself, but provides space in its attractive basin for numerous orbits to variously express its underlying essence. As an abstract principle, it provides the organizing, global-level guidance of downward causality to compose a stochastic simmer into a purposeful flow of order and pattern. Through the course of its evolution from an iconic sensation through the complex mechanical processes of symbol-level enactment, the teleological trajectory originating from the tempest of pre-manifest potential and culminating in order is a vertical domain crossing that is of, but transcendent to, its tumultuous origins. With its effects anticipated in, but not necessarily predictable from the lower levels of causality, the cause on which systemic activities converge draws its full description from past as well as future, while firmly anchored in its current expression.[dxc] Whether an apt analogy or evolution through natural selection, that expression is a dialectical synthesis of interior possibility and external contingency.

Poised at both apex and nadir of the reciprocal interchange of causality that provides the system with closure, final cause is the turning point that conducts and translates mutually supportive currents of intention and information across the semantic and phenomenal manifolds in an oscillating wheel of evolving relations between meaning and form. In the intertwining braids of reciprocal causality, final cause is both origin and goal; or, simply, "Where the beginning is the end will be."[dxci] Describing the foundational nature of this most subtle of causes, Emmanuel Swedenborg writes, "The deepest form of thought, the perception of ends, is actually the first effect of life."[dxcii] Traveling the dualistic route of manifestation, the evolution of consciousness within form represents one pole of final cause, countered and complemented by that of entropy. Both of these final causes, one of light, the other of shadow, participate in all stages of manifestation: feeding, constraining, and ultimately reclaiming the borrowed forms fashioned from chaotic plentitude.

The end toward which intelligence directs energetic resources is rooted in an abstraction whose initial form is intention, and whose final form is a localized instance that conforms to a self-similar pattern despite outward variances demanded by different circumstances. In contrast to its non-directional and passive substrate of conscious potential, intelligence is wholly teleological, funneling latent potency through the canalizing constrictions of ordering attractors whose parameters become formalized into habits which support evolvable complexity. Small-scale final causes constrict a larger energetic flow, attenuating it through their structured dynamics and molding its application toward their collective sustenance, which is a spatiotemporal analog of a final cause as fathomless as the potential that impels it. Teleology is therefore a mental property that is not limited to advanced cognitive capacities. Rather, as Thomas Nagel points out, "It is essential that if teleology forms part of the natural order, its laws should be universal and not just the description of a goal-seeking process."[dxciii] The implication he draws is that in addition to physical law, there are other laws of nature "biased toward the marvelous."[dxciv] Like Peirce's "logic of nature," teleology is a universal property and a non-local principle, open to countless forms of localized expression.

Nagel highlights two criteria for the existence of a "natural teleology:" that the laws of physics are not completely deterministic, and that some possible futures are more eligible than others as steps in the development of complexity.[dxcv] The gesture sketch of intelligence drawn by chaos supplies a cursory template for such universal end-directedness to fill in and refine with organic details supporting the ascent of order. Homogeneous equilibrium bifurcates into broken symmetries, providing the basis for differentiation. The increasing local complexity wrought by differentiation, and overlaid on immutable self-similarity, allows domain crossing to re-integrate the pieces of fractured symmetry at a higher level of interrelation, depth, and meaning. The serpentine fractal threading indifferently through all the phase changes that a dynamic system undergoes preserves the memory of the system in its replicative and scale-free patterns. As a system's final cause, the attractor draws trajectories whose initial conditions are partially located within the agents themselves, experienced iconically as impulses, motivations, and appetites toward fulfilling life's underlying imperatives. Projected at a generalized level, these drives in their countless formal iterations are like the trajectories that reveal the attractor's presence by orbiting its bodiless center.

Heart of an Attractor

While they give form to the attractor that holds them in its thrall, the functions that swirl within the magnetic basin never venture into its vacant interior. Rather, they describe it while remaining asymptotically aloof from the still center that clothes itself with their rough explications of its void presence. Never reaching zero, no matter how closely they trace it, each trajectory populating that probabilistic phase space reveals according to its own path and to its own degree the vacuous central quality that orders it. Likewise, all of manifestation, arising out of the empty stillness underlying iconic firstness, which is the conscious context of all intelligent processes, exhibits to its own degree—no matter how closely it approaches zero—that primary emptiness. Constituting the undefinable perception to which sensory devices relay their inputs, this silent region of origination is separated from its measureable descriptions by an inscrutable manifold at the interface between calculable measurement and the experiential quality that is beyond computation. Neither spatial nor temporal, the discontinuity between experiential awareness—whose contribution of open potential provides the basis for intelligent activity—and measurable phenomena, can only be bridged interpretively, but never directly measured. Surrounded by a substantiating weave of dynamics that describe it like an epistemology but are distinct from that inchoate source of intelligent order, the space between being and expression is the free domain of thirdness, the logic of nature.

Acting like an attractor which contracts potential's wanderings into a small range of state space, the enigmatic orchestrator of intelligent order attenuates the free dissipation of divergent trajectories by entraining them into systems of mutual reliance. The complex forms that diversify within this circumscribed space carry on the dynamics of chaos by replicating within themselves, at every level of organization that nests beneath their symbol-level mantles, a self-similar emptiness of attraction that coheres their multiple levels of organization. This describable, but unmeasurable quality which is the heart of the attractor is iterated throughout the nested hierarchy of complexity and constitutes the subjectivity of the agent. Teilhard de Chardin describes this empty center as "an interior in the heart of beings, as seen through a rent that is enough to ensure that to some degree, this 'interior' exists through all of nature from all time."[dxcvi] Permeating all of nature from within, this "rent" is the primary isomorphism shared among situated entities. As the "force that through the green fuse drives the flower,"[dxcvii] that experiential singularity is the dissipative expansion that evolution alternately mines and counters through adaptive innovations of form and constraint. Although curbed by parameters, the ever-expansive nature of the undefinable quality underlying manifestation tends to create levels of infinity within the bounds that constrain it. The hierarchical tangle of order drives this infinitude irreversibly up the Cantor ladder to its leading edge, drawing potential from depth, as well as the modular breadth that accompanies complexity, to elevate the ability of the agent to contribute to the construction of its own experience.

In critical concert with the orderly regime, chaos is the substrate of creative manifestation from which springs pluripotency at every level of complexity. Like a metaphor, chaos represents a realignment of causal factors within an emergent context and leads to a redefinition of the regularities and probabilities that describe a system. So potent is the meaning that arises through chaos that Carl Jung recognized it as more than "mundane cause-and-effect;" rather, "it potentially marks the birth of a new cosmos."[dxcviii] From the hierarchical superposition of order upon chaos, which yields coherence, ensues all evolution. The meaning that surges upward through all tiers of organization and toward which they bend their activities unites all systems under a singular level of description that lies beyond all individual bounds of surprisal and so bespeaks a universe that doesn't merely possess or contain meaning, but that arises from and embodies meaning. Ortega y Gasset explains its nature: "The 'meaning' of a thing is the highest form of its coexistence with other things—it is its depth dimension."[dxcix]

Through all dynamical phase changes, breaks in symmetry, and shifts in stability, the immeasurable, numinous dimension remains preserved as potential that is malleable to its embodying formal conditions. "The 'true thing' is then the Object that maintains its identity within the manifolds of appearances belonging to multiplicity of subjects."[dc] Its conscious nature requires that meaning is both its form and currency. It is an underlying invariance, or symmetry, that is the basis of agency; the "inside" of the epistemic cut. Transferred intact throughout phase changes and emergently expressed at increasing levels of complexity and degrees of freedom, this undefinable interior—the empty heart of the attractor—is the constant; the universal "elementary conception between the manifold of substance and the unity of being" that is preserved through all evolutionary permutations.

Unperturbed by the chaotic turmoil in which it awakens, the quiescent epicenter of all order silently conducts the dance of evolution around itself; it is at once the initial condition and final cause of all manifestation. "The thing is a rule of possible appearances," says Husserl. "That means that the thing is a reality as a unity of a manifold of appearances connected according to rules. Moreover, this unity is an intersubjective one. It is a unity of states..."[dci] The "intersubjective unity" manifests itself in the myriad of sentient attractors nested within its spacious basin, which embody various depths of complexity and degrees of interrelatedness, and together comprise the sturdy, yet supple and delicately balanced structures which measure and draw the vibrant power of potential up through their orderly rungs, without which, "cosmos returns to chaos."[dcii] With the empty, underlying whole iterated like a localized void at their centers, all unities necessarily incorporate each other to varying degrees into structured ecologies through their mutually limiting or amplifying interactions. Ritualizing regularities into cycles of reciprocally causal closure, agents whose activities coalesce into unique arrangements of formal interactions implicitly enshrine at their small scales the global ordering principle that enjoins the greatest and the least of its expressions into a singular circular mesh. By shedding and ensnaring vagrant trajectories to and from other related attractors, the system foliates into the stabilizing, symmetrical lateral spread of near-decomposability, creating many anchoring platforms from which further elaborations of complexity, with their new depths of meaning, can emerge.

6

Interface

"And in the mind the will to grow and generate, and in the will the power, and in the power the light, and in the light its forth-driving spirit; which maketh again a will to generate a twig, a bud, a branch, out of the tree like itself."
—Jacob Boehme

Whether physical or semantic, the constraints of a system propagate order, releasing unexpressed potential as an entropic byproduct that facilitates directionality, affects coupling, and guides probabilities. As potential evolves through form to access environmental opportunities, it is teleologically challenged to generate emergent properties at its leading, interactional edge. Exhibiting formal and final causality over rest of system, emergent capacities function like attractors to entrain lower-level dynamics to a common final cause, which manifests at the system's symbol level. Across each phase change that yields an escalation in complexity, the system's lower-level dynamics translate themselves into higher levels of capability and degrees of freedom, preserving their essential properties even as they cross into novel domains of both vertical ascent with its concurrent depth, and lateral, modular complexity. Vitalizing the rigor of unadorned order, chaos threads along the boundaries of each phase transition, drawing along a fractal strand whose principles are replicated under different conditions and at different levels of complexity as the system ascends the echelons of emergent, hierarchical order.

Marking the presence of domains to be crossed, boundaries delineate distinct tendencies and mediate commerce between them. The boundary between agent and environment is a two-way interface which selectively draws inward certain semiotic, energetic, and material trajectories, while deflecting others based on relevance. Conversely, the self-declarative surface projects outwardly to prospective receivers. As the interface between inward and outward flows of information and energy, the symbol-level boundary represents a brief description of both the organism and the context in which it evolves. It is a dynamical turning point that integrates interior dynamics into nonlinear loops of reciprocal causality with exterior conditions, while constraining internal potential into persistent regularity by curbing entropic expansion from within and noisy encroachment from without. This nexus of interchange is a haven of chaos, which awakens at the boundaries of divergent domains. The nonlinearity that is nurtured along boundaries also cultivates another, more counter-intuitive side effect: a means of propagating order.

Chaos and Order at the Boundary

When the thermodynamically mandated dispersive tendencies generated by metabolism encounter nonlinear boundary conditions, they can conspire to produce, within a uniform medium, a localized, self-sustaining pulsate of traveling energy. This non-dissipative wave is a soliton, which embodies a high level of symmetry between its medium and boundary conditions.[dciii] It is the offspring of the two intersecting manifolds it traverses: the rate-independent formal conditions that provide the template for its genesis, and the rate-dependent realm of dynamical expression through which it transports order in localized waves.[dciv] As a soliton engages in energetic exchange with its environment during its travels, perhaps using quantum potential to "feel" its way along its route, it extends coherent patterns to localized structures, increasing the system's internal degrees of freedom.[dcv] Its most distinctive feature is its resilience in retaining its form and velocity as it travels—a property that has particular relevance in the context of a living cell. Its resistance to disruption and dissipation allows the soliton to maintain its organization while mediating the orderly and directed movements of molecules, atoms, and fundamental particles that constitute cellular activity.[dcvi] The coherent wave delivers information and order across scales by structuring its medium.

When operative at the molecular level, a soliton is a unified corpuscle of energy and matter capable of transferring localized energy quanta with almost no dissipation.[dcvii] Its directed pulse encompasses both energy and matter by transferring the former in terms accessible to the latter: ordered, measurable information that propagates along a causally defined trajectory. This is what makes a soliton a viable mode of informational transfer, in contrast to a quantum particle. Although a particle can be a repository of information, its ability to relay a message is limited because its mode of propagation is saltatory, marked by discontinuous jumps that leave no traceable pattern. By lending continuity to the movement of quantized energy, a soliton wave provides a means for its energetic "message" to announce itself throughout its propagating medium.

With its capacity to direct the movement of energetic quanta, the soliton presents itself as a plausible driver of one of the major engines of directed particle movement within the cell, catalysis. As the basic mechanism of pushing biochemical reactions far from equilibrium, catalysis promotes certain reactions over others by offering a low-energy alternative route to their completion. Contracted by a solitonic pulse, the distal ends of an enzyme's active site come into sufficient proximity to accommodate the reaction's charge transfer.[dcviii] Because the target of an enzyme is an individual particle, however, the assistance that a soliton provides to a reaction is not merely mechanical. The solitonic energy-matter hybrid instead accesses a deeper level of interface: that between classical and quantum objects.

At the level of protons and electrons, classical modes of contiguous and measurable movement accede to quantum indivisibility—even within very large molecules.[dcix] Enzymatic activity must therefore account for the wave dimension of the particles it is tasked with shepherding. Because the wave function of a particle near a barrier extends into the barrier itself, the narrowed gap between the particle and the targeted reaction site afforded by enzyme activation may allow the probability wave to probe and even fully occupy its new potential position. At the edge of the solitonically shortened chasm between current and potential states, the particle dissolves its form into probabilistically guided potential, rematerializing almost instantaneously in the target site. The enzyme has facilitated quantum tunneling.[dcx]

The quantum movement that catalysts promote is foundational to biochemistry. However, quantum leaps themselves, while they do transfer the energy of the leaping particle, are hypothesized to be acausal, equiprobable, and time reversible, making them poor carriers of information. Without agent-like activity altering their probability of transpiring, such transfers could not occur with enough frequency, rapidity, and reliability to foster biological processes.[dcxi] Cellular activity, however, is replete with agent-like directedness with the possible assistance of solitons. For example, the folding of metastable polypeptide chains into dynamically active proteins, the local unwinding of DNA prior to transcription, and the electron transfers in photosynthesis and respiration may all be the handiwork of traveling quantum waves.[dcxii] Owing their very existence to the convergence of information and energy, soliton waves may be implicated in the emergence of life itself.

Quantum Systems

Beyond the critical fusion of stability with chaos, life spans obverse domains at many other levels: between agent and environment, inner and outer, animate and inert. At the foundation of all other domain dichotomies is the most mysterious of all: that between the quantum and classical realms. The intrinsically probabilistic events of the quantum realm defy classical circumscription. Particularly jettisoned is the mechanistic level of explanation afforded by efficient causality, which demands for every perceivable effect, a proximate and measurable cause. Although quantum behavior ostensibly resists classical, mechanistic causal explanations, it is far from random. Instead, a particle such as a photon or an electron apparently constructs its trajectory with striking purposefulness, "selecting" an optimally efficient path or orbit only after simultaneously sampling a neighboring range of potential from a state of superposition.[dcxiii] In the forking prongs of their entangling probes, querying particles investigate probable outcomes as though through a fractal structure whose branches each lead to different potential endpoints.[dcxiv] The parallel "virtual transitions" of exploring, but uncommitted particles are not merely hypothetical, but can have measurable effects on physical processes. Once a sufficiently long branch develops toward a definitive outcome, certainty sets in and the particle "collapses" from a state of superimposed possibility to one of resolution.

At the classically unfettered level of quantum superposition, there is a completeness akin to Pattee's idea of semantic closure,[dcxv] but which is prior to the epistemic cut, with ontology undifferentiated from epistemology. What is known about the observer-dependent system is what it expresses. Unanchored to material solidity, quantum states—unlike classical ones—are too susceptible to disturbance and easily redefined by measurement to exist objectively. Instead, a quantum system survives ensconced in the self-referential cocoon of its own unitary evolution—an internal space without the external juxtaposition of environmental entanglements demanding distinctions be made or relations be established. Such a seamless state of unity precludes sign processes, since there are no boundaries to cross. Instead, the whole nonlocal system reacts instantaneously to any change or perturbation at any point—such as demonstrated by entangled electron pairs, wherein measurement detects a spin state in one and the other instantaneously resolves into complementarity. Such "undivided wholeness"[dcxvi] precedes information, which relies on the differentiation imparted by objectivity to necessitate meaning, which is always about something, implying division. Meaning and differentiated existence are irreducibly entangled conditions.

The epistemic cut only emerges with the incipient trappings of embodiment, when the ground-state unity of the quantum system yields to the classical epistemic distinction, in which the measured object has an existence independent of the measurer's knowledge of it—an independence which allows it to function as a sign. As the quantum state entangles with its environment, the unabridged potential suspended in unitary coherence gives way to partiality by expressing a single definitive state—an eigenstate—out of plural possibility. Upon this break in symmetry, the wave description decoheres—possibly collapsing, or simply shifting phases so the unexpressed waves do not interfere with the expressed eigenstate—into a particle description, and the perfect memory of the system's unitary evolution, along with the details of the transition, dissipate as entropy while the expressed state takes up a single, irreversible, historically conditioned trajectory.[dcxvii] The decoherence event is the product of a "measurement," with the environment acting as the measurer that draws one of the system's many potential states into interaction—highlighting it over others, amplifying it into the sphere of meaning where evolution takes place. The result of the measurement is a bifurcation from the unified symmetry of latent potential to a state of polarity, with the orderliness of expression counterbalanced by the entropy of dissipated potential.

Quantum Darwinism

By preferentially coaxing a particular aspect of the nondescript quantum realm into the tangible classical one through measurement, the environment may be foreshadowing the selective role it plays in biological evolution. Leibniz describes the founding condition of ready potential, "Everything that expresses essence or possible reality, strive with equal right for existence."[dcxviii] The Quantum Darwinism hypothesis posits that the reduction of quantum coherence is contingent on ambient environmental factors whose interactions with the quantum system favor certain potential states over others by enhancing their probability of being expressed.[dcxix] In the undisturbed superposition prior to classical emergence, quantum fluctuations accrue within the unitary system as a degenerate store of possible eigenstates, all occupying the same energetic state while spanning a range of causal efficiency. Different potential states correlate with prevailing conditions to varying degrees, in direct proportion to their probability of selection. When superposition is destabilized, the Quantum Darwinism model predicts that the most unstable outlier states, as poor reflections of the eliciting environment, will be suppressed through oscillatory interference, whereas the states that are more robust to the distortions of decoherence, known as pointer states, will be irreversibly amplified and stabilized.[dcxx]

The admixture of selection by a changeable environment, degeneracy of possible states, and the ever-present stochasticity of the details of the process itself ensures that multiple repetitions would yield a range of different outcomes, with a limited subset more probabilistically favored. The repeated selection of the same pointer states allows them to multiply more readily throughout the environment than more fragile states, since they are successfully "measured" more often.[dcxxi] The branching fractal model depicts how repetitive selection can ultimately bolster a delicate, observer-dependent state to the level of objectivity. Its branches, which redundantly encode the system's information, develop when different sub-environments interact independently with the system.[dcxxii] The various environmental contexts essentially provide different perspectives on the same information describing the selected state. Robustness to multiple angles of "measurement" allows pointer states to become sufficiently abundant to be detectable without perturbation. Objectivity grows out of robust subjectivity, which replicates itself into what Peirce would consider a "habit" of nature.

Once a successful state expresses itself, it may become increasingly likely to be selected in subsequent decoherence events, reflecting the nonlocal, indissoluble nature of the non-physical substrate underlying physical expression. The "undivided wholeness" implied is the immaterial source drawn from by quantum evolution, which emerges into manifestation under compelling conditions. Entanglements among particles maintain coherence within their interactions like relics of the undifferentiated nonlocality from which they arise, with measurement on one particulate node instantaneously affecting all other aspects of the network.[dcxxiii] As these quantum entanglements spread throughout the universe, however, their frequent "re-measuring" by other classical objects tends to negate their effects at observable levels.

Quantum Intelligence

As favored pointer states multiply, information about them proliferates throughout the environment in the form of regularities that express nature's "primordial habit-making tendency." Upon emergence, the system takes on attributes common to all classical systems. It is constrained by and integrated into a context with vastly higher degrees of freedom than it embodies itself, and which it encounters as surprisal. While the limited system is only capable of interacting with a tiny portion of its environment's degrees of freedom, it can still reduce surprisal by enhancing the regularities it relates to. The habit-making tendency of nature is a harbinger of directed, purposive action.

Acting like a noisy channel, the environment accommodates and conveys information about proliferating systems up to a certain point—the "classical plateau"—beyond which any additional information short of a perfect global measurement can reveal only redundancy rather than new insight.[dcxxiv] Agents within the environment therefore adopt a heuristic model of information collection, reflecting the trade-off between precision and efficiency that inhabits this plateau, shifting ever in relation to changes in the state of the system being measured. One of the tools available to agents seeking to interpret a suite of conditions is computation, which reflects a mode of interpretation that is highly conserved throughout evolution. In extracting from its ensemble of potential a state relevant to its immediate context, a classically emergent system is performing the most primordial computation—and therefore interpretation—in the universe.[dcxxv] With the system coming to a particular conclusion, which is its manifest form, based on a set of premises, which include its intrinsic scope of potential states as well as extrinsic conditions, the computation it performs is a type of inference. The emergence into classicality therefore constitutes the primordial expression of intelligence, as an unmeasurable state of a nonphysical system crosses domains to become a distinct, describable entity. Its symbol-level presentation to the environment is the classical analog of the selected pointer state, which determines the nature and scope of the newly minted particle's interactions with its environment. Like a system capable of learning, the most successful "inferences" propagate through the environment into regularity, or habit, which Peirce deemed synonymous with induction.[dcxxvi] Conversely, the detectable presence of the system's information within the environment makes possible the deduction of its presence and properties. Peirce's "logic of nature" is a formative, bedrock principle from the very incipience of classicality.

The collapse of superposition into a single manifestation is simultaneously a domain crossing and a domain delineation, which invites further crossing. The vertical transition between quantum and classical is a change in kind from which unfold the dualisms of primordial distinction: between inner and outer, semantic and physical, meaning and symbol, icon and index, measurer and measured, and so on. The division between subject and object necessitates the interactive exchange of semiosis, as undivided wholeness trades instantaneous nonlocality for a temporally conditioned, situated perspective that is dependent on boundary crossing to attain some semblance of coherence within the incongruous state of differentiation. The nonlinear, divisive conditions of classicality also impose a new form of memory. Undissipated preservation forsakes simultaneous holism in the transition to contextual contingency and irreversible dynamics, inflected with the guiding semantic constraints of semiosis.

From the very incipience of the classical world, the structuring logic of intelligence not only supports the generation of forms, but also conditions the experiences contained within those forms. Acting through the perceptive vehicle of intelligence, consciousness samples its own potential in relation to environmental information—an activity made necessary by the primordial, cross-domain collaboration between inner impetus and outer expression to accomplish a contextually conditioned act of distinction. By providing an internal, computational complement to the external "observation" of the environment, consciousness selects, interprets, and expresses a single state, while retaining its essential, immeasurable character which is beyond computation.[dcxxvii] In the compression of possibility into manifestation, a complex, nonlocal conglomerate of processes is reduced and summarized into the localization of individual expression. The close entwinement of consciousness, intelligence, and expression is described by Peirce, "Viewing a thing from the outside, considering its relations of action and reaction with other things, it appears as matter. Viewing it from the inside, looking at its immediate character as feeling, it appears as consciousness."[dcxxviii] With matter's dual aspects of measurable form and intangible consciousness, its very advent is concurrent with the unfoldment of intelligence. The computation that brings quantum insubstantiality into manifest form is the initial expression of thirdness, which correlates an internal potentiality with an external condition and presents the result at an emergent symbol level that is an interface of semiotic interchange and evolution.

Just as chaos and order transpose roles according to the level of consideration within a system, the environment and system alternate in their roles as attractor. The environment is an attractor to a particular eigenstate, which when expressed acts like a basin of attraction in reordering its environment. Enjoined in complementary exchange with non-local factors, a localized system engages with its surroundings in a fractal pattern of uncertain boundaries between interchanging roles. The integral importance of the environment in the processes of intelligence indicates that intelligence is not simply concentrated within the agent, but a complex function of contextual embeddedness and interagency. As agency increases in complexity, with expanding degrees of semantic freedom, the burden of selection increasingly shifts from extrinsic, environmental sources to the intrinsic capacities of subjects which are always engaged to some degree in shaping the conditions of their own evolution.

Quantum Life

The gateway between the mysterious quantum landscape and the familiar classical world of law-like behavior becomes more than an esoteric question of physics when considering that biology also spans that strange boundary, carrying out its most mundane tasks in the hazy aura of quantum indeterminacy. Making and breaking chemical bonds, absorbance of frequency-specific radiation, ATP cleavage, and single electron transfer are all quantum effects.[dcxxix] Far from resisting the challenge presented by the probabilistic nature of quantum activity, cells are finely adapted to exploit that indeterminate pluripotency. This is demonstrated by photosynthesis, in which the energy of a captured photon is transported with almost perfect efficiency from the chloroplast's photoreceptors to its reaction centers. Photon-harvesting antenna proteins achieve this remarkable feat by delaying the otherwise nearly instantaneous event of decoherence. The extension of the duration of coherence from the typical 1.5 femtosecond span to as much as 750 femtoseconds allows the captured photon to simultaneously sample the various biochemical pathways to the reaction site that is its destination in search of the lowest-energy route. [dcxxx] Every aspect of the energetic journey along the absorption channels is geared toward forestalling decoherence. Specialized proteins delicately shuttle their non-classical ward through an environment whose noise inputs are finely balanced to optimally mediate efficient transport and whose steep energetic terrain prevents backward transfer. After passing in a soliton-like wave to the reaction centers, essentially taking multiple routes simultaneously, the photon's state of superposition collapses, delivering its energetic cargo almost completely undissipated.[dcxxxi]

Within the cell, the agents most suited to the task of ushering quantum particles within a complex classical environment are, naturally, the measurers—enzymes, calling upon their own quantum potential to execute measurements with rapidity and specificity beyond the capacity of any purely classical device.[dcxxxii] The environment within the cell actively assists the quantum tunneling process in enzymatically mediated reactions.[dcxxxiii] Its interior may act to drive quantum dynamics and maintain coherence by striking a balance between noise—too much of which curbs transport by facilitating the counterproductive quantum Zeno effect that effectively traps the particle—and calm, which in excess allows the particle to wander aimlessly.[dcxxxiv]

The quantum capacity for parallel exploration that is exploited by energy-harvesting chlorophyll molecules is also recruited by other biomolecular systems within the cell. Highly efficient quantum searches utilizing the fractal probes of quantum states can sample and sort nucleotide base pairs during DNA replication and proofreading, and even explore the quantum superposition of mutational genetic states.[dcxxxv] Even tautomerism, with its destabilizing potential for randomness, might actually enhance the adaptability of its host by allowing a potential mutation in a genetic sequence to be recognized in a form that is alternative to the wild type—a feature that can be usefully exploited in the face of environmental change.[dcxxxvi] A source of random DNA mutations, tautomers arise from quantum fluctuations in coding protons that allow them to transition from one position in a nucleotide base to another, forming a modified chemical structure.[dcxxxvii] Any "measurement," such as when the gene is read for transcription, induces a collapse of superposition, with either the normal or tautomeric proton position being "selected." The observation that the most frequently transcribed genes have the highest levels of tautomeric mutations points to the quantum uncertainty hidden beneath classical stability.[dcxxxviii]

Overall, however, random mutations are relative rarities among genomes, which guard against such inner sources of erosion with an abundance of redundantly coded information.[dcxxxix] This is what makes some of the mutations that do occur in cells remarkable. Because a system's size does not necessarily preclude its display of quantum properties, the precise boundary between quantum and classical in a cell is indeterminate—free to travel up and down the cell's functional hierarchy depending on the state of the cell and resources available.[dcxl] This ambiguity of boundaries may point to a potential explanatory role for quantum mechanics in the astonishing ability, considered earlier, among carbon-starved bacteria to generate directed, adaptive mutations. The weakened interactions of the depleted cells with their environments may allow the cell to internally approximate a state of quantum coherence. Once the cell has mostly withdrawn its environmental entanglements, its internally referenced dynamics mimic the pre-classical state of unitary evolution. In this relatively unmeasured state, subtle and symmetrical interactions between the cell's genotype and phenotype play out in defiance to biology's central dogma of unidirectional informational flow, much like the directionless circularity of quantum time. Within the coherent cellular body of internal entanglements, a fluctuating amalgam of wild type and mutant states exist in the equiprobability of superposition as information accumulates without dissipation or loss. Suspended in a unitary state, the cell would be able to generate and sample potential mutational pathways relative to external conditions until an internal agreement with its surroundings would force the proliferation of "imaginary time" potential states to a turning point into real time, not unlike a Wick rotation. The coherence-collapsing measurement would be internally generated, driving the now-externally entangled cell to an intense series of computations informed by its environment toward a directed action—in the case of the carbon-starved cells, a multi-step mutation that enables them to utilize an atypical food source.[dcxli]

Even cells not under duress display hints of quantum talents. The ciliate *Spirostomum ambiguum* uses its powers of quantum computing to learn, store, and select behavioral heuristics to create its own unique repertoire of altruistic and deceptive signaling strategies for the purpose of attracting mates and competing with rivals.[dcxlii] Although the search patterns for learned heuristics vary among individuals and according to social contexts, they show a general pattern, as well as learning-based improvements with subsequent mating encounters.[dcxliii] The initial preferred strategy proceeds according to quantum Bose-Einstein (BE) statistics. If unsuccessful, this state dissipates into a classical computational phase described by Maxwell-Boltzmann (MB) statistics, which allows recursive trial-and-error strategy searches. Interruption of quantum computations with classical MB ones may help drive, like an energy pump, intracellular conditions toward another BE state as a new strategy replaces the unsuccessful one.[dcxliv] The classical phase, in which environmental entanglements predominate and exert an influence on computational outcomes, alters the quantum probability space as the cell continually classifies its learned experiences according to its ever-changing inner dynamics.[dcxlv]

The foundational role that quantum coherence plays in cellular biology was likely just as crucial to abiogenesis. The ability of quantum systems to continuously interrogate their environments and their own potential states may have allowed prebiotic systems to discover and instantiate the rare, low-entropy configurations necessary for life by virtually traveling multiple possible evolutionary paths simultaneously in search of the most viable.[dcxlvi] For example, large biomolecules such as amino acid chains could, under certain circumstances, resume a state of superposition that would allow the growing complexes to sample the state spaces of possible additional peptides relative to the environment before selectively extending the chain, which would again decohere upon entangling with a complex environment.[dcxlvii] Like the successful pointer states of Quantum Darwinism attaining objective status through proliferation, self-replication would "fix" a growing peptide to classical reality,[dcxlviii] much like an index fixes an icon's meaning out of indeterminate potential.

The potential explanatory power of quantum coherence pervades cellular activity, from mutations to metabolism to behavior. Kauffman speculates that vast webs of coherent or partially coherent degrees of freedom may span large volumes of a cell.[dcxlix] Laszlo expounds on the quasi-instant, nonlocal correlations, rather than causal connections, that cohere multicellular organisms as a precondition to maintaining life.[dcl] This vision entails that the intricate inner workings of any organism, from bacteria to elephants, would be indefinitely poised between aspects that propagate quantum coherent behavior and others that decohere toward classical behavior.[dcli] The wavering boundary between quantum and classical is as indistinct as that between the living and inert. McFadden and Al-Khalili suggest that the two distinctions may be closely related, with life's ability to harness thermodynamics in order to retain connection with the quantum realm setting it apart from the inanimate matter from which it is composed. In bridging the two seemingly incompatible domains of physics, life infuses materially and efficiently causal dynamics with the persistent uncertainty of that realm outside of measurement.

Routes to Coherence and Consciousness

In non-biological systems, quantum-like coherence can occur under certain conditions in macroscopic physical states. Superfluidity, superconductivity, and Bose-Einstein condensates can arise when a large number of particles participate in a single quantum state, behaving as one entity with a single wave function.[dclii] In this unitary state of collective behavior, all properties and information entirely overlap. Individuality is subsumed by the homogenizing power of long-range phase correlations that dominate the system's interactions, and individuality breaks down into frictionless wholeness.[dcliii] Marveling at the ballet-like coordination of superconductivity, David Bohm sees mind-like behavior animating the coherent particles in a way that is more like an organism than a mechanism.[dcliv]

In physical systems, such macroscopic states of coherence are only achievable in extreme conditions approaching absolute zero that preclude biological activity. Biological coherence requires another mechanism entirely. One possible mechanism was proposed by physicist Herbert Frohlich. According to his model, the driver of coherence is an electrically polarized ordered state of vibrational oscillators, excited by a continuous supply of pumped energy. Under this scenario, the pumped energy tends to reduce entropy, while the dissipative effects of non-equilibrium counterbalance that reduction. When the energy supplied is sufficiently large compared to energy lost, the system attains a stationary state in which the energy feeding the polar modes is channeled into the states with the lowest frequencies and the system approximates a Bose–Einstein condensation, with most bosons occupying the lowest quantum state.[dclv] Such a condition would bring long-range phase correlations into the system's dynamics, creating a high degree of structure and functional order. The conditions that would support induced coherence would provide a backdrop of non-equilibrium steady states of nonlinear vibrations, a decrease in informational entropy, and fertile ground to spawn those carriers of information and order, solitons.

In the Frohlich model, the dipolar oscillations maintained by hydrogen bonds and non-localized electrons trapped in the hydrophobic regions of proteins along a thin layer of molecules adjacent to the cell membrane are suspected to harbor the coherence that pulls cellular dynamics into concert.[dclvi] Other theoretical quests for the locus of coherence, most notably by Roger Penrose and Stuart Hameroff, have focused on the interior of the microtubule. The requisite dipolarity could be supplied by water, possibly derived from its ordered phase wherein its OH- ions stack themselves into a stable, highly ordered, lattice-like arrangement of hexagons that allows a flow of positively charged hydronium ions through the core of the cylinder.[dclvii] This arrangement may play a role in establishing the macroscopic dipole moment that would spontaneously induce a cascade of photon emissions whose complex interactions would effectively transform disordered, noisy energy into order. With the interior of the microtubule acting as waveguide for the photons, the emitting molecules would interact with their boson cloud collectively and coherently, producing the phenomenon of superradiance. The close, channelizing confines of the hollow cylinder would direct the interactions to propagate a steady-state optical pulse—a soliton, sustained without distortion or decay by the continuous absorption and re-emission of photons that would render the medium transparent, creating the phenomenon of self-induced transparency.[dclviii]

The possibilities of such remarkable micro-phenomena have inspired conjectures about a potential role for microtubules in conscious experience. The ordered electromagnetic waves of superradiance offer the possibility of a holographic form of information processing and representation based on quantum interference.[dclix] Another possible effect perpetrated by the inner radiance of the microtubule's core is to allow a weak coupling between coherent oscillations and the tubulin dimers that compose the tube and display irregular patterns that may conduce to cellular automata-like computations.[dclx] With its inner walls penetrated by photons, each microtubule may function as a quantum encoder in an optical computing network bound by the long-range correlations of nonlocality. This commingling of quantum and classical computations would give the environment an ample role in influencing algorithmic outcomes. As a result of coherence, the computations would be reflective of a cellular mode of consciousness. However, according to Penrose, consciousness itself can only arise in the presence of some non-computational function that would be an inherent aspect of matter.[dclxi]

Under the Penrose-Hameroff model of Orchestrated Objective Reduction, or Orch OR, the key to conscious experience lies in the delay of decoherence, which allows a non-random reduction of the unitary state to an expressed eigenstate. The locus of reduction would be internally, rather than environmentally centered, and would correlate to conscious experience at its most infinitesimal level.[dclxii] Offered as a possible agent of reduction is gravity, which would destabilize sufficiently disparate outlying states, whose causal distinctiveness lies in their slightly different potential effects on space-time curvature. The superposition of energetically degenerate potential states of infinitesimal causal distinction is a source of uncertainty in the system—a potential source of entropy as well as information.[dclxiii]

For models that situate consciousness relative to microtubules, the coherence fostered therein is not limited to its cylindrical incubators, but extends into a network of microtubules separated by hundreds of micrometers to create a long-range quantum coherent macrostate within, and possibly even beyond, the cell. Such a network of nonlocality, if capable of extending beyond cellular borders to synchronize clusters of neighbors, may be foundational to many biological and cognitive processes. The local coherence-generating dynamics, if capable of extending their reach across their borders, with their membranes communicating among each other in a synchronistic "dance," may represent the bottom-up ground state of consciousness that passes influence up the rungs of complexity to the coherent global level of explicit awareness.[dclxiv] Projected across multiple scales, the synchronizing backdrop of coherence would support the many-tiered emergence of coordinated, global-level complexity.

Quantum Brain

One solution that the nonlocality of coherent states may provide is to the persistent "binding problem" of conscious experience, which is simultaneously unitary and highly differentiated. In a quiescent but alert state, the spontaneous activity of unstimulated neurons fluctuates within the basin of attraction of their preferred cortical state (PCS).[dclxv] Although the resting state fluctuations occur in nearly the same manner as during evoked activity, the latter generates a dynamical pattern much like a limit cycle with a well-defined and stable spatial structure. Awareness, therefore, doesn't necessarily increase neuronal firing events, but it does arrange them into an orderly pattern of long-range correlations approaching synchrony.[dclxvi]

While the shift from spontaneous to correlated fluctuations is a local symptom of perception, its translation into an integrated experience invokes the wider context of the brain. One of the puzzles complicating the binding problem is that the synaptic activity that is the physical correlate of consciousness is distributed rather than proximal. The meaning content mysteriously encoded in locally activated neuronal clusters must somehow be integrated with that of other, more distal centers of neural activity. The dynamic core hypothesis conjectures that a conscious experience is comprised of highly differentiated functional clusters of neurons that arrange themselves spontaneously, their composition varying from event to conscious event.[dclxvii] When an excitation propagates into a coordinated network of firing events, they link together into a dynamical chain of transitory states, with widely distributed regions being activated or deactivated to create a novel conscious experience. Temporal order ripples like a "kinetic melody" through the brain in a rapidly executed, teleological order through ephemeral connections that unite different activated subgroups in fleeting solidarity. Only through a balance of rapid integration with a sufficient span of duration can these brief fluctuations be incorporated into coherent percepts.

The integration necessary to bind otherwise uncorrelated neural centers may arise from the same pattern as that of any other complex system: an intricate and modular network of hierarchical order. Founded on the coordinated nesting of alpha, beta, and gamma wavelengths into synchronized rhythms of cross-frequency oscillations, the hierarchy of vibratory complexity twists itself into the counter-spiral of reciprocal causality as the global electromagnetic field generated by local neural activity coordinates that very firing to establish synchrony at a large scale.[dclxviii] Like a pulsating beat binding musical elements into consonant harmony, the nested synchronization of waves would provide the stable energetic structure necessary to entrain the spontaneous local patterns of transient flickers into the coordinated context of cogent experience.[dclxix]

Despite the high level of complexity that underpins cognition, the environment in which neural activity is transmuted into experience is far from rigidly ordered. Neural interactions must rise above a backdrop of noise to create a discernable message. The temporary connections between activated brain regions, and the large numbers of excitatory connections found in the parts of mammal brains devoted to higher-order cognitive functions invite and magnify chaotic dynamics.[dclxx] Neural firing events arise with apparent spontaneity from an indeterminate coalescence of internal conditions that generate, but do not fully explain the events. The top-down property of awareness affects the random firing of neurons within a basin of attraction by synchronizing them and linking them to other spontaneously formed assemblages. This state of emergent order balances at the peak of tension between unbidden chaos and orderly phase synchrony. The resultant "kinetic melody" of neural activation is a time-dependent dynamic that calls upon coherence at the lowest, possibly subcellular level, to grant it features including an extended life span of activated subgroups, reminiscent of delayed decoherence; quasi-instant connection between distal regions, much like entanglements; and global coherence akin to unitary evolution and capable of selecting internal states that align with the environment. At the elevated level of complexity concentrated in brains, mental activities bear a striking resemblance to quantum properties.

Scale Invariance

While the binding problem investigates how sensational plurality can be distilled into experiential unity, a more fundamental question asks how consciousness can extend beyond its immaterial, semantic domain to affect physicality. Reaching across the all of the interfaces that life traverses—including semantic and physical, animate and inert, quantum and classical—the question of volitional expression examines a crossover so essential, yet so significantly at odds with the thermodynamic tendencies of classicality, that life has organized itself around amplifying and preserving that original domain crossing. The processes supporting that fundamental preservation do so by directing its causal efficiency to the maintenance and continued cultivation of order. "Upwardly heritable" in principle, but subject to formal variation and unpredictable outcomes in their rise through the nested tiers of hierarchical complexity, the essential dynamics that support life from its foundations persist throughout all of nature's formal obfuscations.

Along with material and energetic commerce with the environment, informational exchange is a primary support of life processes, serving as a bridge between intrinsic potentiality and extrinsic causality. Embodied at the molecular level in the soliton, whose fusion of energy, information, and matter makes it a semiotic fundament, such exchange is the basis of the regularity that pervades the "universe of signs" at all levels. Driving another organizational fundament of life processes, solitonic pulses enable the catalysis that channels equilibrium into directionality, criticality, and evolution. Catalysis itself, as a mode of subverting structural constraints to achieve transitions to more favorable thermodynamic states, is a process whose principle is preserved across scales.[dclxxi] In disrupting equilibrium by biasing outcomes, catalysis provides a metaphor for the universal creation of order across all domains by selectively reducing possibilities into well-fitted probabilities. Resolving incoherence toward intelligibility, every physical, energetic, symbolic, or syntactic mechanism, pathway, or pattern "specifie[s] its own irreducible perspective on the probabilities of past and future states of the system."[dclxxii] In doing so, every bridge between open potential and directionality, however elemental, constitutes "its own irreducible concept." Representative of a universal tenet of order, catalysis is one among multiple principles that awaken with life and reform themselves in new variations across all scales and domains.

Oscillations, Ergodicity, and Awareness

Preceding even catalysis, a deeper recurring theme in scale-invariant consistency is the presence of waves. In a unitary state of quantum superposition, potential is expressed as waves, with the troughs providing an important source of structure by delineating active crests of potential. Wave interference enables the computing potential of superposition, with quantum algorithms utilizing constructive interference to increase wave amplitudes in the vicinity of an optimal solution.[dclxxiii] This pre-classical precursor to information precipitates the unitary state's collapse as simple undulations behave in complex ways.

While oscillations lead to chaos when they bifurcate, they allow coherence when they harmonize. Like a meaningful message or an entropy-dissipating structure, resonant coherence is a statistical outlier issuing from the intelligent impulse that orders the conditions of its expression. Keeping probabilities from becoming absolutes, critical order breaks the equilibrium of ergodicity—which regards all of its potential states with equal favor—by weighting certain probabilities more heavily and spilling them over into irreversible evolution. While ergodicity dissipates diachronically as entropy through dynamical interactions, its uncritical embrace of possibility is partially preserved within the constraints of manifestation through the increase in potential that accompanies an evolving system's expanding degrees of freedom. Outwardly, a vestige of totipotency is implicitly worn at the symbol level, which invites a potentially infinite array of perspectives, and therefore possible interpretations.

All oscillations, whether coherent or chaotic, resolve at the immeasurable discontinuity that animates the biosphere from within the subjective interiors of agents. Consciousness is the incalculable context that all activities paradoxically constitute measurements of by its filling its contents, without being synonymous with that untouchable ubiquity. With sentience as an ever-present backdrop to life's activities, the experience of an action takes on as much causal significance as the measureable events that surround it. For example, only through a photoreceptor's "experience" of the photon whose collapse it delays can it measure the potential utility contained in that energetic quantum. It is immanent awareness that enables the all-important act of measurement, which describes physical quantities without being circumscribed by those bounds of description.[dclxxiv]

Excitable Media and Travelling Waves

While the amplified crest of a wave is of importance because it can correlate to meaningful causal efficiency, the trough that frames it is equally important in the silent support it offers its active counterpart. Similarly, the refractory zone of an excitable medium—a region of temporarily inexpressible potential—plays an important structuring role in the formation of traveling waves that propagate information in macroscopic structures. Slime molds, for example, act like an excitable medium when the intermittent signals of starving amoebas pulse biochemical cues throughout a population. When the flurry of excitations reaches criticality, the individuals become coordinated into a system, looping themselves into spirals and concentric rings. When unified as a plasmodium, these protists collectively attain a suite of capacities normally accessible only to more complex organisms as synchronization unleashes the power of complexity by cohering and amplifying individual intelligences to a globally unified level like the synchronized bosons in a Bose-Einstein condensate.

Similar to the order-inducing rhythms of the slime mold, neurons' biochemical releases across synaptic junctions are pulsed, with a refractory period in which the binding sites of the receptor cell are unable to receive new stimuli. The action potential that prompts the biochemical release is itself a coherent traveling pulse, while an activated neural system acts like an excitable medium by requiring a perturbation to prompt it beyond a threshold that engenders a burst of organized activity, followed by a quiet relapse into a resting state.[dclxxv]

Like their cerebral counterparts, sensory neurons relay the news of their activation by propagating an electrical pulse along their axons and stimulating connected clusters of neurons to take up the message. Since activating or suppressing areas of an excitable medium amounts to structuring it, the semantic input that the neurons fire in response to orders their energetic configuration in relation to the object that they are perceiving.[dclxxvi] The agile intelligence directing the process of perception ensures that the relationship is far from static. Rather, the anticipatory penchant of interpretation predicts the route of the energy flow, expectantly lighting up regions of the neural web where future connection is probable. These regions become highly coherent compared to surrounding areas, much like the amplified crest of a quantum computational wave. Conscious perception is therefore an act of embodying the metrics of the apprehended object in terms of the nervous system's electrical, biochemical, dynamical, and spatial patterns. Between subject and object arises a correspondence in which a chimeric, dynamical form of the object is represented in the observer. The intentional object is informed, but not constrained, by the same conditions of the object's phenomenal existence: "Quality, light, color, depth, which are there before us, are only there because they awaken an echo in our bodies and because the body welcomes them" (Merleau-Ponty).

The nervous system is a complex interface which unites the manifolds of sensation, perception, cognition, and motor control. While the relationship between stimulus and perception is mediated by an inwardly-conducted traveling wave, the converse relationship between intention and action is structured by an outward flow. The electrical waves engendered in the bodies of neurons propagate through their axonal extensions and into the muscles—changing vehicles at the synaptic juncture via biochemical release—which respond like excitable media by binding acetylcholine in a series of oscillations between activity and latency. Each active period triggers cascades of complex chemical and electrical activity, culminating in the muscular contractions that carry out directed motions. The commonly accepted mechanocentric metaphor of the brain and nervous system as a vastly complex machine misses this crucial aspect of neural functioning, rooted in very simple principles, which accounts for its fluid versatility. For Davia, the nervous system is merely a specialized expression of the simple requirements of life: energy and structure combined with an excitable medium.

The electromagnetic mosaic that fleetingly shimmers through infinitely arrangeable neural patterns is a measurable counterpart of the ineffable mental experience it describes. The observable activity of the brain is at best a metaphor for the mind, expressed in terms of embodiment that do not fully explain or contain the intangible quality that they signify. Not only is brain activity a metaphor for the gyrations of mind, it is also an analogy for it. The plasticity of neural structures arises from their malleability as excitable media, organizing through intention-driven oscillations between activity and quiescence. The thinking mind similarly relies on amplified thought "waves" framed by their concurrent inactive troughs, bounding even thoughts into signs processes.[dclxxvii] Bohm explains, "Thought proper begins...with thought, conscious of itself through its distinguishing itself from non-thought."[dclxxviii] The empty frame of non-thought is not non-conscious; it is unfilled, non-explicit consciousness. It arises simultaneously with thought as a conjugate property that provides the necessary juxtaposition to make its object distinct in a non-physical adumbration of the epistemic cut. Each thought-region, protectively swathed in silence, fills its interior with a unique rendition of the self-similar content animating the rest of the universe: the "intelligent perception which is capable of bringing about an overall harmony of fitting between mind and matter."[dclxxix] Like the rest of the universe, every thought-island only exists by virtue of its relation with every other: "Thought is an interpretive relation rather than an idea known within the mind."[dclxxx] With crests amplifying each other into ascent over the noisy background, the waves surrounding these peak regions cancel each other out into the stillness of an empty frame. It is "the hallmark of the visible [or expressed]...to have a lining of the invisible" (Merlau-Ponty).

The processes that generate the contents of consciousness and fulfill its edicts pass through many levels and forms: cellular, systemic, neural, motor, perceptual, intentional, and beyond. The stratified internal synchrony of a complex system is a microcosmic reflection of the hierarchical environmental nesting into which the agent incorporates itself. The constant that is preserved through all of the changes in form and mode of informational conveyance is the wave. From mechanical and energetic waves such as sound and light are stimulated the electrical pulses of action potentials that release biochemical messengers in ephemeral, coordinated ripples within the brain. In its order-propagating trajectory from source to target, the undulating organizer structures different types of media through multiple vehicles, but according to the same meaning-pattern which passes through transitions like an order-bearing soliton to deliver its message undissipated, albeit translated. Reaching across all hierarchical scales, the order-inducing wave twists and spirals its way through every level of complexity, from that of molecules within cells; cells within organs; organs within systems; systems within organisms; organisms within networks; networks within populations; populations within ecosystems. All participants in the informational dissemination of the many-formed wave are structured by it in relation to each other into the irreducible tangle of system dynamics. Like the fractal that unites chaos through all of its tumult, the travelling wave provides the coherent thread that unites formal and dynamical variation into structured unity. Reverberating tiers of order unite internally localized intelligence in relation to an external counterpart which is general, abstract, non-local, and pervasive. As Bateson surmises, "Epistemology, the pattern which connects, is, after all, one, not many."[dclxxxi]

Long-Range Correlations

Just as the coordinated harmony cohering an organism into unity points to internal, nonlocal connectivity, the coalescence of organisms into a synchronized flock, herd, school, swarm, plasmodium, or other coordinated, mobilized aggregate suggests a similar principle of nonlocality, with coherence extending beyond the bounds of the individual organism to enfold the group into a new level of singularity. When moving coherently, a flock or herd is a concentrated, ordered unit of energy, arising from nonlinear conditions and propagating order through its internal degrees of freedom like a large-scale soliton.

Synchronization emerges in biological networks when all individuals in a group collectively align their behavior, much like the onset of order via long-range correlations in condensed matter phase transitions. Behavioral correlations result from local, short-range, individual interactions, although they may extend their reach to encompass the entire group, depending on the level of noise in the system.[dclxxxii] The dynamics that emerge in mobile, self-organized animal groups are internally conditioned by factors including the constraints of locomotion that vary among species, the necessity to avoid collisions, and the tendency to align with a small group of neighboring individuals.[20] The fluid synchrony with which a coordinated group navigates these structuring variables allows it great sensitivity and responsiveness to external perturbations, like predator attacks, while maintaining robustness. This is because the interactions of participating agents are topologically constructed rather than spatially dependent, allowing the strength of cohesion to remain constant at different densities and variations in shape that even include splits.[dclxxxiii]

One important factor conditioning group synchronization is noise, which is internally generated by individual deviations from the rules guiding the group.[dclxxxiv] Below a critical threshold of noise, order increases, but correlations lengths are shortened, which threatens the cohesion of the group. Above the crucial level, correlation is destroyed as animals continue to maintain their behavioral state but lose sensitivity to neighboring behavior. At the fine-tuned point of balance in between is an optimal level of noise that fosters self-organization. Just as in

---

[20] The size of the group ranges in size, from 3 to 5 individuals for fish such as perch and up to 7 for birds like starlings.

thermodynamic systems, an optimal level of noise is not the adversary of organization, but a crucial feature of its integrity.

When correlations between individuals extend to encompass the entire group, the effective perceptual range of each individual is expanded to that of the entire group, allowing information to pass undamped among all members.[dclxxxv] With this onset of scale-free dynamics, long-range correlations subsume individual variations to grant the group fluid access and responsiveness to information not available at an individual level—an agile cohesion that is analogous to the delicate and undissipated unity of quantum coherence. Like an ensemble of degenerate potential states, each individual contributes uniquely to the intelligence of the whole, pooling the subtle perceptual differences each position within the group affords. As individual epistemic boundaries expand outward to implicitly enfold the entire group within a unifying envelope of coherence, the global increase in degrees of perceptual freedom contracts free energy inward, diminishing surprisal at the individual level far beyond what any single group member could achieve alone. By collectivizing that information into a higher-level leading edge guided by a common final cause, the coherent system efficiently selects an optimal state to express, instantaneously guiding its members to defensive formations, directional changes, evasions, or other behaviors that reflect the environment's demands.

When classical, assortatively linked systems take on coherent behavior, they forego to some degree the process-based mode of classical correlation which lies in the signal transmissions that structure differentiated, semiotic agents into complex networks. Like the agreement of low-energy-state bosons in a coherent condensate, the coordination of a group into a unitary super-organism requires members to drop below their individuated levels of volition and to pool their intelligence into a higher level of organization that circles around to implicitly direct the actions of individuals, like the entailments that guide a metaphor. Simultaneously below and above the individual level, de-localized intelligence produces a form and degree of synchrony that could not be achieved through semiotic means.

Closure Loops

The ergodic unity of quantum coherence finds a classical analogy in a formally divergent and evolving world, bound by semiotic and entropic entanglements that bring different agents into various degrees of interconnectedness through their niche-constructing activities. The reversibility that reigns at the quantum level but is revoked under the influence of thermodynamics replays itself under the time-dependent constraints of classicality through the recursions of complexity such as feedback loops, reciprocal causality, and semantic closure loops—all of which express the same self-referencing principle. Agents enmeshed in ecological interactions affect a similar form of closure in relation to each other; for example, the bison that deplete their pastures at the same time reseed them in their droppings. The stampede-inducing presence of predators, which promote the herd's health by culling it, can turn ungulate hooves into plows that tear up densely packed grasses, aerate the soil, and churn under the next generation of seedlings—autocatalysis writ large.

Intelligent Selection

The scale-invariant patterns that replicate themselves through layers of complexity cohere life in all its forms into a vast, intricately knit system. In the intelligent threads filling and ordering that structure are preserved principles which are not only prior to life, but prior even to manifestation. Like a metaphor that contracts the semantic space between disparate domains to correlate them into a new form of meaning, chemical catalysis favors specific outcomes that remove the system from equilibrium, imposing dynamical directionality that is a classical analog of the primordial contraction of profligate potential into a single selected state. The waves that structure the evolving possibilities of a potential system send their amplified echoes into the material realm, wherein even the most complex information is transported on the crests and troughs of waves and, in much more complex form, through living, excitable media. The non-locality of sub-physical unity resurfaces in complex, integrated systems as long-range correlations, which bring individual aspects of a system into coordinated agreement and channels the intelligence they individually embody to a higher, collective level. This higher level engages with its lowest-level constituents in the reciprocal closure of system identity.

Accepting the tenets of Quantum Darwinism leads to a picture of a universe in which the conditions that evolution imposes on its subjects are self-similar iterations at ever-new levels, rooted in the emergence of objectivity from immeasurability. A reservoir of potential comprised of energetically interchangeable but causally distinct states is reduced in response to environmental exigencies, which act like measuring constraints. Whether degeneracy is supplied by an ensemble of possible eigenstates; parallel branches of quantum exploration; a population of genomes; potential phenotypic expressions of a single genotype; or possible interpretations of a sign, the system summons its internal resources of intelligence to creatively complement its embedding context, offering to the impersonal forces of selection an array of prototypes to engage with, select, and hone. Across scales, the improbable compression of potential into biological functionality disposes natural outcomes toward novelty, complexity, adaptiveness, and sentience. From the evolution of metabolism to its serendipitous invasion by parasitic nucleotides; to the advent of biologically active proteins out of the nearly infinite possible combinations; to the coherence within individuals as well as among them when they coalesce into a synchronized collective state; to the metaphorically grounded feats of the thinking mind, the same general principles and patterns hold sway, acting as law-like habits of nature which apparently incline toward the marvelous.

Conscious Evolution

Implicit from the most basic levels of organization, the emergent features that unfold at higher levels of evolution through the progression of complexity conserve the universal tenets of intelligence through the countless forms that explicate them. Likewise, the principles that bind complexity into autonomous unities are predicted in a more essential form in life's inanimate prelude and preserved throughout all of the evolutionary translations that populate the universe with diversity. The crucial quality preserved among the living is the potency of the quantum realm, which silently propagates its own internal evolution while suspended in an unmeasured state. Obdurate to description, the unitary chrysalis shelters superimposed ripples of immaterial potential that are gravid with subtle seeds of physicality. When stirred by the suggestion of ambient conditions, the equilibrated balance breaks toward expression to infiltrate physicality with otherworldly potential under the guise of form.

Arising with the irruption of immeasurability into classicality is the coeval collaboration between intelligent mentality and material expression. In the space of coherence fostered by the harmonization between those two foundational but diametric poles, and the chaos that proliferates along their dualistic boundaries, the high order of manifestation emerges. Balancing each other to support the evolution of the universe in all its contours and dimensions, each of these dichotomous expressions of unitary origin insinuates its influence on the other's probabilities in a fractal relationship that is at once non-differentiable in the vast complexity of its details, and utterly simple in its condensed presentation of the unifying logic underlying the proliferation of those details. Logic, in turn, localizes itself with the imposition of boundary conditions, which imply the parameters according to which the system's intelligence functions. When those boundaries are contextually aligned, the logic of the system is in concert with that of its environment and becomes a locus of coherence.

In life's preservation of coherence, pre-classical unity is enshrined in the very heart of physicality. The acausal intelligence endemic to that realm expresses itself according to the parameters that circumscribe it into form. It is this mental quality, expressed through iconic, experiential "firstness," that is foundational, as the reservoir of potential, to all expression that follows. It is an intrinsic feature of the universe, as acknowledged by Hameroff and Penrose's Orch OR theory. However, while the Orch OR model situates the first flash of proto-consciousness in the collapse of an extended state of coherence, the role of consciousness as embedding context makes any type of decoherence a spatiotemporal object of primitive experience, rather than the origin of consciousness itself. Decoherence is a localized explication of non-local potential relative to ambient conditions, collapsed into an "interpretation" that presents as matter. Rooted in the relationships that tie a pointer state to its surroundings and ultimately comprise the classical world of relativity, decoherence is a primordial epistemology. It is also an incipient act of self-organization and self-declaration as the selected state assumes a particulate identity, whose symbol-level sheath derives from a nonlocal precedent that is universal in potential. Life's ability to access and exploit this other-dimensional potential is at once the source of its intelligence and the driver of its evolution. Drawing omnipresent immateriality up through the roots and branches of manifestation, intelligence supplies agency to its conscious substrate through localized form. The incursion of the immaterial into formality is attended by the order as well as the chaos of its boundary conditions, offering these as binary correlates to its own intrinsic coherence, which is the initial condition for the whole unfolding evolution that follows. The natural order unfolds from the subjective interiors of all things, thus validating and necessitating perspectives of all levels, depths, capacities, and ranges.

Deftly, expansively, and creatively informing the living radiations of agency, the guiding hand of intelligence binds complexity across all scales through an incalculable order of logic. Like an orderly cloak enshrouding fundamental quantum unruliness, materiality comes to life with the assiduously preserved touch of that immeasurable realm. In lifting molecular activity above the level of mere constraint to that of directionality and control, the phenomenon of life points beyond material and efficient levels of causality to a more ethereal source of potency through which it mobilizes complex formal arrangements to engage conversantly in material, energetic, and semiotic exchange with the very environment it distinguishes itself from. The entanglements that draw a system outward from its internally referencing state of coherence are semantic bonds that index the functional properties of a system to its environment. Reflective of the inner coherence of the system, those intelligent and causally compelling relational features effect a synchronous resonance between interacting unities, which constructs a system at a higher level. Like the degenerate plurality of superimposed quantum states, the multitudes of diverse and unique perspectives that vivify the biosphere in an ongoing, simultaneous concrescence are all participants in a single, unitary, universal evolution. Rising and falling to inner fluctuations of form and dynamics that carry on simultaneously, the biosphere as a whole—and even the universe itself—evolves within a state of unperturbed coherence.

7

Universal Origins

"Observer and observed are merging and interpenetrating aspects of one whole, unanalyzable, indivisible reality; there is flux of events and processes rather than building blocks."
—David Bohm

Underneath classical discreetness is the unabridged unity from which materiality arises. Within this unchartable sea of unvitiated firstness, the indices and symbols of classicality have no place. Suggestive secondness and assimilating thirdness only arise with the division that materializes upon the threshold of classicality. Penetrating the emergent realm of space and time in forking tributaries, naked firstness makes questing, channel-like inroads in the domain of relativity by obeying its foundational laws, which govern, among other regularities, the exchange of semiotic tokens. Rule-based transactions of sign processes affix relations between entities, allowing recurrent interactions to nucleate into complexity. The regularity of universal laws provides a firm underlay for the formally causal relations that accrue into systems, correlated by the self-similarity that preserves those systems' integrity through every evolutionary transformation. Unpredictable spontaneity saturates this orderliness, shaping and coloring it, expressing that measureless pulse of vitality and awareness through which the universe of signs takes on meaning. "Wherever chance-spontaneity is found, there, in the same proportion, feeling exists," says Peirce. "In fact, chance is but the outward aspect of that which within itself is feeling."[dclxxxvi]

In order to survive in the alien environment of physicality, the etheric explorer cloaks itself with an exterior that conforms to the specifications of the conditions it encounters by expressing the tenets of universal laws. Generating functionality through the material trappings that can safely house tender iconicity's emergence is a primordial act of intelligence. Decoherence yields an eigenstate and the foundational epistemic cut, which allows substance-less quality to don the mantle of materiality with the crossing of potential into existence. The shift from a holistic state of unitary evolution to the partiality of manifestation pries open a chasm between the discreet expressions of the self-same ground of being. This gap is partially bridged by the horizontal domain crossing of semiosis, which discriminately highlights limited, environmentally conditioned states of the sender by instantiating some corollary of these in the receiver.

The split between potential and expression that leads to classicality is a primordial symmetry break, or phase transition, between balanced equilibrium and the bifurcating prongs of possibility. Every phase change that transpires throughout classically situated systems is predicated on this initial one. Like all of its successors, the original phase change preserves essential features of its prior state, even as formal relations become wholly re-ordered. The original preserved content is of the intangible realm prior to material, efficient, and formal causes. Beneath every subsequent symmetry break, this immeasurable self-similarity persists as a fundamentally unbreakable symmetry. From phase transition to nondeterministic phase transition, this underlying, ineffable component is preserved throughout classical expression as the internal, subjective state inherited from the quantum realm. Even in the agentless desert of the abiotic physiosphere, subjectivity is still primary. "This is all one can find in the simple substance," reasons Leibniz about his concept of the ultimately indivisible unity, the monad, "that is, perceptions and their changes. It is also in this alone that all the internal actions of simple substances can consist."[dclxxxvii] This inheritance preserved from the original, pre-classical source domain channels spontaneity, and therefore subjective, iconic feeling, throughout classical manifestation.

Transforming through endless guises of form and interaction, evolution is the "movement of consciousness veiled by morphology."[dclxxxviii] It spreads horizontally to create coherence in space, as well as propagating vertically to affect coherence in time.[dclxxxix] While the former drives diversification without necessarily deepening complexity at the individual level, the latter functions along the critical seam between opposing tendencies to support the saltatory leaps of emergence that transform prior dynamics into new levels of complexity. Variously recoded in subtle isomorphisms throughout the permutations of evolution, the immaterial potential suffusing the universal panoply of forms is the original metaphor that expresses itself in terms of material embodiment.

An Insider's Perspective

Sharing the feature of observer dependence, both the quantum and classical realms are predicated on subjectivity, with objectivity arising as a secondary property. Even the most elemental unities distinguish between a subjective interiority and a symbol-level exterior, as described by Leibniz, "The monad's natural changes come from an internal principle, since no external cause can influence it internally."[dcxc] With the constituting fabric of classicality comprised of a "harmony of monads,"[dcxci] semiosis acts as a crucial ordering principle which entails an experiential element, however infinitesimal. Even at the most fundamental levels, semiosis necessitates a border crossing not just between entities, but between material and semantic realms, so that experience may be assimilated as information based on the iconic resonance by which it induces a change in the receiver.[dcxcii]

The current theory of particle physics understands commerce among elementary particles to be regulated by forces and mediated by quantized, indexical force carriers: bosons, which include photons, gluons, and W and Z particles. Each of these fundamental currencies only communicates itself relative to a particle's ability to "interpret" its message in terms of the force it represents. In communion with some unobservable interiority harbored by a particle that directs its responsiveness, forces shape the interactions of their miniscule hosts while simultaneously crafting the entire universe, with no apparent discrimination between their activities' effects at either scale. These omnipresent operators maintain a nonlocal presence not only throughout all of space, but even within the non-spatial interiors of the particles they order.

Fundamental forces act through and in relation to elementary particles as a primitive stratum of subjectivity, playing on an intangible manifold of responsiveness that is cloaked beneath the symbol level of outward presentation. By supporting and structuring semiotic interactions between particles, the forces foster horizontal domain crossing at its most elemental by invoking internal symmetry as its basis. The strong and weak nuclear forces are posited by the standard model to compel effects by interacting with an unobservable aspect of symmetry within receptive particles that is not definable in terms of their interactions with the external world of time and space, but only in relation to the force acting on them. Inferable but not measurable, isospin represents an invariant internal symmetry between the particles—nucleons in the case of the strong force, and doublet pairs of quarks for the weak force—that is recognizable to each respective force, unlike the particles' measurable attributes such as charge and mass. A force's effect is therefore dependent on the properties of its particulate receiver being in some way complementary, or isomorphic, to it. Although its ability to express is subject-dependent, the repeated pattern of the force's influence over all of its constituent particles resolves at a higher, statistically measurable level as objectivity.

Symmetry and Self-Similarity

As the primary signifier among charged particles, the photon occupies a keystone niche at the interface of physics, semiosis, and the epistemic cut. Far from equilibrium with its surroundings, the luminous quantum courier sets and holds the ceiling for the speed at which its "messages" can be transferred between fermionic correspondents, and among interacting entities in the universe at large. This primary arbiter of semiosis is also that of special relativity, which ties the motions of objects to the speed of light as a primary reference frame and measure of how motion diverts itself through space relative to time. By setting the typical message-carrying parameters of semiosis, and providing a subject-dependent point of bifurcation in an entity's relationship to space versus time, light places both epistemic divisiveness, as well as domain-crossing communication at the foundation of physics.[dcxciii] Moving at a constant speed in relation to every reference frame it encounters, light is a fundament of self-similarity. In its utter lack of discrimination among any possible state of position or motion, light announces the deep symmetry that underlies and connects every object it could conceivably interact with by validating every potential perspective.[dcxciv] With its motion fully diverted through space, light is timeless from its own perspective until it encounters an observer to "measure" it. Its farthest reach essentially demarcates an observer-dependent event horizon bounding the universe. As pervasive emissaries of electromagnetism, photons—both real and virtual—penetrate even the darkest depths. Light's ubiquity analogously recalls the ergodicity, or tendency of a system to pass through every potential state, of unitary evolution.

With the invariance of symmetry as its central tenet, relativity is eminently egalitarian, and predicated on the equal application of universal laws throughout space and time. Embodying and enforcing fundamental, universal self-similarity with indiscriminate consistency along with light, is gravity, which likewise makes no distinctions in its relations to objects as it warps space and time around each and all in identical proportion. Drawing a dividing line between the domains of quantum coherence and classical manifestation, gravity's invariant application secures every possible perspective while preserving self-similarity across scales to create a universe that conserves its most essential founding conditions. Leaving an imprint of its influence on the clumps of matter unevenly distributed throughout space, gravity has preserved the essence of the universe in its earliest form, when its own non-uniformity was a central driver of evolution. This early stage of asymmetry, in turn, was reflective of the underlying condition of quantum unruliness, whose probabilistic logic—the "lumpiness of chance"[dcxcv]—made uniformity essentially impossible. The non-uniformity so crucial to the ability of the universe to evolve remains preserved at the vastest of scales in a cosmos unevenly filled with concentrations of matter, interspersed with void reaches of space, to create a great, galactic lattice.[dcxcvi]

As the dynamic, mutable medium of symmetry, spacetime is the embodiment of gravity.[dcxcvii] Its relationship with embedded objects is reciprocal, defining spatial relations between objects while itself being molded by their mass and state of acceleration. The perfect preservation of symmetry between the medium and its contents provides a basis for the enactment of objectivity through subjective channels: both sides of the epistemic cut, observer and observed, are commensurable.[dcxcviii] Like heteroclinic points of stability amid chaos, the symmetry on either side of the epistemic cut provides a balanced point of unity between inner and outer. This mirror-like invariance provides the basis for the entrée of an observer-dependent universe through environmentally induced decoherence, which draws partiality from unity and enjoins observer and observed in a mutual coupling.[dcxcix] Far from being a one-way incursion of the environment into unitary seclusion, decoherence requires that the potential object also has some sort of effect on its observer before it can partake in objective reality.[dcc] When this microscopic influence is reflected back on the unitary system by an "observing" environment, it returns amplified into collapse-inducing disproportionality by the numerous different points and angles of observation populating the macroscopic system that it had subtly interacted with. This principle of mutual affectation is preserved in a scale-invariant way up the rungs of complexity, so that even the structural coupling affected between living agents and their environments is symmetrical from the perspective of either entity.[dcci]

Symmetry provides the basis for domain-crossing, which implicitly pays tribute to the relative nature of all manifestation by expressing the same underlying condition in ever-varying terms, each being validated by the same unifying universal constraints. Universal laws condense into patterned interactions among the localized bodies that are variously acted on by those general principles according to their physical properties. Since any individual entity is limited in its scope for expressing those laws, it is restricted to a metaphor-like selectiveness, highlighting particular aspects out of totality in a specific way that corresponds to efficient causality, while discounting the rest as unexpressed potential. Solidly anchored in the symmetric universality of physical laws, the milieu of interacting particles at the base of the universe all represent different "interpretations" of the same founding conditions, which bestir from materiality the dynamical heterogeneity that propels the universe-creating coevolution of relational structures to complexity.

In a seeming paradox, the deep symmetry underlying all physical and temporal interactions is only able to express itself as evolutionary when it is broken. Symmetry breaks disrupt the uniformity of equilibrium and so accompany differentiation. The forces of the universe themselves are posited to represent symmetrical fissures that were "frozen out" at various stages of universal development as its symmetry dropped, to develop as universal "habits." Deeply persistent beneath apparent symmetry breaks, however, lies hidden a deeper symmetry that is unaffected by the topological deviations that overcome thermodynamic invariance to foster evolution. With universal constants such as the speed of light impartially preserved, each reference frame—from atoms to stars to frogs—represents a distinct, and distinctly valid, "interpretation" of universal laws.

Temporal Symmetry

The perspective-validating quality of gravity-based spatial symmetry has an analog in the temporal invariance of the immeasurable experience of "now" that precedes even iconic representation, and is the conscious context that enables meaning. Immobile despite its ever-fluctuating, directional contents, the presence at the center of the critical suspension between past and future is reflective of a non-dynamical invariance amidst the spatially and temporally contingent movements of a restless universe. Everything in its span of perception happens relative to it, like an obstacle that briefly splits a river's flow.

Just as light provides an indication of the symmetry with which the universe regards its innumerable reference frames, it is also descriptive of the temporal symmetry that lends continuity to the ongoing, irreversible dynamics of the universe. Relativity's light cones are descriptive constructs that illustrate the close commingling of ergodicity with its apparent antithesis, directionality. The structure of the light cone model, with past and future cones concentrating on a singular point with neither temporal duration nor spatial extension, known as a spacetime event, indicates that all events that can have a causal influence on a spacetime event lie in either its past or future.[dccii] From the plunge into classicality onward, every spacetime event is attended by a constriction of potential, even as it likewise heralds a complementary expansion that will converge on a new space-time event. Encapsulated in a spacetime event is a three-part summary, comprised of position, which is historically conditioned; perception, which arises from the deep root of unchangeableness that unites the outward flow of events into experience; and potential, which strives for the future while patterning itself on the past. The converging past cone is composed entirely of light rays that encounter the event throughout their histories, while the future cone radiates toward all possible outcomes propagating from that single event. The expansive hypothetical emanations of the future light cone suggest some degree of eventual entanglement of the future light cone with those of every other spacetime event. Conversely, the span of light funneling into each event-point is laden with a history of entanglements from its overlap with all other past light cones. The majority of past entanglements are not expressed in the collapse of the cone into the focal singularity, just as future entanglements are largely potential, differentiated by probabilistic biases that arise from the interactions of their spacetime events.

Untouched by the adjacency that enhanced probabilities impose on potential, the distant future and past entanglements of the light cones are echoes of the equiprobable wander-space of ergodicity, from which probabilities are extracted and resolved into actualities. The borderless fields that coalesce from the fanning extremities of the cones into unified clouds of past and future appear, in the historical cone, as a haze of initial conditions from which any given space-time event derives, while its prospective counterpart takes on the aspect of final cause; or the attractor toward which events' trajectories evolve. Symmetrical to each other in their potential causal impacts on their spacetime referent, the two self-similar oceans of entanglement, alpha and omega, are separated by a spatiotemporal firmament that is bridged at myriads of junctures of contraction into an infinite swarm of singular space-time events. Those spatially and temporally spanless markers of the passage of potential into expression, of future into past, highlight that experiential quality whose contemporaneous presence is relatively localized by the events that describe it, but remains outside of the measurable parameters of space and time. Husserl ponders the enigma of the causal power of perspective on events,

> "It is inherent in the essence that anything whatever which exists in reality but is not yet actually experienced can become given and that this means that the thing in question belongs to the undetermined but determinable horizon of my experiential actuality at the particular time. This horizon, however, is the correlate of the components of indeterminateness essentially attached to experiences of physical things themselves."[dcciii]

The First Light Cone

Utterly polar to the non-replicable distinctness of internal experience is the universal principle of gravity, which equally and indiscriminately imposes its effect on all matter—although at tiny scales this is virtually negligible. Among physical causes, gravity alone can warp or tilt light cones, thus disrupting their distributional uniformity and altering the probability structures that emanate from affected points.[dcciv] This supremely objective, unbiased force has the same effect from the outside of an event as the most profoundly subjective feature of the event's interiority; its intentionality. Unlike gravity, volitional change can't be accounted for in terms of universal laws; and yet in its potential for shifting the scope of probable outcomes emanating from a spacetime event, the internal and subjective is symmetrical with the external and objective, although they lie on the opposing manifolds of semantic and physical. The two universal, but diametrically opposite features of subjective interiority and objective gravity are brought together in a reciprocally causal circle by gravity-based models of decoherence, wherein potential presents itself to gravity as a range of possible states. By destabilizing the poorly fitted outliers, gravity facilitates the selection of a single state, which in turn, exerts an influence on gravity upon manifestation.

For the coherent unitary evolution prior to an emergent particle, with no past light cone, the future light cone would exist as the pure potential of quantum "feelers," reaching beyond their unitary bounds to interrogate their environment as forking branches of computation. Prior to the primordial moment of manifestation, all light cones would be only in the form of entangled future possibility. No disruptive discontinuity would yet puncture the space-time fabric, altering its homogeneity by contracting its possibility into expression. However, like the commingling extremes of light cones whose expanded scope embraces potential, the questioning probes of coherent states could be envisioned as entangling with each other into a complex composite of potential states as a community of proto-particles. Although not embodied and therefore not wholly localized, the complex of potential would be a subjective observer of the decoherence of the very states that collectively project it.

The dancing wavelengths of potential states would interact, with favored states communally stabilizing each other by amplifying their crests into relative localization, as in quantum beating, in a purposeful choreography ordered by long-range entanglements and internal computations. Regions amplified by the cross-fertilization of many potential systems' wave-described evolutions would ripen with the invitation of localization. At a critical threshold of complexity, the stability of the unitary pre-systems would be overwhelmed by the juxtaposing instability introduced by gravity's interaction with outlying states. As the precarious balance between the opposing tendencies tipped away from equilibrium, the fracture in symmetry would precipitate a spontaneous collapse of entwined evolutions into expressed eigenstates.

The eminently malleable excitable medium of space, supporting an array of crests and troughs of varying amplitudes and frequencies, would facilitate the localization of undifferentiated potential from high-information, but untransmissible noise into decipherable particle-messages. These would largely reflect probable and well-fitted states and so promulgate the directional and sustained progression of material expression, like a primitive catalyst injecting directionality into process.

With the abrupt contraction of potential into limited forms, dissipating potential would flood outward as luminous, photonic entropy riding wave-crests. Rippling through space carrying reports of the collapse, radiant waves of the primordial message-bearers would awaken other evolutionary seeds of potential already on the cusp of particulate form, propagating a self-sustaining, nonlinear chain reaction of expressive efflorescence in an undulating sprint across space. As light begot light in every direction, each incipient particle would be framed by a halo of vivifying luminosity—a nascent light cone describing its material evolution. With the "observation" that propelled the material-making distinction imagined as a mingling of vibrations that harmonized the ripples of potential into localized criticality, particle parthenogenesis becomes a process of distinction affected by domain crossing. It becomes the foundation of a universe in which observer and observed are bound together into a system wherein the properties of every object are determined by their relationships with all other objects.[dccv]

Without past light cones to converge on the definitive event of classical emergence, universal genesis appears acausal. However, it is drawn forward by potential that lies in the future—a final cause that draws manifestation forward by doubling as an initial condition that has not yet been temporally sequestered from its outcome. As the system shifts from pluripotency to singular expression, the circular course of quantum time straightens out into the irreversibility of classical time. The implacable onrush of directionality is pierced by the still center of situated perspective that it is superimposed upon and which necessitates that time exist in a non-equilibrated balance of continuous symmetry breaking between past and future. With the perception of temporal progression suspended in the timeless point of coherence at the branch of bifurcation that is self-similar among all entities, conscious potential is always prior to the phase change a bifurcation ushers in. This unaffected quiescence is the pervasive point of union between the diverging forks of broken symmetry and the evolutionary shift they represent. The dimensionless present moment at the heart of the confluence between past and future is, like a metaphor, a portal and a turning point that conducts spontaneous potential through a new unfolding that is a counterpart of the closure of a previous expansion. Open-ended evolution plays out in reference to the singular stabilizing point that is a discontinuity in the spacetime flow through which embodied perspective peers, and around which the tides of chaos vacillate as interchanging crests and troughs of expansion and contraction.

The universe's abundant population of situated perspectives, which embody that timeless and spaceless state, encompasses countless vantages from which order can be correlated out of chaos. Ranging around that central, still point beyond spatiotemporal parameters, salient and even peripheral events are catalyzed into a probabilistically biased, irreversible flow. As a point of both unity and divergence between converging past and expanding future, that stillness holds both thesis and antithesis; as a convergent point that joins the two together into irreducible logic, it is a synthesis. Insofar as that point is impregnable to the flow it observes, it is forever in a state of unitary evolution, always ensconced in its own promise of potential which it feeds into the stream that flows past it. The "within of form" is the dimensionless space that opens endlessly within situated entities as the non-dynamical, subjective potential that begets temporal interactions through intelligence-guided actions, and is compelled to these by the powerful draws of material and efficient causes. The subjective state at the turning point between space and time is qualitatively different from, but the progenitor of, that which apprehends those physical and epistemological fundaments as separate. It is a depth of consciousness, orthogonal to the horizontal rush of events, which spills into them intelligently as the energetic spontaneity that arranges the formal causes within and around the situated subject that experiences them. About this silently witnessing observer to all temporal change, St. Augustine says, "Eternity is supreme over time because it is a never-ending present."[dccvi] It is the point—spaceless, timeless, and omnipresent—from which flows the potential that is both wellspring and leading edge of evolution.

Implicate and Explicate

Light cones depict discreet, consecutive spacetime events, which entail that proximate and subsequent events' cones would overlap heavily. From a more distant perspective, however, the rapid succession of transitions, with their significant causal overlap, would resemble a flow rather than discreet changes. David Bohm contemplated just such a flow and labeled it "holomovement." While providing an observable, measurable appearance of change and differentiation through the fractured lens of time, the permutations of holomovement actually overlie one continuous, indefinable, immeasurable movement that Bohm refers to as the "implicate order." The inexpressible implicate order offers glimpses of its churning essence via the perceptible explicate order. The action of a force on a particle connects the two orders at their point of interchange, with the law-like regularity of the force "bind[ing] together a certain set of the elements of the implicate order in such a way that they contribute to a common explicate end."[dccvii] This "common end" is only an approximation of the underlying, high-dimensional implicate whole, whose vast entirety is indescribable, and yields low-dimensional measurability only as a secondary product.[dccviii] Although the implicate order is entirely and holistically present at every moment, it is, like a holograph, expressed consecutively at its surface.

Bohm's implicate order paints reality in colors extracted from the quantum mechanical palette. Cast in an observer-like role, the implicate order "sees" the underlying movements animating the world as a series of interpenetrating elements in different degrees of enfoldment all present together, recalling the superposition of unitary evolution. The explicit form that is projected to the viewable surface of the whole enfolded order is determined by relationships of co-present elements much like the selection of a pointer state, or the emergence of new properties that are not predictable from the lower levels of the system that generate them.^{dccix} With the explicate order refracted into countless interacting sub-orders that reveal only glimpses of the underlying intelligence of the whole, presentable forms belie the undisrupted totality that they partially unfold. The relationship between implicate and explicate is reciprocally causal, with the whole exerting a downward influence on its explicated representatives while forming itself out of the activities of their agency.

Encompassing more than mere outer surfaces, the explicate order consists of layers whose increasing subtlety Bohm likens to a series of increasingly finely woven nets. Each level constitutes information that gives form to the activity of each subsequently less subtle level, invoking the poles of mind and matter which information conjoins.^{dccx} The interweave of the layers leaves no unbridgeable gap, and the movement across them—perhaps soliton-like ripples—supplies the experience of mind. Through enfoldment, each relatively autonomous level partakes to its own degree in the overarching whole, while drawing from the property of mind the relative autonomy and stability of microcosmic wholeness that is capable of "interact[ing] autonomously with other wholeness" to foster evolution.^{dccxi}

Although the qualities of mind and matter are invoked to describe the unceasing turmoil of unfoldment and enfoldment that comprises the saga of evolution, the deeper reality that Bohm envisions is beyond either. An effort to understand the origin of force, he avers, "would take us to a deeper, more comprehensive, and more inward level of relative autonomy which, however, would also have its implicate and explicate orders and a correspondingly deeper and more inward force of necessity that would bring about their transformation into each other."^{dccxii} Leibniz concurs, "A soul can read in itself only what is distinctly represented there; it cannot unfold all its folds at once, because they go to infinity."^{dccxiii}

The unity of the implicate order supports Teilhard de Chardin's contention that "the stuff of the universe cannot divide itself but, as a kind of gigantic 'atom,' it forms in its totality…the only real indivisible."^{dccxiv} From the perspectives above and below the levels of individuality, the universe is not fragmented, but unitary. In order to manifest, wholeness relatively divides itself, creating domains to be crossed and whorls of turbulence to be navigated. The regularities that describe the universal laws of nature come from the most fundamental levels of interaction, acting as forces on localized, discreet, individualized concentrations of the whole. The situated condition and dissipative natures of these "monads" provide nucleating surfaces for evolution, which locally conditions the interactions of universal forces. Relativity is the context for the unfolding experience of localization, mediated by the intelligent actions of mind as a liaison of the underlying consciousness that knits—and at higher cognitive levels, perceives the unity among—seemingly disparate elements into coherent, flowing patterns. Attaining such a level of self-perception entails the long, patient, and iterative unfoldment of ever-new expressions of localized intelligence that overlap each other's spheres of experience, perception, and niche significantly in their lateral spread, while their vertical progression foreshadows the emergence of self-similar processes of expression at increasingly refined levels until a change in degree has become a change in kind.

Universal Theories

Bohm's vision of physical motions as small systemic perturbations on top of an infinitely turbulent background corresponds with the concept of zero-point energy—the emptiness of space that he asserts is not a vacuum but rather a plenum. Instead of an unfilled void, Bohm conceives of space as a ground state of infinitude, composed of an enormous store of energy whose perpetual changeability samples constantly from an inexhaustible plentitude of potential states with every miniscule tremor.[dccxv] Erupting along the surface of a seemingly uniform medium, fluctuations become more erratic and less deterministic at increasingly finer scales of resolution and fill even the tiniest regions with discontinuity.[dccxvi] This noisy layer of perpetual background fluctuations has been implicated by more than one theorist as the source material of the universe itself, with particles being merely conserved excitations on top of the vacuum/ plenum. Much like an optimal level of noise within a channel of communication, a cell, or a flock supports the free flow of information, the variable amplitudes of fluctuations of the dynamic zero-point medium provide a basis for atomic stability.[dccxvii]

Somewhere between the zero-point energy of empty space and elementary particles is a gap that quantum physics deems acausal. One prevailing explanation regarding the architecture of space-time and its material artefacts is string theory, which posits a strange world of evolving space-time configurations. Its active ingredients are strings which vibrate at different frequencies, producing different particles. The size and shape of the extra dimensions it introduces into physics have a significant impact on the strings' vibrational patterns, and so on particle properties. To accommodate the higher dimensions introduced by string theory, space contorts itself into evolvable Calibi-Yau (CY) geometries, with energetic oscillations emanating from their porous topologies in patterns that correspond to elementary particles. Empty space itself is a low-vibrational pattern in a CY, according to Laszlo.[dccxviii] As they vibrate through space, strings are able to probe the fine structures of their miniscule environments, but only down to a certain size. Any energy infused into the strings beyond that necessary to probe the Planck length causes the string to grow in size, decreasing its short-term sensitivity.[dccxix] "String theory sets a lower limit to physically accessible distance scales," confirming Bohm's assertion that detailed analyzability is only possible in the classical realm.[dccxx]

Another theory that lends a phantasmal cloak to quantum imperceptibility posits a string net liquid as a form of universal scaffolding. Instead of turning to Landau symmetry breaking as an evolutionary mechanism like many models do, string net theory considers phase transitions that are topological, requiring many symmetrically identical, degenerate ground states.[dccxxi] The topological order is expressed in the random-seeming movements of electrons that, from a higher perspective, are actually coordinated into orderly "dances" which follow particular sets of rules.[dccxxii] In this quantum choreography, each particle is dancing with every other in an organized way that seeks the lowest local energy state to create topological order through patterns of quantum fluctuations that are linked into long-range entanglements.

Superimposed upon each other, strings can take on different dynamical configurations, or "dance" patterns that represent distinctive ground states, and therefore different states of matter. Elementary particles appear in this model, not as building blocks, but as whirl-pool like defects, or excitations above a deeper, lattice-like ground state corresponding to empty space.

The concept of dancing electrons strongly resonated with Wolfgang Pauli. "At the quantum level," he envisaged, "all of nature engages in an abstract dance," whose performers fall under the categories of symmetrical or asymmetrical according to the pattern of their dance.[dccxxiii] Bohm, too, was compelled by the imagery of an electron choreography, orchestrated by the "mind-like quality animating matter,"[dccxxiv] or the aspect that is amenable to information as an organizational principle. This non-material aspect of a particle is its wave function, which exerts physically real influence through its role as a transmitter of information.[dccxxv] Conducting semantic potential through their wave functions, particles actively engage with each other through their movements, which are conditioned by mass, charge, spin, and energy. Bohm's hypothetical ensemble of electrons coordinates its members' motions through the mechanism of "active information," or the ability of an electron to draw information not only from its own wave aspect, but from a common pool of information within a system—including other electrons, and even distant features of the environment as well—that transcends any simplistic, efficiently causal explanation of prior relationships between particles. Such nonlocal information sharing would coordinate individual particles' movements as though they were conjoined as parts of a larger whole. Pauli likewise concluded that "the underlying pattern of the whole dance has a profound effect on behavior of each individual particle."[dccxxvi]

Contrary to quantum mechanics, which presents itself as the lowest describable level of reality, Bohm believes the gap between potential and quantum manifestation is filled with "hidden variables." Similarly offering an alternative to the acausality of quantum mechanics is the "causal indeterminism" of subquantum kinetics, yet another theory of the unmeasurable realm.[dccxxvii] Drawing from the systems theory model of open, dissipative systems which function far from equilibrium, subquantum kinetics envisions a deeper layer of manifestation, whose activities can be described as nonlinear reaction-diffusion processes. Set against an absolute, etheric backdrop of space that is at odds with Einstein's relativistic frame, the actors of subquantum kinetics are "etherons" that constantly interact and transmute to produce macroscopic concentration gradients of the three reacting etheric substrates.[dccxxviii] Spinning in the heart of a critical concentration gradient is a pair of mutually complementary vortices, which respectively conduct opposite reacting etheron species inward and outward from the core of the reaction center, according to their concentrations. The gradient is maintained by nonlinear reactions which convert one species to another; not only perpetuating the spin-inducing gradient, but stabilizing the pattern, which constitutes a subatomic particle, as a dissipative system sustained by a through-flow of reactants. Particles, according to Paul LaViolette, are essentially "space ordering states" whose "explicit order does not prevent chaotic fluctuations from emerging; instead, it dominates their effect."[dccxxix]

Subquantum kinetics agrees with Bohm—and Louis de Broglie—that the observer-dependent duality between particle and wave of quantum physics is actually a continuous particle-wave system—a "wavicle," in Bohm's terminology. Radiating outward from the central gyre of concentrated reactivity are concentric rings of reactant gradients, alternating in polarity and reduced in amplitude relative to the core to generate a Turing wave pattern. The local maximum at the core of the reaction system is the particle, surrounded by a halo of diminishing reaction gradients that are its wave aspect. Within the alternating polarity of the circumambient rings is the force potential which, when enacted, expresses itself as a force that moves the particle, either attractively or repulsively, in response to the field potentials of other particles. On this view, force is a derived, efficient cause emanating from a fundamental, formally arranged, material cause. Etheric Reactions pervade apparently empty space, devoid of matter and field, generating spontaneous, non-critical fluctuations of electric and gravitational potential that fail to sustain their form, but correspond to the concept of zero-point energy.[dccxxx]

Holographic Space

While the exact natures of matter, space, and their relationship invite further investigation, Merlau-Ponty sagely advises that "we must seek space and its content together." Matter, rather than being distinct from space, may actually constitute an ordered configuration of space. Bohm suggests that "what we perceive through the senses as empty space is actually the plenum, which is the ground for the existence of everything, including ourselves."[dccxxxi] A concentrated region of order within an otherwise tumultuous—but on average, homogeneous—sea of fluctuating potential, matter affects its embedding matrix in a reciprocally causal relationship, whether by warping its shape or altering concentration gradients of ethereal reactants. Like the wave aspect of a particle, the pliant fabric of space acts like an excitable medium to propagate information about the macroscopic structures it supports and whose movements it guides—or in John Wheeler's phrasing, "space-time tells matter how to move; matter tells space-time how to curve" as they interact with each other through the gravitational field, the large-scale architect of the universe.[dccxxxii]

According to Rupert Sheldrake's theory of morphic resonance, informational potential underlies form, carried in the invisible wave-aspect shared by all matter, and connects unfolding events that are spatially and temporally separated through a non-local resonance founded on their essential similarity. The fields that implicitly inform and structure the behavior of responsive particles remain operant even in the context of a more highly ordered structure. Just as the form of the structure enfolds the forms of its particles, the global field it generates likewise incorporates and subsumes lower-level wave aspects by its distinctive expression of downwardly causal logic, without being reducible to them. At the same time as it constrains the probabilities of lower levels, the global level of logic invites a new level of possibility. Perhaps encoded in the ripples of space surrounding an event, such as a chemical reaction or organismal development, Sheldrake posits that morphic resonance facilitates future iterations of the same type of event by nonlocally structuring the surrounding informational field, which guides its progression to a given type of end. The abstract, informational counterpart of physicality is the hidden executor of the formal efficiency that conducts the motions of particles into pattern and order toward a final cause.

Closing the feedback loop between the fundamental domains of material form and non-material information, matter informs its surrounding field while being guided by it. Under Sheldrake's theory, evolution does not merely operate on individual structures, but also on the pervasive wave-aspects that complement condensed form. The interface between informational wave and expressive particle is a region of chaos where two dichotomous tendencies, one subtle and the other measurable, conjoin into an emergent expression. Like the entailments of a metaphor, this silent chaos nonlinearly transfers structuring information across distinct domains, guiding the coupled evolution within each in relation to the other. As the immaterial wave directs the observable particle, it adjusts its subtle oscillatory patterns in response to changes that its symbol-level emissary undergoes over time.

Much like the "kinetic melody" of neural activation that connotes mental experience, the whorls that objects imprint on the embedding matrix of space affect the nature of their interactions. In its role of excitable medium, space carries the waves of innumerable entities at all levels of complexity, from the nearly imperceptible patterns of particles to the residual ripples of supernovae. Some of the most fundamental perturbations that matter imposes upon presumably chaotic space are the orderly fluctuations of subatomic wave functions. The information they enfold is locally expressed but nonlocal in potential, theoretically smeared throughout space, although their actual expression is probabilistically delimited. By locally ordering space, matter introduces regularity to randomness and structure to homogeneity much like a signal against a conductive backdrop of noise.

Propagating information about materially sourced disturbances through its fluid-like body, space encodes complex informational interference patterns in its conductive texture. The potential information carried in the perturbance-born ripples of space is analogous to the concentric patterns of a holograph, which, when subjected to a particular kind of radiant energy, become something far different from mere patterns of disturbance by taking on meaning. No clear, decipherable correspondence exists between the concentric patterns that adorn an unilluminated holographic plate like raindrops—or the ripples of order that propagate through an excitable medium—and the epistemic content of their encoded objects. The patterns themselves are empty of meaning until they are translated into a narrative flow that is illuminated by a particular kind of interpreting structure. Only in the self-created context of orderly disturbance does the object acquire significance, with "the interference pattern at each region…relevant to whole structure, and each region of structure…relevant to the whole of the interference pattern."[dccxxxiii]

Like the universe itself, holographic images possess a huge capacity for information storage. Just as the informational content of a holographic surface can change based on the angle at which two lasers strike the film, a perspective-dependent universe—such one in which a probability wave will not collapse for an observer in motion relative to a stationary observer who does see it collapse[dccxxxiv]—similarly encodes reams of information from many facets and angles. The holographic effect predicted by string theory describes physics that takes place on a bounding surface, which is of lower dimensionality than its interiority, like an event horizon. In revealing the aspects of itself that can be translated through a lower-dimensional surface, the higher-level interior would not be constrained to a particular form, but would rather be compelled to express through many forms whose interactions would only disclose a correlated pattern from a higher level of evaluation. Bohm compares this condition of indeterminate outcome to images of a three-dimensional object—he uses the example of a fish tank—taken from different angles. Although the images are not identical, they correlate into a pattern that indicates a single referent. The singular truth condition underlying the outward variances of universal expression is the unitive feature preserved across all domains that allows the inferences that are foundational to the "logic of nature."

Each point in space, including "all the matter in our bodies, from the very first, enfolds the universe in some way."[dccxxxv] The potential for meaning arises in the unfolding flow of the whole that distills essential aspects of itself into discreet parts, which in turn provide the syntax-like structure for the uncontainable meaning that expresses through them in coordinated and purposive patterns of interaction. In arranging themselves relative each other, the multitudes of mutually engaged, many-formed microcosms establish their own frames of reference through which they construct meaning by correlating order from chaos, as though flowing the universal energies through their limited forms as part of a grand narrative that unfolds through many chapters and many versions. External discreetness masks underlying continuity, which is implied through semiotic exchanges that perception renders into a flow. The inner and outer are connected but conjugated like order and entropy, momentum and position, energy and matter.

Cosmic Origins

While space functions like an excitable medium in its wave-propagating and structural capacities, it takes on the role of a conduit in conducting the effects of forces. From a classical perspective, with its empirical emphasis, the fields of forces are states of space rather than matter, although they can interact with matter and share energy and momentum. Quantum mechanics accounts for them as a physical reality, while subquantum kinetics places them on a continuum between the distinct order of an irreversible process, and the randomly active equilibrium of unincorporated space. In their intervening position between matter and milieu, force fields occupy a quasi-material informational realm, and function as efficient causes to subvert the randomness of equilibrium by biasing probabilities in favor of the orderly manifestation of matter. By effectively muting the large majority of spurious interactional possibilities, forces essentially ordain some degree of order by enforcing the law-like regularity that funnels stochastic events toward characteristic endpoints.

Forces, which are indistinguishable at a macroscopic level in the formlessness of equilibrium, manifest themselves when symmetries break. According to the pictures presented by inflationary models of the universe surrounding its earliest moments, the strong, weak, and electromagnetic forces were all originally unified, making the universe much more symmetrical than its current configuration. Gravity had not yet distinguished itself from quantum mechanics.[dccxxxvi] After its first 10^{-35} seconds of existence, the forces fractured apart—following the even earlier fracture of space and time, which became differentiated after Planck time (10^{-43} seconds). In these early symmetry breaks, Jantsch sees evidence that "structuring forces were made available for a simultaneous evolution at microscopic and macroscopic extremes."[dccxxxvii]

The Planck dimension which concentrates space, time, and forces into an almost infinitely proximate starting point from which they diverge with expansion is the lower limit that string theory allows the universe to be compressed into.[dccxxxviii] In this way, the need for an infinitely dense singularity as a primordial point is ameliorated, potentially allowing a prehistory to the universe before it reached the critical Planck length that allowed it to expand and time to move forward.[21] In this scenario, the inflationary bang would have been an event in a preexisting universe, without having necessarily created it.[dccxxxix] Such an episode of outward expansion would have invoked an aspect of gravity not normally attributed to it: a power of repulsion that invaded space with a shattering outbreath of matter and energy racing away from a generative point.[dccxl]

In contrast to the unimaginable magnitudes of energy released by the posited Big Bang, the "immense 'sea' of energy" that comprises Bohm's holomovement reduces the momentous, universe-creating explosion to "actually just a 'little ripple.'"[dccxli] While Bohm doesn't dispute the

---

[21] At around Planck time, time starts to curve around into space and calculations begin moving forward in time instead of hitting zero.

general tenets of the Big Bang and the subsequent 14-billion-years-long unfoldment of the universe, LaViolette does. His theory of subquantum kinetics sees the possibility of a less dramatic emergence of matter onto the universal stage. In his model, matter can arise spontaneously and probabilistically from the noisy fluctuations of the ongoing, randomly distributed reactions that fill the volume of pre-existing space.[dccxlii] The stochastic seethe of short-lived reactions assumed by subquantum kinetics would fail to nucleate into matter as long as the regions of space they occupy remain subcritical, meaning that the concentration of the primary reactant G is not drawn down enough by a sustained transmutation cycle that turns it into the other two reactants, X and Y, to allow a nascent particle to fend off the twin destroyers of gradient diffusion and the erosion by ambient noise in order gain enough size to stabilize.[dccxliii] Critical and protective pockets of space, or "G-wells" develop along with matter, functioning like gravity, as the "G-ons" are consumed at the core of the particle to drive the through-flowing reactions that make it an open, autonomous, dissipative system. The depth of the gravity well corresponds to the mass of the particle that can be stabilized, and recruits random fluctuations of reactant concentrations as the source material for matter.[dccxliv]

Like fertile oases in the desert of space, critical regions foster the spontaneous, autogenic growth of matter, and allow the proliferation of particles to eventually grow into stars and even galaxies, all with correspondingly deep gravity-wells. According to this paradigm, the G-ons responsible for the gravitational effect should actually have a repulsive, or at least neutral effect outside of critical conditions. Only when a well forms around an emergent particle does its attractive potential dominate by virtue of its local depletion, allowing materialization to proceed more rapidly as the well is drawn down. Accordingly, the rate of materialization increases exponentially, propelled by its own success to produce a variation on the Big Bang—dramatically slower, but also more organic than the conventional conception of the universal advent—with over 99 percent of the matter in the universe arising within the past 10 to 15 billion years, and the overall age of the universe being pushed back billions if not trillions of years. According to the autogenic model of manifestation, the "physical world is continuously, ongoingly generated and sustained."[dccxlv] Or, as Teilhard intuited, "Matter is in a constant state of genesis of becoming."[dccxlvi]

Although details of the universe's origin, destiny, and span resist simple explanations, the observer-dependent view from within bounds it with an event horizon that extends as far as its earliest photons have traveled. Outside of this boundary, which, according to inflationary models, the universe generates through an accelerating expansion of space which outstrips even the speed of light, is the unknowable and empyrean region which no observation penetrates. From the tension between totality and its observable limitations arises relativity, leaving no room within the confines of space and time for an absolute. Instead, an analogy of absoluteness arises out of the unitary wholeness of potential that divides itself only relatively, generating perspectives that are necessarily partial because their situated condition turns each frame of reference toward other partial manifestations rather than the totality that gives rise to them.

Division and Reunion Through Spacetime

Universal materialization is founded on the paradoxical incursion of undivided unity into multifarious relativity. Foundational to all formal variations of expression is an unconditioned, universal essence whose nature is absolute. Husserl describes the transcendence of that self-contained quality, "No being which is presented and legitimated in consciousness by appearances, is necessary to the being of consciousness itself."[dccxlvii] Radiating from this all-pervasive center is not only a universe of staggering expanse, but also ongoing expansions of potential within localized bounds, particularly among those rare forms that are able to willfully, consciously express that potential.

In order to manifest a measurable outer form, the substance-less experiencer of iconicity that underlies the quantum and physical worlds deploys the activities of intelligence. Primary of these is the process of distinction, through which the singular state of potential preserves its essential nature despite all of its outwardly variant expressions, providing the foundation for evolution. Beginning with the primordial experience of quantum collapse, potential is measured against its surroundings. Leibniz expounds on the encounter between inner infinitude and outer constraint:

> "Since the nature of the monad is representative, nothing can limit it to represent only a part of things. However, it is true that this representation is only confused as to the detail of the whole universe, and can only be distinct for a small portion of things…otherwise each monad would be a divinity. Monads are limited, not as to their objects, but with respect to the modifications of their knowledge of them."[dccxlviii]

Although object-free in its undivided state, when compressed into the circumscribing horizons of physicality, the ethereal substrate fractures into the dimensions of potential, intentionality, and subjective perspective as it assumes an objective, symbol-level mantle that is describable in terms of universal regularities. The relations it establishes within and among the objects and events that it encounters in its spatiotemporal guise constitute the constraints and contingencies in terms of which evolution proceeds. As fundamental "monads," or irreducible unities, conjoin themselves into structures of increasingly integrated complexity, their relational scope with the environment that they shape and construct simultaneously deepens and broadens.

Underlying the localization of simpler components into increasingly complex form is the non-local counterpart of agent-centered intelligence, whose broad, generalized strokes manifest as universal principles. Forces mediate physical interactions by acting on particles that are capable to differing degrees of reflecting their immaterial attributes. In their generalized applicability, these universal principles lay a steadying hand on processes of hierarchical integration at all scales. Their expressive potential is revealed at the fertile boundary conditions imposed by the discreetness of the unities they interact with. As incorporeal enforcers of fundamental levels of differentiation, forces set the parameters within which intelligence operates as a localized phenomenon. In their adherence to the most fundamental guiding aspects of the universe, all differentiated forms, including living agents, are localized expressions of nonlocal principles. Within the invariant parameters imposed by forces, subjectivity and its semantic entanglements generate an intricate maze of contingency through which flows "the within, consciousness, and spontaneity," which "are three expressions of the same thing."[dccxlix] As different "interpretations" of universal principles interact through material forms that variously convey a singular underlying state, the entire universe evolves as a "self-supported structure of relationships."[dccl]

Common to all manifest multifariousness is the context of spacetime, which supplies the fundamental basis of distinction. Irreversibly propagating outward from the primordial division between potential and expression, the numerous unitary forms that differentially reflect their common origin engage each other in the interactions that support evolution. Although invariant in its application to its constituents, the span of spacetime across all scales makes it profoundly nonlinear and far from equilibrium in its effects. The delineations it places between entities are property-dependent and so impartial, making this approximation of objectivity a solid, counterbalancing foundation for subjectivity, with its arbitrary but non-random distinctions. As executers of universal logic, forces function within the divisions held in place by space-time to set the terms of distinction and interaction among situated entities at the most fundamental levels. As Jantsch observes, the evolution of macrocosmos is based on self-consistency.[dccli]

To the extent that it is synonymous with gravity, spacetime is also the basis, not only of all differentiation, but of universal union as well. "Because it contains and engenders consciousness, spacetime is necessarily *of a convergent nature*," says Teilhard.[dcclii] Its fabric invites fractal branches of potential to extend beyond unified singularity in questioning probes, and entangles them into a directional, non-linear maze, supported by habits, from which they do not readily withdraw. Countering the divisive radiations wrought by the sundering medium of relativity is the intelligent concourse among entities, which reframes spacetime as a unifying context through which "reality emerg[es] through a self-birth, constituted by the living reunion of reflective particles."[dccliii] The firstness that supplies subjective inwardness to situated embodiment embeds within its derivative vehicle of secondness which, in turn, conveys symbol-level thirdness as an observable means of ameliorating the foundational divide between fractionated aspects of totality. The divide between localized carriers of icon is the primal ancestor of the fundamental "breach from one mind to another," which William James sees as "perhaps the greatest breach in nature."[dccliv] Of the semiotic triad, unconditioned icon is the purest reflection of the totality it signifies, as well as the sole route to unity with that totality, and therefore affords resolution to the foundational "breach" of nature.

In the semiotically effected "living reunion of reflective particles" is the enactment of *logos*, which collects or draws together fractionated facets of a singular whole according to their materially conditioned affinity for each other. Uniting within the context of a higher-level engagement that fosters the proliferation of formal diversity, this "living reunion" ultimately leads to the evolution of forms capable of supporting explicit, sentient volition. At once discreet—that is, internally integrated—while simultaneously incorporated with their surroundings at every level, all intelligence-hewn forms participate in the universal cultivation of complexity. As complexity evolves, its scope deepens and broadens to encompass the intelligence of the lower hierarchical levels that comprise it. By gathering the capacities of lower levels within its global mantle, the intelligent system which envelopes them centers their functionality within itself and draws its description from their emergently rendered capacities. The constraints placed on the lower hierarchical tiers from above are restrictions of their developmental potential, like the refining branches at the tip of the fractal tree.[dcclv] At the same time, that potential is channeled upward to a new level of expansion, concentrating within the microcosm of the system's evolution a reenactment of the unfolding potential throughout the evolving universe as a whole. "If we include in our nature everything that it expresses," declares Leibniz, "nothing is supernatural to it, for our nature extends everywhere."[dcclvi]

While an initial condition to all subsequent evolution, the universe-begetting incursion of limitless, subjective sensation into the selective sieve of classicality is at the same time a primordial final cause. Drawing quantum probability into measureable form like an attractor ensnaring diverging trajectories, the universe constructs itself out of material that is ultimately immeasurable, and modeled according to the "primordial image" of the semantic domain that is prior to time's dynamics. With initial conditions and final cause fluctuating as conjugate variables into each other's roles, the acausal impetus to manifestation is only ever partially fulfilled because of the infinitude of potential relative to expression. That potential continually fuels evolution by pushing it toward more complex arrangements of attractors, or more inclusive final causes. Harmonizing the spontaneous chaos of unmitigated potential with its stabilizing rhythms, intelligence exercises both local and nonlocal sway over the dance of manifestation, efficiently arranging material and formal causes into platforms that favor its expansion. As complexity grows and facilitates the unfolding expression of agent-centered volition and mentality, the initial condition reveals itself as an ultimate final cause: that of explicating conscious awareness.

Intelligent Evolution

Just as fundamental as change in form over time, the evolution of a universe constructed through the integral relations of all its parts is dependent on the adaptation of interactional properties among its elements, and, crucially, of mental properties to more complex patterns of information. The mutually embedded contexts of informational wave-aspect and expressive particle-aspect that constitute a physical unity entail that epistemic evolution accompanies distinction of form. Accordingly, even the most foundational instance of formal differentiation is predicated on an informational distinction. The degeneracy of potential states within a coherent evolution is only disrupted when the causal variations in some are amplified relative to a contextual condition, which serves as a structural reference point. This amplification of potential into form and corresponding, externally referenced meaning, is in direct contrast to the object-free wave patterns evolving in the unitary chrysalis prior to manifestation. Whereas in the latter, the self-correlated fluctuations promote isolated, internal cohesion, after reduction transpires, the selected state takes on meaning by correlating with the external referent it is "measured" against. Perspective, while sourced in the inwardness of subjectivity, is a cooperative property between measurer and measured that is context-dependent. The alignment of situated potential with its surroundings constitutes what Leibniz calls the "modifications of knowledge."

Upon the fracture of the ineffable synchronic unity into the diachronic unfolding of materiality, the wave-states that survive into manifestation face the challenge of criticality that demands a balance between synchrony—which, if complete, would reduce all states into unity—and noise, which if excessive, dissolves into incoherence. Only in the critical balance of these opposites does meaning emerge and evolve. In their complementary superposition lies the basis for unity between the inner and outer duality assumed upon manifestation: "It may prove to be that 'psyche' and 'matter' are actually same phenomenon, one observed from 'within' and the other from 'without.'"[dcclvii]

As small-scale observers of a vast environment, situated entities relate to their environment by the arbitrary "measurements" they make of its local properties, scaled to their dimensions and scope of salience. Internally, these are experienced as the Umwelt or lifeworld of the subject. Externally, they are reflected in the interactions of systems with their surroundings as material, efficient, and formal causes. Therefore, even as the observable interactions of particles follow law-like behavior, they must internally invoke some degree of interpretation—which, although it may asymptotically approach zero, is never completely absent. Due to the limitations of manifestation, which impart attributes, conscripted forms are compelled to derive meaning from relatedness; by referencing or being about something else. This necessity of interconnection is the origin of the propagative directionality of semiosis, the semantic driver of physical evolution. All classical activity transpires within the epistemic bounds of semiosis; experienced, relayed and interpreted by innumerable situated perspectives actively engaged in enacting the "logic of nature." Rooted in relationships, epistemic structures are interpretive and emergent semantic catalysts which guide the probabilities of an entity's actions and interactions. Over the course of evolution, individualized, embodied "measurers" change and develop in scope, nature, and depth of the semantic leading edge by which they structure their interactions. Accordingly, the signs they respond to and their interpretations shift and alter, imparting on the selfsame context a multitude of perspective-dependent meanings.

At the most fundamental levels of matter, epistemology and interpretation are essentially undifferentiated from material and efficient causes. As causes and effects of the properties that a system acquires through situating constraints, both of these forms of causation become entrained into formally, dynamically efficacious structures that channel potential from plasticity to the narrow and irreversible specifications of expression. Functioning within the parameters of physical law, formal and final causes work in tandem to localize the effects of nonlocal forces in emergent ways that outwardly express intentional states. Thirdness is the guide that skirts the boundary conditions of semiotic interchange, working with the "insideness" of situated entities to manifest their latent semantic landscapes. In the directed passing from intention to expression is teleology, or purpose.

Reliant as it is on non-local principles for expression, intelligence is only a relatively localized property. Rooted in a domain that is neither spatial nor temporal, mind has access to "unconditioned perception that is a direct response to order in universal flux," and that is the "single source" of "intelligence and material processes" according to Bohm.[dcclviii] Individual carriers of subjectively concentrated intelligence sample from all available totality, delimited by perspective and salience to a probabilistically proscribed, localized portion of that totality. Outside of those bounds is the inscrutable region of free energy, guarded by surprisal which negatively enjoins all localized expressions of sentience in its impenetrability. Intimately entangled with observable aspects of its immediate surroundings, subjective intelligence includes the environmental aspects embraced by the inner faculty of Umwelt by building its epistemic structures in relation to these. Inner and outer potentialities are balanced, or measured against each other through mutual modifications between agent and environment. Emerging from that harmonizing balance is meaning as a particular interpretation of the local interaction of universal principles with specific boundary conditions.

Nonlocal intelligence is a passive, indiscriminate, coherent substrate within which the living turbulence of chaos can germinate into order and evolution. Such immediacy within a "universe of experience," which demands the vibrant participation of all of its members, is in line with the idea of "cosmic ecology" advocated by Freeman Dyson, in which life and intelligence are on equal footing with general relativity as factors influencing the evolution of the universe.[dcclix] Penrose similarly concludes that "a scientific worldview which does not profoundly come to terms with [consciousness] can have no serious pretensions of completeness." This is simply because "consciousness is part of our universe." [dcclx]

Within the overlapping contours of the two as-yet theoretically non-unified realms of quantum physics and relativity is ample space for a vitally conscious "cosmic ecology" to flourish. Across the presentable differences of these disparate levels of description is preserved a deep self-similarity rooted in the "undivided wholeness"[dcclxi] that each realm views from different scales of perspective. The view from within the subjective interior of all matter is presented by quantum mechanics, which brings from a unified substratum the entanglements that bind classicality's measurable effects into a single, unitary universe. Relativity's external view of the surfaces of events likewise proclaims the irreducible interdependence of every object, force, and parameter of a singular universe that evolves as a unified totality rather than just at the level of its parts.[dcclxii] Both viewpoints derive from subjectivity as the underlying basis for objectivity—implying that objectivity is, at best, relative.[dcclxiii]

Whereas relativity divides its subjective components according to their reference frames, quantum mechanics divides itself in response to the frames of sufficiently powerful observers. The unifying principle in which all of the different perspectives of the universe is held is the ultimate context for all intelligence and meaning—that of consciousness. As physicist Amit Goswami summarizes, "Consciousness is not a phenomenon; all else is a phenomenon in consciousness."[dcclxiv] Complete understanding of the physical universe and its metaphysical basis is beyond the scope of minds hemmed in by cognitive and perceptual limitations. The route available to the seeker of universal knowledge therefore lies "not only [in] resolving its mysteries, but also by immersing…within them."[dcclxv] As Teilhard concludes, "To perceive cosmic energy 'at the fount' we must, if there is a *within* of things, go down into the internal or radial zone of spiritual attractions."[dcclxvi]

Ground State

Classicality is a turning point that that places the consciousness it channels under the sway of non-local forces and their localized expressions. Physicality is the differentiable vehicle that conducts intelligence, the active counterpart of consciousness, through its formal and epistemic evolutions. Through the medium of materiality, witnessing mind acts as the coherent point of convergence between the chaotic upwelling of spontaneous potential and the complex order that cogently expresses it. The narrow band of critical agreement between the two is a "rent" in physical nature through which perceptive mentality peers as through a window. In its passage through the decohering gateway of manifestation, consciousness localizes within form by preserving the immeasurable essence of that unitary state as the complementary adversaries of perception and its looming shadow, surprisal.

While potential evolves in relation to subjectivity's objects, it is ultimately rooted in the inchoate realm below the level of expression from which it derives. This singular substrate is the source of the symmetry underlying multiplicity, passively validating each reference frame to support the integrative work of domain crossing and the creativity of interpretation, through which intelligence unfolds into an ever-turning kaleidoscope of perspective and potential. Although void of quality in its unexpressed state, the infinite divisibility of pure consciousness holds latent the potential for all forms, as well as all entropy that obscures its wholeness from the limited view of conditioned perception while providing both fuel and traction to the irreversibility of evolution.

In the formless nether world suffusing all matter, patterns—which only manifest as intelligible information in the presence of interpreting minds—are only implicit shudderings of the imagination of a fundamentally conscious universe. Beneath the outer extension of symbol-level physicality and even the activating interior of subjective intelligence, lies an immaterial, uncaused core. Like the hollow heart of a strange attractor which turns away the direct approach of any orbiting function, the numinous interior of materiality is described by endless iterations of physical expression. From this non-differentiable core, which is paradoxically common to all differentiated forms, emanates the incredible diversity of universal articulation, woven into a seamless unity by the logic of nature which never changes except in form. The evolutionary radiation unfurling from the immeasurable state reflects, in its "present reality…the mysterious center of our centers, the Omega."[dcclxvii]

In their coeval integration, each aspect of the unitary universal evolution provides every other aspect a context in which to function, making the system as a whole ultimately self-referencing. The resultant complexity that emerges provides a focal point for the convergence of physical expression and its intangible meaning. Mediated by forces, physical activities center the locus of meaning upon themselves, connecting the measurable domain with that beyond measure by creating acts of meaning. The organic arising of the symbol level that is the emblem of thirdness imbues outer expression with semantic content that is internally, subjectively instantiated. As turning points between two otherwise unbridgeable domains, all semiotically engaged manifestations within this "universe of signs" are essentially enacted metaphors. With a bodily frame of reference and access to the huge volumes of potential information afforded by its ability to shift perspectives, metaphor acts by recognition, perceiving a facet of itself in a differently oriented reference frame and creating a complex system founded on that self-reference. This deep and subtle act of recognition turns all substance into symbol, and clothes the transformative capacity of thirdness in classical, material form. From the first, matter is an interpretation, as well as invitation to further interpretation. It is the effect of an incalculable cause.

8

The Conscious Cornerstone

"And in the mind the will to grow and generate, and in the will the power, and in the power the light, and in the light its forth-driving spirit; which maketh again a will to generate a twig, a bud, a branch, out of the tree like itself."
—Jacob Boehme

"Our sensory experience turns out to be a floating condensation on a swarm of the undefinable."
—Teilhard de Chardin

Whether a seething yet methodically choreographed mass of string-like superposition, or a reaction-diffusion system of transmuting reactants amid a sea of ethereal flux, the immeasurable, sub-Planck universe dwells far below the level of classical observation. Measurement, space, and time coil back upon themselves when classical methods are employed to probe this mysterious underworld's inscrutable weft. While no measurable attributes exist in "that primeval chaos in which there [is] no regularity," it is not, as Peirce intuits, a "blank zero."[dcclxviii] Rather, this is the realm of the pure experience underlying icon, compensating for its lack of appreciable form or content in its "intensity of consciousness feeling" and "endless and innumerable diversity of chance utterly unlimited." Viewing the same condition from the opposite end of the spectrum—extinction, rather than inception—Husserl is similarly inclined to identify "absolute consciousness" as the only "residuum after the annihilation of the world."[dcclxix]

This object-free region of sheer, unabridged awareness is anathema to the theories, empirical measurements, and proofs that uncover and describe the workings of classicality. Although speculatively intruded upon by the oblique and abstract theoretical probes born of rationality, the region prior to manifestation has traditionally been the province of the sacred, the source of illumination accessed by mystics of every tradition. The undivided totipotency that exists at inaccessibly tiny scales, while at the same time underlying the whole of the cosmos like a silent ocean is, like the Buddhist notion of Atman, pure existential Self that is at once smaller than small and larger than large.

Awareness of the realm of undivided consciousness, so we are told by its explorers, means access to the very foundation of the universe's creative potential. Jacob Boehme describes the physical world, or the "external generating," as an "unbeginning birth."[dcclxx] The "visible world," he tells us, is a "procreation, or extern birth; or as a substance expressed, or spoken forth, from both the internal and spiritual worlds."[dcclxxi] In her revelatory encounter with divinity, Julian of Norwich held in her hand a "little thing the size of a hazelnut" that represented all manifestation. From this experience, she intuited three elemental, describable truths about the object that she held: that God made it, sustains it, and loves it. However, its essence, as infused by its maker, keeper, and lover, could not be known without uniting with it.[dcclxxii] It is omnipresent, at once concentrated in all localized entities, while simultaneously nonlocal. The second and third universes of experience float like mere bubbles of expression atop an ocean that cannot be charted, only merged with.

Ancient Philosophies

Over the course of its ages-long mystical quests, India has spawned several schools of philosophy, including the rationalistic system of *Samkhya*. With its clear division between *purusha* and *prakriti*, or spirit and primordial, undifferentiated nature, Samkhya proposes a model of evolution propelled by three natural qualities, the *gunas*. Prakriti is the uncaused root-cause, while purusha is transcendent; neither cause nor effect.[dcclxxiii] Like Aristotelian proto-matter or Einsteinian mass-energy, gunas are both substance and energy that support evolutionary changes, while themselves being conserved as underlying principles that infuse matter with potency.[dcclxxiv] While their natural state in relation to each other is one of equilibrium balanced by tension, the three gunas—*tamas, rajas,* and *sattva,* corresponding to inertia, change, and mind—become unbalanced and pushed far from equilibrium when purusha expresses a magnetic attraction to sattva, the quality it most closely resembles. This union is of neither necessity nor causality, but rather a resonance between ineffable consciousness and the mind-like property it inspires. "Divine nature is not our possession but is joined to us," says Emmanuel Swedenborg.[dcclxxv] Through the active medium of rajas, or dynamical change, the resonance of activated intelligence echoes all the way to the material level of tamas, allowing mind to move physicality.

Disrupting the balanced tension of natural properties with its polarizing incursion, spirit acts as the acausal propagator of disequilibrium, inciting the oscillations that can mark a system's descent into chaos, or conversely, its ascent to order. As the passive source of consciousness, purusha is the supernatural context in which intelligent manifestation unfolds; it is the subjective witness to the experience that is intelligently orchestrated through the medium of sattva. In turn, intelligence, its engine rajas, and its vehicle tamas, express themselves locally as differentiated "infinitesimals;" non-locally as field-like "all-pervasives;" and abstractly as principles.[dcclxxvi] Leibniz expounds on this idea:

> "Each portion of matter is not only divisible to infinity, as the ancients have recognized, but is also actually subdivided without end, each part divided into parts having some motion of their own; otherwise, it would be impossible for each portion of matter to express the whole universe."[dcclxxvii]

The first offspring of the prakriti-purusha union is *mahat*, a state of cosmic consciousness in which there is no differentiation between subject and object. Although Samkhya predates the triune Hindu godhead[22], the concept of mahat aligns closely with the Son aspect of the Christian trinity. As Paramahansa Yogananda explains, "Christ Consciousness, present in all specks of creation, is the only undifferentiated, pure reflection of the Absolute, God the Father."[dcclxxviii] This primordial descendant of the marriage between consciousness and nature is the "firstborn of all creation," "through [Whom] all things were made."[dcclxxix] All evolution proceeds from this primary ground state of perfect consciousness reflected through the lucid prism of pristine intelligence. "Divinity as source is the father, Divinity as human [or manifest] is the Son, and Divinity as emanating is the Holy Spirit.," explains Swedenborg.[dcclxxx]

Permeating every aspect of a universe whose parameters are astonishingly fine-tuned to produce conditions conducive to life, the "only-begotten Son" of Christ Consciousness provides a coherent matrix that knits its many-formed progeny into a singular, nondeterministic pattern. However, as Yoganada explains, this sentient intelligence is "not the active element in creation," but rather serves an advisory role to "the distinct, active, differentiated conscious intelligence that brings into manifestation all particles of vibratory creation." This is "the Holy Ghost, which is imbued with the only begotten Son...As Cosmic Vibration, all things are one; but when Cosmic Vibration becomes frozen into matter, it becomes many." The sacred sound Aum is the Hindu counterpart to the Holy Ghost, carrier of the primordial syllables through which manifestation is exhaled: "A stands for *akara*, or creative vibration; u for *ukara*, preservative vibration; and m for *makara*, the vibratory power of dissolution."[dcclxxxi]

Within the dualistic framework of Samkhya, the parent substances are of two different natures, one absolute and the other relative; both

---

[22] The Hindu godhead consists of Brahma the Creator, Vishnu the Preserver, and Shiva the Destroyer.

complete and balanced in themselves. When pure consciousness couples with the intelligence-harboring capacity of sattva, nature becomes unbalanced; immaculately impregnated with potential and incomplete in her partial, relative capacity to express absolute consciousness. Tripartite prakriti then occupies the creative role of Holy Ghost through the endlessly varied modifications of the gunas across all scales of time and space. These scale-free iterations are phenomenal expressions of a deep, numinous ubeity that is "nonspatially present in all space and nontemporally present in all time."[dcclxxxii] The parents' aspects are preserved throughout manifestation as all-pervasive *akasa*, or ether, and *buddhi,* or intellect, and are not reducible to the infinite gradations of form that arise in the criticality of their confluence.

The Kabbala, with its emphasis on the esoteric significance of natural numbers, charts the original creative unfoldment through the enumerations of the *Sephira*.[23] Represented numerically, the Sephira represent the hidden ideas of creation lying latent, or "equiponderated," in the first emanation, *Kether*, which corresponds to the number one and contains all creative potential.[dcclxxxiii] Prior to Kether is *Ain*, the primal negatively existent essence whose undefinable being becomes positively extant when defined, or measured. Ain—along with *Ain Soph*, or limitless expansion, and *Ain Soph Aur*, or illimitable light—are the three veils of the "negative," or non-manifest, existences that formulate the hidden ideas of the Sephira not yet called into being.[dcclxxxiv] Drawn out from negative potential through the mystical enumerations, order affords its ethereal forebear a positive, or expressed existence. As evolution proceeds from the empyrean essence signified by zero into a positive, definable mode of being, it takes on a distinct form: "The limitless ocean of negative light does not proceed from a center, but it concentrates on a center, which is the number one of the manifested Sephiroth."[dcclxxxv] Boehme similarly refers to the primordial contraction into single-pointedness: "In creation, the inbreath preceded the outbreath that gave rise to space and all else."[dcclxxxvi] This is a form accessible to mystical

---

[23] Likewise, the term *Samkhya* refers to an enumeration, as the system lays out a sequential lineage of "evolutes" that comprise the principles of the manifest universe.

perception, as attested to by Julian of Norwich, who learns that God is in all things when she sees the whole godhead concentrated on single point.[dcclxxxvii]

Due to its singular nature, Kether can neither be multiplied by itself nor divided. Its only route to succession is through self-reflection.[dcclxxxviii] Once it manifests a reflection, Kether establishes a vibration between the poles of changeless zero and the second Sepiroth, *Chokmah*, which denotes wisdom. Singularity oscillates between conscious potential and intelligent expression to generate the creative vibration, which spills outward into cosmic fecundity with the all-pervasive silent witness tucked metaphysically into the concealing folds of microcosmic expression. The vehicle that enables the creative unfoldment of potential and wisdom through evolutionary expression—much like the Father Creator whose reflected intelligence perfuses the created Son—is the third Sephiroth, known as *Binah*. This feminine emanate embodies understanding, and enables the creative power of Chokmah, thereby completing the first trinity of the Sephira.

Duality

Primordial creation is described in the Kabbala Denudata in monad-like dimensions of simplicity:

"The beings created by the infinite Deity through the First Adam were all spiritual beings, viz they were simple, shining acts, being one in themselves, partaking of a being that may be thought of as the midpoint of a sphere, and partaking of a life that may be imagined as a sphere emitting rays."[dcclxxxix]

With its potency concentrated on a single point, the unfilled midpoint is a balancing, stabilizing center for all of its emanations. Swedenborg describes this central source, "Everything is alive or responsive to life where the heart is at work through the channels it extends from itself."[dccxc] Vacuous and self-contained within its own center, consciousness explores beyond physically imposed boundaries by radiating questing streams of potential to carry its inexhaustible flow outward. The ray-like emissions bespeak the "emanation" that Swedenborg describes as the function of the Holy Ghost, which is synonymous with the creative vibration Aum, gravid with pure but passive universal intelligence.

Guiding the purposive play of manifestation are the dual domains of consciousness and intelligence, as described by Swedenborg: "An action…gets its reality from love and its quality from intelligence."[dccxci] Love, the conscious but inactive and formless divine essence, utilizes intelligence, whose first function is to make distinctions, as a vehicle: "Love has neither sensory nor active life apart from discernment…love leads discernment into all functions of the mind." From the primordial apportionment of absolute unity into infinite articulation through the intelligent refractions of the Logos, the divisions at the fount of evolution are antithetical to the undisrupted symmetry they impose measurement upon. Of this dichotomy, Peirce notes, "Consciousness, the feeling of the passing instant, has… no room for rationality."[dccxcii] Only by conjoining, or "marrying itself to"[dccxciii] the structure-building capacity of "divine wisdom," which attenuates energy's free dissipation into channels that grow into habits of intelligent structure, can pure Being engage in the activities of creation, at once ontological and epistemological.

The foundational distinction that apparently divides the primordial substance into many discreet forms is not only a lateral division between formally and epistemically distinguished fragments of totality, but also a vertical demarcation between the ethereal and the embodied. Although the former underlies as well as transcends its solid-seeming yet ephemeral expression, the two domains are of fundamentally different natures. The consequence is described in the Gospel of Phillip, verse 21b, "Flesh and blood cannot inherit the kingdom, what it shall not inherit is that which is upon all of us." Because presentable materiality and conscious ineffability are of distinctly different natures, "correspondence [is] the means of union between spiritual and physical things."[dccxciv] From this correspondence arise all of the scales of manifestation that weave themselves into a universe of experience.

Even below the measurable level of classicality, the constituent and constructive qualities of divine love and divine wisdom are creatively engaged in corresponding activities, according to LaViolette's interpretation of the subquantum realm. In the Neolithic myths of Egypt and the Near East, he reads an encoded documentation of an ether-based physics of creation. Revisited in the Egyptian myth of Atum and Osiris, the Sumerian myth of An and Ki, and the Babylonian myth of Tiamet and Marduk is a theme of separation between earth and sky. This refrain, he contends, resounds as a reference to the "condition of disparity between two interrelated species" of etherons that bifurcate themselves into alternating patterns of dominance that comprise the Turing wave-pattern that he believes to constitute a particle.[dccxcv] Carl Jung likewise detects a dualism operant in manifestation: "The spirit (pneuma) has, since time immemorial, stood in opposition to the body. It is turbulent air, in contrast to the earth."[dccxcvi] Swedenborg agrees, envisioning the spiritual and earthly spiraling in opposition to each other.[dccxcvii]

The distinction between noumenon and its phenomenal shroud features a tension that Wolfgang Pauli deemed paramount in classicality—a tension not between matter and dynamics, "but between *indestructability* (energy) and *time*."[dccxcviii] The creative vibration, imbued with the intelligence of the Son, is the Word, or Logos that is "in the Beginning." Like a two-faced Janus, the Word translates at the interface of infinitude and constraint, looking to the domain of indestructibility from which pours the illimitable energy sustaining the universe, and at the same time gazing upon the time-dependent individuation of that same energy. In that Word, according to St. Augustine, "all is uttered at one and the same time, yet eternally. If this were not so, [the] Word would be subject to time and change."[dccxcix] The "never-ending present" that is eternity becomes enfolded into space-time strictures through the intelligent agency of the primordial Word, to be "spoken" through the divine "mouthpieces" of manifestation in a realm "in which each word has a beginning and an ending—far, far different from your Word, our Lord, who abides in himself forever."[dccc] Pointing to the mysterious depths contained in that Word that are beyond mere expression, Fr.

Thomas Keating instructs us that "the original language is silence. Everything else is a poor translation."[dccci] Incomplete in their measurements, words are insufficient conveyances of the ineffable substance of reality.

Many From One

Prior to the body as the primary frame of reference is the precursor to pure, self-existent icon that is not dependent on anything else for its being, and whose "immediate character [is] feeling." Through its activating union with intelligence, consciousness allows some degree of determinateness to impinge on its freedom in exchange for the ability to manifest. The price exacted for expression in the constrictive realm of physicality is the relinquishment of unlimited degrees of disembodied freedom, dissipated as the entropic feedstock that fuels the very process of evolution through which that freedom is regained. Rumi describes the cruel capture of his evanescent spirit, compelled to forgo ideational liberty in favor of the fleshly chains of incarnation:

"I used to roam among souls, like a hart's flight, winglessly roaming and celestially happy…Suddenly, suddenly I was summoned by love to prepare for a journey to the temple of suffering. I cried desperately; I begged and pleaded and shredded my clothes not to be sent to this world… I was frightened, then, to make my descent."[dcccii]

The collapse of potential into singular expression is framed by the dissipation of entropy—the rapidly disseminated pluripotency whose forgetful loss Rumi laments. The only route to its restoration is through the construction, via divine wisdom, of complex, epistemically conditioned structures capable of driving consciousness upward toward reclaimed knowledge of its undivided essence.

In its situated condition, consciousness becomes locally blind to that unbroken essence, forgoing omniscient holism for a fractured perspective capable of highlighting and expressing only tiny swaths of potential at a time. As Merlau-Ponty explains, "The soul thinks according to the body, not according to itself." Guided by the limited perspective that it takes on in situated form, potential radiates itself into the diverse plurality which is an expressed analog of the vibrant core of all entities. Constrained by the conditions of spatial and temporal localization, the individualized, subjective consciousness is presented with the illusion that it is separate from the greater whole. Swedenborg corrects this false appearance, saying, "The divine nature is not different in one subject than it is in another. Rather, one created subject is different from another." He also notes that, "heaven's form…is the same [even] in its smallest manifestations."[dcccii] Similarly, Boehme speaks of the universe-begetting singularity as "the only one essence [that] has manifested itself with the external birth in the desire of the similitude, how it has manifested itself in so many shapes."[dccciv] Boehme further describes the underlying self-similarity of all manifestation: "For God, who is a spirit, and also a being, hath manifested Himself by the external world in a similitude, that the spirit seeth God in the essence and lustre of the majesty, and the same likewise in itself, and its own fellow-creatures like itself."[dcccv] The impetus underlying the manifold world of form is rooted in the simple desire "that God might behold Himself in the resemblances and ideas of the creatures, and have joy in Himself with the beings created out of His own wisdom."

The spatiotemporal measurements that fathomless eternity distills into spontaneously and dynamically arrange themselves to unfold the evolutionary saga of universal existence. Expression, although offering a route to completion for a tiny portion of potential, continually generates new levels and forms of potential with every act of fulfillment. On this treadmill of closure and regeneration, the dichotomous twin poles of possibility and manifestation chase each other in a self-driven, non-equilibrium cycle of perpetual evolution. At the center of the intractable loop is a double vortex leading to a still place at the center.

The Spiral Dance

Teilhard de Chardin visualizes at the heart of creation a "vortex which grows deeper as it sucks up fluid at the heart of which it was born"—a very centering image that invokes the gravitational well postulated by subquantum kinetics, wherein the reactions that lead to order devour their transmuting substrate rapidly enough to create the conditions that enable the stable persistence of their process-based, higher-level forms. In their clairvoyant observations of the elements, Leadbeater and Besant likewise detected the body of the "ultimate physical atom," finding it to be "composed entirely of spirals" that whirl in relation to each other to create a heart-shaped form that conducts the "flow of life-force"—analogous to the Hindu concept of *prana*—vertically through its center, as well as laterally through its spirals.[dcccvi]

From its most fundamental expressions, the nature of materiality accommodates consciousness and all of its entailments. As described by Teilhard, this space of prehnesion is the "interior in the heart of beings;" the "rent" which necessitates that "there is a double aspect to the structure of everything."[dcccvii] This metaphysical interior is the seat of iconicity, and echoes the Buddhist insistence that form is emptiness and emptiness is form.[dcccviii] While Thich Nhat Hahn clarifies this as meaning that everything is "empty of a separate self" in a profoundly interconnected world wherein "none can exist by itself,"[dcccix] Leadbeater and Besant suggest that there may also be a more literal interpretation. During their psychic foray into the infinitesimal, the seers found that at our scale of perception, space and matter appear in a relationship that is a direct inversion of their appearance at the barest levels of manifestation. Instead of empty space, incipient matter is surrounded everywhere by a dense substance they term "koilon." The particles that cooperatively arrange themselves into matter, by contrast, are empty: "Matter is not koilon, but the absence of koilon, and at first sight, matter and space appear to have changed places, and emptiness has become solidity and solidity has become emptiness." These miniscule voids "are filled with the breath of the Logos" that divides impenetrability and fills it with emptiness. Then, seeking itself out in other localized spaces of emptiness, it engages with other forms through which it encounters itself in an intelligent choreography of patterns that circulate sustaining energy through themselves, changing it "in character" according to the pattern they dance.[dcccx]

The spirals composed of unimaginably minute spheres of emptiness envisaged at the foundation of creation also have a long history of being celebrated as the grandly cosmic movements of evolution itself. Among the most ancient symbols revered by humanity is the spiral, whose significance for early people is described by Monica Sjoo and Barbara Mor:

> "The ascending spiral is matter transforming into spiritual/psychic energy. Simultaneously, from the descending spiral, the materialization of the spirit, comes the manifestation of the whole manifest world. The spiral involution of energy into matter is the primary movement of the universe, into created beings; the spiral evolution of matter into energy is the creative movement of these beings, consciously evolving back to their source."[dcccxi]

The in-coiling spiral draws information and sustenance inward to meet its outgoing counterpart, which projects action and entropy onto its surroundings. Through these counter-flows, the system declares itself, replenishes its resources, and maintains its adaptive agility by incorporating novel information. At a critical balance of in-coil and out-turn, the twin vortices touch, at the same time, both the foundation and the limit of perception: the inner and outer bounds of surprisal. Piercing the depths of individuality—which, even in its simplest forms enfolds infinity—while simultaneously radiating outward into a network of interconnection, the double vortex of evolution orchestrates its oppositional tendencies concurrently to cultivate complexity through the binding effects of recursive feedback loops and domain-spanning redundancies overlaid on dissipative dynamics that emanate away from their source.

The Original Source Domain

Pervading all variegations of form is the subtle invariance of self-similar potential that is preserved throughout the universe's supercritical radiation. "Truth is single, but its names are many for our sakes, to teach us lovingly this one thing through many things."[dcccxii] Frequently associated by mystics with light, the singular numinous vitality underpinning all form "personifies itself by veiling itself, and the personification is only stable when the veil is perfect."[dcccxiii] The "veil" is made "perfect" through the cyclic closure that is characteristic of any system, whether physical, biological, ecological, or semantic. The ontic traveler that develops from "negative" potential to "positive" expression is the "Light that shineth in the darkness,"[dcccxiv] which the "world" and "darkness" fail to comprehend because it is inaccessible to the measuring apparatus of the phenomenal world, offering only symbol-level clues to indicate its transcendent essence.

Set within a context that is essentially of itself, woven with threads of its own substance-free, non-spatial body that pre-exists localization, boundless consciousness condenses into embodied forms that are inextricably embedded in a wholeness of "immeasurable extent, older and younger than [individualized] consciousness,"[dcccxv] in that it is both nonlocal backdrop and emergent local outcome of intelligent evolution. Concentrated in every form, the tiny ember of conscious potential carried over from unitary evolution smolders internally, recalling within delimiting bounds an infinite origin and providing the context in which events take on meaning. "Constituted unity [is] inseparable from the original constitution itself," observes Husserl.[dcccxvi] And according to Leibniz, "Every substance is like a complete world and like a mirror of God or of the whole universe, which each one expresses in its own way...Thus the universe is in some way multiplied as many times as there are substances."[dcccxvii] Yasoda, mother of Krishna, uncovered this truth when, peering into the divine child's mouth in search of the butter he had mischievously stolen, instead beheld the entire cosmos.[dcccxviii]

Attesting to the omnipresence of consciousness, Boehme states, "For the Being of God is undivided; it needeth not any room or place."[dcccxix] In each manifest form, the self-same universal logic expresses itself uniquely through a different situated reference frame. When circumscribed by boundaries, the original source domain infinitely expresses its now-hidden nature through continuously evolving forms, categories, and possibilities for interpretation. In their various individual capacities to express the underlying, quality-less property of consciousness, all unitary entities participate to their own possibility- and probability-proscribed extent in unfolding the ongoing emergence of the three universes of experience: "Each of us dichotomizes the Kosmos in a different place," in the phrasing of William James.[dcccxx] Every localized iteration of the universal pattern represents a particular instance of nature's logic—a sharply enunciated counterpoint to non-local generality, participating to its own degree and with its own quality in stretching apart the chaos-fostering boundaries between abstraction and manifestation. Within the boundaries of the reciprocally causal closure between these two poles is an interiority that hosts the spaceless and timeless germ of coherence; the fertile ground in which potential ripens toward expression. Acting as anchoring portals to secure the threads of the cosmic fabric into a dynamic and irreducible interweave, all embodied carriers of universal wisdom uniquely contribute to the evolutionary drama, whose fathomless unfolding inspired Boehme to marvel, "Doth not God impart and reveal His wisdom to us diversely."[dcccxxi]

Divinely infused embodiment is the metaphysical logic of a universe whose nature is the fundamental and profound interconnection of all of its components. Explains Teilhard, "The concentration of a conscious universe would be unthinkable if it did not reassemble in itself *all consciousnesses* as well as *the conscious*."[dcccxxii] Captured in the opulent imagery of myth, the endlessly interconnected nature of the universe is conveyed by the many-jeweled net of Indra, which portrays a cosmic web of infinite interpenetration. Reflected in the shining jewel that occupies each cross-section of fibers is every other jewel in the net, along with its endless series of reflections, each of which contains its own multitude of reflections, ad infinitum. The jewels' eternally iterated reflections locate each facet of the universe in the interiority of every other, highlighting the paradox articulated by Thich Nhat Hahn: "'Everything has emptiness as its own nature.' And that is why everything can be."[dcccxxiii] The Gospel of Mary 2:2 affirms the essential inter-penetrability of universal forms: "Every nature, every modeled form, every creature, exists in and with each other." As partial reflections of universality, everything from particles to the systems they evolve into is a uniquely expressed microcosm of the self-same totality. This is why Buddhism considers every particle a potential Buddha, participating in the universal teleos: consciousness becoming through form what it already Is. The cohering condition of "interbeing" (Hahn) implicitly entangles every situated agent, binding each instance of individuality into a greater, indissoluble unity—the universal monad.   The body as source domain is secondary to the ultimate, ontological Source which surveys itself through the many-formed mirror of embodiment, "for the external world is generated out of the internal, and created into a comprehensible being, the wonders thereof belong unto the beginning."[dcccxxiv]

Semiotic Universe

From its seamless state of unity, free of the spatial divisions that call on semiosis to bridge perceptual discontinuities, the subtle source domain supplies its essential character to the "endless and innumerable diversity"[dcccxxv] of its embodied reflections. "Because He sees things, they exist," declares Fr. Thomas Merton[dcccxxvi]—but He "sees," or measures them, through the vehicles of embodiment. Condensed into particulate forms, multitudinous seeds of intelligent agency dance to variations on a pattern that converges on progressively higher levels of description. Engaged in a play of reminisce for the unitary origin whose self-same essence they declare from different localized vantage points, all manifest forms participate in establishing the informationally mediated correlations that build meaningful order.   As semiotic actors, each particle presents itself within the "universe of signs" at the interactive symbol level, using sign processes to reconnect, in a new form, what has been fragmented. Initiated from inside parameters set by the divisions of Logos, wherein subjectivity is free within its bounds to unfold its unique endowment of infinitude, domain-crossing semiosis highlights and coaxes different aspects of implicative potency into explicit causality like a melody threading through points of rhythm.

Epitomizing the invariance that "recodes" itself throughout systems at all levels, the universe as a whole embodies the principle of semiosis that structures its constitutive levels into dynamic relations. Founded on icon, the semiotic triad is based fundamentally on resemblance—whether objectively, as an image, or relationally, as in the diagrammatic structures which Peirce understood to particularly include algebraic equations and language. As a single instance of the universal pattern, language alludes to its referent not only symbolically through its signifiers, but relationally through its iconic structure. Conducting meaning into intelligibility, syntax creates a pattern of niche-like roles for a range of categorically distinct signifiers to fill—a pattern that is homologous to the ecological ordering of the physical and biological systems which likewise portray localized versions of universal logic via the animating interplay of order and meaning. As adumbrations of the form which structures linguistic patterns, these world-creating systems must also be diagrammatic, and therefore iconic, representations of a referent whose significance they do not fully contain. Emergently constructing a rendition of universal meaning through the condition of embodiment, which conveys subjective experience in terms of enactment, the dynamical and fungible "fillers" of syntax-like ecologies partake in the metaphorical pole of construction, with its demands of similarity fulfilled relationally across all scales and domains.

By collectively implying a referent whose form is not explicit, participants in the "three universes of experience" exemplify epistemology: they are "about" something, referring to it without resolving into it, and indicating it without explicating it. In this way, manifest form is indexical as well as iconic. As the embodiment of semiosis, it is also symbolic. Occupying the highest tier of semiotic expression, the interpretive "logic of nature" that occupies the third "universe of experience" is symbolic in its endless entanglements of associations, all oriented toward a single, subsuming level of description. A point of stability amid pervasive mutability, the symbol level encapsulates an intricate array of events and conditions, past and future, in its pithy presentation. Carried implicitly below, above, and within the presenting symbol level, the relational entanglements that bind unities into systems are localized reflections of the universal condition of penetrating interrelationships. With the mandates of higher levels of organization implicitly anticipated in the lower, each aspect within a system is united to every other by a network of indirect references to something that is larger than itself: the complete whole. Conjoined in the anticipation of correlation at a higher level, all apparent disparities of form and process that populate the universe resolve into unity as they all contribute to the expression of the same totality. This quality of anticipation is innately connected to the properties of symbol, as described by Peirce, "The being of symbol consists in the real fact that something surely will be experienced if certain conditions be satisfied…The value of a symbol is that it…enables us to predict the future."[dcccxxvii] Tracing its essence to the future, symbol indicates a referent forever beyond its own limited scope. As the highest and most encompassing level of symbolic description, the entire universe, by its own logic, must likewise signify, without fully expressing, something eternally beyond itself.

Evolving Through Chaos

"There was a chaotic something, yet lacking nothing before Heaven and Earth," we are told by the Tao Te Ching—a formless shadow that could be regarded as the "Mother of the World."[dcccxxviii] Indelibly linked from ancient times with primeval maternity, the chaos at the foundation of the universe is sourced in the same duality that fosters harmonizing coherence. "For I had a thorough view of the universe as in a CHAOS," Boehme relates. "Wherein all things are couched and wrapt up, but it was impossible for me to explicate and unfold the same."[dcccxxix] Much like Bohm's infinitely enfolded implicate order, or Leibniz's monad whose perceptual restrictions alone prevent its deification, Boehme's rapturous vision of the creative universal matrix provides an unsettling glimpse of its turbulent grandeur. Infinitely fracturing into the elements of evolution, reposing wholeness stirs itself into the chaos that yields to order only by transcending its own erratic propensities. Ever at odds with its invariance-preserving foil, symmetry, which faithfully reflects its singular origin in the subtle isomorphism underlying form which calls together order, chaos is enervated by multiplicity and, while availing itself to the demands of order, also harbors entropy. Precipitously balanced between the poles that stake out primary dualities—the poles of potential and form, quiescence and chaos, creation and destruction, nothing and everything—is their generative fusion which sees the birth of a universe.

Like the gravitational singularity hypothesized to inhabit the center of a black hole, the discontinuities that puncture the space-time fabric with perception are calm epicenters within the tidal oscillations of chaos. Replicated in myriads of infinitesimal centers, the primordial differentiation awakens into a sea of relatively uncorrelated expressions which quickly entangle, through their microcosmic emanations of relation-structuring waves and computational tendrils, into hubs of complexity whose order represents an abstract, logical type that is amenable to endless expressions. Curbing the boundlessness of the Absolute into measurement and partiality, the spatial and temporal dimensions of classicality dictate evolution as the means for consciousness to enact its ideational potency on the universal stage, "veiled by morphology." As Swedenborg explains, "No one can be created directly from the Uncreated, the Infinite, from Reality itself and Life itself, because what is divine is one and undivided. We must be created out of things created and finite, things so formed that something divine can dwell within."[dcccxxx]

As the context common to all manifestation, the underlying substrate of conscious intelligence is the self-same initial condition for all evolution. Once the journey of spatiotemporal constraint has been embarked upon, however, a variety of physical conditions intervene on individual evolutionary trajectories, forcing the tremendous divergence from predictability that ultimately enables the evolution of complex systems. In the unstable seethe of noisy, uncorrelated fluctuations, information production becomes maximal as individual trajectories veer wildly away from their own probabilistic paths. Conveyance, in contrast, drops to negligibility until a few improbable paths seed the way to order. Although the individual probability of any particular region in space spawning order is vanishingly small, the sheer vastness of fluctuations sampling their possibilities makes the onset of order almost inevitable under appropriate conditions. With the creation of new, orderly phase spaces balanced between information production and transmissibility, the probability of order amplifies.

Evolution at any level, of course, is more than simply a game of chance. It is the confluence of chance and necessity (Pauli); directed in part by the agent that purposefully shapes the world to its own advantage, biasing probabilities in its own favor through intelligence. Although handicapped by its entropic adversary from a probabilistic point of view, the ascent of order from chaos has an adaptive advantage that arises from the subjective capacity of thirdness. Swedenborg describes this unlikely weighting of the probabilistic scales: "[The] function [of the union between love and discernment] looks to what is good, and the form of their function looks to what is true…The good," or divine love, "looks to the true"—discernment—"for its manifestation and the true looks to the good for its existence."[dcccxxxi] While accounting for the good and the true as the foundational dyad of manifestation, much like the self-extant semiotic system which icon and index conspire to create, the third aspect of the transcendental triad has a distinct role: "Beauty is [love's] intelligence."[dcccxxxii] At once an outward property of the objective symbol level and inward judgment of subjectivity, beauty is the expression of the primal, ontological need for self-declaration that is requisite within a "universe of signs." Within the tumultuous radiation of life and its interactions—all ultimately traceable to common originating initial conditions, and therefore far from random—is the urge to higher levels of expression: more elaborate displays, more beautiful colors or patterns, or more perfect camouflage; all reflections of consciousness in its many forms striving for maximal edification. As the elegant elucidation of nature's logic, beauty is wholly within the province of thirdness—one of the two universes of experience Peirce deemed independent of the creator, rendering it eminently subject-dependent and contextually conditioned. Driving evolution through its fertile artistry, the interpretive scion of consciousness and intelligence unfolds through beauty, biasing manifestation "toward the marvelous."

In both the downward flow of order and the upward surge of radical spontaneity, self-similarity conserves the system's essential nature throughout each symmetry bifurcation, which renews the cycle of evolution from a fresh point of convergence between the manifolds of physicality and semantics; localization and non-locality. The enlivened threads of interconnected intelligence which dance to the dulcet tones of inscrutable attractors reinvent their patterns across domains, expanding in diversity and deepening in complexity through their labyrinthine journey toward reunion with the strangest of Attractors. Although itself formless and immutable, that ontological singularity is endlessly interpreted and described by the ever-changing, ever-refining interplay of forms and relations that array themselves in circular homage to its universal essence. The invariance underlying every aspect of manifestation is the ground— the Alpha—in which evolution is rooted, providing both the material and efficient causes of interactional potential when it shatters into form. Like a meta-attractor, the Attractor behind all attractors, it also supplies the teleos, the Omega toward which systemically supported wholeness propagates, molding evolution with its unspecified formal and localized final causes. The "radiation" of evolution is "a present reality of the mysterious center of our centers, the Omega," says Teilhard de Chardin of the universal march he perceives toward the explication of that divine center common to all."[dcccxxxiii] The center radiates from itself—only relatively—in the outflowing vortex of its exhale. Simultaneously, it holds all of its spacetime "metaphors" into a structured grammar through which "God is constantly speaking only one thing…In this one utterance he speaks his Son and at the same time the Holy Spirit and all creatures," each of which "exists for the perfection of the entire universe."[dcccxxxiv]

Reflecting the foundational and aspirational wholeness which frames it, universal evolution is an ongoing, simultaneous act of unfoldment at all levels. Composing its countless individual components into a collective harmony capable of embodying intelligent consciousness, the cosmic concert manifests evolvable order only through "a supremely improbable coincidence of the totality of elements and causes."[dcccxxxv] Leibniz encapsulates this unlikely condition: "The very idea or essence of the soul carries with it the fact that all its appearances and perceptions must arise spontaneously from its own nature and precisely in such a way that they correspond to what happens in the whole universe."[dcccxxxvi] Revealed in the deep, multi-level entanglements within and among entities, nature's teleology threads through all manifestation, its malleable relational fibers conjoining its members like the interpenetrating weave of a mystical, jewel-hung net.

Dialectical Ascent

Threading its filamentous way through a self-woven, self-reflective web, the singular, non-spatial omnipresence inspires form with a vivifying causality that is distinct from the unperturbed quiescence of infinite potential. The irreducibly complex tangles woven by capillaceous strands of emptiness connect with each other in nonlinear cycles of correlation and causality that churn and coil asymptotically around the physically insubstantial heart that is the core of all manifestation. Active at even the smallest of scales as an attractor of local dynamics, the unspoken, yet ever-speaking Word is the center of ordered interactions, extending them lattice-like into robust, fractal complexity, and nesting them into a sentient hierarchy whose leading-edge degrees of freedom climb with every emergent ascent. The broad, exploratory, lateral spread of diversity provides a stable platform and endless repository of potential source domains for the vertical expansion of consciousness that forever strains beyond its boundaries in a circuitous, striving meander which simultaneously deepens even as it extends.

From the primordial foam that smolders at the universe's base rises the "perfect spontaneity" that "every substance has"[dcccxxxvii] as a metaphysical inheritance, scaling the tiers of complexity toward increasing degrees of freedom. Nondeterministic and creative, potential—which is of the unmeasurable, experiential realm that imbues events with meaning—is the foundational ingredient for all forms of evolution. Offering itself to the creative work of building order, the constructive chaos of potential precedes any incursion of order into space and time, and lingers like a residual mantle around its expressed object. Forming the bottom-up current that infuses spontaneity into a system, unruly chaos colludes with irreversibility to channelize salient regularities into order-building habits. In their unincorporated states, the primitive precursors of order roam the wilds of vacuous space, following inscrutable trajectories rooted in their own tiny suites of causality. When curbed into orderliness, they lend their minute potency to the structures they help comprise, their freedom channeled upward to accommodate system-level demands. Like a process of domestication, the potential congealed in the "wild" particles of chaos are subdued, assimilated, and conscripted to a final cause. Through the evolutionary ascent of structure, "the beasts may be tamed, the herds broken in, and the serpent lose its sting."[dcccxxxviii] A discontinuity within chaos, the structure that houses interiority is a "rent" in the underlying fabric of space that co-opts its local, desultory dynamics and imprints on them an echo of its own intrinsically sourced logic. Between the poles generated by volatile possibility and stabilizing regularity arises the coherent backdrop that enables the creative capability of evolution.

Although apparently autonomous at its own focal level of description, each situated subject plays an integral and well-ordered part in some higher-level system. Sampling potential attractors in terms of present conditions, intelligence draws itself toward the future. Malleable threads of potential arrange themselves below the level of presentation to become powerful, temporally persistent organizing principles that guide events within and between systems through a host of tacit entailments. As complexity accumulates, with its vertical ascent supported by a broad and diverse lateral span at every level, more holistic patterns emerge out of the integration of lower levels.[dcccxxxix] Attesting to this anticipatory quality, Teilhard de Chardin tells us, "Nothing could ever burst forth as final across the different thresholds successively traversed by evolution… which has not already existed in an obscure and primordial way."[dcccxl] Similarly, Salthe contends that all emergent features that appear later at higher integrative levels would have been implicit during earlier stages, with potential and actualized configurations "rehearsed many times." The self-similar patterns that reassert themselves with every ascending coil of complexity's spiral are "rehearsals" for their own emergent reconfigurations at higher levels of freedom within different conditions, contexts, and domains.

The continually transposing flux between chaos, order, and higher potential is a dialectical trinity imposed upon raw potential by the directionality of time, process, and entropic generation. Evolving through emergent saltations, each microcosmic system within the universal macrocosm binds its lower-level dynamics into a presenting level at which they correlate, and translates them as though across a nonlinear line of symmetry to a new level of potential. At the highest, most encompassing level of description, all entities and dynamics are enfolded in the universal system. Teilhard touches on the deeply entwining nature of this chaotic-seeming tangle of causality when he wonderingly describes the "formidable coincidences" involved in "forming even smallest thing." He continues, "Life does not work by following a single thread, nor yet by fits and starts. It pushes forward its whole network at one and the same time."[dcccxli] Like a genome whose changes and expressions only occur within the context of an entire body, evolution at even the smallest scales reverberates throughout the entire intelligent web, connecting the greatest with the least via nested and complex cycles of reciprocal causality. With self-transcendence implied even in the lower hierarchical tiers that support global systemic order, a new synthesis is forever poised for emergence at the critical juncture between chaotic thesis and ordered antithesis.[dcccxlii] Cradled in that precipitous symbol-level cusp is the turning point around which the reciprocal web of evolution twists and projects itself, with potential both embedded in and unfolding from the focal level—a reflection of the originating dialectic of being, intention, and expression, creatively aligning to conceive a universally nested hierarchy of unitary evolution.

Pushing the intricate and meaningful network of interactive agents to integration at higher levels of complexity, the anticipation of a higher-level attractor spreads itself non-locally to affect the entire evolving universal nexus at once. Recalling Jungian synchrony, the fortuitous arrangement of elements and interactions through diachronic channels advances the evolution of the whole system simultaneously. From the elevated perspective at which lower-level dynamics converge into a pattern, causality—a heuristic device of understanding tied to the delimiting bounds of embodiment—cedes its explanatory power to convergence, which all of evolving nature participates in synchronically. In a continuous culmination of unfolding potential and novelty, nature's multitudes of forms all participate in a display of grandeur whose collectivity deems that "the whole universe together participates in the divine goodness more perfectly, and represents it better, than any single creature whatever."[dcccxliii]

Converging Branches

Through every form and at every level of expression, consciousness persistently performs its inherent task of "reduc[ing] the manifold of sensuous impressions to unity" by intelligently correlating randomness and complexity into a higher-level, simplifying description. The improbable and fortuitous thereby become not only commonplace, but governing principles in every domain of evolution. As causally efficacious principles active from evolution's incipience, consciousness and the non-deterministic intelligence it deploys to create structure—Swedenborg's divine love and divine wisdom respectively—are truly foundational universal principles.

Within the scope of possibility set by the constraints of physicality, every system "has within it an indication of its possible plentitude."[dcccxliv] The interactive levels that a system harbors beneath its symbolic aegis contain the potential for subsequent evolution based on what it has preserved of its historical inheritance. Each level of expression—whole and self-contained in its "perfect veil" of closure—is anticipating, beneath the limited information it presents outwardly, the emergence of a new level of holism, with new resolutions as well as bounds of surprisal, and new degrees of freedom. Aligning itself in relation to a limiting condition like the pool of relevant inferences conjured by the restrictions of an analogy, formless potential simmers at the threshold of expression when drawn by the magnetic pull of constraint. Inquests of potential penetrate physicality with a characteristic form and dynamic:

"For the works of mortals on earth are like branches,
Nothing has but one fate in mind, but all things
Revolve in a circle, nor is it lawful to abide in one place,
But each keeps its own course wherewith it began."[dcccxlv]

The probing fractal branches—whether of a mobilizing electron, a pointer state establishing objectivity, or a radiating phylum—form the many-pronged shape that is conducive to evolution. "The biosphere," explains Teilhard, "has so far been…a network of divergent lines, free at extremities."[dcccxlvi] As possibilities extend from a common origin to explore in parallel different relationships with the environment, evolution leaves a Linnean trail of bifurcations in its ever-travelling wake, which is "lawfully" incapable of "abid[ing] in one place."

The extension of outreaching branches is countered by an opposite tendency. For Orpheus, it is the "revolution in a circle," while Teilhard elaborates on a particular manifestation of that loop: "By effect of reflection and the recoils it involves, the loose ends have been tied up, and the noosphere tends to constitute a single closed system."[dcccxlvii] Contra to the outwardly extending, diversifying reach of evolutionary differentiation, potential simultaneously recoils upon itself in the bounded interiority of embodiment, where it encounters—much like in its exterior reach—a varied environment whose modular, intertwined functions maximize the range of information that resonates from multiple experiential angles into unified subjective experience.

Particularly captivating Teilhard is the internal reference at the core of cognition, which leads him to conclude that, "The noosphere (and more generally the world) represent a whole that is not only closed but also *centered*."[dcccxlviii] Like their outwardly extending counterparts, the inwardly coiling spirals of intelligence interact with each other in nonlinear ways. The "psychic centre, once turned in on itself…centres itself further on itself by penetration into a new space," he explains. "At the same time it centres the rest of the world around itself by the establishment of an ever more coherent and better organised perspective in the realities which surround it."[dcccxlix] This self-referencing "centering" is the basis of all autonomous agency, wrought through the arduous cultivation of biological evolution into adaptable cognitive flexibility. Mirroring the hierarchy of cyclical closures that support its ascent, conscious evolution eventually circles back around on itself, sealing a semantic circuit at an emergent level of expression.

In the nonlinear, dialectical symmetries of causality and evolution, the cognitive leading edge comes to supersede its embodied context by penetrating into new evolutionary terrain that is biologically supported and informed, but not conscripted. Evolution in the cognitive sphere entails not just an increasing breadth of knowledge, but also, the "growth of within." Arising from the "continual tension of organic doubling-back" that comprises the universe "both on the whole and at each of its points," the inward penetration of subjectivity is part of a universal process of "interiorization."[dcccl] As it assesses the probabilities of possible futures, intelligence strains against perceptual limitations to ascertain patterns according to which it might refine its anticipatory quests. Counterbalancing the external limit of accessible knowledge is an internal region of surprisal that likewise resides beyond the filamentous touch of intelligence, which interrogates its intrinsic space with the same tools it applies to ambient environs. Just as the surprisal hemming in perception and cognition impels adaptiveness, the unknown wilds within semantic spaces cajole the internal spiral of intelligence deeper into its own core. Like any other unknown and potentially chaotic region, the unexplored interior harbors potential dangers. Yet as an attractor that summons internal dynamics to order, this intentional locus of agency is also the source of structure and keeper of nature's universal logic within each individuated frame. Patiently probing into that endless center with its tendency toward increasing refinement, intelligence gradually unfolds the potential within its own center for explicit and even self-awareness, ultimately becoming capable of perceiving the true Nature underlying the world of appearances.

Deepening and expanding within the conscious domain as a semantic corollary of physical and biological evolution, the growth of intelligence toward explicit self-awareness is an unfoldment whose ordering transpires outside of space and time. Enmeshing entities within their environments by molding perception to form, and inner environment with outer, the tendrils of intelligence conjoin the myriads of sentient jewel-like centers, each one enacting infinity through its own form and to its own degree of disclosure. By individually and collectively tapping into the many-leveled universal rhythms, the agents who creatively explicate the vast potential opened by the evolutionary foray into mental domains consciously participate in the generation of a pattern of such a high order of logic that it is beyond the capacity of finite mind to fully correlate it. The deepest, most enduring tempos that underlie the flourishes and accents particular to specific forms of manifestation are the self-similar cadences of the foundational template of primordial intelligence, with which nature strives to align itself and thereby declare. Continuously refashioning itself from endless well-springs of orderly energetic iterations, formal manifestation clothes the uncontainable plentitude of conscious potential with intelligently wrought garments of complex, autonomous structure through whose evolution explicit awareness unfolds.

The way to liberation, according to Vedic tradition, is to realize that the Atman, the pure numinous self, being, or experience beyond phenomenological identification, is identical to Brahman, the universal Creator. Passing oppositionally through the passive gate of universal intelligence, the oscillating transposition of outgoing creative vortex and incoming transcendent vortex shreds to nothing on the inbreath everything that had clothed that pure Being on the outbreath. Expressing within, but from beyond, the ultimately self-referencing context of Teilhard's "giant atom," the final unity that evolution's individuated expressions seek already Is. Beyond sensual apprehension, that promise of fulfilment is poised at the apical turning point in the reciprocally causal interchange—a quiescent discontinuity between inner and outer bounds of surprisal, beyond the reach of both.

Unbeginning Birth

Ensconced as they are within nested layers of universal constraint and the form it enables, localized, sentient subjects represent the evolving leading edge of the semantic systems that, in some forms, allow explicit understanding of the conditions of embodiment. Plicating the universal fabric into intricate patterns that support wholeness, the immeasurable discontinuities of subjective consciousness situated within microcosmic forms semantically unfold the macrocosm which physically enfolds them. From mere self-reference to full self-awareness, the deepening interior leads the situated and subjective consciousness to an even more fundamental source of awareness. The inward, recursive gyre of intelligent evolution within the subject is both microcosm and leading edge of a universal involution, through which consciousness becomes revealed to the only property capable of perceiving: itself. The Gordian knot of universal self-reference is perpetuated by localization, which relatively imparts perspective on localized quanta of evolving consciousness and allows subjective differentiation within objective frames of reference. The continuous invitation to sever that knot by reuniting individualized consciousness with the boundless swells of conscious potential below and above the level of cognizant mind is a promise of creative renewal to the self-aware visitants who consciously seek that replenishing center. By linking back to a center that is pure potential and the source of limitless energy, a recursion to the source, or origin, "not only restores strength, but also creates the possibility of recognizing and bringing into play ever new chreodes and new developmental lines."[dcccli]

Because the relative nature of spacetime precludes the full habitation of the absolute singularity, the fractionating prism at the boundary of physicality renders indivisible wholeness outwardly particulate, while preserving its completeness as an inward quality. Evolving within a fractured context that directs the focus of perception outwardly, the inner space—the differentiated drop of totality—correlates itself to its experiences, leading to the founding delusion of partiality. Only when intrinsic wholeness, scrupulously concealed beneath the folds of expression, has evolved sufficient structural strength and flexibility to at last perceive its ontological heritage, destiny, and being, is the illusion of limitation finally reversed. Rather than internalizing what it perceives externally as a truth condition, the liberated consciousness is freed to radiate its internal emancipation outwardly, reconnecting with itself in other forms, and creating a new kind of non-physical structure through which the rediscovered divine energies can circulate and flow. Says Boehme, "The external world is likewise of God, and from God, and man is to that end created into the external world, that he might bring the external figures into the internal, that he might bring the end into the beginning."[dccclii]

As evolving agents deepen their vertical integration through increasing complexity, their volitional ability takes on a more active role in selecting the potential that they express. Taking its place in the systematic flow of reciprocal causality, humanity serves not only as a local maximum among many that channel the cosmic flow between Alpha and Omega from different heights, depths, perspectives, and capacities, but also provides a self-aware leading edge to the universal project of conscious evolution. The integral embeddedness of humanity within the intelligent fabric of conduits that channel wholeness through their partiality like rivers connecting two oceans is described in the Tao Te Ching:

"[The Tao is] widening until the circle is full….
…Man rounding the way of earth,
Earth rounding the way of heaven,
And heaven rounding the way of life [the Tao]
Till the circle is full."[dcccliii]

Beginning and end are interrupted by a spatiotemporal interlude founded in chaos as purpose evolves through means toward end. As each pole of beginning and end—intention and expression, initial condition and final cause, past and future—takes the place of the other in a directional flux, it acts as the ground of the other's being. Together, the dualistic, vacillating currents generate a boundary, within which coherence can blossom to support intelligent activity, and along which chaos can supply the conditions that germinate expression. Instead of infinite regress in the fluctuations between ground state, chaos, and final cause, there is only infinite interchange between potential and expression, beginning and end, inner and outer, and all other outposts of multiplicity that seek convergence on the still, one-pointed center of consciousness. Ultimately, Alpha and Omega are unitary, oscillating in relation to each other as conjugate variables, bounded into apparent distinction by a region of creation that conveys timeless immateriality in temporal terms that prevent them from simply resolving into equilibrated, non-evolving unity.

The complex coexistence of the diametrical poles of world-begetting oppositional tension necessitates that all manifestation is essentially a metaphorical conveyance of an ineffable condition that is embodied in the irreducible duality of inner and outer. Conjoined at the metaphysical point at which events become meaningful but the laws of physics dissolve, the fluid and chaotically oscillating overlap of the two domains of expression, semantic and physical, generate that curious foundation of manifestation, paradox. Like the realm of manifestation it structures, paradox is upheld by a balanced tension of opposites. Interposing between its antithetical poles is a discontinuity that holds them in relation to each other while containing neither. Also like manifestation, paradox itself is built upon a paradox: although fundamentally incomplete in its reliance on a discontinuity for its existence, it is within that very vacuity that completeness resides. As the essence of the symbolic, paradox is the turning point within metaphors and symbols—including the metaphorically constituted "living symbols" that populate the semiotic universe. Representing the union between metaphor's dichotomous poles of source and target, which are apparently contradictory but coexist in relation to a discontinuity that transposes meaning and form into each other, paradox propagates singular meaning throughout evolution by allowing it to continuously change form. Because of its roots in paradox, warped by the turning point of discontinuity, the universe and its evolution are ultimately beyond analysis, but available to the openness of experience.[dcccliv] Immaterially situated in the equilibrium amid the chaos of opposing tendencies, this experience is a sacred one according to Thomas Merton, who finds that "to be holy is self-contradictory."[dccclv]

Universal Epistemology

The parallel extension of potential through a multitude of spatiotemporal conduits of entangled intelligence is the proliferation of a grand Idea borrowed from another dimension. Translating the singular omnipresence into a rainbow of forms, perspectives and relationships, evolution construes an intricate web whose every fiber contributes supportively to each "growing branch in the life-tree of God in Christ."[dccclvi] Space and time act like nonlinear sieves, filtering from totality limited expressions that integrate with each other into structures of complexity through an evolutionary process that makes "something out of everything" through "intelligent subtraction."[dccclvii]

From the formless, progenitive ocean of unified consciousness whose mystical name is I AM, all manifest expressions derive their universally self-similar logic, which is simply *to be*. As the basic condition common to all existence, "to be" is also a common final cause for all potential striving for existence, diversely iterated through the panoply of perennially evolving forms. As the foundational and universal logic, "to be" is sufficient, adequate, and self-contained as a final cause—up to the point of manifestation. At that critical juncture, when unified singularity fractures into untold multitudes, the epistemic condition of situated form applies an addendum to the self-existent truth condition, transforming it into the imperative "to be about" something; to reference something as though separate from it; and to interpretively mold the active faculty of intelligence according to that "aboutness." From the analogies that all agents construct of the world as they encounter it arise their particular forms of logic, which guides the activities, meaningful interactions, and relationships that allow the conscious potential seated within physical vehicles to develop and unfold into the patterns of perception that underpin the structure of evolution at every point.

Perpetuating the ongoing creation and transmission of information instantiated with the onset of classicality through a plurality of forms and interpretations is the intelligence of the fragmented Original Memory seeking to reconstitute itself through the far-from-equilibrium material, energetic, and semiotic channels available to it. According to Swedenborg, the tendencies toward "useful functions" which are inherent in self-organized systems "have within them…a striving to return to their origin by the means at hand."[dccclviii] Driven by the mandate of this universal final cause, manifestation replicates its characteristic patterns at all scales. From the negotiations of energetic flow and entropic erosion that characterize lower levels of description emerge not only the material and energetic exchange, but also the meaningful semiotic interactions that structure cooperation, competition, trophic relations, and social structures at higher, cognitively mediated levels of semantic capability. Through the unfoldment of the evolutionary drama, with its universal conditions and spontaneous flourishes, autonomy bolsters itself into agency and deepening levels of conscious awareness. Within the intentional landscapes that arise like variegated manifolds against an interpretively malleable backdrop, the regularities and nuances of the grand saga reveal themselves from different angles and various degrees of clarity to minds increasingly centered in their own volitional potentialities. Uniquely enacting at their respective depth and from their distinct vantage points the universal flow that binds manifold expression into coherent unity, all universal actors creatively participate in crafting the fluid storyline of the cosmic narrative.

9

The Journey of Consciousness

"In the end the law of nature, irrespective of its obviously empirical derivation, is always a psychic form as well...and has its origins in psychic premises."
—Carl Jung

"Consciousness does not grow out of any activity that is inherent to it; rather, it is constantly being produced by an energy that comes from the depths of the unconscious and has thus been depicted in the form of rays since time immemorial."
—Carl Jung

Upon becoming bound by dynamical knots to immanent form, nonlocal universality assumes countless discreet forms that are subject to contextual and historical conditioning. Primordial substance congeals itself into matter that is animated by its own energetic conjugate, which flows through open systems in an ethereal wave that dances them into an ongoing evolutionary crescendo. In this flow, at once universal and individual, is revealed not only the logic that Peirce saw as expressed in sign relations, but also a deeper logic permeating all nature. Evident even in the workings of less differentiated levels of evolution, whose random-seeming movements align into a patterned choreography at a higher level of description, is the intelligibility of order that pulses together with chaos in a quixotic harmony that projects macroscopic order from microscopically unpredictable patterns. Endlessly iterated throughout manifestation—from the rhythms of brain waves to heart beats, to the patterns on leopard fur and mollusk shells—this union of complementary opposites fosters within its chaos-laden bounds the inscrutable coherence whose very emptiness issues the summons to order. Even slime mold amoebas dance themselves into self-exciting concentric circles and spiral patterns as though the most primordial shapes of the universe were seeking archetypal expression in those gelatinous little bodies.

Both creative and logical, nature's fusion of unpredictability with order at all levels is an assertion of its primal condition of chaos bearing the imprint of intelligence—the "inactively active Christ Consciousness or Son [that] is the conscious Presence of God's intelligent divine plan in creation, and the Eternal Witness of the work of the Holy Ghost."[dccclix] When expressed as a localized phenomenon, this is the intelligence that guides an agent within its evolved parameters and local context. The individual's "interpretation" of this universal intelligence is what is presented at the symbol level. In this way, as Jung quotes Goethe, "all that is outside, also is inside." Jung adds the distinction, however, that the inside has an *a priori* structure.[dccclx] Serving as an initial condition that is self-similar for all of manifestation, while also subject to evolvable variation, this "*a priori* structure" is the non-deterministic and endless suite of semantic, and therefore physical, forms that lies latent in primordial, undifferentiated intelligence. Compelled to various externalized manifestations by its natural corollary, final cause, internal self-similarity establishes a polarity with contextual conditions to enable evolution by providing material, efficient, and formal causes with an abundance of loci to array themselves in terms of. With its basin of attraction always at least partially in the future, the inner is pulled outward to expression, with the symbol level as its canvas. The implicit and probabilistic *a priori* structure takes form in the system's presentation and interactions. "For the external world is generated out of the internal, and created into a comprehensible being, the wonders thereof belong unto the beginning."[dccclxi]

Although organisms express internally sourced patterns of potential in emergent ways more discernably than non-living entities, they are not unique in this capacity, but rather are displaying at a high level of complexity a condition that is universal. Salthe and Teilhard de Chardin both contend that all patterns of manifestation must be expressed in some form at a lower level of integration, where seeds of future, symbol-level, leading-edge presentations commingle implicitly, as though still suspended in an unmeasured state of unitary evolution. Similarly, Julian perceived that "everything was set in order before it was made."[dccclxii] The order, however, is implicit potential; etheric wisps that have not yet nucleated a physical corollary. Order only becomes explicit through the dynamical channels of interpenetrating relationship; the kind found in a world where everything is describable in terms of its relation with everything else.

Independent of their physical effects, potential objects stir the conscious pool of possibility that each agent samples from, differentiating degenerate potential states and mobilizing channels of organization by aligning them materially, efficiently, and formally between initial condition and final cause. Lying outside of the measurable parameters of space and time, potential guides and is in turn structured by these conduits of its own explication. Its unexpressed and untapped potency underlies and supports manifestation like a Platonic world of ideal forms casting oblique reflections of its perfect dimensions on the physical universe. Such a world is considered by Roger Penrose "primary, a logical necessity, and both other worlds—physical and mental—are its shadows."[dccclxiii]

Cognitive Evolution

Along with the organisms which harbor it, cognitive capacity adjusts, modifies, and adapts itself throughout evolution to maximize its reach and occupation of niche space. Flooding its banks like a rain-swollen river, potential expands laterally, replicating itself in as many diverse forms as its environment can be coaxed into sustaining. Each excursion into diversity yields a new potential platform from which the probing tendrils of possibility may extend and explore, as consciousness seeks new shades of expression and new angles of niche colonization. While the safest and most plentiful niches exist as a mean, or central tendency, they are forever open at the extremes. From the diminutive to the herculean; the cryptic to the flamboyant; the sedentary to the athletic, outlying tendencies invite exploitation at the atypical edges of expression. For cognitive capacity, a niche is always open at the top, drawing potential upward like water lured by the sun's heat to transpire through arboreal columns. "Life," Teilhard de Chardin reminds us, "being an ascent of consciousness, could not continue to advance indefinitely along its line without transforming itself in depth."[dccclxiv] Consciousness painstakingly erects the relational hierarchy of semantic trusses that flexibly support its vertical climb through the forms it enlivens and evolves within. As novelty supervenes upon establishment over the course of evolution, systems are compelled to tune their internal relations to accommodate increased complexity, and the symbol-level façade that functions as a semantic transducer adjusts to declare its acquired capabilities.

Whereas the symbol level of physicality is the body, for cognitive systems, it is explicit awareness that is built along the leading edge of an "immeasurably vaster constitutive framework provided by [the] cognitive unconscious."[dccclxv] Providing a metaphor for the structure of consciousness is the brain itself. Much like the outer symbol level of a deeply complex, hierarchical system, only a very thin sheath of neocortex is actively involved in the thinking and computing that we identify with explicit awareness. Beneath this relatively membranous interface of activity is the vast apparatus that supports it, built up over eons of evolution. Through the course of its evolution, this supportive interior has gradually layered new strata of complexity upon the old, downwardly altering the expression of those ancient functions. Invisible to the system's interactive presenting level, the deep layers of complexity represent both an ancient evolutionary inheritance and the interior region of surprisal that consciousness struggles to perceptually penetrate through the dual motion of deepening and ascent that characterizes its evolution. Only with the advent of brain structures such as the prefrontal cortex and its analogs in other species, with their extensive and recursive back-linking, are the contents of various other brain regions drawn to the surface level of conscious awareness, and transmuted into higher-order cognition. Beholden as it is to less complex structures of consciousness, the glimpse of its own inner workings afforded to explicit awareness is the foundation of self-awareness. In accessing some perception of the dark and supportive regions of cognitive surprisal, the subject touches upon the evolutionary inheritance of its own psyche, filled with indirect but integral connections to the whole evolution of the cosmos. Through the "rent" of self-aware consciousness, "that which looks at all things…[can] also look at itself and recognize, in what it sees, the 'other side' of its power of looking" (Merleau-Ponty).

As the leading, downwardly causal edge of mentality, explicit awareness is largely guided by the proscribing constraints that flow upward from the more foundational rungs of the semantic hierarchy rather than being capable of issuing its own, independently formulated directives. Like their physical counterparts, cognitive constructs are many-layered and hierarchically nested, with the majority of activity continuously operant below the expressive level. Consciousness, therefore, is far more encompassing than mere awareness. "Mind," according to Swedenborg, "means everything involved in our volition and discernment."[dccclxvi] Jung believed that the balance of causal efficiency in affecting volitional processes is tilted so strongly toward the non-explicit, underlying motivations and biases secreted throughout the psyche that he declared God to be "left-handed."[dccclxvii] Potent but unseen organizers of behavioral expression, the activities of what Jung deems the "unconscious" play a role that is somewhat analogous to the invisible forces that sculpt the universe within their parameters. The deep physical seam from which forces emerge has a mental counterpart in the "archetypal contents" that guide the mind and likewise derive "from a deeper, timeless stratum."[dccclxviii] The predictable invariance with which forces act is a primordial expression of the "universal habit-making tendency." Similarly, the unconscious accrues, through the historical channels of phylogeny and ontogeny, certain "habits" of behavior sensitive to particular stimuli that express themselves as instincts.

In connecting the spirit, or the life-force "pneuma," and matter on the basis of some subtle isomorphism shared between them, the unconscious acts as a bridge between life's two constitutive realms by regarding them as not only equivalent but actually identical.[dccclxix] Like a fractal that at once conjoins chaos and order even as it delineates them, the psyche is an interface between the numinous and the phenomenal: "Whenever something material exists, the psyche is also partially involved."[dccclxx] Like the critical and creative wedge between chaos and order, mind is suspended between its physical context and the intangible, nonlocal dimension of consciousness. Although it has left no discernible fossils through the course of its evolution, the unconscious mind manifests itself through complex behaviors and prescient knowing in instinct-guided organisms, while its ghosts fill the unattended corners of the human psyche.

Conscious and Unconscious

Deciphering the nondescript workings of the cognitive unconscious, particularly as they express themselves symbolically and through dreams, was the focus of Jung's life work. "Just as the human body represents a whole museum of organs, each with a long evolutionary history behind it," he reasons, so likewise the mind "can no more be a product without history than is the body in which it exists."[dccclxxi] Just as the brain preserves a cryptic evolutionary record within its structure, Jung believed that the psyche's historical development is likewise conserved in intelligible ways. More expansively, William James describes the brain as "an organized register of infinitely numerous experiences received during the evolution of life."[dccclxxii]

Layered like sedimentary strata, more primitive levels of intelligence underlie and inform the successive states they eventually yield to. Subsumed as they are by the global-level leading edge of consciousness, the more basal levels receive and process information without registering most of it as experience at the explicit level. Bateson describes the resultant system, "Perception is governed by a system of presuppositions" that have woven themselves into distinctive patterns over many generations. The entire epistemic edifice is "a whole philosophy deep in the mind but beyond the consciousness."[dccclxxiii] In a complex tangle of both lateral and vertical domain-crossing and reciprocal causality, the numerous nested tiers of semantic organization methodically interact with the physical domain to allow intentional states and directives to be parlayed into expressed interpretations. The majority of these do not rise to the level of conscious explication, but they do frame and focus the contents of awareness and bias its probabilities of enacting certain outcomes over others. Potential expressions not highlighted for enactment or preservation become unconscious content and recede back into the dark recesses below the threshold of lucidity.

The importance of the unconscious in structuring the boundaries and loci of conscious attention underscores its role as the generative matrix of awareness. Like the empty heart of an attractor, the unconscious does not have an objective existence, but rather is defined by the effects of its influence, and the forms it takes on when it presents itself to the consciousness. Jung depicts a holographic projection across the boundary of the two domains, with unconscious content bifurcating at the critical threshold—retaining its unconscious character while projecting a form across the liminal boundary of perceptibility.[dccclxxiv] Conversely, externally sourced stimuli are translated through the senses into psychic events, simultaneously being perceived and incorporated into the formless, unknowable substrate of the unconscious.[dccclxxv] A subtle symmetry is implied in the double reflection across the interface between the conscious and unconscious: in order to encounter oneself at a higher level of consciousness, it is necessary to delve deeply into the layers of the unconscious.

Self-contained, like an icon whose existence is independent of its semiotic derivatives, the unconscious is free to function independently of its conscious progeny.[dccclxxvi] The relative autonomy between begetter and begotten generates a tension of opposites that, when balanced, allows creative emergence. However, when this natural and necessary polarity is not tempered by integration, which reconciles the emergent pole of consciousness to its more instinctual forbear, the former can forgetfully uncouple from its very source and function as though independent of its chaotic shadow. With its roots shorn from the depths of its constitutive potential, the conscious mind is no longer fed by the upwelling currents of the unconscious, nor is it able to direct that swell of potential through the intentional exercise of downward causation. Unmoored from the top-down control of an integrated consciousness, the unconscious mind becomes an unstable ally at best, equally prone to helping and hindering conscious processes.[dccclxxvii]

The unconscious is at once a generator of the order that supports the emergence of higher levels of organization, while also the formless yet logically ordered pool of chaos, whose strata are reflective of both the mind's individual development and its evolutionary predispositions. An increasing capacity for conscious awareness enables increasingly complex epistemic structures, based on a broadened source domain and increased interpretive flexibility. This expanded compass, with its diversity and potential for novel connections, is a semantic cauldron of self-organization that supports a whole domain of conceptual evolution which branches and nests into interlinking subsystems. When these organized gestalts form part of the specie's collective epistemic inheritance, they are instincts. As they take on more role-based functions that incorporate individuals into an elaborate social structure, they evolve toward archetypes.

Instinct and Archetype: Patterns that Connect

While Jungian archetypes are not synonymous with the mathematical transcendence evoked by Platonic ideas, Jung contends that they are of the same kind, except that the former are linked to physiological processes.[dccclxxviii] Their commonality is in their *a priori* existence: "The phenomenon we call spirit depends on the existence of an autonomous primordial image which is universally present in the preconscious makeup of the human psyche."[dccclxxix] These "primordial images" are part of the unconscious heritage of every kind of creature, from Uexkull's notable pea weevil and ichneumon wasp to humankind. The "preparedness" with which so many animals encounter their surroundings begged for Uexkull questions regarding the "meaning transfer of the primal image."[dccclxxx] While the mechanism of transfer was never settled for him, the fact that it is transferred enables creatures to recognize and respond to signs from each other and their environment in species-appropriate ways. Uexkull's favorites—the weevil, the tick, and the wasp—conform very closely to a tight, inherited script with little room for new interpretation. Other species, such as the many birds that rely on various forms of imprinting, allow space between endemic and acquired knowledge. For all of these creatures, the internal response to the stimulating factor is deeply ingrained in the collective history of their species—a potential object waiting for an external affirmation to connect the circuits within the mind, enabling the creature to fulfill an expression of that image.

Humans likewise respond in patterned ways to signals from the environment, observes Joseph Campbell.[dccclxxxi] Instincts, which guide their carriers' activities and delimit the contents and quality of their experience, are adumbrations of the "autonomous primordial image" within the human psyche that Jung invoked. This "image," or archetype, is a mental structure that "occurs spontaneously and possesses an autonomous numinosity."[dccclxxxii] It is an unconscious specter that broods over formless potential until summoned by circumstance to assume a mental shape. Prior to its active projection, archetype lies latent in a non-dynamic, unmeasured state like the superposition of potential eigenstates in unitary evolution. In the same way that instincts responsive to external cues broadcast from the mental "inwardness" of agents to "[reach] far out into the world...and '[psychify]' time and space,"[dccclxxxiii] likewise "archetypes imprint their stamp on matter so physis and psyche form an indivisible connection."[dccclxxxiv]

Fluidly adjustable to changeable external conditions, archetypal expression enacts thirdness from a timeless, unconscious stratum rooted deeply in humanity's shared history. Spanning the gulf between local and nonlocal, archetypes arise from what Jung deems the "collective unconscious," a portion of the psyche he describes as a "deeper inborn layer not derived from experience but [that] is universal," and which "presents a level in which individual distinctions of consciousness are more or less extinguished."[dccclxxxv] William James reached a similar conclusion about the influence of evolutionary history on the human psyche by stating his belief that "the human mind owes its present shape to experience…of the ancestors as well" as to personal experience.[dccclxxxvi]

Archetypes preserve the functional proficiency of their instinctual predecessors in that they are impulses to particular types of action, prompted by conducive conditions. However, unlike instincts, they reflect the more sophisticated elaborations of human epistemology by portraying the objects of their actions.[dccclxxxvii] As denizens of the unconscious, archetypes represent something that is inherently unknowable, and "not entirely contained in time," [dccclxxxviii] but that is inferable by its effects, much like the chaotic functions which bear testimony to the empty presence that they frame. This indeterminacy is the foundation of the open-ended scope for expression carried in every archetype, which allows limitless interpretive variations on its underlying template. Woven into highly ordered patterns from threads originating at lower levels of organization, archetypes supply, limit, direct, and constrain the evolution of behavioral probabilities from potential to expression, manifesting themselves through recurring motifs that flexibly adapt to ambient conditions.

According to Jung, archetypes represent a "probability of psychic events;" they are "symbolically anticipated result[s] of … psychic statistic[s]."[dccclxxxix] Like any other semantic structure, archetype is an attractor which channels and routes the flows of energy and events toward a probable set of outcomes. Only when activated by a convergence of supportive circumstances does an archetype take on form by entraining actors like nodes into the network of its field-like pattern. Like a current oscillating between the conscious and unconscious poles of the psyche, the mobilized archetype reveals some aspects of its enfolded information through its players' activities, much like the interpreting agents of DNA convert limited aspects of the semantic potential of its cryptic syntax into dynamical functionality.[dcccxc] With agents acting as centers of attraction, the field they sustain by playing out a temporal analog of the archetype's encoded information links them into a coherent network of complexity in which proximate causality is obscured. The nonlinear boundary conditions, portrayed through archetypal actors in their roles as living symbols, disclose the system's logic.

In their relative autonomy, archetypes take on some agent-like properties. They are niche constructors, enacting regularities in relation to certain stimuli. Like Umwelten, they arrange incoming data according to the form of their peculiar logic. The patterns of events within an activated archetypal field can manifest as Jungian synchronicities. As a necessary corollary of diachronic time, synchronicity arises through affinity between relational dynamics and the situations that elicit them—a condition that Jung sees as a causal force more potent than causality itself.[dcccxci] Eschewing the narrow and surficial focus of proximate causality, which separates cause from effect, Jungian synchronicity invokes nonlocal connectivity, contextual contingency, multiple realizability of expression, and domain crossing from internal process to external mapping, to converge the otherwise uncorrelated trajectories of random-seeming events into a single archetypal basin of attraction.[dcccxcii]

Synchronicity is the leading edge of archetypal self-organization, open to evolving new patterns. Behind its manifestation, Jung assures us, an archetype has been at work for a long time in the unconscious mind, skillfully arranging circumstances that will lead to the "crisis," or symmetry break, that allows novelty to surface.[dcccxciii] A biological analog of Jungian synchronicity lies in the ability of a genome to silently accrue potential changes below the level of expression. When these changes epistatically crystalize into phenotypic novelty, an evolutionary saltation transpires much like a quantum leap, leaving no obvious, traceable record behind it. As Teilhard de Chardin discerns, life proceeds "not by fits and starts, nor a single thread, but the whole network pushed forward all at the same time."[dcccxciv] Similarly, within the balanced tension stretching between archetypal poles, consciousness has an opportunity to develop and adjust, evolving in essence and form.

Just as a genome can be breached by a virus, an archetype can parasitize the interpretive capacities of a hosting consciousness that is not sufficiently powerful to maintain its distinction in the face of the compelling pull of unconscious undertow. Like any other unconscious upwelling, archetypes "double" themselves at the interface of consciousness, offering their contents to the localizing power of an individuated intelligence capable of immediately integrating them into its conscious experience.[dcccxcv] If recognized and integrated, the archetype can be brought under volitional control. Otherwise, the dark reflection below the conscious surface retains its full autonomy, which often plays out at odds with dictums of the rational intellect. The Apostle Paul apparently struggled with the frustrations of unintegrated archetypes: "For that which I do, I know not. For what I would do, that I do not; but what I hate, that I do."[dcccxcvi]

Jung details how the structure of archetype is mirrored in the very physiology that embeds it. The cerebrospinal aspect of the nervous system—the structures supporting explicit sensation and consciousness—comprehends surfaces. It is the domain of categorization and reason, perceiving entities as separate and in isolation. As the presenting symbol level, this system gives expressed archetypes their outermost forms. In contrast, the sympathetic nervous system is in touch with that underlying realm that is, says Jung, like water, with "no inside and no outside, no above and no below…where all life floats in suspension."[dcccxcvii] The analogy of water implies a route to the intentional access of the mental strata that harbor archetype. Unlike Narcissus, enamored of the form appearing on the water's reflective surface, Jung advocates a deep penetration of the encompassing realm underlying the surficial veneer, "where I experience the other in myself and the other-than-myself experiences me." Only through a descent into the shadowy depths of the hidden unconscious, the interiority from which the exterior arises, can consciousness ascend to unexplored heights. Under the guidance of archetype, this descent marks a return to the original, constituting consciousness that is the source of all potential, channeling the psyche's currents into the "flow [that] is prior to what forms and dissolves in it."[dcccxcviii] Immersive integration of individual consciousness into the deepest and most universal of conscious strata breathes invigorated potential up through all layers that support explicit awareness. With the forces of life thus renewed, chaos yields fresh opportunities for the emergence of creativity and order.

Metaphor and Symbol

Welling up from within the chaotic, non-rational depths of the unconscious to project a self-similar motif on externally various circumstances, fluid archetype lacks a distinct, literal correspondence between its meaning potential and outer modes of expression. Because of its fundamentally non-rational, non-literal nature, the primary vehicle for the expression of archetypal content is metaphor.[dcccxcix] "A word or image is symbolic when it implies something more than its obvious meaning. As the mind explores the symbol, it is led to ideas that lay beyond the grasp of reason," explains Jung. "Because there are innumerable things beyond the range of human understanding, we constantly use symbolic terms to represent concepts that we cannot define or fully comprehend."[cm] Metaphors and symbols are different modes of the same function, which divines potential lying beneath surfaces by drawing from the associations that support the emergence of the symbol level. Metaphor allows a concept, whose instantiation is mental but whose locution is firmly locked in the dimensions of time and place, to expand in its capacity to conjoin and convey meanings across domains, activating the hidden entailments that attend a mental object much like a wave attends a particle.

By forging its domain-crossing spans based on implicit and subjectively ascertained likenesses well below the symbol level, the interdimensional penetration of metaphor affects an efficiency of a deeper order than reason, which divides along planar surfaces. With its inward reach, metaphor complements this highest manifestation of categorization, whose focus is on the presentable attributes of the objects it measures. While categorization establishes the outposts of the mental structure that intelligence must construct in order to interpret, the multileveled interconnections that metaphor establishes among those points reveal and fulfill the potential depth of meaning within the delineations of form. By transposing potential into meaning via association, the tools of intelligent domain crossing explicate the subtle entanglements uniting all domains.

Likewise a symbol, with its manifold potential for meaning, speaks to the mind beyond rational consciousness, mobilizing the more experiential, and vastly more expansive interpretive potential of the unconscious.[cmi] Symbols are "natural attempts to reconcile and reunite opposites within the psyche,"[cmii] prompting a vacillation in the mind's focus between the physical form and its meaningful intimations until the current between the two poles of consciousness supports coherence.[cmiii] Symbols play a structural role in the psyche's functions by connecting the consciousness to the archetypal narratives that direct the flow of its energies. The manifold of potential meanings that await awakening in a symbol points to the profound non-linearity it embodies. Like a metaphor, a symbol is a turning point—a region of coherent discontinuity surrounded by chaos—between distinct domains whose disparity is resolved only through interpretation. The semantic closure that interpretation affords between subject and object generates an emergent context, structured by entailments whose distinctive logic constrains and guides the creative activities of intelligence.

In embodying meaning beyond itself, a symbol is a metaphor whose full power can only be accessed by active participation. Sourced in the mental realm of potential, a symbol's meaning is not pre-determined, formulaic, absolute, or single. Just as the potential to create a metaphor lies latent within any domain, any object can act as a symbol; a stabilizing placeholder on which many insinuations of meaning can converge. In the observer-dependent relationship of symbolism, a symbol's significative pluripotency is collapsed—relative to a particular reference frame—into a single selected state aligned with the interpretive priorities of the observer. Neither wholly intrinsic to interpreter nor object, the act of interpretation is a dynamic interface between the association-making intelligence of the observer and the relations that person perceives as the symbol's definitive properties. The stratified manifolds of surface-level features, associative relations, and subjective experience are cohered into the unity of a single stable point of understanding betokened by the symbol, which represents a binding seam where criticality simmers between the expansive chaos of potential and the defining, contracting order of interpretation. Through the emergent integration of object and meaning within subject, the transformative capacity of interpretation affirms and enriches the associative scope of the unconscious mind, and integrates that abundance with the continuously evolving, differentiating activities of the conscious mind.[cmiv]

In eschewing the boundaries imposed by literalness, metaphors and symbols demonstrate the relativity of measurable phenomena. Initiated in consciousness rather than materiality, all manifestation is indelibly metaphorical. The Gospel of Phillip, verse 59, describes this condition: "Truth did not come into this world naked, but came in types and images." The outer patinas apprehended by rational mind serve an indispensable function when understood as signifiers of a deeper level of truth. Guiding interpretations when approached as symbols, literal images point beyond the limitations of perfunctory, surface-level features to a more numinous reality that is ultimately the self-same beneath all external heterogeneity.[cmv] Ortega y Gasset cautions that "we dwarf the meaning of symbols by demanding meaning, or that deep should appear in same way as superficial; things that present only that part of themselves are strictly necessary to enable us to realize that they lie concealed beneath it."[cmvi]

Ritual

As if re-enacting and thereby entering into rhythm with the universal regularities whose coterminous cadences unfold evolution, humans have turned from their earliest roots to ritual as a means of seeking the icon enfolded within the symbol, synchronizing the conscious flow within the group on the basis of the immersive experience of shared meaning. Providing a crystalizing seed of order, the imputed meaning of a symbol informs how agents within a semiotically aligned group orient themselves in relation to what they perceive as its message, which contains its causal power. Ritual, as an enacted symbol, is vested with the purpose, according to Campbell, of "conduct[ing] people across thresholds of transformation that demand changes in both conscious and unconscious life."[cmvii] By synchronizing the focus of both levels of consciousness, the structures of awareness are able to align with the intention that is intimated in the ritual in order to actively express it.

The rituals carried out by animals and humans are highly ordered iterations of the habit-making tendencies of nature. As with metaphors and symbols, both poles of consciousness are engaged when a ritualized pattern refers to a meaning not derivable from the act itself, but rather from the associations it conjures in the minds that interpret it. A ritual is a scripted flow of intention that takes its actors into the iconic, unmediated heart of the symbol which encapsulates the meaning they seek entry into. Underlying the symbolic façade that provides moorage for the rational mind is a deep homology between participants and the ritual's referent, which is ultimately a non-rational, iconic state of being that ritual enactment ushers the experience of its participants into. Bent as they are around the ineffable components of consciousness—experience and meaning—rituals allow the conscious mind to drop to the common experiential ground of manifestation, from which participants can renew their connections among themselves, as well as to their vivid, living environments. In an inward-turning reversal of sign processes, ritual begins with a symbol and leads its actors into a shared iconic experience akin to unified coherence. It reverses the outwardly reaching tendencies of intelligence and redirects them inward, shifting the fruits of interpretation from anticipation and prediction to insight and revelation.

Metaphors, symbols, and rituals serve as organizing principles that summon to creative order the ocean of potential underlying expression. Deriving their powers of meaningful reference from the contexts in which they arise, these tropes, like all other complex systems, start out as arbitrary, relatively autonomous units that become fixed into emergent, ecological orderings of epistemic gestalts that encompass their components without being reducible to them. As these orderings fledge into a complete paradigm, its downwardly causal constraints entrain the emergent, constitutive tiers of semantic scaffolding toward its support, maintenance, and propagation. By creating structures of explicit expression to correspond with conditions of internal perception, paradigms iterate the pattern of evolution, which differentially adorns fundamental self-similarity in context-dependent trappings. The most fundamental paradigms address the most primordial, universal experiential conditions. One of the most prominent features of that universality is chaos.

Ocean of Chaos and the Birth of Consciousness

The intrinsically unknowable noumenon pointed to by archetype, symbol, and ritual is nothing less than the "living mystery."[cmviii] The undivided consciousness at the source of manifestation appears to the rational intellect as a place of deep darkness and chaos. In ancient myths and rituals, experience of this energetic ocean is sought and celebrated as the great, generative Mother. The third Sephira of the Kabbalistic trinity is Binah, is the "supernal Mother, co-equal with Chokmah, and the great feminine form of God, the Elohim, in whose image man and woman are created."[cmix] Although her primary attribute is understanding, her chaotic form is alluded to in the Kabbala's reference to her as the "great sea." Concealing mystery in its formless depths, the dark region underlying phenomenal manifestation ebbs and flows well below the reach of rational, conscious mind. Its chaos is the logic of the unconscious. It is this living, energetic ocean that is tapped by the roots of the Trees of both Life and Knowledge, and explicated along the orderly lines of forking branches, which unfurl a bounty of fruit and vibrant leaves, upturned toward the radiance of the sun.

Like its oceanic counterparts of the earthly realm, the primordial tumult teems with living forms, its piscine symbols identified by Jung with the maternal attributes of life force, renewal and rebirth, and products of the unconscious. In his exploration of world myths, Joseph Campbell finds at the source of many a watery abyss a cosmic serpent, representing divine life-creative energy. The serpent's shedding skin denotes renewal both physically and spiritually on many levels, from the cyclical changing of seasons that bring annual resurrection to the slumbering earth, to the epiphanies that replenish the human spirit from within. As the third edge of the primordial trinity, the emergence of oceanic Binah creates a closed, triangular boundary much like the "self-closing form of the serpent [pursuing its own tail which] delimits creation" [cmx] and localizes wisdom and singularity as thirdness and firstness respectively; universal collaborators in the expression of transcendent meaning through the conscripting channels of immanent form.

The water that invites the consciousness to baptismal descent signifies the spirit which becomes unconscious over the course of its evolution, demanding that each leading edge eventually succumb to an emergent successor. This dark sea with its mysterious inhabitants hidden from conscious view is the source of what Jung calls the "other Eucharistic food."[cmxi] The fish represent salvation, which Fr. Merton defines as a "deep respect for [the] metaphysical reality of man."[cmxii] The apostolic vocation as fishermen, harvesting their food from the sea, conveys this significance. When the resurrected Jesus ordered disciples fishing in unproductive waters to cast their net on the right side of the boat, the yield was both a bounteous catch and recognition of his divinity. Beneath the water's concealing surface, the fish sought by the net were merely abstract potentials from the perspective of their pursuers. The starboard cast of the net bespeaks explicit volitional consciousness, whose mastery alone can coax from the featureless obduracy bounding the realm below from that above the treasures it shields from view. Only when the hidden denizens of the deep are entangled in the net's confining mesh, which has become an attractor ensnaring their previously free-roaming trajectories, can the fishermen at the surface "measure" them, transforming their potential into realized value by awakening consciousness to the perception of divinity embodied.

In their awakening epiphany, the fishermen become capable of partaking of the body of Christ at the highest level of transcendence, but only by retrieving this subtle sustenance from the depths of darkness. The fully realized consciousness of Jesus displays its mastery over the aqueous shadows which he freely walks across, indicating that he has utterly submerged himself in the very realm that is now under his command in order to attain divine heights. By harmonizing with its watery foundations, the highest leading edge of consciousness becomes free to inhabit them without succumbing to their drowning sway. Like the infinitely reflective net of Indra, or Bohm's many-layered gradations of mesh, the conscious mind has the capability, if strengthened into focused awareness, to skillfully troll beneath the opaque boundary of the unknown in terms of the known to collect to the surface the deep-dwelling fish-offerings of the unconscious. Glistening under the rational light of cultivated awareness, the silvery bodies from that ineffable domain convey the insightful fruits of chaos that allow it to be purposefully and creatively rendered into new expressions of order. Through the play of conscious creativity, humanity accesses its unique heritage as an intentionally active participant in evolution, capable of reproducing what Merton refers to as the "divine idea."[cmxiii]

Hovering above the level of constitutive chaos, it is the function of consciousness to harness and express selected aspects of the formless "divine life-creative energy."[cmxiv] Drawing from potential below while also tending, with or without intentional awareness, toward the silent pull from some higher basin of attraction, the leading edge of conscious evolution is always poised at the crossroads between two poles of potential: compositional and aspirational; Alpha and Omega. The attractor stationed at the very boundary of surprisal, always coaxing eager evolution toward the unknown, is portended from creation's very inception: "In the beginning the earth was without form and void, and darkness was upon the face of the deep. And the Spirit of God moved upon the face of the waters. On the second day, a firmament in the midst of the waters divided the waters from the waters, above and below."[cmxv] In the multi-dimensional division of waters, past was split from future and evolution became directional, shrouded by a penumbra of unconscious potential that lay not only below the leading edge of awareness, but above it as well.[cmxvi] Husserl detected the embedding unconscious context in which intentionality arises: "Actional [mental processes] are surrounded by a 'halo' of non-actional mental processes; the stream of mental processes can never consist of just actionalities."[cmxvii] Merton corroborates: "The conscious mind of man is *exceeded in all directions* by his unconscious."[cmxviii] The potential from which consciousness evolves thereby maintains a balanced opposition to the potential that transcends it.

Shortly after dividing the dark regions, creating preliminary delineations of categorical order within non-rational chaos, God spoke, "Let there be light." With that pronouncement, the light of the conscious became cordoned off from its unconscious shadow, and the destabilization of equilibrium through differentiation propelled consciousness and matter into a mutually reliant, yet oppositional tangle of relations that rolled forward into time and evolution. The leading edge of consciousness became like a line of symmetry, a dividing line that can activate its force of attraction to stir up stores of past experience and selectively apply them to enactment. At the same time, its attractive draw can also pull from unexplored, unexpressed potential that lies ahead of its current level of expression, situating causality not only at, but also below, above, and within a given hierarchical level.[cmxix] By reifying the self-awareness implicit in the two poles of potential, humans have a means by which to access the stable point that represents the critical fusion between them: "Faith enables us to come to terms with our animal nature and to accept the task of trying to govern it according to the Divine will, that is, according to love. At the same time, faith subjects our reason to the hidden spiritual forces that are *above* it."[cmxx] When consciously balanced as a symmetrical line that at once divides the ebbing potential of the past from swells of new possibility, humans embody the Logos, the original intelligent power of division which engenders manifestation based on a foundational paradox: what it ostensibly divides is indelibly unified—laid together or collected—within its own centered body.

Myth

From its earliest dawn, the human enterprise has located itself within a story line. Events and regularities have accrued meaning via subtle layers of association held in place by symbols, which serve to guide the flow of meaning within the narrative. This meaning is amplified and consecrated when the story's receivers accept the symbol's invitation to immersion into its experiential interior, where ultimately all of the domains that meaning crosses resolve into singularity. Early societies sought coherence in ritual around important events, like puberty, marriage, death, a hunt, a harvest, and various seasonal and celestial events. Marking as sacred the significant turning points in cosmic, local, and personal cycles allowed cultures to trace the universal flow of energy at its various scales, etch it into their collective consciousness, and harmonize their lives according to it. One vital vehicle for accomplishing this multi-level integration was myth. Campbell defines mythology as "an organization of images conceived as a rendition of the sense of life."[cmxxi] Ordered into a flowing narrative, these images are used as a template for organizing people within a society by providing a consensus understanding of their origins and history, and therefore their relationship with their surroundings across scales. In this way, myth becomes the "secret opening through which inexhaustible energies of cosmos pour into human cultural manifestation."[cmxxii]

Like a ritual summoning the antipodes of consciousness into congruence, myth addresses, according to Jung, the "primitive" need to assimilate outer experience into inner events.[cmxxiii] It is a tool of cognitive niche construction originally used to establish and incorporate the human microcosm within the nested rhythms of the macrocosmic symphony. This most primal of needs finds a symbolic encoding in the images of myth—which "originate in a spirit that is not quite human, but rather a breath of nature"[cmxxiv]—and the omnipresent infusion they imply of the sacred into every dimension of life. Mythical symbols "touch and release our deepest centers of motivation"[cmxxv] and make them consciously accessible from different angles, including by offering analogies through the characters and events they describe. Codified as myths, the guiding precepts of a culture represent an interface between the order of society and that of nature by which its surprisal is acknowledged. The unknown events from without are correlated with those mysterious regions within because the numinous depths of the unconscious are not merely projected, but actively enmeshed in the natural world. By integrating themselves into their surroundings, myth makers are, by proxy, consciously inhabiting their own unconscious minds.

Although the outer trappings of myth are assayable by rational explanations which measure and assign properties to their objects, these can at best highlight only partial aspects of a myth's meaning potential, leaving the rest enfolded in the timeless suspension beyond the ken of surficial cognition and its time-dependent interpretive frame. From within, however, the view afforded is one of unitary coherence. Entry into myth, and the rituals and symbols that attend it, engages each participant as a "living symbol," instrumental in conducting the omnipresent energies of universal sustenance through his or her own body. Within the sacred interiority of the symbolic, those engaged in its thrall find the still, unitary point of coherence which persists through even the decohering collapse wrought by surface-level measurement; which turns outward to the world as entanglements; and which resides inwardly as the unequivocal voice that "speak[s] to the wonder of the universe."[cmxxvi]

By presenting themselves in the "types and images" that alone convey truth to minds conditioned by embodiment, myths—like metaphors— provide a sensorimotor bridge between visceral iconicity and expressive symbolism; between instinct and intellect.[cmxxvii] Viewing nature's mysteries—even those contained in oneself—"plain and naked"[cmxxviii] is not an option for the uninitiated mind. This bitter warning was delivered in the myth of the hapless archer Actaeon, who, upon accidentally glimpsing the unveiled beauty of the nature divinity Artemis, was transformed into a stag, to be shredded by his own pack of hounds; his animal instincts. The danger they present to the mind incapable of sustaining them is why, according to Phillip, the mysteries burrow themselves away from the sensory and rational devices of external description, and only divulge themselves, in their irreducible array of endless potential, in the presence of "interpretation furnished by wisdom."[cmxxix]

In a layered progression that embellishes a founding motif with locally relevant details to convey a universally symbolic meaning, suffused with divinity, myth is an imaginative projection of the unconscious, which, unlike the surface-apprehending conscious, can delve into an order of knowledge that is beholden to rationality. Its substance is grounded in the natural processes of intelligence: the continuity of memory, the distinction-making at the base of rationality, and particularly the metaphorical play across domains, which sustains the dynamical emergence of interpretation. The poles of self-referencing are frequently switched, as the environment is anthropomorphized, and then referenced as a source domain. This inversion is a necessary "step outside the system" (Hofstadter) that allows for more objective viewing. Closing a subtle semantic loop by drawing all outward projections back to their originating human center, the psychic circulation engendered by myth feeds the ongoing drive of evolution in the cognitive domain. Unconscious attributes projected onto the surrounding environment are made visible to the analytical power of the observing mind, thereby providing a crucial scaffold for burgeoning self-awareness to anchor to by facilitating integration across domains, including those of the conscious and unconscious, while fostering the capacity of nuance from which grows reason.

By embedding the conscious mind within the non-rational context of the unconscious, much like an autonomous agent carves a niche which deeply integrates it into its surroundings, myth unites the poles of the psyche into emergent union. As Campbell observes, "the soul comes to full power by assimilating beings thought to be outside it."[cmxxx] In Wilber's terminology, when the forces and phenomena that are thought to be "otherworldly" are incorporated into the experience so that they are accepted as "this-worldly,"[cmxxxi] the capacity of the psyche to assimilate its experiences has at once deepened and centered itself more fully within the localized center of human consciousness.

The imperative for integration, present for all life, became an increasing challenge for humanity's ancestors as cognitive structures began their own radiation of evolution on top of animal experience.

While a seemingly straightforward process, the integration of increasingly higher levels of consciousness with their implicit underpinnings becomes more complicated as the gap between intellect and instinct grows. The example of imprinting, for instance, demonstrates a cognitive bypass for onerous genetic encoding. Its functionality hinges on the proper alignment of external circumstances with an internal readiness—a simple bias synchronicity. As the gulf between genetics and cognition widens, however, and the agent becomes even more dependent on non-biological transmissions of information, the integration of mental domains becomes more intricate, arduous, and fraught with opportunities for failure. The capacity of speech in particular introduced for the first time the possibility of a barrier between the surface level of awareness and the immediacy of experience. Objective, rational descriptions are alien encroachers on the numinous, fluid, and interconnected landscape of the non-rational. Myths circumvent that challenge by speaking in the language of the unconscious, deepened by the richly associative and meaning-laden imagery of nature, and rollicked along by the prosodic flow of narration; the music of event tied to that of speech.

The elements of myth seem so far removed from our rationalistic, scientific modern worldview that they appear from this vantage point simplistic, even whimsical—the product of minds naïve enough to believe in their magical, supernatural, and profoundly nonscientific premises. However, the generation of myth is thoroughly natural, arising from the intrinsic spontaneity at the foundations of complexity in general, and manifesting in the psyche through the medium of intelligence. Like the self-similar fractal, myth often offers very little self-evident information in its presentation. Unlike some of its more specialized descendants such as allegory—whose symbols map in a relatively direct correspondence to their referents—myth is profoundly ontological, setting its actors within a cosmological framework that they occupy according to its storyline. By conducting their lives as symbolic enactments of the meaning embedded in their myths, participants channel the deeply sourced, upwelling vital current that is always prior to rationalization, and always hovering at its descriptive boundaries like unassimilable surprise. Anathema to rational explication, the flow of this meaning-current can only be explicated through a lived interpretation. As such, myths embody an element of evolution that is not amenable to the scientific method in the same, objectively measurable way as the many habit-like regularities of the universe. The mechanistic worldview that has successfully explicated so many structural and relational patterns of nature lacks—rejects the very premise of—adequate metaphors to apply to the creative element of natural play that engenders myth.[cmxxxii] It is playful spontaneity, however, that supplies natural selection with the fodder of abundant potential to be reduced through measurement into realized outcomes.

The Play of Creation

The ascent from the swirling abyss of potential into form, cause, purposiveness, intention—all intelligently wrought tools of consciousness—is conceived of in Hindu systems of thought as *lila*, or the play of God. Indeed, it is through the "fanciful spirit …on the border-line between jest and earnest"[cmxxxiii] animating mythology that cultures sought to draw divinity into their daily workings. A game of belief, Campbell tells us, is the first step to divine seizure—the very seizure sought and celebrated by mystics, forming the basis of religion.[cmxxxiv] The power accorded to symbolism within mythological systems amounts to a "highly played game of 'as if.'"[cmxxxv]

While habits, or chreodes, act as the guiding channels that structure consciousness through constraint, it is in the freedom of play that these potential pathways are sampled and tested. Individually, play is formative in developing the physical and mental capabilities of its human and animal participants, while at the same time availing social structures to important modifications. Under different circumstances, play can provide relief from the rigors of hierarchies when dominant individuals temporarily subordinate themselves. Conversely, play can help establish and enforce hierarchical roles, such as through non-aggressive contests of strength.

At the same time as it promotes individual development and social stability, play is a vital contributor to the evolution of consciousness toward self-awareness. Through a complex act of semiotic layering, play effectively negates its apparent referent when behaviors from one context, such as aggression, are applied to the more agreeable pursuit of non-competitive play, in which participants invoke the "as if" element by portraying an emotional state they are not in.[cmxxxvi] Partners in play explicitly set a semiotic context in which to interpret the meaning of their ensuing behavior. In conducting this "metacommunication," or messages about the messages they send, the participants of play are collaboratively constructing a mutually understood referent that is entirely mental, based on a shared volitional state, which alters the meaning of the interaction that follows.[cmxxxvii] The "as if" element of play leads communication to a higher level of expression by compelling a coil of self-reference that allows players to engage, with explicit intention, in an emotional state that is not necessarily expressed in their behaviors.

The postural, gestural, vocal, and facial means that animals use to communicate playful intentions are essentially nonlinguistic metaphors. For example, the canid "play-bow" depicts non-aggression by lowering the body physically to imply willful vulnerability and non-offensiveness.[cmxxxviii] Metaphor itself is a game played in the conceptual and linguistic domains. Just as playful activity among agents requires that they use a system of meanings to establish a new shared motivational state that allows the transfer of behaviors endemic to other domains, metaphor functions by rearranging categorical boundaries within semantic domains. With its unscripted creative potential and its self-referencing recursions, the play of metaphor is hemmed into coherence by the strict, logical guidelines of selectivity.

The spontaneous vitality flowing upward from the lowest levels of systemic integration carries the experiential, metaphysical substrate of all manifestation. As an expression of potential—which finds abundant accommodation in the vastness of the unconscious before expressing in the relatively narrow swath of explicit consciousness—play is prior to austerity, just as expansion is prior to contraction; meaning to syntax; and radiation to the orderliness of canalization. Although integrally dependent on structure for expression, potential cannot be fully contained or described by the constraints that "measure" it. Ever at play, this uncontainable vigor is the joyous expression of the forward impulse to life that precludes evolutionary stagnation and dictates that "[we] were not created for pleasure: [we] were created for spiritual JOY."[cmxxxix]

The bottom-up flow of natural play, whose counterpart is conscripting, top-down selection, becomes increasingly explicated with higher degrees of semiotic freedom within agents. The survival urge apparent in even the simplest of life forms comes to reveal and even be eclipsed by its ebullient underpinnings. This uncontainable force is the "exuberance of an internal activity that had outstripped the material needs of life."[cmxl] A lifetime of studying wild chimpanzees led Jane Goodall to conclude that "it is a sense of wonder and awe that we share with them."[cmxli] Thomas Merton sees such "spontaneous awe at the sacredness of life, of being"[cmxlii] as the fruit to be sought from contemplation. Whether non-randomly dancing through a ballet of electrons, hovering at the localizing cusp of constrictive selection, splashing over bodies and landscapes in improbable varieties of colors, sounds, and patterns, or spilling over the brim of complex consciousness into myth, symbol, art, insight, or ingenuity, the vibrant pulse of life that supplies meaning beyond quantifiable, measurable parameters is ever at play, vivifying the universe.

The Egg and the Hero

Myths employ symbols to create a spiritual roadmap of their makers' past, which acts as a guide to incorporate its recipients into their present context. Rooted in the primordial mystique of the Goddess, who contains all of creation within her womb and nurtures life with the bounty of her body, the earliest myths trace the genesis of the universe to a state of darkness or chaos. Some renditions have the Great Mother skimming along the surface of chaos—originally by herself, and later embracing a lover—and dancing it into order. Other traditions variously envision universal parturition as the emergence of social order from some nebulous, pre-manifest realm such as a dark subterranean womb from which people ascend; or a supernatural "dreamtime" populated by heroes and deities; or a cosmic egg that splits apart its thin shell to reveal the higher-dimensional seed of life it had been incubating beneath that protective bounding surface.[cmxliii] The themes shared among all myths of the cosmogonic cycle are the emergence of the current, familiar order from a prior age of a supernatural, unrecognizable order; maintenance of the present order; and eventual progress to universal dissolution.[cmxliv]

In myths set in a world already unfolded from its umbilical center, the timeless realm becomes the destination of adventuring heroes. The hero's journey transpires between the twin poles of generation and destruction as he seeks to bring the power of the great Beginning and End into the present time and incorporate its blessing into life's daily rhythms. Like any system of symbols, the hero motif lends itself to numerous interpretations on many levels. Campbell and Jung trained their focus on its metaphor for consciousness, whose leading rational edge strives for balance within the context of its non-rational foundations. Through the course of his adventures, the hero embarks on a journey into the unknown, which parallels a descent into the unilluminated portions of his own projected unconscious. His triumphant return from distant regions of peril is the successful integration of the two poles of the psyche. The journey is one of faith—accessing the spaceless, timeless dimension in which intention and expression align in synchrony to rise above mere probability and enable an otherwise impossible mission.

In pursuing his quest in an unknown target domain, the hero detaches himself from his known and accustomed world and ventures into the dark dream worlds of the cosmogonic birth. These are the subconscious keeps of archetypal wraiths and chthonic spirits, which appear to the quester as supernatural guides to offer their sometimes inscrutable assistance through the dark and ambiguous region to the power source it guards.[cmxlv] The adventurer must pass through the uncertain terrain of the unconscious to reach the spiritual region of higher consciousness. In order to engage in the immersive, unmeasured experience at the foundation of life, the hero passes through a threshold that divests him of his former concepts of his self; his ego-identification. It is a "self-annihilation" that is the opposite of self-abnegation. Rather, it is a "reconciliation of the individual consciousness with the universal will."[cmxlvi] Paradoxically, the closer individualized consciousness approaches the singular ground of all manifestation, the more powerfully differentiated it becomes.[cmxlvii] This supremely revealing and expanding act of self-surrender allows the adventurer to fulfill the role of the hero, as described by Ortega y Gasset: "A hero means to be one out of many, to be oneself. If we refuse to have our actions be determined by heredity or environment it is because we seek to base the origin on ourselves and only ourselves."[cmxlviii]

Along with the treacherous journey, the dangers of the call to heroism lie within the hero himself and his conscious response to his experiences. Like the entropic shadow that encircles order as both aid and adversary, the begetting unconscious is not entirely benign in relating to her progeny's intrepid invasion, as the terrifying archetype of the Terrible Mother warns. At once generatrix and destroyer, the dark, maternal chaos swirls indifferently even should she resorb the rational intruder into her undifferentiated core.[cmxlix] As a normal part of mental functioning, conscious and unconscious regularly switch poles of dominance, with previously conscious elements sinking under while new ones supplant them in the cycle of death and rebirth associated with the Great Mother.[cml] However, the consciousness risks the loss of its individuated identity on the pyre of entropic oblivion that the dark regions represent to those unprepared for entry. The natural secrets that Acteon was unable to face are the same as those encountered by the seeking hero. "Though the world was made through [the light], the world did not recognize [the light]."[cmli] Conscious mind, uneasily aware of the perils that guard its source from penetration, protects itself from the fearsome objects and entities it imagines to inhabit its deepest abysses. The terrors of the dark realm are called into being through the mind's own lack of recognition as a sort of prophylaxis: "Anyone unable to understand a god sees it as a devil and is thus defended from the approach."[cmlii] The fearful recoil of the unprepared consciousness rebuffs a direct encounter with its own shadows. While this reaction helps the consciousness to maintain its rightful place above the non-rational tumult, it also proliferates within those unvanquished realms demons empowered to resist efforts of reconciliation.

Only after sojourning through the labyrinthine dreamscape of the non-rational unconscious without any guarantee of success and uniting it with the surface-level rational consciousness, can the hero be effective on earth by bringing his hard-won guerdon back to his place of origin.[cmliii] The hero comes to consciously explicate Teilhard's "rent" that runs through the "interior in the heart of beings… [that] exists through all of nature from all time." Fully possessed of the knowledge of unity within multiplicity, the hero returns home with the new dispensation to "release …the flow of life into the body of the world"[cmliv] by disseminating his cultivated wisdom.

Even after his journey has been fulfilled, the hero is still within grasp of the self-sought danger that attends great responsibility. Although his perspective, newly deepened through integration, may leave the hero confounded by the "baffling inconsistency between the wisdom brought forth from the deep, and the prudence" of daily life, it also burdens him with the grave responsibility of bridging these two worlds without adulterating the principles of one with those of the other.[cmlv] Compounding this source of danger is the possibility of a consciousness which resists the humbling power of the mysteries it uncovers, instead assuming the mantle of master. Instead of receiving the mead of nobly gotten gains, it puts itself in danger of sinning, which, according to the Gospel of Mary is not a simplistic distinction between right and wrong acts, but of improper mixing of spiritual and material natures.[cmlvi] When the ego usurps the judgment seat of the universal Self to Whom it owes its tributes, consciousness remains confined to the outer, "light-reflecting" surfaces of phenomena, blind the their true, numinous nature.[cmlvii] This well-recognized danger was a common theme in myths, leading to misbegotten monstrosities like the Minotaur; or tragedies like Icarus, whose quest for solar radiance was untempered by an appreciation for the palliative protection of the watery depths, which ultimately swallowed him out of his brazen but unskilled flight. Instead of laying claim to the throne of consciousness and redirecting its powers of intelligence to the frivolous pursuit of arbitrary impulses, it is rather the job of the ego to help make real the totality of the psyche, which is "inborn but hidden" as Jung says, or "implicate," per Bohm, or "enfolded," according to Boehme. The wholeness that is prior to and latent within the psyche becomes a powerful tool of positive transformation only when it is fully realized and lived. As the Gospel of Thomas, verse 70 admonishes, "If you bring forth what is within you, what you have will save you. If you do not have that within you, what you do not have will destroy you."

The hero's quest is the retelling of a saga that occurs not only within the human psyche, but in some form throughout all of manifestation, in which the critical summoning of order from chaos is fraught with uncertainty and danger at every level. The fine balancing of life, with its concomitant evolutionary drive—laterally into diversity of form and vertically into diversity of depth within form—that is a consequence of the open, dissipative nature of the forms assumed by potential, is inherently uncertain, with the dangers of misalignment between conscious and unconscious poles of mentality increasing along with complexity and the degrees of freedom that make a system flexible enough to perceive itself and strive for heroism. In the ordering of chaos, heroism is akin to a trajectory leaping outside of its most probabilistic basin to chart its own course toward a self-chosen eventuality. Says Ortega y Gassett, "Nothing prevents heroism—which is the activity of the spirit—so much as considering it bound to certain specific contents of life."[cmlviii]

Disintegrated Psyche

Like every other emergent structure, that of explicit consciousness is optimally autonomous when integrated with its context, which includes not only its external, but internal environment as well. The integration of the conscious with the unconscious, which is what facilitates the intentional alignment of potential with expression, is the process of individuation that localizes the universal functions of intelligence within the contingent frame of the individual. So fundamental to the ripening of conscious capabilities, individuation is simply a matter of, in Jung's words, "the individual becom[ing] what he always was."[cmlix] As consciousness develops, the leading edge must forgo its privilege and yield back into the devouring unconscious in order to allow a new level of emergence to express and explore its potential. This process is only sustainable when the emergent leading edge incorporates previous layers of achievement, which have surrendered themselves into the unconscious loam which incubates new possibilities, enriching its depth and orderliness. Midway between the individuated consciousness and the primordial mythological moment, the archetypal "treasure in the realm of shadowy thoughts"[cmlx] presents itself as a support and asset to a robust consciousness heroically capable of integrating with its own unconscious. This, according to Jung, is where archetype serves the conscious mind, functioning to "keep our highest and most important values from disappearing into the unconscious. For when these fall into the unconscious the whole elemental force of the original experience is lost."[cmlxi]

When the degrees of freedom that a semantic system's evolution releases to its leading edge are supported by a deep well of potential that is not pushed away as a dreaded dark side, but inhabited as a bottomless wellspring of understanding, the leading edge of consciousness is liberated to coil back into the "involution" that Teilhard envisioned as the basis of mind's evolutionary leaps of progression. Once the system is able to see itself in its integrated depth, it has insight into the underlying play of forces that reverberate through the semantic complexes of motivations and interpretations that conscious evolution has painstakingly crafted into an individuated expression of universality. The dynamical functioning of the system necessitates that the leading edge of explicit consciousness, while inhabiting its formative structure like a kingdom, also maintains itself above the level of the forces that drive it and fill it. This generates the tension of opposites whose complementary poles balance each other and create a critical region of creative evolution. However, when the low-dimensional bounding surface of consciousness locks itself away from contact with the secrets of its unconscious foundation, it can only reflect the deeper and more profound truths of the latter as pathological contortions.[cmlxii] Unable to stir its own depths, the surface-dwelling mind risks stagnation and ultimately its own destruction, as it is unable to draw deeply from the replenishing current of upward causation but is rather confined to its own shallows and their limited capacity for perception, retention, cultivation, and growth.

Only by maintaining itself in balanced tension above its unconscious foundations can the conscious mind foster its own evolution by actively utilizing and directing the flows of unconsciousness. In eschewing its rightful capacity to recognize and intentionally engage with unconscious structures, the unguarded leading edge of awareness is in very real danger of "falling into the archetype by identification."[cmlxiii] With this adulteration of levels, which subordinates the power of conscious determination to lower-level impulses, the harmonious flow of reciprocal causality is distorted and volition surrenders its autonomy. Instead of exercising the liberty of willful determination, it is condemned to act out the archetypal energies as though they were puppeteers rather currents to be purposively fashioned and intentionally guided. In such an imbalanced condition, the buoyant and fertile balance of opposites becomes a catastrophic bipolarity that fails to contain the destructive powers of chaos within creativity, instead unleashing the levelling power of entropy in which consciousness has no power. Jung perceived this condition as prevalent when he noted that the "psyche is far from being safely synthesized; on the contrary, it threatens to fragment only too easily under the onslaught of unchecked emotions."[cmlxiv] He warns that the result is a conflation of id—personal and cultural appetitive drives—with the unconscious, thereby eroding the integrity of the conscious mind.[cmlxv]

While an unintegrated consciousness may defensively seek to purge itself of archetypal uprisings, Jung warns very clearly that ridding our minds of archetypes is a type of suicide, akin to ridding the body of its organs.[cmlxvi] Instead of seeking to control, repress, or dissolve the contents of the unconscious mind as expressed through archetype, the task at hand is to "dissolve the projections" that have become hardened through literal interpretations, and "restore their contents to the individual who has involuntarily lost them by projecting them outside himself."[cmlxvii] Proper reintegration of the psyche entails ousting the tyrannical regime of excessive top-down control and restoring consciousness to its rightful place above but in balanced relation to the compelling gyres of archetypal flow that have, in the meantime, subsumed it.

A relatively modern malady of arguable origins, the condition of unintegrated consciousness has been a powerful source of influence on the currents of recent history. Although long and variously cultivated, rational thought accelerated toward criticality in the awakening of medieval Europe toward modernity, spurring the radical re-ordering of peoples' conceptions of the world around them and their place in it through revolutions in exploration, philosophy, science, and technology. When emissaries representing the Age of Discovery embarked to foreign shores in search of favorable routes to sustain their markets, the drama of cultivated but unintegrated rationality forced to confront what it had turned into its shadow side was played out in the events that transpired from the numerous encounters that ensued.

The terror that shook the Western mind, fiercely protective of its rational achievements, was not born of an encounter with the centered and holistic power to be attained through the heroic quest of integration. Rather, with low-dimensional rationality only able to perceive veneers instead of constitutive numinosity, the potential for spiritual and psychological richness could only be modeled through the pathological lens of a dissevered psyche. Instead of seeing a mirror to their own humanity reflected in the dusky faces of native inhabitants of untamed shores, the conquerors saw only degenerate Calibans whose best hope for any kind of redemption was under the authority of the more "advanced" civilization. The pathology of top-down control that is not refreshed by the deeps of its own upwelling revealed its destructive penchant by shattering countless lives and cultures under the ensuing tyranny it imposed. Without the integrating grace of myth to move them to humility and awe at the virgin beauty they encountered of nature and humanity, mercenary explorers, as Frederick Turner describes, turned to the powers of cold calculation to inoculate themselves against the humbling effects of majesty and began taking an inventory of the abundance that would eventually succumb to their despoliation. "For them," explains Turner of the destructive invaders, "myth was the hideous error of the ancient past that they were here to oppose and finally destroy."[cmlxviii] The invitation to integration offered by abundant nature and earthy people was repellent to fearful minds whose shallow rationality only saw demons rather than their own light. To venture near the possibility of a deeper understanding, these minds were sure, would lead nowhere but to a deathbed penance gasped in a mortifying flash of remorse, "The horror! The horror!"

Although the tragic lack of understanding that impels uncoupled rationality to turn on its own foundations acknowledges the importance of maintaining the mind's leading edge above the levels it integrates for fear of dissolving back into the constitutive milieu, it fails to recognize the equally sinister dangers of allowing too much space between the two poles of mind. In its dread of dissolving into unconsciousness, tyrannical rationality endorses the ordered regime at the expense of generative chaos, creating structure that is too rigid to propagate information and thereby evolve. Such rigidity is supported by the universal habit-making tendency, which channels consciousness into patterns that persist with minimal volitional input. Although potentially an efficient mode of establishing order, habit disconnected from an adaptive context and a deep understanding of its own logic and repercussions can quickly and perniciously erode consciousness by failing to connect it with any source of regeneration or mode of efficient dissipation. Shattering under the unaccommodating brittleness of its own structure, excessive order breaks into its nemesis, rampant entropic chaos, which drowns all structure in its depth of unconsciousness.

The rigid grip that the rational mind seeks over its own level of achievement, along with the living history of its own evolution which surrounds it, sustains it, and never ceases whispering to it in the language of universal truths, is the inevitable outcome of a reciprocally causal loop imbalanced by an inordinate top-down flow. The leading edge of consciousness seeks to enthrone itself, rather than remembering the cycle it is part of—the cycle of life, death, and emergent new beginnings. In striving to entrench its symbol-level, and therefore inherently incomplete and temporary form into a permanent reign, the rational mind ironically undermines its own foundations by devaluing the very thing it does not fear losing: the internal and external integration which brings all participants of consciousness into balance within their individual centers, which are foliations of the all-encompassing original Center. Both the means and the end of that balance is the spontaneous joy drawing from the deep and empty heart of the Attractor that animates the "deadness" of material structure into a playground of spirit.

Spirit, the loving connectedness that recalls the singular origin of all manifestation, must accompany rational growth in order for it to be sustainable. Swedenborg expounds: "Our discernment has necessarily been given the ability to be lifted above our own love into wisdom's light, which is beyond our own love."[cmlxix] Although cognitive capacity is granted license through its fractal probes—well suited for exploring future potential—to move ahead of, unyoked to, the divine love that comprises its reality, too great of a chasm between them leads to a catastrophic shattering of the rational structure. As Jung points out, slow-developing "psychic evolutions don't necessarily keep pace with intellectual developments."[cmlxx] There is a need, he remonstrates, "to bring a consciousness that has hurried too far ahead into contact again with the unconscious background with which it should be connected." Much as the arrogant grandeur that sought to leave earth and pierce the heavens by erecting the Tower of Babel ended in shattered ruins, rational structures of consciousness that grow too far beyond their primarily experiential underpinnings are destined to be razed to the level at which love dwells, so that the two might be able to evolve together, says Swedenborg. Tragically, unfettered rationality often accompanies a desiccation of love, the immediacy that grounds it, and the empathetic domain-crossing it fosters that would turn otherwise shallow rationality into deeply grounded wisdom. Under these bipolar conditions, the presumptuous over-reach of consciousness dooms the loveless edifices it constructs to an especially precipitous fall.

Return to the Center

The mythological roadmaps handed down from ancient times are like mirrors of our very evolution and constitution, predicated on the symbolic which, "unlike despotic orthodoxy…favors independence," according to mystic PD Ouspensky. He adds, "Truths can easily be turned into monstrous delusions when people attempt to express them in language without symbols."[cmlxxi] Centered on the source of constant renewal, symbol and myth are autogenic and self-organizing, conveying the self-similarity of history while evading the linear path toward decay by embodying the essence of the timeless dimension of meaning. From the original radiating point of manifestation—the primordial moment sought by myth—emerges the foundational duality between coherence and irreversible dynamics. This tension between synchronic omnipresence and diachronic progression is internalized into human concepts and modes of expression, particularly demarcating the wholly different logic of poetry versus prose. While the poetic reframes a central theme from many angles, "in prose, the reverse process is at work: successivity prevails over simultaneity."[cmlxxii] The straightened trajectory of diachronicity is the irreversible march of history, with coherence reduced by entanglement to a prosaic succession of events. In contrast, the synchrony of poetry, wherein metaphor reigns supreme, is a linguistic representation of coherence—a center from which a diversity of perspectives and descriptions of the same "attractor" can emanate. As portals to synchronic holism, the non-literal devices of myth, symbol, poetry, and ritual are "the mirror-opposite" of historical progression.[cmlxxiii] This is why myths, although ripe with potential interpretations in many domains, are notably refractory to a literal reading. The intangible truths of the soul kept and revealed by the sacred tropes do not avail themselves to the weighing and measuring devices of surface-level analysis; as Campbell concludes, "When poetry of myth is interpreted as biography, history, or science, it is killed."[cmlxxiv] While the fecundity of metaphor affords numerous angles from which to poetically expound on a single theme, that synchrony dissipates into a single, low-information dimension when stretched into diachronic linearity.

Restriction to the literal realm of history at the expense of the surrounding, irreducible synchrony beyond rational mind's pattern-making reach places severe limits on the scope of truth that can be apprehended. In contrast, mythology's organic growth from a unified psyche wraps and folds its layers of actionable meaning into an often simple presentation. This understanding led Bateson to point out that "most of the really important stories aren't about things that really happened—they are true in the present, not in the past."[cmlxxv] With their symbol-level simplicity encapsulating a suite of universal conditions that are preserved through every magnification of complexity, symbols and symbolic narratives are applicable at many different levels concurrently, and so endlessly open to interpretation and adaptation. The interpretive penchant of the self-aware mind finds in myth the selfsame truth projected into innumerable angles and levels. This insight is revealed in the Lotus Sutra, when a vision of countless Buddha lands is conjured, revealing in each different land the self-same Buddha preaching the exact same Sutra.[cmlxxvi] Occupying all forms of creative manifestation omnipresently, the single transcendent truth can be declared simultaneously from infinite perspectives. Rendered into unity through the complex relations that entangle them into complexity, all of these perspectives coexist like superimposed potential of an identical ground state, iterated through many causally distinct variations.

Rather than a chronicle of history, myth is "the story of the soul."[cmlxxvii] The story it tells in its many renditions is of the mythological moment sought by ritual and symbolism, which is synonymous with the first presence of consciousness in nature, and is always now, in the Beginning. In the mythological moment, expansion and contraction overlap in the selfsame movement, as the non-local universality of synchrony parlays itself into historical unfoldment. The implicit meaning of a myth or ritual requires dynamical reenactment to attain causal efficiency; to invoke the forces not contained in its simplified description, but rather at the heart of its explication. The reentry into that Moment, unbound by logic, through the vehicles of symbol, ritual, and myth conjoins participating agents with each other in the context of that primordial, experiential, and timeless eternity, each experiencing and expressing the self-same, unalterable essence in unique and ever-creative ways. With the tools of metaphor and symbol to intelligently direct the flow of meaning across the differing domains of outward expression by connecting their tiny tributaries to a single vast underlying channel, the depths of universal experience are galvanized into a vitalizing circulation whose powers of rejuvenation and centered totality can become manifest realities.

10

The Road to Crucifixion

"I am the "Provider of Attributes" serpent with many coils,/ I am the scribe of the Divine Book which says what has been and what is yet to be...I extend everywhere, in accordance with what was to come into existence."
—Iru-to, Serpent of Egyptian mythology[cmlxxviii]

The growth of semantic freedom that accompanies deepening complexity enables evolving agents to engage with their experiences in increasingly refined and even symbolic terms. Each emergent level of cognitive evolution resolves to some degree the uncertainties of lower levels, but at the cost of opening up new arenas of surprisal in domains previously inaccessible to individualized intelligence. As intelligence unfolds its questioning tendrils toward its own development, the constitutive layers that implicitly frame and guide conscious functions weave themselves into increasingly intricate arrangements. Fostering integration between inward depth and outward extension are the stories that humanity has been telling throughout its sojourn within the "three universes of experience."

Summarizing the need to connect with the unconscious through metaphorical channels is the assertion of Phillip that truth conveys its "naked" essence only through the "types and images" of the forms it assumes, because the "world cannot receive it in any other way." The bridge between linguistically enabled consciousness and its pre-rational foundation is symbolic. The symbols that became codified into cornerstones of religious lore are symbol-level expressions of "secrets of the soul," which "they set forth…in glorious images."[cmlxxix] These are the images—collective in origin and nature—which Jung believes animate the collective unconscious. Campbell similarly traces all of the world myths to a common fund of motifs. He refers to these as "mythologems," which radiated from their originating center like an evolving phylum, differentiating according to the niches their bearers constructed.[cmlxxx] Throughout all of their formal metamorphoses, the numinous referents underlying multifarious symbol systems are preserved because they and the integrating function they provide to the conscious mind are universal.

Over the course of its evolution, myth shifted, altered, and ultimately reformed itself into world religions, including Christianity, whose central tenets reach back to some of the earliest mythological motifs. Joseph Campbell points to Christianity as an evolutionary culmination of many threads of mythology and theology. He found Christ to be implicit in polytheistic religions, while "in the Old Testament, prophesied; and in the New Testament, revealed."[cmlxxxi] The savior is variously represented by many pre-Christian deities, including Orpheus, Tammuz, and Osiris, while the theme of the deity's descent, sacrifice, burial, and resurrection has taken on forms as diverse as the death of the horned moon followed by its resurrection three days later, to the descending god who, after being slaughtered by the people, re-emerges from the ground as a food-bearing plant.[cmlxxxii] The theme of divine descent, sacrifice, and resurrection as food is a deeply ancestral mythologem.

According to Campbell, the foundations of the Abrahamic religions roughly reflect a confluence between the myths of two major ontogenic streams that had long ago parted ways: those of the plant cultivators, and those of the animal cultivators. At the point of contact erupted the chaos that inevitably attends the meeting of different tendencies, and the resultant system harbored, sometimes inadvertently, aspects of each. Written from the perspective of a successful group of nomads who roamed the outskirts of settled Near and Middle Eastern cities in perennial search of fodder for their herds, the five books of the Torah are a story told from the outside. The wandering pastoralists were viewed askance by the settled agrarians, who walled themselves off from the dangers of the wilderness—particularly the numerous tribes of militant nomads, although the Israelites' presence was uneasily tolerated in part because of the bulwark it provided against other potential invaders.

The people of the Torah distinguished themselves from their earth-worshipping agrarian neighbors by shifting their reverence away from earthly, motherly, and chaotic deities and instead directing their devotions skyward, where the scorching Father held Himself aloof from—unintegrated with—terrestrial things. The power of distinction He seared down upon His chosen ones created a new order of relations between humanity and nature—a split between the begetting matrix and the rational structures of consciousness that had evolved from her tempestuous womb. In the anthropocentric worldview that came to overrule the prior, holistic order that honored the obliging Mother and her abundant provisioning, the splendid came uncoupled from the terrible, unleashing angels as well as demons. Under the solar-oriented paradigm that came to supplant earthy rootedness, the divine presence felt by the nature-worshipping pagans as pervasive withdrew from its intimate connections with the earth, whose seasons and cycles nested themselves within the astrological wheel, and fled to the sun to become concentrated as the great, fierce, and jealous Ruler and Father.

Similar to the myths it derived from and succeeded, the religion established by the Hebrew desert fathers was inscribed with imagery that reflected very little of its truth-content at the presenting symbol level. St. Augustine addresses this inscrutability with his explanation that "scripture presents this truth to us in one way only, and there is only one way in which the words can be shaped by the tongue. But it may be understood in several different ways without falsification or error, because various interpretations, all of which are true in themselves, may be put upon it."[cmlxxxiii] Rooted like every other quest for the divine in the primacy of the mythological moment, the scriptures revered by the conquerors with a burgeoning sense of history begin in a synchronic state of potential, envisioned as a paradise for nascent humanity. The intangible reality of the garden's bliss is the longed-for estate of righteous humankind, but from which they are debarred by the limitations of carnal flesh. Re-entry through its guarded gates is the hope of a people awaiting a savior's redemption.

Eden and the Fall

Beneath the chronology of events that unfold in Eden and their arc toward the future, is the timeless story of the many divided out of the One, all embarking on unique journeys through time and space. Suggestive of an idyllic and non-temporal epoch prior to the struggle between order and entropy that characterizes the evolutionary process, the Garden of Eden is endowed with imagery from the opulent gardens in the walled-off cities around which the nomads foraged, and which they would later declare to be their own promised lands. Death was not yet the source of life, so animals were at peace with each other; and the timeline of senescence had yet to unfold for an as-yet ageless humanity. Untouched by the far-from-equilibrium pressures of sequential time, Eden existed in a unitary state of coherent potential, in the peaceful prelude to chaos, after whose unleashing a living could only etched through the sweat of one's brow.

Eden remained blissfully ensconced in synchronic stasis until,

"Adam...did perish in his perfection and become earthly; did it not come to pass by *imagination,* because he induced his desire, longing, and lust into the outward, astral, elemental, and earthly kingdom, whereupon he in his desire, lust, and imagination was forthwith impregnated, and became earthly, and thereby he fell into the sleep of the external *Magic*."[cmlxxxiv]

The soul of Adam, says Jung, is like the "wick of a candle containing innumerable strands."[cmlxxxv] The potential of the entire human race is compressed into this single prototype; or, in Julian's phrasing, "Everyman is one man, and one man is everyman."[cmlxxxvi] In the unitary seclusion of paradise, this potential could freely sample its range of states, untouched by the conscripting exigencies of a challenging environment. Sheltered in a protective cloister impervious to the outer world's tumult, the garden shielded its germinal possibilities from decoherence until a volitional movement from within responded to observation-like promptings from without by sending questioning branches of potential beyond its boundary and "falling" through entanglement with the external environment.

Fertilized by the suggestive impulse to life, the Edenic ovum shifted from a balanced state of potential to active becoming, releasing its creative capacity to venture into the world like a hero answering the call to adventure. In its "fall" into the diachronic flow of the physical world, the perfect fullness and preservation of potential forsook its equilibrated stasis in response to a signal that penetrated and "measured" it from outside its bounds. As a result of the fall, pure, unembodied firstness became enmeshed in a world of forms, boundaries, epistemology and surprisal—a state of manifestation whose scope of expression is contingent on its context and history. The plunge of self-contained potential into the Darwinian tumult is, for mythology, the primal moment of birth, or separation.[cmlxxxvii]

Swedenborg traces all life properties back to divine love as the basis of volition, and wisdom as the basis of discernment, while Samkhya presents the beginning of evolution as the affinity felt by transcendent purusha, or spirit, for natural sattva, or mentality. The purushas' acasual adoration is an act of volition not tempered by the power of discernment—the cultivation of which becomes their route back to freedom.[cmlxxxviii] Yoganada identifies feminine Eve as the feeling aspect of humanity, from which arises volition.[cmlxxxix] According to the interpretation he presents, when non-rational impulsiveness is favored over the capacity of discrimination, masculine rationality is led to plow the fields of natural evolution until it can raise divine love back up to its heavenly stature—the unitary paradise whose inhabitant is the androgynous, archetypal Perfect Man, the ideal human prototype fully possessed of complete consciousness. Discernment develops only through the gradual construction of individual and evolutionary experience, which transforms agents through their own power of interpretation. As cognitive structures evolve and stabilize into habits, individual consciousness becomes increasingly capable of bringing mental concepts into refined focus as the dividing, or measuring, capacity of categorization grows in flexibility and subtlety. As the primal division of unity into duality, Logos develops through the distinction-making that is the basis of all intelligent activity. Its dividing power is instrumental, according to Swedenborg, in creating structures through which love—the passive subjectivity underlying intelligence—can rise to higher states. When the complementary dyad of volition and discernment ripens together into fullness, the entrapped purusha is released from the cycle of evolution back to its native realm of ideational bliss.

The god of the primordial paradise injected into that beatific abode implicit warnings to its unwise denizens about its limitations. In exchange for protected bliss, they must abstain from autonomy, maturity, and differentiated experience. At the seductive urging of the serpentine drive to evolution, they undertook the arduous task of incubating and cultivating the power of discernment, and so were compelled to make their living in the natural world, naked and vulnerable to its exacting, selective measures and precarious balance on the razor's edge of criticality. Adam and Eve became capable of shame as soon as they became incomplete, losing paradise to experience the visceral and conditional. As a layer of protection, God clothed the neophytes in animal skins, concealing their tender innocence in the cover of a "dead thing."

Although rendered by orthodoxy as the darkest moment of humanity's past that indelibly shackled all future generations with the bondage of sin, Julian offers a different perspective of the fall. Although the "greatest wrong ever done was Adam's sin," she says, it was absolutely necessary for Adam to fall because "the making of amends is greater than the sin was bad."[cmxc] The fall from unitary existence paved the way for the entry of Christ consciousness into the domain of physical manifestation: "When Adam, or everyman, fell Christ fell, rejoicing, into the depth of the virgin's womb."[cmxci]

The Serpent and the Son

The presence of the serpent in the garden is an atavism of a previous age of mythology. Prior to its Christian association with Satan, the serpent was a symbol of the Cosmic Mother, winding a thread of order through the primordial, life-giving pranic stew simmering below physical manifestation, and whispering secrets of oracular wisdom to the priestesses who held sacred the mystical fecundity of the all-begetting Goddess. Ferociously mirroring the dialectical evolution of new structures of consciousness—which demands that in tilling under prior levels of attainment to make way for a new generation of perspective, the leading edge keeps itself disentangled from the lower levels it arises from—the cultural succession that supplanted the wisdom of the serpent with the jealousy of the Father strove to purge the memories and symbols of its predecessor. Campbell describes this turnover as the heaven of one level of mythology becoming the hell of the next as a new paradigm replaces a previous order.[cmxcii] Shards of this transformation are perceptible throughout the mythology and edicts of the conquerors, designed to suppress and vilify the paradigms that governed the people they defeated which were antithetical to their own claim to dominion. For example, as new images and associations came supplant old ones, swine and dogs, two early achievements of domestication, becoming unclean while the ovine flocks and bovine herds of the pastoralists become tokens of God's favor.

In Eden, the serpent's original implications of vital earth energy and chaotic, generative potential are recast as the instigators of all human sorrow when he leads the woman, like a fallen priestess still in his thrall, into his devious treachery. The role played by Satan as tempter and deceiver is comparable to the Vedic conception of *maya* as the cosmic deluder whose function is to create the appearance of individual distinction from Absolute Unity.[cmxciii] This universal illusion is also known as the "measurer," since it is tasked with measuring infinite spirit into localized forms forgetful of their inherent and originating unity. The purpose of such a memory-erasing deception is to set a stage for the convincing unfoldment of lila, the play of God in which the One takes on a multiplicity of forms. The impulse to fall is not precisely causal, but rather an internal acquiescence to the lure of maya, which enkindles an evolutionary radiation through the passive but intelligent prism of Christ consciousness which knits all emergent creation into a mutable system, far from equilibrium, bound into coherence by an infinitely high logic.

Intelligent Logos and delusive maya are equally implicated in enacting universal evolution. Both measurers of the unmeasurable, these complementary antagonists comprise the primordial duality of nature, when light and dark are differentiated and segregated as rulers of distinct provinces. The point of solidarity from which the two poles of measurement bifurcate is affirmed in the Gospel of Phillip, verse 47: "Messiah is a double term, meaning both the Christ and 'the measured.' Jesus in Hebrew means 'atonement.' Nazara is truth, so the Nazarene is therefore the truth. Christ is what is measured, and the Nazarene and Jesus are those who have measured him." Atonement—"at-one-ment"—bespeaks unmitigated prelapsarian unity, while its measurement is the localization of universality based on the founding illusion of separation.

Creation through the "first-born of all creation" transpires upon the critical fusion of the opposing states of singularity and profusion. Manifestation becomes prolific only with the aid of the delusive measurement that erases the perfect memory of unity, dissipating its unexpressed states as fertile entropy to push the evolution of the whole forward. The perfect, primordial intelligence that is the source of nature's logic can only take form through the illusory delimitations of constraint. In a highly enacted metaphor for the unitary coherence that is the ground and destination of spiritual striving, the situated entities that can only partially channel the transcendent logic of universal wisdom due to the intrinsic incompleteness of the physical condition collectively comprise a greater, self-contained whole.

Symbolic of this wholeness is the serpent, which surreptitiously continues to fill its archetypal role betokening creative wisdom, despite the ignominy assigned to it in Eden. Creating the oppositional tension necessary for the coherence that allows criticality to rise within its bounds, the serpent locks itself into a closed circle as it strains to grasp its tail. At the point of contact is a discontinuity that is the paradox of self-reference. The centered subjectivity of bounded coherence "warps" its internal semantic space in response to its form-specific interpretation of the imperatives common to open systems, much like space-time melding itself in conformity to matter or energy. Within this simple coil is encoded the entire arc of evolution in its adherence to the cryptic guidance of God's postlapsarian dictum structuring the adversarial relation between the two measurers when he instructed the serpent: "And I will put enmity between you and the woman, and between your seed and her seed. He shall bruise you on the head and you shall bruise him on the heel."[cmxciv] The two poles of the divided singularity—one embodied, the other ethereal—occupy distinct domains that are separated by an expanse of discontinuity, which is the coherent resonance through which the wordless voice of God speaks. The ophidian pole with its chaotic "seed" of material generativity pulls apart from the human pole, whose semantic "seed" grows through rational intelligence. Within the relativistic bounds of this separation, infinity unfolds creation. Projected into duality through physically imposed dimensions, initial condition must translate itself into material, efficient, and formal means to traverse the rupture that intervenes between origin and final cause. This is the logic of the universal system, iterated into endless, self-similar, microcosmic variations at every possible scale. Local, sign-mediated domain crossings build up the robust, scale-free webbing that spans the poles of creation in countless intelligent interpretations of that logic. Across this self-constructed bridge of relational entanglements, chaotic potential reconnects with itself in the form of its fulfillment: explicit, self-aware consciousness. In the dramatic denouement of the evolutionary saga as revealed in Genesis 3:15, when the serpent winds around to complete its intelligent spiral of self-reference, it reaches to grasp, not a reptilian tail, but instead a human foot—a supportive foundation of conscious intelligence, grounded in earthly energy.

Although maya obscures the original memory, all-permeating Christ intelligence provides the means for reassembling it. This is the toil humanity is driven to as it carries on the evolutionary vocation of explicating consciousness. With its privileged access to domains of higher cognition, humanity faces the unique challenge of evolving conscious structures that grow local expressions of nonlocal truths through intentionally active agency, guided by wisdom.

Eros and Agape—Divine Love in Creation

Like all other instances of evolution, including of mythologies, Greek legends of cosmogenesis underwent their own changes over time. In Plato's telling of the unfolding divine pantheon, Eros—hermaphroditic like the prototypical Perfect Man—is numbered as first of the gods, although Hesiod's prior chronology had him emerging after Chaos, Gaia, and Tartarus. In later myths, after being re-rendered as the son of Aphrodite, Eros absconds from his rightful estate among the immortals to pursue his beloved, mortal, nature-bound Psyche, echoing the purushas' lovelorn pursuit of nature's mind-quality.

Penetrating space with the branching fractal tendrils of possibility, divine Eros chases his manifest beloved with a creative, generative passion through a self-made labyrinth whose walls are mayic veils. At the core of the capillaries he pierces through the fabric of space-time is the singular expression of consciousness in its created aspect of primordial Christ intelligence, which is at once the source of formal pliability as well as intrinsic self-similarity. The consciousness concentrated within the threadlike core of Eros is the "rent" of infinite expansion that multiplies potential within boundaries, and that grows complexity into vehicles of agency and volition. The intangible ever-expansiveness within the Erotic veins, akin to the yogic concept of *nadis* or energetic channels, is the balanced non-discrimination that sees the deep isomorphism between the juxtaposing poles of quiescent awareness and the chaotic tidal oscillations that roil the spatiotemporal discontinuities that are singularities into evolution. As the "divine nerve"[cmxcv] that pierces, permeates, and vivifies the very fabric of creation, stirring it into forms that enfold yet more space in caverns of localization, Eros is the impulse to life within order and the unifier of oppositional domains. The structuring, presenting level of ardent Eros is none other than the divider Logos, in whose presence time differentiates into past and future, space into directions, and unity into infinity.

Stirring through an inexhaustible array of forms, each with its own characteristic intelligence, Eros is driven insatiably forward by the inevitable partiality of any offspring of his union with Psyche. Surrounded by conditions which invite the anchoring entanglements of intelligence, which in turn establish regularities that flourish into everything from universal physical laws to local accretions of dynamical order, blind Eros is guided solely by self-affinity. Swedenborg describes the creativity inherent in this pursuit, "Each thing sees the other as a kindred with which it can unite its whole function and with which it can realize its whole purpose in actual results."[cmxcvi] Seeking a complementary representation of his own primal image underlying the manifold accoutrements of outer form, Eros unites on the basis of invariances deeply hidden from superficial view; or, summarized by Leadbeater and Besant, "consciousness can recognize only consciousness."[cmxcvii] Once evolution transpires, and partial Umwelt overrides holistic perception, perfect knowledge is impaired. It is the challenge of Eros—the vital impulse of creativity; godhead in a seeking, piercing, channeling form—to reassemble itself into a manifest mirror of its perfect, non-physical, formless form.

Guided by the active expression of primordial intelligence to purposefully pursue self-affinity, Eros orders itself through different components into often disassortative networks cohered around localized attractors that guide their interactions into sustainable cycles. Through the evolutionary channels it constructs, poetic Eros preserves synchrony by re-presenting the same theme throughout all form, rippling self-similarity into a rainbow of forms and perspectives, evolving them into further layers of complexity, adaptiveness, and intelligence. Inspiring the radiant diversity of form that is its most visible effect, Eros guides evolution by a nonlocal corollary to local constructive principles. The microcosmic self-affinity Eros relies on to create local structures of order also resonates at a universal level, as the ultimate nature—the absolute Attractor—behind spatiotemporal Erotic excursions calls its "prodigal son" back home to itself. Matter-entangled Eros can only answer that insistent, subtle summons by incorporating a vertical axis of development to complement the vast lateral spread of diversity.

The upward pull to criticality that incites evolution is Eros, urging all the forms he inhabits to self-transcendence through the attractor-like domain crossing that allows new "interpretations" of the structures that form out of space, from atoms that combine into molecules, through evolutionary transitions in individuality, on up through all of the plurality that the universe supports. In the joyous but urgent drive to expand into new degrees of freedom and creativity of expression, the upward flow of Eros is necessarily counterbalanced by a downward flow to complete the creative and functional loop of reciprocal causality. The downward current is a different expression of divine love, Agape. The function of this feminine counterpart, the shadow side of virile Eros, is to carefully attend to all prior steps in the evolutionary procession, shepherding the accomplishments of physical and mental form into an ordered structure that supports the leading edge of further evolution amid the ever-changing conditions of the universal life cycle. In its highest form, Agape represents the unconscious—whose nature is of complete entanglement, or interrelationship with everything else—in both the individual and the whole of nature, which supports the advance of the leading edge. Ken Wilber sums up the functions of the two currents of divinity coursing through nature by describing Eros as the yearning reach of the lower for the higher, while Agape is the compassionate embrace of the higher for the lower.[cmxcviii] In turn, it is the Agape of higher dimensions, or as-yet non-manifest attractors, which pulls forward the Eros of the manifest level.

The fall into differentiation—through the lure of Eros and the divisions of Logos sustained by the veils of maya into habit-like regularities—coincides with the urge to liberation; the basis of Eros' drive to upward expressions of intelligence overlaid upon its endless lateral divisions. "Passion aims toward becoming whole," says Jungian psychologist ML von Franz.[cmxcix] Eros therefore acts as an active expression of Logos' passion for wholeness—the divider of ontology into epistemology seeking reunion through the redemption of creative domain crossing and the transformation of interpretation. Eros' passion is complete and full within all the forms it vitalizes, and yet inexorably drawn by self-affinity to the higher levels of expression that will allow it to more fully encounter its own ultimate nature and to fulfill "the strongest and most ineluctable urge in every being," which is "to realize itself."[ml] The loop of self-reference is closed in the mutual recognition between Eros and Logos, wherein each fulfills the promise of the other: Eros ripening the epistemology instantiated by Logos into profound wisdom that flows from the depths of existence, and Logos dividing the waters anew to perpetuate the play of creation in ever-new forms. The demiurgic adventure of Eros is an all-encompassing tale of the hero's journey outward into unknown lands of adventure. After his earthly sojourn, the Greek Eros regains his eternal home, while Psyche, after fulfilling challenges set for her by Aphrodite, is likewise raised to immortality. When they ascend, it is in response to the lure of the ultimate Attractor from Whom Eros is fashioned. Through a nested, hierarchical maze of lesser attractors, Eros ascends toward its final cause, in Whose form it was created, by first attaining a clear perception of its true universal essence through the vehicle of embodiment.

From its formless yet vividly experiential chaotic roots, and all throughout its fecund manifestation, "nature is pregnant with the future."[mli] From matter, such as stars and galaxies propagating parthenogenic novelty, to the abundant biosphere whose cycles of richness established early humans into rhythms of celebration, to the perceptivity and inventiveness of intelligence in its countless organismal frames, all of nature supports within its ongoing propagation the unfoldment of increasing degrees of self-realization. This is implicit in the unconscious penumbra of potential that extends not only below the level of the consciousness, but above it as well. "Animals," notes Peirce, "all rise above the general level of their intelligence,"[mlii] with exemplars as surprising as the findings that pigeons' conceptual abilities border on the abstract, and that even lowly reptiles—alligators—are capable of tool use.[mliii] Similarly, humans naturally reach beyond our own level of cognitive expression. Merton expounds, "Contemplation is above our nature but it is our proper element, we can breathe this new atmosphere on earth."[miv] From the realm of contemplation, through which consciousness seeks its non-manifest condition, Agape carves channels to be filled by Eros that reach down to rational mind, guiding its ascent into the transcendently non-rational, which is why in Swedenborg's telling, discernment adventurously uncouples to a limited degree from its volitional complement. The function of individual intelligence is not to build for itself aggrandizing tributes to its outer egoic cloak, but to find and unite to a higher love—the Agape of the higher level. Although wisdom is of the realm of potential above us, drawing us toward it, we are capable of drawing it to ourselves for present manifestation; according to Julian, "Love makes might and wisdom come down to our level."[mv]

Mandala and Cross

In the idyll of Eden, Jung sees a mandala; a "symbol of individuation," implicative of "the pre-existent meaning hidden in the chaos of life."[mvi] Jung extensively explores that potent symbol, which he understands to represent the self as a psychic totality in which everything is related to everything else through a central point in a "concentric arrangement of…contradictory and irreconcilable elements."[mvii] Sheltered within the maternal confines of the garden, the prelapsarian development of human potential is allowed to proliferate unperturbed. Upholding the coherence of the protective cloister are two pillars suggestive of the duality of material existence and foreshadowing the impending motifs of evolution, crucifixion and resurrection. The Tree of Life, akin to Swedenborg's conception of divine love, and the Tree of Knowledge, or divine wisdom, stand in the garden's center, roots penetrating downward to the generative chaos of life energy underlying manifestation and branches attentively stretching upward toward future possibility from without. It is the presence of the latter, the Tree of Knowledge, with its power of discernment inherently predicated on mayic divisions, distinctions, and measurements, that makes the fall and subsequent evolution inevitable: "That tree killed Adam…The law was that tree…It did not prevent him from evil nor preserve him for good, but it created death for those who have eaten it. For when he said, 'eat this, do not eat that,' it became the beginning of death."[mviii] In his "killing," Adam loosed his potential into the material world.

In the round, Platonic perfection of the mandala is reflected the undifferentiated, androgynous Perfect Man. Its dyad of trees foreshadows the cross whose function is to consummate the vision of Eden in striving humanity by dividing the mandala into a quaternary, wherein godhead—concentrated on a point at the heart of intersecting crossbeams—finds its highest expression. One of the revelations imparted to Julian was a mandala-like vision of a heart's center, like a bounded quaternary inside of which was a "blessed kingdom…a most glorious city. In the midst of it sat our Lord Jesus, God and Man…His Godhead rules and upholds both heaven and earth…in us he is completely at home."[mix] In the sacred center of the encompassing round, symmetrically balanced at the midpoint between ascent and extent, "the self is enthroned."[mx] Rendered as both "jewel" and "beloved city," the non-spatial point centered at the heart of both mandala and cross is a turning point between the dimensions of materiality and mentality that allows spontaneity and vitality to inform all active physical expressions. For evolving consciousness, its central placement indicates a perennial turning point between the horizontal spread of evolutionary play, and the vertical ascent fed by the "sweat of the brow" that labors toward divinity.

Only when its balanced maternal sheath is pierced by the masculine, sword-like cross does the Edenic mandala quicken with potential, balancing the poles of expression on the central point that at once carries the "germinal secret of the father" and the "umbilical point of the mother," and from which the "inexhaustible energies of eternity break into time."[mxi] The emanations of that central point, which Julian recognizes as the concentration of godhead, bear witness to its phenomenal creativity as well as its indelible numinosity. In all of its radiations are carried the "present reality of the mysterious center of our centers, the Omega"[mxii] toward which Eros strives.

The cross dividing the encompassing orb like lines of symmetry reflects in its discriminating capacity a unifying core that rises and recedes through manifestation as the birth and death of temporal bodies, while the timeless and dimensionless thread of consciousness infiltrates every detail within the intricate ladder of evolution through which it strives upward. The hemispheres cleaved by the crossbeams that connote a transection of the Trees of Life and Knowledge are not irreconcilably sundered, but rather represent the "matched hemispheres, light and dark, of a single sphere, which is being itself."[mxiii] The alchemical trees referenced in the cross unite spirit and matter for Jung, just as for Julian our two parts are reconciled into one through the Christ nature implied in both tree and cross.[mxiv] Through the division and cohesion simultaneously signified by the cross, Logos reaches toward the reunification of its fragmented, matter-identified individual selves with the holistic bliss of its undifferentiated origin, which is its destination.

The capacity of discrimination at the foundation of intelligence—unlike unitive metaphor, which seeks and draws together cohering threads of hidden self-similarity—is of the family of division that gives rise to "aboutness," or epistemology. "I come not to bring peace but to bring a sword," says Jesus, embodying the archetypal function of the universal Logos.[mxv] The shearing and discriminating sword, while the source of delusion, is at the same time key to its resolution. In placing its objectifying cuts, the power of discrimination imbues its objects with an "outside" that it can categorically assess, slicing through the ambiguity of unresolved chaos in order to make new domains available for creative recombination into emergent structures of consciousness. As it evolves into rationality, the power of distinction facilitates the expansion of degrees of freedom that ultimately circle the intelligent system around so that it may objectively encounter its own localized self, allowing the subject to become its own object. The segregating power of external Logos is mitigated by the cohering power of Eros, which climbs and extends through the interiority of the ladder of manifestation represented by the cross. Unitive and urgent, Eros threads through the core of the dividing arms, encountering at the extent of its reach a circular track that guides it into greater spiraling depths of consciousness within itself.

Always contained by the fertile margins of the mandala-mother, the sword divides from within, manifesting verdant fecundity inside those nurturing bounds. Julian's revelation revealed this condition when she perceived how we are incorporated through Christ into Mother Mary. Goodness, she discerned, comes through the Mother, while strength is supplied through the cross.[mxvi] By providing the spirit that moves through intelligence with a material cloak, the Mother represents access to wisdom, without which "knowledge of Christ is only speculation."[mxvii] Only through embodied birth can direct experience of that transcendental, yet foundational wisdom be attained by volitional, individuated consciousness. As the "long silence from which everything begins and in which everything ends,"[mxviii] the empty Mother is the reposeful backdrop "in which alone Christ can be heard" like music.[mxix] The inseparability of Christ and the Mother, or primordial intelligence embedded in the actively creative cosmic vibration, means that "she who is the Mother of our Savior is Mother of all...Indeed, our Saviour himself is our Mother for we are forever being born of him, and shall never be delivered!"[mxx] The integration of Christ within the Mother to become intelligent Logos and creative Eros is alluded to in medieval allegories in which Mary the mother of the Lord was also his cross.[mxxi] In addition to her role as the bearer of divine life, Mary, in these allegories, also takes on the destructive role of the Terrible Mother, embodying simultaneously the generative womb of creation, and the entropic tomb of dissolution. Here she reprises the role of the Goddess—the Great Mother who contains all of creation in her womb, including its death.[mxxii] The mandala's boundary in which all creation is conceived is also the recess into which it eventually wanes.

The mandala's protective embrace maintains the poles divided by Logos as a singular system of complementary opposites that resonate into coherence rather than splitting into the fragmenting oscillations of chaos, and harnesses the fiery passion of Eros into a many-formed play rather than the "unbridled dissipation" (Jung) of randomness free of channelizing structure. By binding the opposing poles of chaos and order in a balanced tension, the parameters set by the natural Mother support the creative fusion that conducts spirit through matter. Deviation from the delicate balance between freedom and constraint would promulgate a dissipative sundering, with all of the vibrant potential of Eros reduced to unproductive entropy. By warding off the noxious potential of a bipolar schism between the vital poles that uphold nature, the cross in a circle "has an apotropaic effect, because, pointed at evil, it shows evil that it is already included and has therefore lost its destructive power."[mxxiii] The opposites contained within nature's enveloping form yield deleterious, entropic chaos when they strain apart, but when joined at a unifying, stabilizing point, they critically converge to produce creative emergence.

As the epitome of evolution, Jung understood the mandala's circumscribing boundary to be a conservative guardian of a pre-existing order that simultaneously hosts the burgeoning, as-yet unexpressed potential carried in the reach of the cross that radiates toward the unknown.[mxxiv] Contained in the new order is the older pattern expressed at a higher level, rendering evolution an upwardly spiraling fractal dance of circularity. The cyclicity implied by the mandala's annular perimeter is celebrated in the Round Dance of the Cross from the Acts of John:

"I [will] be wounded, and I [will] wound.
Amen.
I [will] be born, and I [will] bear.
Amen."[mxxv]

The self-referencing loop of wounding and bearing, death and new life, circle each other in the perpetual race of entropy and order, dark and light; the serpent seeking its tail.

"Life in Christ is life in the mystery of the cross," proclaims Merton.[mxxvi] This supernatural mystery, he continues, is "a *sacred action* in which God Himself enters into time." The crucifixion is a metaphorical synopsis of incarnation, with the divine sacrificing its transcendence by descending into embodiment, and at the same time possessing the means of redemption into spirit. The transition from the irresolution that accompanies the explosive diversity of early levels of evolution and development to a more precisely defined state that subsumes wide-ranging potential with a more finely modulated balance is demarcated by invisible lines of symmetry that amplify certain attributes out of a broad span of potential and recast them according to a new formal arrangement fitted for a new domain of experience. The silent divider is a perfect point of balance between simmering possibility and emergent expression. It is a non-linear mirror that projects potential into expression in a non-traceable, re-materializing "quantum leap" that leaves the archives of evolutionary evidence marked by causal discontinuities rather than linear progression. Hidden in the space between leaps are the unceasing cycles of potential, expression, selection, amplification and propagation, and finally a recession whose ends feed into the next cycle like an autocatalytic loop. As the semantic corollaries of these stages of self-organization begin to ripen toward explicit awareness, an agent's intelligence becomes increasingly instrumental in its own progression. In the rarified reaches of the mental domain where self-awareness arises, the rational subject facilitates leaps of cognitive evolution through self-reflection across the pure prism of Christ consciousness which functions as divisive Logos, unitive Eros, and delusive maya, which bears the imprint of historical memory in its many-leveled coils. The image rendered through the transformative mirror of subtle symmetry is reflected at a higher level, shedding prior constraints in favor of new degrees of freedom that enable self-reflection, spurring the spiral upward as though through the increasingly urgent spinning near the epicenter of a vortex. The ages-long epic of the evolutionary unfoldment of consciousness replays the story of descent and transcendence myriads of times in anticipation of the liberation represented by the holy marriage between intelligence and unlimited divine consciousness, expressed through circumscribed form.

The Feminine: A Non-Rational Guide

The union of Eden and the cross in the quartered mandala points to the overriding Christian theme of redemption from the fall, or spiritual transcendence of the physical realm. Jesus himself bore an imprint of the mandala on his suffering body as he languished on the cross. From his pierced side flowed blood and water, invoking the maternal power of the birthing goddess. Inside the wound, according to Julian's privileged glimpse, was space enough for all creation to "rest in peace and love."[mxxvii] The all-encompassing puncture is a poignant reminder that, in the words of Thich Nhat Hahn, "a large open heart can accept the sharp thing."[mxxviii] Triumphant over trial, compassion is the attainment of the spiritual emptiness that enables material transcendence and reprises, at a new level of fulfilment, the promise implied when nature first takes into her balanced body the divine impulse to manifestation. The Alpha-and-Omega reciprocity of the life cycle reveals itself as the wound becomes a womb, indicating the inextricability of the transcendent Son with his natural Mother, as he mirrors her creativity at the higher level of apotheosis: nurturing spiritual children in a pierced womb that they might be divinely begotten in a new arrangement of paradisical union.

Ensconced within the womb of the Great Mother, Christ also inhabits the feminine within Eve and the serpent, who together draw the man away from his cordoned-off paradise into evolution. It is also through feminine guidance that he makes his way back to the Christ who is in and of the Mother. The androgynous Perfect Man experiences his first differentiation, or bifurcation, with the excision of Eve from his side. This prelude to a future wound that would one day be seen by a visionary mystic as containing the whole world points to more than an extraordinary and arbitrary means of physical creation. Rather, something deeply internal is explicated through the non-volitional wounding of the self-contained prototypical human that will enable evolution. The caveat, however, is that the organic process of life is inevitably attended by death. "If the female had not been separated from the male, she would not die with the male. His separation was the origin of death. For this, Christ came, so that he might correct the separation that has existed from the beginning, by uniting the two together."[mxxix] Adam, as the biological pole of evolution, floods the world with potential that is ultimately fulfilled in the purposeful attainment of Christ consciousness, wherein all of the dualities riven by Logos and sustained by maya are resolved into the unity at the foundation of manifestation.

The woman who is extracted—or projected—from the man's depths presents him with a new sort of awareness that that she visibly embodies. She, along with the law governing the Tree of Knowledge, is a prerequisite to the type of knowledge that entails "tilling the fields"—the willful, directed action analogous to the directionality of irreversible processes. Latent below the surface of his rational apprehension, an implicit, primary sort of knowing that is a bridge between natural and supernatural is carried in the unconscious—furled like a scroll that documents the evolutionary journey of body and spirit alike. Although the gift offered in this "helpmate" of Adam's is that of spiritual awakening carried in the unconscious, Jung warns that the "unconscious lets its creatures go only at the cost of sacrifice."[mxxx] The feminine guide accordingly offers the non-rational fruits of sacrifice; the spiritual epistemology that is the initial condition whose many outcomes include the cultivation of reason in the field of consciousness. As the keeper of secret knowledge, Eve represents to Adam *epinoia*, the Awakener who guides the uninitiated Perfect Man, or field of human potential, along the spiritual path of *via negative*. Inaccessible to rational thinking, the spiritual truths that grow along this path must be imparted through "hints and glimpses, images and stories, that imperfectly point beyond themselves toward what we cannot now fully understand."[mxxxi] Although she is a guide to rational development, the *epinoia* can neither appeal to nor be appealed to by rationality directly—as though a veil or curtain hangs between them. Instead, through premonition, intuition, and internal reflection, she urges human development toward spiritual truths that transcend rationality but invite experience.[mxxxii]

Presented to Adam in the tangible form of Eve prior to his fall is the promise held in his own unconscious, of potential for an awakening that would "restore him to his full being" after his travails in the fields of exile. Her gift is of "teaching him about the descent of his kind, and by showing the way to ascend, the way he came down."[mxxxiii] The final truth that she reveals to him is not one of factual knowledge, but one that will lift his consciousness from bodily confines to the transcendent goal of Eros through the experiential gateway whose name proclaims that I AM.

This knowledge is alluded to by Jesus in the final verses of the Dance of the Cross hymn:

> "For you could by no means
> have understood what you suffer
> unless to you as Logos
> I had been sent by the Father.
> …If you knew how to suffer,
> you would not be able to…"[mxxxiv]

The fruition of this knowledge, which presents the limited and so "suffering," contextually bound self as an object in the field of unabridged universal awareness, is in the union of the two hemispheres of the human psyche—the rational consciousness with the unconscious bridge to the profound mysteries of existence and evolution through and toward which all manifestation is called. The fundamental motif of the union of opposites is so essential to the unfoldment of conscious potential that it is iterated through countless dualities whose creative resolution is the expression of generativity, including those between feminine and masculine, chaos and order, and matter and spirit. The last duality is symbolized in the biblical saga of fall and redemption through the First and the Last Adam, who together embody the two poles of evolutionary potential which merge their separate streams into coherent overlap in order to evolve together through each other. With Adam representing the initiation of evolution from its Alpha, his messianic successor betokens its culmination toward the Omega, both of which are of identical essence. The localized form of Jesus exemplifies a microcosmic embodiment of the universal principle of consciousness as the pure reflection of God the Father:

> "The first man Adam became a living being; the last Adam, a life-giving spirit. The spiritual did not come first, but the natural, and after that the spiritual. The first man was of the dust of the earth, the second man from heaven. As was the earthly man, so are those who are of the earth; and as is the man from heaven, so also are those who

are of heaven. And just as we have borne the likeness of the earthly man, so shall we bear the likeness of the man from heaven."[mxxxv]

The descent of divinity into localization precipitates the dance of creation, with its progeny radiantly carving for themselves evolutionary pathways that exalt them into fuller expressions of what they already are through the paradoxical method of appearing as what they are not. Even as spirit undergoes the ritual of life cycles through all the complex systems it forms and intelligently inhabits, the embodied descendants of that animating consciousness become forgetful through estrangement of their essential unity. The insistent pull of Eros, however, whispers remembrances to its scattered, particulate reflections of their true, undivided nature. In its perfect Light, that otherworldly messenger urges its spiritual offspring toward a restoration of their native freedom from entanglements, in order to free illimitable spirit from the "suffering" of delimiting physical parameters with their corresponding perceptual confinements. By transmitting this message through the "types and images" endemic to the unconscious to the receptive conscious mind, the Illuminator brings resolution to the cycle of cosmology by appealing to the living forms that spirit has taken on through voluntary sacrifice. In "accepting earthly contact and suffering," spirit evolves into a soul that can be "transformed into a mirror in which the divine powers can perceive themselves."[mxxxvi] As they become awakened to that role and thereby reclaim their birthright to spiritual emancipation, redeemed souls fulfill the "word" spoken by God, and conclude their season of labors in the fields wherein they "experience the inevitable as the hard to gain."[mxxxvii]

Rational Food

The Christian drama culminates in the redemptive sacrifice of Jesus on behalf of Adam's fallen offspring, offering the opportunity for a reunification of individualized consciousness with its source. The countless variations of this motif in prior mythologies all emphasize the sacred nature of this killing as the means by which divinity provides his own body as sustenance for the people. In the ancient Polynesian mythologems that presage the crucifixion, the earth receives the spilled blood and entombs the god's lifeless body, transforming it into food-bearing plants which sprout three days later. Similarly, Jesus, as a human embodiment of Christ consciousness, offers to his disciples his flesh as bread and his blood as wine. These are distinctly foods of transformation, requiring human agency to intentionally change them from their raw forms. Laborious, directed effort cultivates their ingredients, collects them together in harvest at their time of ripeness, and finally renders them into a form ready to be changed—not merely in degree, but in kind—by inviting the transubstantiating ministrations of fermentation.

From the initial "laying down" of the divine into form, or the deity's development from the negative existence of Ain Soph to the positive existence concentrated fully *en potentia* on Kether, its dynamical mode of existence has created a universe of continual change and transformation, rather than of stasis. The elements that intelligently coalesce into open systems take whatever kind of "food" is appropriate to their form, replenishing their structures and energetic flows. Like attractors drawing loose trajectories into themselves, open systems rearrange the flows they collect to themselves according to their own bodily patterns.

While physical food sustains the physical body, the internal semantic support of manifestation deems that the "body is as much symbol as substance." The food of conscious evolution is the exchange of information. Through the many-formed, localized intelligences harbored by living agents, consciousness adjusts the scope and filter of its attracting Umwelt "net" in order to procure its semiotic sustenance. It variously ingests and renders chemical, tactile, olfactory, visual, and auditory perceptions into refined and meaning-laden signs. And just as bodies adjust their food requirements according to niche, evolving consciousness likewise demands fitting informational fare throughout its excursions into complexity. Accordingly, linguistic communication became a new kind of "food" which fueled the evolution of the noosphere. In the unitary state of Edenic bliss prior to humankind's exile to the realm of manifest form, however, there is no need for semiotic exchange of any kind. The Gospel of Phillip describes this condition in verse 17: "Before Christ came, there was no bread in the world. It was just as in the garden, where Adam was, where there were many plants as nourishment for animals, but no wheat as food for mankind, so people ate like the animals." For most animals, content in the second semiotic universe, the scope of knowledge and informational exchange is eminently species- and niche-appropriate, and highly contextually bound. Not until they were led by the sibilant persuasion of the serpent to plow evolution's higher fields did humans cultivate and partake of their postlapsarian diet, with its powers of liberation from bodily and contextual immediacy. Only through the striving sweat of their brows could humans bring forth the transformative semiotic vehicles that elevated their ability to express nature's logic to new heights. Such new cognitive vistas made available to questing humanity the transcendent and transformative "food" of spirit, enriched with new depth and reach when expressed in the terms of the third semiotic universe.

The cognitive depth and expansion invited by symbolic language is one of degree in that the evolutionary principles that structure every other domain with diversity are equally at play in the consciousness. However, the transition is one of kind in its power to expand the horizons of the semiosphere in all dimensions, including the inward coil of a consciousness increasingly centered on itself. The inward expansion allows for the insight, higher-order conceptualization, and abstraction necessary to support self-awareness as the "tender thing" of immediate experience wraps itself in the rational clothing of its slain animal tendencies, which were its prior leading edges of consciousness. "By a tiny 'tangential' increase, the 'radial' was turned back on itself and so to speak took an infinite leap forward."[mxxxviii] Like the judicious addition of yeast to wheat flour or crushed grapes, the transformative capacity of a complex symbol-system is a distinctly human enactment of universal thirdness at a new level of functioning that generates the structure necessary to support rationality. As the highest manifestation of discrimination, and the finest-probing tool accessible to consciousness as the basis of intelligent activity, rationality is a metaphor for the Logos: the conscious center around which the dance of intelligent evolution, the Dance of the Cross revolves; the line of symmetry that reflects the lower in the higher and represents their confluence. As a line of reflection across which to evolve, the grand purpose of rationality is be transcended.

Sacrifice

Like the leading edges of other complex systems, a symbolic system subsists on the circulating flows conducted upward through its lower tiers of organization. In the constructive turnover of hierarchical growth, each leading edge basks at its apex before being plowed under the soil to feed the next level of emergence, guiding its expression like the implicit entailments of a metaphor. Laid down as though into a dark tomb of unconsciousness, logical and cognitive structures support new seasons of growth that are distinct, and yet dynamically bound to the remembrance of previous emergences. The supervening of a new global-level form upon a previously established order is at once the laying down of the prior leading edge into the dark, tomb-like space of the unconscious, and raising up from the same a new leading edge expressing the transformative thirdness of interpreting intelligence. As Jung writes, "We are confronted, at every new stage [of] differentiation of consciousness…with the task of finding a new *interpretation* appropriate to this stage, in order to connect the life of the past that still exists in us with the life of the present."[mxxxix] At the collective level of society to which Jung is referring, the leading edge of consciousness may be lionized into a savior, which underpins his insight that to lose contact with what came before is to lose the savior that emerges therefrom.[24] Just as the constitutive levels of consciousness ultimately render their sacrificed "saviors" into food for new levels of emergence, the leading

---

[24] The savior is the culmination of a cycle of ascending heroes throughout mythological evolution, beginning with the trickster, passing to the transformer—embodied in the Hare among some Native American mythologies—followed by a stage distinctly belonging to the human hero Campbell dissects at such length, followed by invincible Twins who, upon having vanquished all of heaven and earth's monsters, turn on the supports of the earth itself. Lest they destroy the pillars of survival itself, the Twins' deaths are necessitated in a cyclical return to the theme of sacrifice. The Twins, originally united in the same womb, "essentially constitute a single person." Although forced apart at birth, and exceedingly difficult to unite, they belong together. This decline portion of the cycle, marked by prideful, egotistical overreach, was sometimes forestalled in ancient societies by human sacrifice, a propitiation whose accompanying rites were directed toward "tam[ing]…individualistic and destructive impulses"(Henderson in Jung 1964, page 107).

edge, in drawing sustenance from a broad base of unconscious dynamics, likewise subsists on the offerings of the lower levels in a balance of reciprocal exchange.

The climatic sacrifice of the crucifixion was the consummation of a long history of animal sacrifice, which released the people, according to the vision of the Apostle Paul, from the prior covenant that had bound them to a particular kind of interpretive relationship with their god. The countless animals ritually offered up to the desert god were reflective of a yet earlier order, when the act of sacrifice was an immediate and integral necessity of life. The hunt was in part a ritual of obeisance to the revered flow of life, whose violent taking was envisioned as a voluntary surrender that required propitiation. Hunting rituals entwined the primordial motifs of death and rebirth, in which the animals sacrificing their bodies for the peoples' survival were individual expressions of a larger, more inclusive spirit into which their own spirits retired and then sprang from afresh during the season of renewal. In this deeply foundational stratum of human consciousness, the act of killing for food became sacramental, depicting "the absorption by humans of the nonhuman, or cosmic flow of forms."[mxl]

In the herdsman, sacrifice became a distinct act, removed from the immediacy of physical necessity as reverence shifted from the life force within the animals to the solar symbol of its origin. In the redirection of the human consciousness from the earthy and embodied to the distant and abstract was enfolded the metaphor of slaughtering what Origen describes as the "sacrificial animals in the self,"[mxli] or subordinating instinctual impulses to the individuating power of rationality that engages in evolution in the elevated reaches of the human mind. Previous orders of understanding were called upon to subordinate themselves, and like the domesticated flocks and herds of the Israelites, divest their autonomy in service to the new systemic ordering they came to constitute. Like the non-rational garden of animal awareness, unplait by darkening distinctions between good and evil, the human unconscious is to a large degree indentured to its biological heritage, which speaks in instinctual as well as appetitive promptings. By applying rational awareness, though, humanity can willfully affect evolution—"the idea of God"—on the animal impulses it inherits by aligning rationality along the critical seam between the lower, animal pole and the higher, transcendent pole that is the destination of Eros.

Ultimately, the symbolism of animal sacrifice yields to a higher sacrifice: "God is an eater of man. So man is sacrificed."[mxlii] The outcome is summed up in a contradiction: "[Animals] were offered up alive, but once they were offered up they became dead. Yet men were offered up dead unto God, and became alive."[mxliii] The "living sacrifice, holy and acceptable"[mxliv] reverses the flow initiated in the offering of animals, and the loop of reciprocal causality closes. The "animals of the self," whose slain bodies become assimilated into the rich humus of the unconscious, proffer from their sacrifices the means of lucid, conscious ascent beyond the entangling confines of matter-identification.

Although intimately tied to physical processes, the evolution of consciousness is distinct from the phenomena that support it. Unlike so many other bifurcations, even those that guide evolution into uncharted domains, the bottom-up constraints of consciousness evolve to support its expansion to the point where it meets, not just the mundane top-down counter-current necessary for systemic closure, but an expansive reconnection to its original "expanded Self."[mxlv] Like a delta that releases a river's conscripted flow into oceanic freedom, this transcendent turning point channels evolution, not to a point of completion, but to the beginning of the very cycle that will replenish it. The nonlocal intelligence toward which subjectivity strains is none other than the Christ Consciousness door of I AM that leads to even more profound levels of awakening beyond individualized consciousness. "The next step not a step," say Merton. "It is to be changed by degree; you are now fruition, experience."[mxlvi] As the experiencer merges with experience itself, the confines of situated perspective dissolve and individuality and even metaphor break down. Shedding the protective, physical "animal skins" that had swathed it in form upon its departure from Eden into the wilds of manifestation, Eros flows with joyous release into the oceanic destination whose nature it had expressed in so many forms during its material sojourn.

In this ultimate transmutation, humanity, the eater of god, at the same time transforms into food for the god. In order to become divine food, the consciousness is transformed according to the attractor above its level that continually calls the Eros-trajectory into its beatific ambit with the invitation to partake in the "kingdom of God," the intangible state of conscious unity underlying physical manifestation. It is the call to fulfill the most original, primordial sacrifice at the very bedrock of the universe: the descent of omnipotence from absolute transcendence into the limiting and relative context of incarnation.[mxlvii] Phillip tells us in verse 5, "Not only did he lay down his soul when he appeared…but he had laid it down since the day the world began. Then he came to take it back"—the circularity of Alpha returning to Omega. Similarly, Isaiah 55:11proclaims, "So is my word that goes out from my mouth: It will not return to me empty, but will accomplish what I desire and achieve the purpose for which I sent it." The spoken "word" only returns to its source when it has ripened like wheat ready for rendering, fulfilling the promise of evolution intimated in the twin pillars of Life and Knowledge by uniting divine love with wisdom.

Once reunited with its undivided nature, Eros becomes more than the driving pulse of spontaneity channeling through the parameters of form, by swelling into an unoccluded river whose flow from an inexhaustible source washes down all of the strata supporting evolution. The moment of Jesus' death depicted this monumental yet subtle shift, when "the curtain of the sanctuary was rent down the middle."[mxlviii] The veil separating daily life from view of the Holiest of Holies—much like localization sundered from apprehension of the ultimate—opened up at that climactic moment, because "some from below had to ascend."[mxlix] The "rent" that allowed the ascent of those "clothed in perfect light" also allowed the downward currents of ineluctable draw to reach their solicitous grace to lower levels of expression, vitalizing them and drawing them higher. Through this transcendence a new channel opens between manifest and non-manifest, deepening the flow of reciprocal causality: "Those who are above opened to us the things that are below, so that we may enter into the secret of the truth...by means of types...[that] are humble in the presence of perfect glory."[mli] The spatiotemporal curtain dividing Alpha from Omega—initial condition from final cause—acts as a vital conduit between them, allowing the teleology of final cause to craft countless fresh avenues through which to ripen its intentional seeds into mature expressions. The reunion of Alpha with Omega transpires through the conduit of sentient agency, which acts as a "rent" through the density of matter to allow spirit to transmit like a sacred message passing through a channel to find each side of the spatiotemporal division to be selfsame.

Locked in a cycle of reciprocal causality stretched between the poles of Alpha and Omega, "God assumes the life of man and man releases the God within himself at the mid-point of the cross-arms...God descends and Man ascends—each as each other's food."[mli] By donning the accoutrements of matter and form in its great world-begetting sacrifice, the divine becomes "the food-substance of the world" as both eater and eaten; the chaotic matrix from which new potential manifests and then lays itself back down.[mlii] The sacred descends, naked and vulnerable, into the coarse-grained material interpretation that clothes it in the protection of "animal skins," whose symbolic function conveys its essence in "types and images." This secondary covering presents totality as partial. In turn, partiality lifts itself back up to the subtlety and completion in which meaning expands endlessly into indissoluble omniscience. The conscious structure that supports this interchange is one of self-aware intelligence, whose discriminatory capacity can maintain those complementary currents without inappropriately mixing, or adulterating, them by conflating the higher potential with the form of the lower, nor by disparaging the lower, up-surging pulse of spontaneity that fuels the emergence of the higher.

By reflecting infinite potential through the perfect pattern of the Son, who is carried into manifestation on the transformative breath of the Holy Ghost, the Father enters creation as conscious intelligence that coheres all of manifestation into differentiated singularity, locating the "kingdom" within as well as ever transcendent of the bounds of form. In this way, "The world was made a paradise that god might descend into it."[mliii] Every participant in the drama of creation actively partakes in the body of Christ; the invitation extended to the apostles was to do so consciously. In order to accept the invitation, summoned beings are compelled to become sacrifices themselves, offering away the limitations of proximal material constraint to a higher form of consciousness. This was the mission of the human emissary of Christ consciousness: "Jesus came to crucify the world,"[mliv] but only through the willing "consent" spoken of by Fr. Keating, fulfilling the mandate that the seeds of enlightenment and transcendence "must be planted in our liberty."[mlv]

Descent

As a localized repository of chaos, the lower, physically identified self is an "an abyss of confusion to be saved from," according to Merton. However, it is also the conduit of the novelty and regeneration that swell up from the lowest levels, as well as the epicenter of organization to the extent that it perceives and arranges order out of surrounding chaos. With its evolutionary entailments offering themselves to the revealing light of consciousness, the lower self embodies what must be fully descended into. Willful descent of the conscious mind into its own dark shadow acknowledges the profound power accessible through the illumination of objects of darkness in a tacit yet "bold acceptance of this dark region's power for both destruction and reconstruction of the conscious structures of those who seek to access them."[mlvi] By laying itself down in the dark maelstrom it is born of without dissolving back into it, a conscious structure can be radically transformed, while fundamentally preserved, by being converted into a new and highly ordered layer of chaos that will be incorporated as a guide into a new level of emergence. The ongoing sacrifice on behalf of transcendence is a baptism through which depths of potential accrue to a system, becoming more transparent to the fearless rational understanding that seeks that inner source of profundity, and thereby gains higher levels of resolution.

Through the integration of developing cognitive structures with the instinctive wisdom of their visceral forebears, surface-dwelling rationality simultaneously deepens its reach and extends its breadth. The environment that the subject relates to comes to include more than external conditions, but also an increasingly complex inner landscape as well. Sign processes emanating from the inner caverns of subjectivity are incorporated into the conscious mind's repertoire and recognized as aspects of an inner source domain, rather than externally originating effects. Through descent into the lower realm of internal surprisal, which is archetypally expressed, ascent is enabled into the higher realm of unconscious potential beyond mind's explicit reach. The contents of the psyche become localized sources of power, rather than irrational, destabilizing projections. Liberated from its stygian catacomb through conscious integration, the wealth of evolutionary potential that fills the unconscious envelope of explicit awareness becomes a tool to facilitate transcendence.

The revitalizing potency of replaying the original sacrifice by plunging the consciousness into the non-rational depths was widely recognized throughout many of the bygone cultures of myth. Many rituals acted out the "sacramental bond between [humans] and the natural world," which was "the primary factor in our evolution—not simply as a physical species, but as conscious beings."[mlvii] Dionysiac wine rituals, for example, served as a downward counter-flow to esoteric practices seeking the illuminative heights of contemplation.[mlviii] The value in pursuing the "divine enthusiasm that overturns reason" was in lowering the consciousness to animal levels in order to access secrets of nature, that the "forces of destructive-creative dark might be released."[mlix] Engaging with the enervating flows that animate intelligent but non-rational psyches and forms avails the seeker to a deep and lucid connection with the dynamic pulse of creation in a purer, freer, more elemental flow.

Exemplifying the symmetry that is reflected across the focal level of consciousness between the lower and higher levels of unconsciousness, the animal intelligence sought in descent is symbolic of both the bestial subhuman, as well as the daemonically superhuman, according to Jung.

In conjoining the earthly with the transcendent at the midpoint of explicit awareness, the prelapsarian balance, wherein animals and humans, or instincts and consciousness, are integrated in a single peaceful corpus of evolutionary potential that is unitary, rather than Darwinian, is consciously re-attained.^{mlx} United in a coherent psyche at the finely balanced interface between constitutive non-rationality and mystical transcendence, the quieted "animals of the self" become amicable compatriots in whom the oppositional distinctions between spirit and body, or "pnuema" and "earth," cease spinning the adversarial wheels of evolutionary change and resolve into singularity.

The descent of divinity into form is the primordial essence of metaphor—the ineffable and indissoluble expressed in terms of substance and partiality. Of this primordial, yet ongoing event of creation and renewal, Pope Francis homilizes,

> "The Lord, in the culmination of the mystery of the Incarnation, chose to reach our intimate depths through a fragment of matter. He comes not from above, but from within, he comes that we might find him in this world of ours. In the Eucharist, fullness is already achieved; it is the living centre of the universe, the overflowing core of love and inexhaustible life."[mlxi]

The cosmogenic event is ritually replayed throughout the universe in all of its expressions, from the ongoing creation of new matter, to the world-filling potential contained in every living body. Relayed through myths and religions is humanity's search for access to that ever-present moment that is forever in the Beginning; the still point of eternity that hovers at the interchange between the in-spiraling and outgoing counter-currents of manifestation and dissolution. In the ceaseless flux between spirit and matter, wherein the sacred is profaned and the profane is sanctified,[mlxii] the interchange discloses its function of renewal by invigorating the mutable dance of dynamical form with the spontaneous vitality of the gravid, fathomless depths of stillness that quench the roots of transpiring order.

11

Unfolding Evolution

"Multiplicity that does not reduce to unity is confusion; the unity that does not depend on multiplicity is tyranny."
—Blaise Pascal

*"It cannot
Be called our mother, but our grave...
Where sighs and groans and shrieks that rend the air
Are made, not marked; where violent sorrow seems
A modern ecstasy."*
—William Shakespeare (*MacBeth* 4.3)

*"This thing of darkness I
Acknowledge mine."*
—William Shakespeare (*The Tempest* 5.1)

When cognitive structures first sent their questing branches of potential above the level of indexical communication to construct a symbolic niche above a new threshold of criticality, they opened up an unexplored domain in which to apply the self-similar rules that govern evolution in every other sphere. Within this novel landscape, the targets of selection are informational, roaming well outside of the bounds of biological necessity and contextual immediacy. With some forms of heritable information now uncoupled from genetic codes and even the molecular modifications that revise their expressive probabilities, new modes of transmission including symbols, rituals, myths, and other cultural constructs came to span the breach between phylogeny and ontogeny by establishing relational norms within groups. Although not without some degree of precedent among other animals, the human penchant for cultural transmission as a form of intergenerational information transfer was undertaken with symbol-abetted elaboration that precipitated a turning point between degree and kind. Eventually, as the growth of discriminating Logos reached out and established itself at new levels of cognitive emergence like the fine-grained branches at the free extremes of a phylogenetic tree, the outer world came to be viewed as a less perfect mirror for the inner, and the power of discrimination refined itself into the dexterity of rationality.

The cultivation of rationality is one human contribution to a story whose pages have long unfurled through countless forms of intelligence. Accompanying the widespread meanders, braids of converging and diverging channels, and countless eddies of specialization throughout its evolution, the vertical ascent of cognition pushes toward ever-new turning points of criticality which entangle order and chaos into increasingly higher-level flows of mutual, balanced exchange. Carving its niche within a cognitive landscape whose referents include logical structures, abstract thinking leads sensory-based experience into uncharted conceptual landscapes.[mlxiii]

Instituted in the simplest levels of categorization, the discriminative capacity that sets the parameters for intelligence branches into an intricate substrate of relational mappings, which comprise the semiosphere. Subjective fibers of semiotic construction consist of the ability, endemic to all intelligence, to recognize relationships across categories. Among animals, relational reasoning ranges from broad, general overlaps among seemingly spurious sets of categories—such as chicks with the freedom to see their own toes becoming more successful foragers of mealworms than those which hadn't—to refined and directed, such as chimps who have played with boxes meeting with greater success in using them as tools than chimps without the benefit of playful familiarity. The ability to transfer knowledge, even implicitly, across domains is a foundation for more sophisticated cognitive elaborations such as analogical reasoning, which recognizes that two different things can be treated as the same.[mlxiv]

Indexed to the bodily source domain, relational perception expresses itself endlessly in non-linguistic applications. One widespread example of the abstract logic of similitude is tool use. Its implementation requires not only recognition of relationships across domains, but also an abstract perception of absence between present and desired states. As intelligence samples the recondite realms of potential in search of a physical bridge between those incongruities, explicit representation is invited as an efficient means of sifting through possible solutions.[mlxv] Like a catalyst contracting its target's active site, a tool contracts the disparity between problem and outcome by offering a physical metaphor for the intangible isomorphism between an extant state and one that aligns with a more favorable intentional representation. Eminently subject-dependent rather than inherent, the exact form of the connecting bridge is thoroughly open-ended according to the desired effect, as well as the subject's apprehension of material, efficient, and formal causes within the given context.

Just as the perception of functional similarities among objects facilitates relational understanding in the physical domain, symbols can likewise promote relational reasoning among semantic objects; namely, other symbols, such as words.[mlxvi] Although symbol-supported learning is demonstrable among animals, the adaptations of the human mind make it a specialist par excellence in the abstract domain of relational reasoning. Facilitated by the abundance of semantic tools that comprise symbolic language, higher-order specializations uniquely enable explicit representation of complex relations across a broad range and depth of domains. The links that relational labels establish across domains support the fine-grained nuance and wide-ranging flexibility characteristic of rationality and its tools, including analogy.

By effectively constricting the semantic space between otherwise unrelated domains, words function like tools, catalysts, and microcosms of their own metaphor-based framework by generating directionality—intentionally promoting connections that could have happened at random, but with very low odds and at a very low rate. In the process of catalyzing the development of the neural structures of rational thinking, words affected a shift in the evolutionary order by acting as expressively flexible carriers of information capable of rearranging the relationships of their users toward the environment and each other to an unprecedented degree. By amplifying the converging potential of lower hierarchical levels into a vertical reach toward criticality, cognition surpasses the threshold between degree and kind when it establishes itself in rationality. Built upon a structure that had taken hundreds of millions of years to erect through the arduous processes of biological evolution, abstract thinking compressed the timescale of semantic evolution to that of learning when it brought the time-dependent realm of dynamics closer to the timeless realm of symbolism.[mlxvii] Evolution increased in tempo as well as depth when its spiral coiled into semantic space.

Natural Logic of Metaphor

As the structural frame which guides the binding logic of complexity, the embodied understanding expressed by metaphor is foundational to the higher-order distinction-making of rationality. Although the syllogistic logic of clear-cut correspondences enabled by speech appears wholly apart from its bodily informed precursor, the chaotic order of non-linguistic logic—Bateson's "syllogisms in grass"—is the encompassing substrate of the rational order. Not only are language and the conceptual systems it reflects metaphorically constructed, but even the logic guiding the construction of grammatical relations is of the preverbal kind in its reliance on nonlinearity."[mlxviii]

The interconnection of ideas in the preverbal realm, uncut by the distinctions of rationality, is an overlapping continuum among closely related mental objects, with boundaries incised through non-rational associations. With its functionality rooted deeply in the subjective recognition of similitude, "each term of a metaphor is manifold" and contains its own "internal complexity."[mlxix] The many-tiered logic of association that comprises metaphor condenses its expansive and nondeterministic implications into a deceptively simple presenting level. Irreducible to its components, metaphor is at once emergent and monad-like in its relation-dependent wholeness. With its open-ended amenability to possible source and target domains, metaphor blurs the distinction between potential and expression, interchanging them to various, context-dependent degrees. Its holistic logic arranges lower levels of chaos into malleable hierarchies that support the unfolding order of emergence while preserving the essential ingredients of spontaneity and coherence through recursive upward twists along the autocatalytic, self-referencing spiral of increasing cognitive depth and flexibility.

The inclusive logic of metaphor is reversed by the partitioning capabilities of its rational, language-enabled descendants, which have the ability to dissever themselves to some degree from their non-linear underpinnings. Suspended aloft a deeply nested web of non-rational, but logically coordinated structures, rationality and the language that enables it together represent a powerful leading edge of guidance over the dynamics of cognition. The differentiation that language enables exerts a radical downward re-structuring effect on conscious perception, freeing it to speculate beyond the boundaries of Umwelt and even incorporate unseen elements from the outskirts of surprisal as prospective causal properties.

With its passage through the turning point of symbolic language, the psyche incorporated itself into a cosmic narrative in its outward projection. As the exuberant exploration of awakening intellect became increasingly tempered by historical contingency, flowing its evolution down the forking channels of radiation, the orderly regime of rational mind began calling for heroes to battle against the inscrutable and supernatural ferocity of the chaos from which they ascended, and thereby attain new heights of conscious structure. Through the course of the successional stages of cognitive maturation toward rational self-awareness, conscious mind resorbs its unconscious projections by coming to understand what it had previously considered supernatural as thoroughly natural, creating a fertile substrate for further development.[mlxx] Even the structures and means of conceptualization come potentially within the purview of analysis and understanding as the cognitive system attains the requisite degrees of freedom to become consciously self-referencing. However, as its syllogistic touch fans out to explore each domain it encounters in the efficiently causal terms accessible to theory and empirical evidence, surface-dwelling rationality inexorably banishes perception of the ubiquitous divinity that enfolds and sustains it, always beyond its measure.

The Rational Divide

In keeping with the distinction-making power of its own rational leading edge, linguistic capacity is unique among evolutionary adaptations in the degree of potential separation it introduces between agent and context. By separating perception from the immediacy of experience with a barrier of description, language presents a substantial integrative challenge for its host. The linguistic subject must balance the vistas of conceptual and relational possibilities availed by language against the "unquestioned belonging" that embeds the non-linguistic agent into its environment on all levels.[mlxxi] Peirce draws the distinction between immediate experience, which, through sensation, is ever-present; and mediate experience such as thought, which "having beginning, middle, and end…cannot be immediately present to us, but must cover some portion of the past or future."[mlxxii] Along with advancing cognition, a potential wedge also develops between not only one's experience and environment, but also between experience and one's own body. Even the neural apparatus that support the complexity of speech shift the channels of perception away from sensorimotor immediacy to more austere cerebral connections, which efficiently circumvent the more onerous pathways of bodily experience to create approximate summaries of these in their brief circuits.[mlxxiii]

As language developed, its early hosts were presented with the same integrative challenge as any other autonomous agent faces within its environment. Supported by the universal penchant for regularities, the most natural response was to formalize shifting and expanding relational understandings into symbols and rituals, thereby codifying networks of associations and the iconic states at the center of all of these. Incorporated into narrative flows, these stabilizing reference points unfolded into myth, the foundational tool used at the human level of evolution to integrate into a unique niche within the biosphere and establish a complementary landscape within the mental domain.

Also ameliorating the divisive potential inherent in speech is its metaphorical structure, which echoes universal constructive principles. Just as myths are metaphorical bridges by which to engage in energetic flows at various scales within the nested cosmic hierarchy, the metaphorical architecture of language and its non-linear syntax connect the thinking mind through a fluid bridge to pre-rational mental structures. By acting as a turning point between different sets of dynamics—symbolically representational order and non-rational, experiential meaning—metaphor in all of its forms binds the rational mind into chaotic orbit with its antithetical foundation. When it engages in a high-level, emergent relationship with rationality, metaphor's role in all other spheres of evolution is explicitly recapitulated: as a localizing, contextualizing, and conditioning point of convergence between universal dynamics and the immutable, agent-bearing interiority beyond physical description that is the individualized bastion of final cause.

For much of human evolution, the balance between rational and non-rational has been tested by various degrees of separation under different cultures and societies, but the two domains have generally maintained critical and complementary contact with each other. Even the foundations of western philosophy enfold ontology within epistemology by conceiving of the mind as directly able to grasp an actual essence rooted in nature.[mlxxiv] However, the journey of rationality has long sown seeds of differentiation between itself and its non-rational foundations as humanity has extended the range of domains whose guarded secrets it deems ripe for conquering through rational methods.

Tools of Rationality

As the basis of ecological structure, niche construction is inwardly instantiated and outwardly projected. The niche an organism carves and occupies is therefore a direct reflection of its perceptions, interpretations, and adaptations. In human society, niche construction becomes elaborated by layers of culture, which from the beginning has situated itself both locally and cosmically. When this primal necessity was critically inverted, laying bare the individual self to the piercing discernment of fine-grained rationality, the western conception of human individuality gradually developed, crystallizing during the intense introspection of classicality, and systematizing into the idea of person-as-agent. Following a centuries-long quest by pre-Socratic thinkers to present a rational account of events in terms other than of the mutable vagaries of deities, the locus of agency gradually transitioned from outside of the individual to within via what St. Augustine would eventually describe as "the will."[mlxxv] This shift implied that the structure of the universe was intelligible and therefore available to human understanding. After the Cartesian rift opened a chasm between the human mind and the rest of the world many centuries later, however, the question of "how do we know?" became newly pressing.[mlxxvi] Without the certitude of a deep natural connection between intention and extension, rationality bereft of its ontological moorings faced new independence as well as new insecurity.

Influenced in its long evolution by the Cartesian divide was the scientific method, whose systematic processes and empirical metrics helped allay the insecurity of uncertainty by rapidly erecting a scientific framework founded on the study of efficient causes as a means to understanding and subduing nature. This new mode of understanding, with its reproducible methods, precipitated an inflation of knowledge along with countless applications in the domains that it was newly opening up. Seemingly liberated through knowledge and the technology that it engendered, humanity tasted the euphoria of domination via technological transcendence that tacitly set aside the question of integration and tantalized the imagination with the prospect of a route to pure, objective knowing about a universe availed to subjugation through human knowledge.

Although science was viewed by some as the ultimate panacea to human ignorance, others were more restrained in assessing its potential. Even as august a logical positivist as Henri Poincare had no need for an absolute epistemic value in science because he saw a trajectory of theories being supplanted by more highly refined, or as he termed it, more "convenient" hypotheses and theories.[mlxxvii] Like math, which was likewise widely assumed to reflect objective and immutable truths, science is constrained by the conundrum articulated by Peirce that "we can't know how large of a portion of the whole we are looking at."[mlxxviii] Because of the limitations of perception and conception, science and math occupy a hazy middle ground as a product of the human mind that is neither "independent of literal meaning," nor "reducible to it either."[mlxxix]

Much like language and rationality, science cannot escape from its non-literal foundations. Arising out of a metaphorically structured conceptual system and conditioned by evolutionary and cultural entailments, science, like any other product of the mind, is an interactive, contextually sensitive process of symbolic activity.[mlxxx] A field opened by language, science constrains language even as it is guided by it. The language that hypotheses are conveyed in adapts itself to their needs, taking on technical forms of meaning that are locked in a one-to-one reference to the framework in which they function, in contrast to the more fluid and accommodating polysemy of non-technical words. Such fine-tuned interpretive adaptations rule out the possibility of any neutral language, concludes philosopher Thomas Kuhn.[mlxxxi] The contextually determined specializations of both the language and the techniques deployed within the radiating branches of the scientific universe reveal the evolution of science to be self-similar to that of any other domain.

Kuhn's analysis of scientific revolutions was transformative because it set in sharp relief the presumed function of science as educing a final, objective truth condition, against its actual relative, metaphorical basis which constructs a guiding framework of belief to inform its methods, tools, and objects of pursuit. Bounded by the constraints of subjectivity, the objectivity toward which science strives encounters a basic barrier noticed by Kuhn: "It is hard to make nature fit a paradigm."[mlxxxii] Like any other symbolically based system, a scientific paradigm points to an idea without expressing its entirety, indicating an implicit web of associations that is always larger than what is expressed.

Acting as the symbol level of a complex system which entrains the dynamics of lower hierarchical levels through its downwardly causal exertion, a paradigm reflects the inherent constraints of perception in its tendency to stratify information according to pertinence. Without the hierarchical structure of a paradigm to render data intelligible by ordering them in relation to each other, all of the facts that observation and experimentation could amass would resemble an equiprobable milieu, similar to the degeneracy of potential eigenstates that have yet to array themselves in relation to an external parameter.[mlxxxiii] Through its logical arrangement of facts into a system of ideas, a paradigm creates a presentable, orderly framework—but pays the cost imposed upon all expression by foregoing the completeness of undifferentiated potential. Selectively guided by the paradigm's entailments, theories and hypotheses emerge to act as lower, supportive levels of organization which closely guide the types of questions asked and the angle from which they are examined. In conformity with these defining parameters, certain evidential aspects are highlighted, and others minimized, creating around the paradigm an event horizon bounded by surprisal—the hallmark of partiality which indicates that the proper role of a scientific paradigm is not as a description of an absolute truth condition, but rather as part of a more comprehensive, interactive system of understanding. The unincorporated spaces between paradigms are haunts of free energy and chaos. Meaning, like an organism and its perception, is bounded.

In the practice of "regular science" versus the saltatory transitions of paradigm shifts is a highly explicated analogy of the evolutionary process and its meaning-based bifurcations of domains. Within a paradigm, research is "committed to the same rules and standards," yielding incremental changes.[mlxxxiv] Inevitably, however, anomalies accrue that are outside of the explanatory bounds of a theory, precipitating a crisis in which the old framework breaks down and a new theory takes its place. Such a non-linear, non-incremental change in kind constitutes a paradigm shift, which often requires re-evaluations of formerly accepted facts and explanations.[mlxxxv] These previously established relations must be formally realigned under the new rubric of explanation, like the emergence of a new level of order that is not reducible to the components it is comprised of. As the new paradigm takes known facts further from their prior state of understanding, they forge a new and unpredictable course whose deviation from the probability tied to their previously settled theoretical orbit acts like the information dimension of a chaotic system, with its sensitive dependence on initial conditions drawing a trajectory arbitrarily far from its starting point to establish a new path around a different center of attraction.

Although drawn at oblique angles to the complex wholeness they seek to describe, paradigms and their hypotheses connect human understanding to the natural world through their very incompleteness and discreetness, by which situated minds can apprehend them. At the indeterminate margins between theory and apprehension, the *elan vital* of uncategorized ontology seeps in, guiding the evolution of understanding, while at the same time dooming the created structures of theories to a finite temporal span. In its turn, each paradigm must yield to a refined and emergent leading edge that rearranges understanding in order to accommodate the surprisal excluded from a previous order. Mind is mistaken, therefore, to deem any scientific system of understanding complete. This is why Bohm could warn with certainty that "to take any physical theory as absolute truth must tend to fix the general forms of thought…and thus to contribute to fragmentation."[mlxxxvi]

While science reveals itself to be one selectively changeable aspect of an evolving universe, its high logical order confers on it a potent role in structuring the perceptions of its human constructors. His extensive contemplation of paradigms led Kuhn to remonstrate, "One suspects that something like a paradigm is prerequisite to perception itself."[mlxxxvii] Darwin likewise concluded that "theories come before knowledge."[mlxxxviii]

Because all knowledge is embodied and so must pass through the prism of metaphor on its way to comprehensibility, the value that science offers is not that of pristine objectivity. The rationally trained positivist is therefore presented with the need to make the ultimate sacrifice and relinquish the linear notion of progress that assumes that changes in paradigms lead closer to an absolute form of truth.[mlxxxix] Without an objective platform to which knowledge can be anchored, positivism is again at the mercies of its self-made insecurities, born of conflating a surface-level presentation with totality. However, this very uncertainty and the non-determinism it bespeaks is actually an avenue to liberation for those willing to pursue it, by releasing humans from the passive role of faithful transcribers of predetermined truth conditions beyond our reach, into the active role of creators of reality.[mxc]

Following the same routes to stability as other human enterprises, science has developed its particular standards of performance, regularizing them into analogs of ritual. However, as the hyper-rational embrace of sheer empiricism grew into logical positivism with its intolerance for the non-rational surprisal that roams the boundless empyrean outside of neatly circumscribed theory, facts became increasingly separable from their broader contexts. The quest for truth and understanding that spurred the scientific revolution became ritualized into data gathering and formalization of findings. Natural philosophy, which encompassed the numinous nature within phenomenal form, was displaced by the increasing rigidity of informational measurement and analysis, whose intense focus on efficient cause restricted the scope of questions that could be asked by excluding the unmeasurable and non-assayable.[mxci] "Science," laments Merlau-Ponty, "manipulates things and gives up living in them."

Along with the scientific flensing of the sublime from the measurable, methodical rationality has proceeded to systematically contract and fragment the purview of every previously holistically conceived inquiry and endeavor it has been applied to. True to its discriminating origin, the empirically bolstered rationality of the Age of Reason sought to create a distinction between its proclaimed mantle as arbiter of truth, and its earlier dramatic, poetic, and metaphorical incarnations. Much like the straight road of history that was unwound from the mandala of myth, poetry's simultaneity was supplanted by the linear progression of prose, with its serviceability to the analytical aims of rationality. Metaphor, the embodied union of experience and meaning, was eschewed as deviant, along with all else corporeal, natural, or cyclical. The entry into the cooler, more prosaic realm of rationality made way for the increasingly scalpel-like refinement of discriminatory power to come uncoupled from its metaphor-bound, poetically discursive forbears with their broad, inclusive overlap of intertwined gestalts. The heaven of metaphorical holism became the hell of the Age of Reason.

Shadow of the Split Psyche

When human consciousness emerged above the fray of biological evolution, it embarked on its own radiation of evolution in the noosphere. The choice harvested from the Tree of Knowledge lifts its keeper's intellect into the landscape of moral agency, colored with god-like hues that incorporate into the natural evolutionary process of bifurcation an element of conscious choice. Just as evolution had previously moved beyond the relatively deterministic logic of physics into the vastly more complex ratiocination of the biotic domain, the yet higher logical order of mental evolution brings up its own complications: "I put life and death before you, blessing and curse."[mxcii] The unheralded innovation of conscious, moral choice emerged as the centered point between two novel potential symmetries that consciousness could break toward: the triumphant ascent of wisdom leading love back to divine transcendence; or alternately, the despotic claim of rationality to ascendancy over its ethereal counterpart. The two poles of divine favor and wrath juxtapose against the capacities of the animal mind, whose unmediated contact with the numinous is largely implicit. Self-awareness, however, explicitly confronts the decision to either "choose life," and swell the progress of evolution by participating with full, conscious intention in the "idea of God;" or conversely, to sink into the inevitable stagnation and entropic dissolution that results from dissevering from conscious mind the upwardly flowing replenishment of the non-rational order. While the former path is one to paradise regained, the latter one is an earthly damnation that contorts the pure conscious light of the living, "pneumatic," experiential realm into grim shadows of ignorant projection, perverting its "original spontaneity" into an "adversary of soul."[mxciii]

At once profound and precarious, the attainment of rationality presents a new level of integrative challenge to the human organism. With the world of higher-order potential accessed by rationality, the fissure between biological wisdom and cognitive capability widens into a yawning chasm. Heavily reliant on learning and experience to bridge phylogeny and open-ended, high-level expressive potential, the supremely complex structure of human cognition invites the possibility of error into the gap between those poles as the entropy stalking the growth of order ascends in kind. Along with new cognitive heights comes the peril of rationality straying from the "straight and narrow" balance of criticality that is the binding seam of manifestation. The differentiation of consciousness enabled by rational self-awareness and its attendant moral agency urgently demands integration with its "root condition," warns Jung, otherwise risking "severance" and the collapse of discrimination's structures when they stray too far from the level of their love.[mxciv]

Although necessary to the process of differentiation, the separation Jung cautions about is viable only when immured within nature's maternal bounds, which foster the coherence productive of evolution. When those nurturing bounds are instead ravaged by the discrimination-based power they foster, intelligent constraint loosens its structured hold on vital Eros, and the vigorous yet delicate balance of evolution devolves into the "unbridled dissipation" of unintegrated potential. The extreme separation of the two poles of consciousness fosters confusion instead of coherence. Rather than being confined to the human psyche or even society, these effects ripple out to affect the rest of nature in the downwardly causal tide that issues from a system's leading edge. Romano Guardini explains, "The moment that energy or matter or a natural form is grasped by man, it receives a new character…The thing of nature becomes involved with, even partakes of, human freedom; in so doing it also partakes of human frailty."[mxcv]

With evolution precipitously balanced between order and chaos, an excess of either can lead to the same dire consequence of systemic dissolution. Just as Eros—representing the ascendant freedom and spontaneity of lower levels—loosed from the attenuating constraints of structure unleashes destructive chaos, intemperate application of the rational cuts of orderly Logos likewise undermines systemic balance by introducing countless, potentially destabilizing interstices into the stability of structure. Excessive emphasis on rationality at the expense of its holistic and non-rational counterpart engenders a catastrophic split between mind and spirit. Once that fracture transpires and the rational mind becomes tyrannical, reason loses contact with its context and so, circularly, its meaning or rationale. The reciprocal current that rises to close the autocatalytic loop of causality is no longer the intuitively wise voice of the wordless shadow side, but instead a destructive pulse of irrationality spawned in the untended schism between the two disconnected poles of consciousness. Uncoupled from the numinous, non-rational, and chaotic "swarm of the indefinable" upon which awareness floats, the divisive scythes of rationality, too thorough at their job of holding the leading edge above unconscious depths, discard this direct energetic connection with spirit as unholy chaff. The gathering power of internal logos is jettisoned when the rational acquires preeminence over the relational, as is its external reflection which is the enfolding womb of the mandala within which all of creation, including rationality, is balanced. Inner depth and its intimate evolutionary entanglements with the rest of the universe are abandoned in favor of the "light-reflecting surfaces" of the apparent and surficial—mere husks of form which are inadequate replacements for the succulent fullness of potential that ripens through deep interconnection.

With the uncoupling of the emergent level of consciousness from its own roots, the replenishment otherwise afforded to every adjuvant hierarchical rung of the psychic structure by the sustaining upward current of the ideal reciprocal balance desiccates into neurotic, contextually divorced recursions. Conversely, the top-down guidance whose beneficent reign ought to summon supportive levels to purposeful order, shrivels into a despotic and insecure compulsion to control. The vibrant fluctuation between downward teleology and upward-flowing spontaneity is supplanted by a macabre battle between tyranny and insurrection. The choreographed abandon wherein creativity meticulously plays within the critical thread between logical order and exhilarating chaos forsakes its freedom for a brittle and defensive posture, while inner and outer surprisal darken from keeps of spirit and vigor to rotting entropy. The sword-like cut of Logos is distorted when turned on its own roots, shearing itself from its larger, native context, and isolating itself from its own expressions in other bodies. Without access to the deeper, encompassing, shared, and fluid intelligence afforded by meaningful interconnection, surface-level consciousness is in a precarious position that encourages defensiveness. Without the necessary semantic structure to bring order to the inner domain of the unconscious, dissociated consciousness projects its innate impulse to create and guide as a compulsion to fear and control.

When its wordless and symbolic offerings are not admitted into the compass of rational understanding, the unconscious mind retreats into shadow. Alienated from its own essence, rational mind becomes incapable of seeing "infinite light" as anything other than darkness.[mxcvi] The shadow of the psyche, which is hostile only when misunderstood or ignored, becomes a fearsome menace to the unintegrated rational mind.[mxcvii] Rather than engaging with the intuitive gifts of *epinoia* from the unknowable regions and thereby turning onto the path of the paradise of deep, experiential interconnection with all other aspects of the singular universal body, disunited rationality prefers to enact its own vision of ordering which, when excessive, shatters from brittleness into its own deepest-seated fear of entropic disarray. Instead of bringing forth emergent levels of novelty and creativity, such mental dissociation produces emergent levels of pathology. This fractured wasteland becomes the new self-image that people learn to identify with in a distorted rendition of individuation. Heaven becomes a promised land to be conquered, and the ego is driven to build up a Babel-like spire of rationality, extruded from context and straining skyward with the piercing intent of storming heaven.

As the two poles of consciousness—whose difficult union is the critical fountainhead of intelligence, creativity, and evolution—strain apart, the formally causal, domain-crossing girders of association that knit them into a robust and cohesive system fray and disintegrate. "Mankind is now threatened by self-created and deadly dangers that are growing beyond our control," Jung asseverates with no uncertainty. "Our world is, so to speak, dissociated like a neurotic. Currently we are threatened by self-created dangers growing beyond our control; we are creating a neurotic, dissociated world, our shadow."[mxcviii] This is because, as Guardini explains, "[Man] has extensively mastered the immediate forces of nature, but he has not yet mastered the mediate forces because he has not yet brought under control his native powers."[mxcix] Failure to recognize the deep rootedness of the unconscious mind in the natural world impels the rational but insecure mind, haunted the demons of its projections, to invade both nature and the unconscious like a menacing alien driven by a "will to destruction"[mc] against these non-rational supports, and therefore ultimately against itself. The intrinsically self-referencing nature of intelligence prescribes that the expanding gloom of surprisal, reflecting back hellish images to the collective psyche that unwittingly projects them, leads the dissociated consciousness toward the very irrationality and destructiveness that it sees all around it in its inability to correlate chaos into order—to the point of turning violently on its own body. By applying its dissevering cuts to the levels that underpin it, the rational mind cleaves its conscious entanglements to the natural pantheon of Chaos, Eros, and Gaia—the creative unconscious, ordered vitality, and sustaining nature—and instead projects these as dragons for slaying.[mci] In resisting the contextually contingent condition of embodiment, rationalism fearfully seeks to divorce itself from its non-rational, unconscious foundations, repressing these and in the process destroying the human capacity to respond to numinous symbols and ideas, which puts conscious mind at the mercy of the psychological underworld.[mcii] In the ironic twist of a self-made hell, by eschewing its connection to the lowly and formative, conscious mind inadvertently condemns itself to the compulsive enactment of those lower-level patterns. The free will that ought to flourish as the leading edge of a cognitive system marked by artful mastery of the degrees of freedom which its lower levels offer as tributes, is instead paralyzed by an utter lack of understanding of the nature of those forces, allowing them to overwhelm it.

As the emblem of rational mind's attempt to divest from its own ground, "Cogito, ergo sum" resonates as the apex of the extrusion of thought from its context. Unmoored from the workings of dendrites and axons, blood and bones, thought stands alone. This is, in turn, is the logical consequence of the extraction of humanity from its supportive context of nature and evolution. Arising as a counterbalance to the unlawful divorce of mind from embodied nature is materialism, which erroneously ties spirit's identity to dependence on the measurable mechanisms of efficient causality. The collapse of universal depth into a low-dimensional surface reduces the numinous creative potency once celebrated as the splendid and fearsome Great Mother—rich and overflowing with potential and life—to dead, soulless matter[25].[mciii]

The shift of consciousness away from the encompassing embrace of the mandala toward the divisive cross borne within that life-giving circle incurs the deceptively simple choice of Deuteronomy between blessing and curse. While the sunward reach of questing intellect brings the blessing of increasing individuation through access to higher-order levels of cognition, the curse that is potentially embedded in that evolutionary foray lies in abjuring the humbling principle of sacrifice that integrates unfolding emergent properties into their context. Although the most highly refined application of the discriminative faculty, rationality is like any other product of evolution that is a small part of a larger whole, requiring meaningful and many-leveled integration with its context in order to maximize its functionality. Applied without deep interconnectedness, rationality sequesters itself from the contextual

---

[25] The word "matter" is believed to derive from Latin *mater,* which implies mother, source, or origin.

relations that would ripen it into wisdom through meaningful, reciprocal exchanges within its environment, inner and outer.

Losing Paradise

While rationality dissevered from its roots is a prevalent modern condition, it is not the only form in which humanity has expressed its highest intellectual gift. Eden and the many other versions of golden-age bliss that inhabit the legends of ancient civilizations may allude to an earlier time of cultural, societal, and technological achievement. Encompassing high degrees of development in the arts, religion, plant and animal cultivation, and governance with a focus on communal well-being, the agrarian civilizations that were vanquished by the numerous tribes of invading nomads represented to their subjugators a far-off ideal of aspirational beatitude. The greatest distinction Riane Eisler draws between the two types of societies is that, in contrast to the cultures that celebrated the gifts of the Earth as a bounty, "at the core of the invaders' system was the placing of higher value on the power that takes, rather than gives life."[mciv]

Embedded in the prevailing mythologies surrounding the shift from a more egalitarian, matrifocal social system to the rigid dominance of a linear hierarchy is also a metaphorical account of rationality's split from its generative unconscious matrix. The ancient Babylonian epic of the conquering hero, Marduk, is the saga of how he wrenched from the Great Mother Tiamat the world-creating power she had been accorded in earlier times. Much like the division in Genesis between the heavenly dome and abyssal depths, Marduk divides the weeping goddess and forges from her rent carcass the starry sky and the habitable earth, claiming for himself the mantle of creator by virtue of his bloody conquest of monstrous chaos.[mcv] The feminine dragon, embodying the earthly energy and wisdom of the serpent, becomes the foundational sacrifice for a new society in which rationality is applied to combative technologies rather than to cultural cultivation. Ushered in with this early matricidal triumph was a new era in which the sun-gods, versed in militant arts, routed and subdued the people whose mythological outposts were the seasonal and celestial cycles that bounded their synchronic consciousness in sacred rounds of nested regularities. Turning those spiraling heavens into their hell, the conquerors rolled out from the unitary evolution of circularity the diachronic timeline of history, written in patrilineal genealogies and punctuated by military conquests. In sloughing off the skin of a prior evolutionary era in which time was sacred and cyclic, and the generation, rather than control and destruction of life and creativity were honored, the course of conscious evolution straightened its trajectory from the encircling mandala to the "straight and narrow" pathway that led to God only through great effort and trial, rather than experiencing the omnipresent divine touch through all manifestation. By unraveling the cycle of myth, with its rhythmic oscillations between death and rebirth, the ongoing and spontaneous renewal embodied by the Goddess was replaced by a timeline of events wherein fall, redemption, and salvation became one-time historical events.[mcvi] Although the decimation of the earlier societies, with their rich cultural achievements, led to a dark time of cultural regression as recounted by Reisler, eventually the foundations of modern civilization arose, to be particularly articulated during the classical Greek period.

Within the paradigm of dominance which supplanted that of integration, reservoirs of ingenuity were tapped and applied to the taming of natural elements as well as other groups of people. However, the triumph of the rational man-hero over the chaotic nature-goddess-turned-monster saw the uncoupling of the rational order from its generative roots, which alone could supply the oppositional balance needed to ensure the sustainable integration of his achievements with the world over which he exercised them. The numinous and fathomless dimensions which beckoned entry through rapturous abandon became cordoned off by a jealous god, whose revelations were now revealed only to His elect, priestly servants, leaders of His people. By supplanting originating metaphors that enjoined humanity in the ecstatic agony of ongoing cosmological birth with those that recast the lot of the chosen people as one of violent domination and asceticism that is its own goal rather than a means to liberating self-mastery, the vivifying upward flows of organic spirituality dried up. The rivers of blood let through the ritual of sacrifice—whether the priestly slaughter of beasts or the military conquer of God's many land-holding enemies—in order to appease the fiery and aloof warrior-father were inadequate replacements for the spontaneous vitality whose life-giving fountains could not replenish a destructive and unintegrated people.

A desiccated spirituality cut off from its source is the result, Jung believes, of imputing too much reality to the "artefacts," or outward "forms of relating to the supernatural."[mcvii] In contrast, the semi-fluid play of "as if" invoked by myth could readily transport participants beyond their literal bodily confines to the rapture of "divine seizure" that revealed the deeper and higher levels of interconnection between people and their world. Such spontaneous, uncontrollable play had no place among a people who affirmed their identity on the basis of history, with its clear evidence of God's dealings with them, whether favorable—awarding them the spoils of plundered civilizations—or punitive, to bring them in regimented steps to the lands He had promised them. The top-down force of control necessary to pilot a vast population through a marginal existence to military triumph left little room for the organic role of symbolism to test and invite the non-rational psyche. Symbols accordingly stiffened from gateways to the supernal to a system of one-to-one correspondences that constricted wide-ranging interpretive potentialities into rigid casings that could only narrowly reflect their intrinsic light.

Not only physical objects, but even the archetypes which, in their manifold potential, offer limitless transformative wealth that leads through associations to the numinous depths of experiential immediacy, can fall prey to the urge inherent in discriminating intellect to establish "singleness of meaning."[mcviii] Demanding literalness from the metaphorical invites the "hardening of categories" that objectivist and positivist philosophies spring from.[mcix] Such idolatry, which the Israelites were emphatically warned against, dries up the fountains of faith—whose power is only tangentially alluded to in symbols and forms—into "mere objects of belief."[mcx] This is a danger in beholding only surfaces and presuming they present a totality—a danger which extends beyond the misplaced adoration of objects. With its outward orientation, an excessive emphasis on rationality can lead its beholder to idolize that capacity itself and become forgetful of the need for baptism in the replenishing and deeply interconnected baths of life. Religion based on outer forms becomes far removed from immediate, conscious experience and becomes reduced to a system of moralistic codes—tamed like a tiger in a zoo, but with a dangerous side when brandished by tyrannical hands. As Campbell wisely warns, symbols are vehicles of communication, not final terms. Mistaking the two, he cautions, can lead to spilling of blood.[mcxi]

False Self

Once shorn of its awareness of cosmic connection, rational mind in its relatively isolated condition enshrines itself as the new source domain from which it assesses and understands all which transpires around it. From his years of peering into the psyche, Jung concluded that the greatest danger in the development of the self lies in the identification of the ego with the self, producing an inflation which threatens the ego with dissolution.[mcxii] The simple distinction Jung makes between the self and the ego is that the former includes the unconscious—with its deep and subtle entanglements to all of the rest of nature.[mcxiii] In contrast, the presumptuous ego inserts itself into the role of self when fractionated consciousness lays claim to totality, curbing the potentially expansive and nonlocal purview of mind to the apparent and literal confines of localized individuality.

Merton warns that referring things to the false, egotistical self is the means by which "we alienate ourselves from reality and God."[mcxiv] Localized ego loses sight of the universal power that sustains it when it equates that vitality with its own limited perception and attempts to appropriate the bounty of infinitude into its discreet nature. Such untenable hoarding leads to the breakage begotten by attempts "to imprison the divine paradox" within an unnaturally narrow framework.[mcxv] The glorious enthronement of embodied divinity in the "sacred city" at the heart's center is usurped by a splintered ego blind to the patterns that connect it to the whole of the cosmos, which participates fully in evolution at every moment. Jesus implored his ignorant listeners to perceive their dilemma of spiritual entrapment when he reminded them, "Is it not written in your law: 'I have said you are gods?'"[mcxvi] As microcosms of the self-similar truth condition that unites all manifestation into indissoluble interconnection, each member of his audience was in full possession of divine nature. However, the limited dimensions of ego, whose apprehension of surfaces only allows it to identify with sensually and rationally presentable things and constructs, veiled the perception of his accusers to his true nature as well as their own. This was the group that would eventually crucify the divine emissary because, in Merton's ironic words, "God did not measure up to man's standard of holiness."[mcxvii] Identifying with the small and localized attractor of personal identity rather than the all-embracing, higher-Self attractor is a blinding fall from paradise into animal skins that paves the road to crucifixion.

The counterintuitive reason that the persecutors and killers of Jesus failed to recognize the divinity he embodied is precisely because it was embodied. When God is exalted from the immanent intimacy of natural forces to austere greatness, inaccessible to "fallen" supplicants unworthy of paradise, His "humblest and nearest attributes" become reviled and repressed.[mcxviii] Under the guise of extolling greatness, worshipping God only as creator leads to "animosity toward spiritual awareness."[mcxix] Similarly, when followers of Buddha glorified him as unique, his status as a human being was sapped along with his universal appeal to enlightenment, which was then deemed a privilege of the elect.[mcxx] However, as Merton explains, God "emptied" and "hid" Himself "as if He were not God but a creature" because "He could not bear that His creatures should merely adore Him as distant, remote, transcendent and all powerful."[mcxxi] This is because "if He were merely adored as great, His creatures would in their turn make themselves great and lord it over one another." Julian offers a ready antidote to the misery and strife of a psyche riven into bipolarity by failing to see God as both great and humble: "It is more honoring to God to see him in everything than in any particular thing…the fullness of joy is to see God in all things."[mcxxii]

Filling even the least of created things with its full measure of divinity, omnipresent consciousness takes on infinite forms and perspectives. Not only does a fully rounded spirituality embrace God as immanent, transcendent, creative, and created, it also encompasses shadows. The dark gods and goddesses were given their due respect in ancient mythologies as participants in the cycle of birth and growth, maturity and ripeness, and finally dissolution followed by rebirth. With the banishment of these dark ones to the hellish underworld of unconscious suppression, modern humanity has no guiding archetype to provide wisdom about the pain that is part of the full experience of life. Instead, the split and unguided psyche naturally turns to the pursuit of pleasure, which eschews the rigor and discipline required for the challenging process of individuation, with all of its potential for actively and intentionally fomenting new births at new levels. Only by forgoing lesser, more banal pleasures in favor of establishing affinity for higher, subtler ones can the things of the dark spaces pass into the light. As Jung appreciated, "accepting darkness does not change it into light, but it can be illuminated."[mcxxiii]

Spiritual Crisis

In "putting asunder" what "God hath joined together" by thoroughly divorcing conscious awareness from the instinctual forces that inform it from the depths of evolutionary experience, modern humans have, in Jung's words, "increasingly divided our consciousness from the deeper instinctive strata of the human psyche, and even ultimately from the somatic basis of the psychic phenomenon"—a condition that allows the instincts relative autonomy.[mcxxiv] Merton delves into the metaphysical repercussions of this psychic disaffection, saying of the Christ-matrix that enjoins all manifestation: "His mystical body is drawn and quartered…by the devils in the agony of that disunion which is bred and vegetates in our souls."[mcxxv] Diverted and dissipated by the myriads of tiny snares of ego-entrapped psyches, the universal flow of consciousness scatters from cohesive structure into the random milieu of disintegration, dismembering and dissolving the coherent network of manifest universal intelligence.

Disjoined from the energetic flows that enliven the cosmic body from every situated angle, the leading edge of consciousness devolves into internecine warfare that tragically leaves the painful sacrifice of crucifixion unfulfilled, and so doomed to Sisyphean replay throughout the entire body of Christ, the "costly and copious flow of [whose] most precious blood overflows the whole of earth."[mcxxvi] The rapturous urgency of Eros is skewered into a tormented passion that leads to neither redemption nor salvation, and is felt by "all creatures capable of suffering pain…even heaven and earth [languish] in their own way"[mcxxvii] by the pathological perversion that weaponizes the sacred wholeness of the quaternary into a sword of division. Like Mary suffering along with her son at the foot of his cross, the maternal womb of nature that clothes conscious intelligence in form mourns the desecration of the fertile ground of life as it transforms into an unwilling tomb to receive back shattered creation. "Just as her pierced heart mourned the death of Jesus, so now she grieves for the sufferings of the crucified poor and for the creatures of this world laid waste by human power."[mcxxviii]

Modern crises—ecological, social, economic—are the final-causal outcomes of a deep, internal and collectively projected spiritual dysphoria, which generates a context utterly foreign to human nature. "'The external deserts in the world are growing, because the internal deserts have become so vast,'" laments Pope Francis, adding, "For this reason, the ecological crisis is also a summons to profound interior conversion."[mcxxix] Minds that cynically excise the sacred wonder from living nature register little compunction in precipitating its ruin "without any consideration for what had been thought inviolate or untouchable…ignor[ing] that strong sense of the sacredness of nature which had endured within mankind's earlier vision of the world."[mcxxx] Such cavalier dismissal of an order once held sacred leaves humanity stripped of its connections to the rest of the universe, doomed to slow death by "cosmic loneliness"[mcxxxi] and yet unable collectively conceive of an alternative to planetary and spiritual despoliation. As the logic of domination subdues the vivifying forces ever ready to percolate to the surface with revitalization, the wild things that once populated the psyche and its stories with their ferocity and wisdom are tamed, depleted, banished by extinction, or safely contained "by a thousand bars...wherein there stands benumbed a mighty will" [mcxxxii]—an apt description of the animal as well as human condition when deprived of enlivening immersion in deeply experienced, meaningful Umwelt.

By damming rather than circulating the vital cosmic flows, the human mind, with its god-like potential for perception, moral agency, and conscious participation in the unfoldment of evolution, turns into a tiny prison by mistakenly identifying individual consciousness with the form that it occupies and fostering the insidious creep of self-abasement and even contempt that deems any individual—human or otherwise—unworthy in themselves for the magnitude of grace promised by redemption. Such misplaced despair grants free license for committing atrocities against every form of creation, thereby expanding the moribund kingdom of entropy.

Regaining Paradise

In his heavy-hearted survey of the crises facing the modern world, Pope Francis articulates their root, "We lack an awareness of our common origin, our mutual belonging, and of a future to be shared with everyone. A great cultural, spiritual, and educational challenge stands before us, and it will demand that we set out on the long path of renewal."[mcxxxiii] Offering a critique as well as an avenue of relief from the current state of planetary malaise, Merton notices that "we have to a great extent lost the sense of sacrifice."[mcxxxiv] The call to sacrifice is a call to martyrdom, and thereby resurrection. Through its natural function of laying down a valuable leading edge to nurture emerging possibilities, the humbling principle of sacrifice offers liberation from the tyranny of rigid and excessive top-down control.

Instead of a singular and inimitable event long past, sacrifice is a ritual of celebration played out in all birthing, sustaining, and dissolving forms—whether physical or mental—that partake in the body of Christ. The ongoing renewal and redemption of the sacrificial cycle are catalysts of purposive new growth, rather than mere propitiation for past failings.

Attributes cultivated at the leading edge of any effort or activity ripens into food, whether beneficial or deleterious, to be consumed by and incorporated into some other aspect of the self-sustaining web in which all creation plays a part. The modern challenge of sacrifice entails in part a critical appraisal of the fruits yielded by the unchecked growth of rational constructs divorced from the grounding context of consciousness which Swedenborg understood to be synonymous with love. Rational development apart from love is an edifice founded on its own destruction, as affirmed by Jung's observation that, while the gains of civilized society are great, they come "at the price of enormous losses, whose extent we have scarcely begun to estimate." Conceding that "progress and development are ideals not lightly to be rejected," he cautions that "they lose all meaning if man only arrives at his new state as a fragment of himself."[mcxxxv] Offering some hope, however, Jung believes that, although "civilized consciousness has steadily separated itself from the basic instincts…[they] have not disappeared. They have merely lost their contact with our consciousness and are forced to assert themselves in an indirect fashion."[mcxxxvi]

For a modern people so inured to separation and division, the task of reconnecting the shattered fragments of psyche and planet alike seem so painful that Merton likens the task to "resetting [a] body of broken bones."[mcxxxvii] The ecological and cognitive structures so delicately crafted over the ages of biological and, more recently, cultural evolution, which connect experiential primacy with integrated, purposive intelligence, have fallen into disrepair through both active violence and apathetic disuse. In order to rebuild the vital channels that connect rational capacities of creation with their numinous reality, the challenging and non-rational regions of the unconscious need to be tended like a garden. Conscious cultivation of that potentially fertile ground with the intent of redeeming the ignorance and hatred, both born of dissociation, which have left it increasingly stripped and sere will yield new cycles of causality that promulgate virtuous, rather than pernicious closure loops; new habits of action through which the two domains of apparent and essential can connect in emergent ways, heralding a revival of the enriching, constructive creativity that is a willful, conscious act of choosing life. This re-establishment of the ruptured connection between humanity and sacramental nature constitutes what Jung describes as the "painful experience of the union of opposites."[mcxxxviii] Only by enfolding into conscious experience its non-rational construction can humanity reclaim rightful access to the numinous forces that animate all of manifestation from well below the apparent level of surface presentation. This is the process of individuation, which is ultimately a process of coming to terms with inborn wholeness.

The task of individuation is an appeal to expand the scope of explicit, rational consciousness by incorporating its supportive levels. This invitation was offered to the Apostle Paul in a vision of ceremonially unclean animals. "Get up, slaughter, and eat," he was instructed, with the understanding that his ministry could be extended to all races. However, the vertical axis of that directive is a reminder of the importance of embracing the fruits of prior evolutionary steps. As cognitive evolution ripens implicit understanding into explicit knowledge, this precarious achievement is at risk of dysfunctionality if not incorporated into its own matrix to yield balanced cohesion between its expression and its shadows. Even when rejected as inferior or "unclean," the structures and specters of the unconscious crave the light of conscious awareness, which they can connect to the deepest flows from within. Jung therefore urges that we "consciously surrender to the power of the unconscious," because in the archetypes housed there, "we are still part of nature connected with our own roots."[mcxxxix] In their spontaneous and vivid upward flow, the lower levels nourish the roots of the achievements and aspirations of higher levels by their self-similar adumbrations of the qualities that will be emergently expressed at the leading edge. As Teilhard de Chardin understood, "Love appears in humans because it appeared at the lowest levels."[mcxl] Individuation is the cultivation of ever-new ways of intentionally expressing the universal truth condition of divine love.

A New Dispensation

Like the thwarted tower of Babel, the pursuit of conquest and control that has accompanied rational development at the expense of integration is rebuffed by the very spiral gods whose corpses are laid at its foundation. The straightened trajectory that ego-blinded builders sought to erect all the way to heaven failed to accomplish their malevolent goal of insurrection against the natural order because of the cyclical nature of evolution, which binds even its most adventurous trajectories into non-wandering, recursive sets that loop and fold upon themselves even as they transcend prior levels of expression. Even the gruesome enactment of evolution through perverse feedback loops is still governed by a corrupted analog of natural law, cycling through the rise and fall of birth, maturation, and dissolution.

As the edifice constructed by ego-driven rationality crumbles to the level of its untended love, its ruins scatter themselves like seeds along the very substrate that can redeem them: "The root of Christian love is not the will to love, *but the faith that one is loved...by God.*"[mcxli] The redemptive possibilities for renewal availed by the discontinuous twist between death and rebirth provides an opportunity for a structure to be built anew. For relatively recent semantic constructs, with their shallow root bases and easily toppled, yet eminently destructive columns, the challenge is to remake them according to a pattern that propagates renewal—a pattern that has been vigorously repressed for thousands of years. Despite the magnitude of challenge such an effort of cognitive, spiritual, and cultural transformation presents, it is part of the responsibility that humans uniquely shoulder as active participants in the "idea of God."

Enfolded into the conscious creativity that allows humankind the intentional pursuit of life or death is the judicious power of dissolution. Willful and conscious deconstruction of semantic barriers to meaningful and loving engagement with the forces of life in their countless guises is the deep and contemplative work demanded of a self-aware species, freeing habit-hewn ideological structures into the spontaneity of unstructured, universal essence. Once liberated, potential again becomes available for the purpose of new construction that will be sustainable and progressive if grown through wisdom and founded on love. As Teilhard de Chardin concludes, "A universal love is not only psychologically possible; it is the only complete and final way in which we are able to love."[mcxlii] The power of love lies in its unifying, cohering capacity:

"There is, therefore, in love an extension of the individuality which absorbs other things into it, which unites them to us."[mcxliii] Unlike the reactionary insecurity of unintegrated, surface-dwelling rationality that tears at its own connections to the rest of the world and recoils from the humbling sacrifice necessary to accomplish the tender task of "[resetting] the body of broken bones," love accepts the pain of reunion.[mcxliv] From this painful but joyous reunion arises a renewed opportunity to construct an integrated system capable of accessing its own base of intelligent support, not only from the deepened and heightened vertical axis of profundity and ascent, but also the horizontal spread of differentiated perspectives that generate and amplify new meaning.

The collective task of awakening to and redeeming the incredible extent of loss inflicted on the living fabric of the planet at all levels "will make such tremendous demands of man that he could never achieve it by individual initiative or even the united effort of men bred in an individualistic way."[mcxlv] With the emergent level of capacity as well as potential for disarray—the blessing and curse—presented by rational self-awareness, semantic structures can be constructed at new levels to fulfill the role of mythology by re-integrating humanity into our own world, both natural and self-created, with the guidance of unexpressed entailments silently and non-rationally acting as ordering principles. The measure of that worldview's validity would be its success in incorporating humanity into our physical surroundings by restoring our connection with the numinous, and thereby awakening with the touch of conscious awareness the sentient pulse of Eros that resonates all manifest forms into the sublime canticle of universal creation. In such an "act of knowing humans imitate something of god's creative love for creatures."[mcxlvi]

The responsibilities of human consciousness received a subtle signal as to their elevated duties in the Middle Ages, around the 9th century, when the traditional Greek cross, with its deeply earthy as well as astrological connotations, yielded to the Latin variation in popular imagery. With the crossbeam lifted and shortened, the perfect Platonic symmetry of the geometrically balanced mandala was disrupted. The new, more precarious state of balance carried in the new image indicates a less ideal adaptive integration with our environment, demanding from us a new and higher form of symmetry.[mcxlvii] The new center of balance is lifted up to the heart center, the fourth energy center in the Vedic chakra system that draws the energy from the lower, body-centric chakras to the higher, spirit-apprehending centers. This balanced, but asymmetrically positioned center is the doorway between the corporeal and the supernal domains; divided from creation's foundation, but rejoined in the heart of humanity to affect an untold alchemy between earthly, rational, and spiritual levels of awareness. Through this transformative portal between lower and higher is the ever-present choice for beings of free will—a crossroads—to arrive at a place of equilibrated complexity in counter-flowing currents rather than the destructive strife of rigidity and repression on the part of the higher directed toward the lower, whose inevitable countercurrent is the striving of the lower to overthrow the higher. Instead, the open heart, the "sacred city," invites a meaningful, self-referential connection between the highest directive levels, and the flows of life from their most basic level. Through the Christ-door of I AM, spiritual supplicants are granted access to their own ground of being. Passage through that rarified gateway is to transcend Beyond Being.

The distinctive form of balance introduced by the awakening of the *anahata* chakra of the heart center comes from the reciprocally causal order it introduces between higher cognitive, creative, and spiritual human capacities and their foundations of animal energy. By unfolding the higher potentialities that rise up from heart-centered awareness, novel ways can emerge to fulfill the mandate that a dying Fr. Bede Griffiths transmitted to mystic Andrew Harvey: "Feed the growing body of the Christ."[mcxlviii] Fed and grown through any creative act that binds love with wisdom, from the coalescence of atoms into molecular systems, to the ecological march through successional stages, to radiating phylogenies, to human ingenuity, the omnipresent body of Christ centers itself in its own singular heart, which is iterated illimitably in all situated forms, making Christ both the core and horizon of all experience. The pathway opened by this transcendent center of expansion is a non-deterministic, evolutionarily novel way to salvation and redemption. The symbol of the cross, ancient and ecumenical, received the Christian blessing of becoming indelibly associated with the tragic grace of "Forgive them, they know not what they do"[mcxlix]—a compassionate and complete embrace of all contingencies, which poses a reminder that even damage wrought by acts of willful ignorance has an opportunity for redemption through that fourth gateway betokened by the central point of the cross, which upholds and uplifts the structure of all creation at every level.

Only by overcoming the force that humanity has uniquely loosed onto the world—that of ignorance—can connection be re-established between the conscious and unconscious minds, and thereby between the leading edge of awareness and the entire rest of the cosmos. By becoming conscious conduits for the many gradations of sentience threaded through our own bodies and minds, connecting us in subtle entanglement to the rest of the universe, we become accommodating epicenters of evolutionary teleology as enunciated by Teilhard, "The Universal and Personal (that is to say, the 'centered') grow in the same direction and culminate simultaneously in each other."[mcl] As Thomas Aquinas understood, the most sacred and holy thing in the cosmos is the integrity of creation's totality. The "grand... purpose of all elements of creation," says Swedenborg, "is an eternal union of the Creator with the created universe."[mcli] By creating "subjects in which [divinity] can dwell and abide,"[mclii] this grand purpose is emergently realized through what Maturana and Varela describe as an "ongoing bringing forth of a world through the process of living itself."[mcliii] Merton reveals the benediction inherent in created form when he tells us, "The God in us allows his love to shine on each other in ways that couldn't happen were it not embodied in us."[mcliv] Endowed with the capacity to partake in the "idea of God," our highest sacred duty is to participate in the upholding and the unfolding of the whole of creation, birthing it as through a womb rather than devouring it as into a tomb.

To choose life is to choose an inward path of awakening, in which potential unfurls and traces many exploratory routes through the immense capacities contained in a human. This inner radiation is the perfect, complementary mirror to the outer radiation, diversification, exploration, and play of chaotic Eros in critical engagement with the ordered regime signified by Logos. Ortega y Gasset reflects on the fundamentally ecological ordering that supports every hierarchical level of creation when he urges, "It is necessary for us to multiply the facets of our mind so that an infinite number of themes may penetrate it."[mclv] Mirroring the macrocosm of the universe, the mind flourishes when diversity radiates through many channels and provides a wide range of perspectives on the same underlying conscious condition. Likewise, the quickening breath of Eros, when structured and channeled, foliates into ever-new patterns of beauty, intelligence, productivity, and potential. In its lateral spread, Eros begets complexity and diversity, which are living repositories of potential that support the spread and flow of life and mentality throughout the universal system. Self-contained at every level, exuberant creativity unfolds a world in which "wholeness interacts with persistent wholeness."

Spirit and Nature: Closing the Loop

It is through the Great Mother archetype, Jung believes, that humankind can restore our own bitterly divided natures.[mclvi] The violent break away from epistemic structures that hallowed nature's cycles saw the pantheistic omnipresence of divinity resolve into a single-pointed monism, marking the beginning of a new epoch in human thought. The inclusive embrace of the Mother fragmented into the projected arrows of militarized Eros, deviating from their shared level of attainment like trajectories in search of a new attractor. The dramatic rupture, projected onto the bipolar desert god Yahweh, saw masculine differentiation surging out of the soil of feminine consolidation. Like a hero following the call to adventure, intrepid consciousness left its level of stability to establish a new angle from which to explore the world and its place therein. In order to complete the cycle, the adventurer must return with his hard-won knowledge to his place of origin, that the novel may be integrated with the established, and that the lion of rational striving may lay down peacefully alongside the lamb of deep interrelationship. However, mirroring the unquenchable ferocity of his implacable deity, the warrior has yet to bend his fiery will in the humility of beneficence.

Rather than plowing the laboriously wrought achievements of rationality into the receptive loam of the unconscious to yield a fertile substrate for new growth, that desert-bred consciousness persists in scorching the earth into barrenness.

Having precipitated the fracture between ego-limited identity and the rest of nature, rationality's consuming fear lies in the mistaken belief that to reconnect with the severed ties of its own evolutionary foundations is to discard its considerable attainments in favor of pig skulls on pikes. However, bereft of the life-giving flows from more foundational evolutionary levels, the high achievement of rationality is unable to fulfill its most vital task of bringing the highest of final causes to fruition in the context of conscious self-awareness. Only by relinquishing its compassionless categories whose hardened boundaries it defends as though they were its true identity, and instead surrendering itself to the vastness that supports and encompasses it, can ego finally exchange the contortions of an artificially limited purview for the natural flow of cosmic embrace. Guardini offers a simple and unequivocal prescription for accomplishing this end, "Man must again learn to become a true master by conquering and by humbling himself."[mclvii]

By reviving and expanding connectivity with the fundamental flows that enliven the rest of nature, the striving urges within humanity regain an expansive source domain whose vitality and potential utility can support the upward surge of intelligence in explicating new forms, depths, and angles of meaning. To that end, the integrative wisdom cultivated and codified in the Neolithic Goddess myths and their serpent-lore patiently awaits the return of her heroes, to assimilate their gains at a higher level of complementarity. A metaphor for this hoped-for reintegration is carried along the human cerebrospinal column. The serpent of enlightenment coils latent at the base of the spine, resting in the cavern of earthly connection known to yogis as the *muladhara* chakra. Upon the summons to awaken, undulating *kundalini* ascends to the sun center—the *ajna* chakra—of the third eye, and engages both earthly and solar poles into a harmonious resonance that liberates the life energy along its path. In this act of "lift[ing] up the serpent in the wilderness,"[mclviii] dormant potential rises through the levels of chaos that support the order of the human organism to unite with its estranged opposite and converge on a sublime and liberating level of potential, chaos, and new expression.

A pattern for re-establishing the forsaken channels of connection was set by the people of Israel through their much-lamented expulsions into the wilderness. Over their protests, the wandering faithful were led again and again to the purifying forces of nature through their intense, compulsory intimacy with it. In the peoples' reluctant return to the harsh desert was the subtle blessing of a natural, redemptive asceticism that forcibly integrated the solar consciousness revered by the people with the earth that they strained to turn away from. Both asceticism and redemption receded when the people gained a much-sought sedentary life, which priests tried to compensate for by flooding their permanent temples with riverine purifications of sacrificial blood.[mclix]

The cycle of wandering, natural asceticism, and the letting of blood repeats its elements in the fulfillment of the messianic prophecy, with the Redeemer presaged by the pieties and privations of the Essenes—among them John the Baptist, who was the "voice crying in the wilderness," declaring the earthly and embodied visitation of the divine. Aside from its function of aiding the unfoldment of the prophetic narrative, the preparatory role assumed by John has a more universal—and simultaneously more personalized and intimate—connotation in the awakening of Christ consciousness within the mind of the devotee. As Paramahansa Yogananda explains, "The real wilderness, where no mortal thoughts, restlessness, or human desires, intrude, is in transcendence of the sensory mind, the subconscious mind, and the superconscious mind—in the cosmic consciousness of the Spirit, the uncreated trackless 'wilderness' of infinite bliss."[mclx] The "voice in the wilderness" announces the impending, illuminating experience of conscious contact with universal wisdom through which our true nature as the "manifestation of ground of being"[mclxi] can be experienced. Because this is knowledge beyond the reach of rationality, the only way to access it is to experience the dissolution of isolating ego into the oceanic, cosmic awareness that is reflected in every individual expression of creation. According to the Gospel of Phillip verse 96, "If you become a spirit then the spirit will unite with you. If you become Word, then the Word will unite with you. If you become light, it is light which will couple with you."

The upwelling spontaneity from the generative source is the foundational iconic experience that beckons the conscious level of awareness and upholds criticality at every level. However, it exists outside of the framework that allows the categorizing, surface-dwelling property of rationality to be the means by which it is understood. Although infinitely divisible by categorization, the living mystery is also always beyond categorical strictures, leading them on an endless and hopeless chase of infinite regress if they should decide to try to corral it. Of this illimitable potential, envisioned as the "perfect man," verse 90 of Phillip says, "Not only will the perfect man not be able to be captured, but he cannot even be seen. For if they [structures of consciousness] saw him they would seize him. In no other way can one be begotten of this grace unless one should put on the perfect light and become perfect light." Outer, explicit consciousness can only see the light of potential as darkness. In attempting to "see" the complete wholeness implied in its perfection, measuring awareness "seizes" the divine light, collapsing it into partiality. Admittance into the holy enclave of numinous realization requires that seekers "play the games of the gods"[mclxii] by relinquishing the analytical grip of the positivist mind and, like Nature who "retained nothing of herself, in no way resisted god,"[mclxiii] re-enter the unitary interior of experience at the heart of all manifestation.

Transcending Rationality

Rationality lifts the consciousness to a pinnacle of freedom from which it is able to reflect on itself, with its own nature potentially becoming visible to its own localized awareness. From this height, it becomes possible to perceive everything—our myths, our systems of understanding, our rituals and bodies, our "cloud-capp'd towers," "gorgeous palaces," and "solemn temples;" even "the great globe itself"[mclxiv]—as metaphors, signifiers pointing to something else, which they are of and yet are not. Integrated rationality has the potential to explicitly observe the vital pulse passing through form and process in a cycle that connects all it creates into an intricate, circular weave while affording each jewel in the web a distinct variation of the self-same logic. Seeing this, and understanding its own part in the ever-rising heave and the ever-falling sigh of energetic breath, integrated rationality has the capacity to open the door to reverence. Guided by humility, integrated rationality can understand the universal, animating grace as at once tender, to be nurtured and protected; magnificent and all-pervasive, to be held sacred and in awe; and purposeful, to be gainfully fashioned along the harmonious critical seam of balance, creativity, and generativity that fulfills the imperatives of life and mind at all levels.

The rationality-aided ascent toward universal bliss-consciousness is a reprisal of the promise of Eden, yet at a level of self-awareness elevated by maturity. The structures—conceptual, relational, technological—that we have built along our evolutionary journey comprise the platform, the structure from which we seek that beatific state. In order to serve its purpose, the rationality that has allowed for so much cognitive innovation must, like any other evolved structure, be transcended. Expressing Logos at the leading edge of conscious awareness, rationality becomes the savior to be sacrificed in order to allow for "greater works than these"[mclxv] to ensue. When subsumed by a higher and subtler emergence, rationality becomes a support in a structure capable of revealing the causal "substance behind the seeming,"[mclxvi] or the universal Experiencer beyond the conditioned subjectivity of manifestation.

The guardianship that rationality assumes over the gates of paradise is on display from the beginning, in the flaming cherubic sword at the eastern gate of the Garden. Protecting the way to the Tree of Life, the sword whirls itself into a mandala of flame, applying the primordial cut that propels unitary spirit into the labyrinth of evolution by fragmenting it into physicality. Debarring access to the Garden's eastern gate of rebirth into transcendence, the blade of discernment is the "highest spirit of reason," which Nicholas of Cusa describes as the "wall of paradise" that conceals God from our view.[mclxvii]

In depicting the stages that lead the evolutionary sojourner past the shredding oscillations of the cherubs' swirling sword-gate, the Baghavad Gita sets the scene for the soul's sublimation on a metaphorical battlefield.[mclxviii] Former allies along the evolutionary path become as enemies to the seeker when a faction of Arjuna's family turns against him in response to his striving against the compelling forces of nature for enlightenment. In this metaphysical battleground of the soul, sensuous tendencies and desires range themselves against the discriminative faculties by which matter-bound spirit—the entrapped purusha—reclaims its liberty. Although intellective rationality must be surmounted in order to partake of the ineffable, in the final surge to emancipation, it isn't Reason who is slain by Arjuna. The liberating sword-thrust fells the most intimate and entrusted advisor of King Ego: Drona, the archetype of habit.

Weaving the very fabric of the universe and binding all its actors into complex epicycles, habit is the structural substrate that supports the foliations of order which direct energetic and informational flows, and which reflects the same intelligent, guiding principles across all scales. Within the realm of physics, habit manifests as regularities and laws. Among the living, it reflects as instinct and Umwelt. For the spiritual aspirant, this closest of counselors supports the tendencies that bring him or her closer to self-realization—as well as those that undermine the same pursuit. In all its guises, habit constructs its channels according to the leading edge of intelligence and its contextually conditioned interactions, conducting consciousness into "concatenated discharges" of "sensation not attended to;" "so organized as to wake each other up successively."[mclxix] With the end result an act of "volition of which thought no longer plays part,"[mclxx] habits perform their constructive action by muting the feeling and spontaneity of pure consciousness. By rising above this universal regulator and measurer, the reclaimed soul is liberated into the transcendental abandon of unconditioned, conscious spontaneity, freed to drink, as would Rumi, "like a flower that drinks, without lips or throat, of the wine that overflows with laughter and joy."[mclxxi]

Evolution and the Word

"In the Beginning was the Word. In him was life, and that life was the light of men."[mclxxii] Silently speaking through embodied representatives, the Word projects into being a realm whose life and light evolve through the channels of physicality, informed by the mental currency of information. All expressions of that realm beyond the reach of physical or semantic structure are metaphorical and epistemological, open to endless interpretive variation. Reposing in immutable singularity, the silent center that is reflected in each universal microcosm is forever unchanging, although the formal, perceptual and relational interpretations that constitute creation continuously evolve, adjust, adapt and refine. Its aspirants seek transcendence beyond the bounds of words and epistemology, and even beyond metaphor, to the plane where all experience merges without distinction.

"I am the Alpha and the Omega, the first and the last, the beginning and the end."[mclxxiii] The universal drama unfolds through the serendipitous alchemy of structure and chaos, bringing undivided wholeness into relative expression through the two poles of structure and semantics. Each requires the other for meaning and expression respectively; although irreconcilable to each other, they come together to create an irreducible whole. Fusing a vast hierarchy of coherently engaged unities into the singularity of cosmic expression, the "universe of signs" assembles itself into interconnected marvels through the dynamical flows of material, energy, and information. Signifying the nonlocal principles that provide the constructive logic of the universe are the discreet and localized forms whose various properties reflect the selfsame principles in a multitude of contributory ways. Below the measurable level of efficiently causal interactions are the subtle entanglements that arise from the wave-like penumbra of supportive, unexpressed potential that silently attends a unity and informs its actions. This less localized intelligence is that of the unconscious, which tacitly functions with the subtle wave-aspects of other unities to align the dynamics of a system into synchrony. Always beyond the scope of containment is meaning, which can never be fully conveyed, but only intimated, indicated, or referred to. Because of its imprecise nature, intangible meaning compels evolving agents to compose epistemic templates, which are contextually and evolutionarily conditioned interpretations of the basic conditions of life, according to which they pattern their activities.

"God utters me like a word containing a partial thought of Himself. A word will never be able to comprehend the voice that utters it."[mclxxiv] The components that construct the universe are metaphors for a willful, potent essence that is transcendent of them yet somehow unites them in a unitary logic of infinitely high order and variation. Pulsing through the innumerable "words" of manifest form, the deific vitality that orders creation into a purposeful "syntax" reforms itself endlessly like a single meaning through a multitude of dialects. Providing a deeper, more enveloping structure than the goalless envoy of entropy, ergodicity, is the penetrating, often inscrutable, but unchangeable logic of nature that cordons off initial conditions from final causes, with evolution unfolding in the space between.

"The invisible is revealed by the visible, and the hidden made secret by the hidden [or unknowable]. Some things are hidden by visible things."[mclxxv] The numinous is indicated by the phenomenal, which only highlights partial aspects of its totality. Underlying potential implicitly persists like the silence that frames words and empowers them to meaning by channeling through them something instead of everything,[mclxxvi] and only disclosing nothing in the absence of order. Although the overwhelming infinity of potential that is not revealed in material, efficient, formal, or even final causes is concealed and unknowable to the rational, apprehending mind, it is sourced in the "peace of God, which surpasses all understanding,"[mclxxvii] but which invites conscious union. At the turning point of manifestation, the two manifolds of essence and form are joined together by unitive *logos*, the word; bound like an object and its reflection in a pool whose surface hides its depth. At the same time, they are driven to the asymmetrical dichotomy of directionality that perpetuates evolution's flow by the dividing sword of Logos, the Word from whom all issue and in whom all are gathered. Demanding conscious integration, the numinous and phenomenal domains that intelligently knit themselves together into manifestation pose to the developing power of evolving humanity the choice, at once personal and collective, between life and death, blessing and curse. This summons to the dispensation of conscious evolution will not allow regress into the pool of reflection, where the freedom of consciousness is drowned, nor a leap toward the sun where the uninitiated burn if lacking the water's salve. With the guiding light of rational perception, the ongoing imperative to transformative evolution can be recognized as self-similar at all levels, in all forms, in every act of evolution at its own level; the generative fractal thread of union between meaning and structure that fuels the explosions of critical, creative emergence.

Manifestation is a metaphor in providing bodily habitation for what it is not: the pure, transcendent consciousness that is the ground of all being. The metaphor of embodiment is a turning point which, like a homoclinic interlude in a chaotic storm, unites the opposing tendencies of higher, animating potential, and lower, expressive materiality inside its calm center. Preserving the essential similarity that underlies all form, metaphor allows that essence to be projected into a universal holograph of infinite forms. Proliferating countless variations on the single evolutionary theme, manifestation constructs an indescribably complex network of relations and entanglements that impel deterministic but often unpredictable interactions. Reaching below the surface-level bifurcations of rationality to unite domains according to subtle, well-hidden levels, the metaphor of phenomenal manifestation is an interface at which the hidden shadows of the unconscious and the unknowable light of transcendence converge from below and above.

Manifestation evolves into polysemy, with many possible meanings channeling into each form. Conversely, a singular meaning expresses through all forms. The radiations of plurality construct themselves into a rich structure of reference, and ultimately self-reference, by translating one interpretation of the universal language into another to craft a protean evolutionary montage. From the countless translations of the selfsame essence and the various shadings it takes on through a kaleidoscope of perspectives, meaning is localized, sustained, amplified, and tailored to its contextual conditions. Congealed into a unitary subject through the active medium of intelligence, localized meaning is an interpretive construct of nonlocal principles interacting with local conditions. With formal constraints delimiting the Absolute into partial expressions, manifestation is metonymic in implicitly referencing ever other form, and in promulgating the ever-rising tide of evolution by connecting all universal aspects in indissoluble continuity.

Manifestation's countless nested layers of hierarchical organization are letters, words, and phrases ordered into a structure that supports and invites the flow of meaning. Guiding and expressing through these cosmically uttered phrases are the properties of logic: the singular generalizes into a multitude by preserving self-similarity under different guises of form. Habit-like channels establish regularities: an induction whose basic unit is chaos, whose guiding principle is nondeterminism, whose mechanism is emergence, and whose products are novelty and complexity. With its final form unpredictable from its underlying premises, the logic of induction reveals the universal to be intertwined with, rather distinct from the particular.[mclxxviii] Multitudinous forms, locally bound by entanglements of contingent meaning, reach beyond themselves to spread their potential throughout all of space, binding each facet of existence with every other into a concrescent singularity that points to a single conclusion: a deduction of final cause that is self-same as the initiating premise. Beyond definitive expression, that deduction is also an inference.

Upholding the entire cosmic edifice is a relativistic syllogism: if this, then everything else in the universe. At the helm of the structure—at once ordered, fluid, conservative, radical, differentiated, singular, coherent, and experiential, the language of creation meets itself in awareness through symbolic form: "Language was never invented by anyone only to take in an outside world. Therefore, it cannot be used as a tool to reveal that world. Rather, it is by languaging that the act of knowing…brings forth a world."[mclxxix]

Beyond all words and thoughts, which are separated from the potential that incubates them by the beginnings, middles, and ends of individuation, is the silence that speaks them from the ever-present Beginning, which is beyond the milieu—chaotic, orderly, creative, and destructive—of manifestation. The ultimate response to the encounter with the silent meaning behind all words is expressed by Jesus, who instructs his apostles:

"…see yourself in Me who am speaking,
and when you have seen what I do,
keep silence about my mysteries."[mclxxx]

Clothing the begetting silence with intentional meaning is the spoken word, that uniquely human heritage by which we bring forth our evolving understanding of the world. Although liberated into cognitive realms inaccessible to non-rational minds, the human position at the leading edge of semantic transmission is hollowed and made shallow if this is the only form of language we avail ourselves to. A more universal language, ever in search of more tongues to speak it, marches the cosmic procession across the sky; awakens, ripens, and lays to rest the fertile earth in a repetitive and restorative succession; foliates and blossoms through the implicate vegetative wisdom that provides a structural and ecological context for the active expression of animal intelligence, with its numerous articulations of that generative whisper; and overflows through the body, mind, and achievements of humanity in an unfolding, refining, vital, and exuberant cascade. Humans are called, not merely to interpret these natural dialects, but to take our place within the unfoldment of the meaning declared continuously since the beginning through the universal language. By holding the structure of that sacred syntax together at a unique point of emergent depth and self-awareness, humanity brings to fullness the Idea that never ceases to seek channels of expression, leading the cosmic choir in a holy canticle that honors every contribution from every perspective in the living fabric of manifestation. Each word in the song, each note in the hymn, is an embodied representation of something ineffable; each a turning point that presents itself in form while at the same time reaching into the formless heart of totality.

End Notes

Introduction

[i] R Jakobson, Language in Literature (The Belknap Press of Harvard University Press: Cambridge, MA; London, 1987) 98
[ii] Jakobson 105
[iii] Jakobson 110
[iv] Quoted in G Jona-Lasinio, Analogies in Theoretical Physics (*Progress of Theoretical Physics Supplement* No. 184, 2010) 1-15
[v] Jakobson 378
[vi] Quoted in D Leary, Psyche's muse: the role of metaphor in the history of psychology (in *Metaphors in the History of Psychology*, D Leary (Ed): Cambridge University Press, Cambridge, 1990) 50
[vii] Jakobson 100
[viii] E Jantsch, The Self-Organizing Universe: Scientific and Human Implications of the Emerging Paradigm of Evolution (Pergamon Press, 1980) 296
[ix] Jantsch 261
[x] E Husserl, The Essential Husserl (Welton, D, ed. Indiana University Press, Bloomington and Indianapolis, 1999) 175
[xi] G Lakoff and M Johnson, Metaphors We Live By (The University of Chicago Press, Chicago, 1980) 19
[xii] Lakoff and Johnson 1980, 184
[xiii] Jakobson 113
[xiv] CS Peirce, Pierce on Signs: Writings on Semiotic by Charles Sanders Pierce (Hoopes, J; Ed. The University of North Carolina Press, Chapel Hill and London, 1991) 23
[xv] WA Wallace, The Modeling of Nature: Philosophy of Science and Philosophy in Synthesis (The Catholic University of America Press: Washington, DC, 1996) 120
[xvi] Jantsch 183
[xvii] Jakobson 427, 443
[xviii] Jakobson 378
[xix] Husserl 84
[xx] Husserl 143

[xxi] P Teilhard de Chardin, The Phenomenon of Man (Harper Perennial Modern Thought: New York, 1955/ 2008) 71
[xxii] Jantsch 162
[xxiii] T Nagel, Mind & Cosmos: Why the Materialist Neo-Darwinian Conception of Nature is Almost Certainly False (Oxford University Press, 2012) 67
[xxiv] A Goswami, The Self-Aware Universe: How Consciousness Creates the Material World (Jeremy P. Tarcher/Putnam, Penguin Putnam Inc: New York, 1993) 51
[xxv] T Merton, New Seeds of Contemplation (Abbey of Gethsemani, Inc, 1961) 3
[xxvi] J Boehme, Jacob Boehme (Ed. Robin Waterfield, North Atlantic Books, Berkeley, CA: 2001) 92
[xxvii] Merton 81
[xxviii] Boehme 74
[xxix] R Guardini, The End of the Modern World (ISI Books, Wilmington, Delaware: 1956/1998) 82
[xxx] Guardini 35
[xxxi] Guardini 70

Chapter 1: The Primacy of Metaphor

[xxxii] Quoted Jakobson 106
[xxxiii] A Juarrero, Dynamics in Action: Intentional Behavior as a Complex System (Massachusetts Institute of Technology: Cambridge, MA, 1999) 190
[xxxiv] CE Shannon, A mathematical theory of communication (*The Bell System Technical Journal*, Vol. 27, 1948) 379-423, 623-656
[xxxv] W Weaver, Recent contributions to the mathematical theory of communication (*ETC: A Review of General Semantics:* Vol. 10, No. 4, 1953) 261-281
[xxxvi] Shannon 1948.
[xxxvii] Lakoff and M Johnson 1980, 14-15
[xxxviii] Lakoff and Johnson 1980, 14, 115-120
[xxxix] Quoted in Leary 6
[xl] Leary 6
[xli] KJ Holyoak and P Thagard, Mental Leaps: Analogy in Creative Thought (The MIT Press: Cambridge, London, 1995) 219
[xlii] G Lakoff and M Johnson, Philosophy in the Flesh: The Embodied Mind and its Challenge to Western Thought (Basic Books: New York, 1999) 542: "[Philosophy]…helps us put our world together in a way that makes sense to

us and that helps us deal with the problems that confront our lives. When philosophers do this, they are using our ordinary conceptual resources in very extraordinary ways. They see ways of putting ideas together to reveal new systematic connections between different aspects of our experience."

[xliii] HA Simon, The architecture of complexity (*Proceedings of the American Philosophical Society,* Vol. 106, No. 6,1962) 467-482

[xliv] Lakoff and Johnson 1999, 366-373

[xlv] Wallace 137-143

[xlvi] Quoted in Leary 1990, 1; Lakoff and Johnson 1999, 376

[xlvii] Quoted in Lakoff and Johnson 1980, 130

[xlviii] Lakoff and Johnson 1999, 383

[xlix] Lakoff and Johnson 1980, 190

[l] Quoted in Leary 1990, 9

[li] Quoted in LD Smith, Metaphors of knowledge and behavior in the behaviorist tradition (in *Metaphors in the History of Psychology*, D Leary (Ed): Cambridge University Press, Cambridge, 1990) 239

[lii] Lakoff and Johnson 1980 and KJ Gergen, Metaphor, metatheory, and the social world (in *Metaphors in the History of Psychology*, D Leary (Ed): Cambridge University Press, Cambridge, 1990), 267-295

[liii] Quoted in Lakoff and Johnson 1999, 394

[liv] Quoted in Lakoff and Johnson 1999, 396

[lv] Peirce 134

[lvi] E Kant, The Critique of Pure Reason (JMD Meiklejohn, translator, Project Gutenburg E-book # 4280, 1781/ 2003) 4

[lvii] E Zahar, Poincare's Philosophy: From Conventions to Phenomenology (Open Court Publishing, Chicago and La Salle, 2001) 4

[lviii] Wallace 201

[lix] Smith 244

[lx] Smith 251-4; Gergen 282

[lxi] Lakoff and Johnson 1980, 186-188

[lxii] Lakoff and Johnson 1999, 510: "Truth for a language user…is relative to our hidden mechanisms of embodied understanding."

[lxiii] Husserl 179

[lxiv] Lakoff and Johnson 1980, 14-19

[lxv] Peirce 17

[lxvi] Lakoff and Johnson 1999, 56-57

[lxvii] HR Maturana and FJ Varela, The Tree of Knowledge: The Biological Roots of Human Understanding Revised Edition (Shambhala Publications, Inc. Boston, Mass: 1987) 34

[lxviii] M Sheets-Johnstone, The Roots of Thinking (Temple University Press, Philadelphia:1990) 371

[lxix] S Lacy; R Stilla; and K Sathian, Metaphorically feeling: comprehending textual metaphors activated somatosensory complex (*Brain & Language* 120(3), 2012) 416-421.

[lxx] Lakoff and Johnson 1999, 346; Sheets-Johnstone 374; SC Levine and S Carey, Up front: the acquisition of a concept and a word. (*J. Child Lang.* **9**, 1982) 645-657

[lxxi] Lakoff and Johnson 1999, 30-45

[lxxii] J Hoffmeyer, Biosemiotics: An Examination into the Signs of Life and Life Signs (University of Scranton Press, Scranton and London: 2008) 230

[lxxiii] Sheets-Johnstone 7

[lxxiv] Wallace 151

[lxxv] Wallace 123-137

[lxxvi] J Ortega y Gasset, Meditations on Quixote (WW Norton and Company, Inc, NY: 1961) 90

[lxxvii] J Fodor, Concepts: a potboiler (*Cognition*. 00100-0277/94 Elsevier Science B.V. 1994) 95-113

[lxxviii] Sheets-Johnstone 61

[lxxix] S Carey, Bootstrapping & the origin of concepts (*Daedalus*. Vol. 133 (1), 2004) 59-68

[lxxx] Lakoff and Johnson 1980, 10

[lxxxi] R Hoffman; EL Cochran; and JM Mead, Cognitive metaphors in experimental psychology. (in *Metaphors in the History of Psychology*, D Leary (Ed): Cambridge University Press, Cambridge, 1990) 190: "Perceptual experience is believed [by Hermann von Helmholtz] to be not of the world, but of an analogy of the world—the results of the operations that process sensations by adumbrating or supplementing them through inference or memory."

[lxxxii] Smith 244

[lxxxiii] Lakoff and Johnson 1980, 193

[lxxxiv] Gergen 272

[lxxxv] AR Damasio, The somatic marker hypothesis and the possible functions of the prefrontal cortex (*Phil. Trans. R. Soc. Lond.* **B 351,** 1996) 1413-1420

[lxxxvi] SA Bunge; C Wendelken; D Badre; and AD Wagner, Analogical reasoning and prefrontal cortex: evidence for separable retrieval and integration mechanisms. (*Cerebral Cortex*: 15, 2005) 239-249

[lxxxvii] Holyoak and Thagard 10; DJ Chalmers; RM French; and DR Hofstander, High-level perception, representation, and analogy: a critique of artificial intelligence methodology (Center for Research on Concepts and Cognition: Indiana U) Technical Report 49, 1991

[lxxxviii] Chalmers et al 1991

[lxxxix] Husserl 92

[xc] BA Spellman, and KJ Holyoak, Pragmatics in analogical mapping (*Cognitive Psychology* **31**, 1996) 307-346

[xci] Spellman and Halyoak 1996

[xcii] Holyoak and Thagard 101

[xciii] Holyoak and Thagard 15

[xciv] Peirce 21

[xcv] Peirce 145

[xcvi] This is the premise of Lakoff and Johnson 1999

[xcvii] Hoffmeyer 227

[xcviii] Peirce 106, 141

[xcix] Hoffmeyer 214; Peirce 67

[c] Peirce 72, 75, 143,188

[ci] Husserl 68

[cii] Peirce 68

[ciii] Peirce 191

[civ] Peirce 28

[cv] T Deacon, The Symbolic Species: The Co-evolution of Language and the Brain (W.W. Norton & Company, Inc: New York and London, 1997) 77

[cvi] Peirce 192

[cvii] Peirce 190

[cviii] Peirce 244

[cix] Hoffmeyer 290

[cx] Deacon 89-93

[cxi] DR Hofstadter, Godel, Escher, Bach: an Eternal Golden Braid (Basic Books, Inc: New York, 1979) 360

[cxii] Deacon 1997, 96

[cxiii] Deacon 1997, 93

[cxiv] Peirce 1991, p 255

[cxv] Quoted in Leary 2005, p 46

[cxvi] W James, The Writings of William James: a Comprehensive Edition (McDermott, JJ; Ed. The University of Chicago Press: Chicago, 1978) 34
[cxvii] JR Van Eenwyck, Archetypes & Strange Attractors: the Chaotic World of Symbols (Inner City Books: Toronto, 1997) 84
[cxviii] Husserl 30
[cxix] Peirce 17, 28, 26
[cxx] Hoffmeyer 218
[cxxi] Peirce 231, 234
[cxxii] Peirce 229
[cxxiii] Hoffmeyer 302
[cxxiv] Husserl 147
[cxxv] JR Averill, Inner feelings, works of the flesh, the beast within, diseases of the mind, driving force, and putting on a show: six metaphors of emotion and their theoretical extensions (in *Metaphors in the History of Psychology*, D Leary (Ed): Cambridge University Press, Cambridge, 1990) 117.
[cxxvi] Peirce 236
[cxxvii] Peirce 83
[cxxviii] Sheets-Johnstone 135
[cxxix] Sheets-Johnstone 4

Chapter 2: Animal Intelligence

[cxxx] MR Papini, Theoretical notes: pattern and process in the evolution of learning (Vol. 109, No. 1, 2002) 186-201
[cxxxi] G Bateson and MC Bateson, Angels Fear: Toward s an Epistemology of the Sacred (MacMillan Publishing Co: New York, 1987) 27
[cxxxii] L Marino, Cetacean brain evolution: multiplication generates complexity (International Journal of Comparative Psychology, 17, 2004) 1-16
[cxxxiii] DC Penn; KJ Holyoak; and DJ Povinelli, Darwin's mistake: explaining the discontinuity between human and nonhuman minds (Behavioral and Brain Sciences 31, 2008)109-178
[cxxxiv] Deacon 1997, 449
[cxxxv] Sheets-Johnstone 1990, 128
[cxxxvi] D Rendall; MJ Owren; and MJ Ryan, What do animal signals mean? (Animal Behavior, 78, 2009) 233-240
[cxxxvii] Rendall et al 2009
[cxxxviii] CM Heyes, Imitation, culture, and cognition (Animal Behavior 46, 1993) 999-1010.

[cxxxix] JW Bradbury and SL Vehrencamp, Principles of Animal Communication, Second Edition (Sinauer Associates, Inc, MA, 2011) 310
[cxl] MA Nowak, Evolutionary biology of language (Phil. Trans. R. Soc. Lond. B 355, 2000) 1615-1622
[cxli] Nowak 2000; Penn et al 2008
[cxlii] Heyes 1993
[cxliii] S Carey, The origin of concepts (Commentaries in *Journal of Cognition and Development*, 2000: 1) 37-41
[cxliv] Bridgeman and Suddendorf from Penn et al 2008
[cxlv] MD Hauser, The Evolution of Communication (The MIT Press: Cambridge, MA, 2011) 41; Deacon 1997,
[cxlvi] HJ Jerison, and HB Barlow, Animal intelligence as encephalization (Philosophical Transactions of the Royal Society of London. Series B, Biological Science, Vol. 308, No 1135, Animal Intelligence, 1985) 21-35.
[cxlvii] Bradbury and Vehrencamp 310
[cxlviii] Bradbury and Vehrencamp 310; Nowak 2000
[cxlix] Griffin 8; VP Bingman, Making the case for intelligent navigation in animal thinking: contemporary issues in comparative cognition; Menzel, R and Fischer J, Eds. (The MIT Press: Cambridge, MA, 2011) 43
[cl] Deacon 1997, 336
[cli] Deacon 1997, 276; J Bruner and CF Feldman, Metaphors of consciousness and cognition in the history of psychology (in *Metaphors in the History of Psychology*, D Leary (Ed): Cambridge University Press, Cambridge, 1990) 234
[clii] SJ Shettleworth, Cognition, Evolution, and Behavior, Second Edition (Oxford University Press: New York, 2010) 77; Deacon 1997, 335
[cliii] Shettleworth 188
[cliv] Deacon 1997, 232; Rendall et al 2009; Hauser 244. AH Bass; EH Gilland; and R Baker, Evolutionary origins for social vocalization in a vertebrate hindbrain-spinal compartment (*Science* 321: 5887, 2008) 417-421
[clv] Sheets-Johnstone 319
[clvi] Smith in Leary 2005, 244
[clvii] Shettleworth 7
[clviii] For example, DR Griffin, The Question of Animal Awareness (New York: Rockefeller Press, 1976)
[clix] Shettleworth 17
[clx] Leary 39
[clxi] T Deacon, Incomplete Nature: How Mind Emerged From Matter (W.W. Norton & Company, Inc. New York and London: 2012) 510
[clxii] Hauser 85; Shettleworth, 4

[clxiii] Hoffmeyer 214
[clxiv] Simon 1962
[clxv] Husserl 165
[clxvi] Hoffmeyer 206
[clxvii] J Von Uexkull, A Foray Into the Worlds of Animals And Humans with A Theory of Meaning (O'Neil, JD, trans: University of Minnesota Press, 1934/2010) 119, 126
[clxviii] Uexkull 144, 167
[clxix] Hoffmeyer 55
[clxx] Heyes 1993
[clxxi] Husserl 32
[clxxii] Uexkull 126-132
[clxxiii] Hauser 6; Shettleworth 162
[clxxiv] Uexkull 202
[clxxv] Bradbury and Vehrencamp 3, 4
[clxxvi] Hoffmeyer 26; E Jablonka and MJ Lamb, The evolution of information in the major transitions, (*Journal of Theoretical Biology*, 239: 2006) 236-246
[clxxvii] Bradbury and Vehrencamp 166
[clxxviii] M Ruggeri; JC Major, Jr; C McKeown; RW Knighton; CA Puliafito; and S Jiao, Retinal structure of birds of prey revealed by ultra-high resolution spectral-domain optical coherence tomography (*Invest Opthalmol Vis Sci*: 51 (11), 2010) 5789-57952010
[clxxix] Bradbury and Vehrencamp, chapter 5
[clxxx] S. N Archer and J. N. Lythgoe, The visual basis for cone polymorphism in the guppy, *Poecilia reticulata* (Vision Research 30, 1990) 225–233
[clxxxi] GD Bernard and CL Remington, Color vision in *Lycaena* butterflies: spectral tuning of receptor arrays in relation to behavioral ecology (*Proc. Natl. Acad. Sci. USA* Vol 88: 1991) 2783-2787
[clxxxii] A Treisman, Feature binding, attention, and object perception (*Phil. Trans. R. Lond.* B, 353: 1998) 1295-1306
[clxxxiii] Shettleworth 79
[clxxxiv] LF Jacobs, The ecology of spatial cognition: adaptive patterns of space use and hippocampal size in wild rodents (In E. Alleva et al (eds), *Behavioral Brain Research in Naturalistic and Semi-Naturalistic Settings*, Kluwer Academic Publishers: Netherlands, 1995) 301-322
[clxxxv] JK O'Regan, Solving the "real" mysteries of visual perception: the world as an outside memory (*Canadian Journal of Psychology* 46: 3, 1992) 461-488
[clxxxvi] Gregory Bateson quoted in J Lovelock, The Ages of Gaia: A Biography of Our Living Earth (WW Norton & Company: NY, London, 1988) 204
[clxxxvii] Penn et al 2008

[clxxxviii] Shettleworth 550
[clxxxix] JA Fodor, The Modularity of the Mind (MIT press: Cambridge, MA, 1983)
[cxc] Shettleworth 165
[cxci] JA Hogan, Structure and development of behavior systems (*Psychonomic Bulletin& Review*: 1 (4), 1994) 439-450
[cxcii] Simon 1962
[cxciii] Simon 1962
[cxciv] MR Papini, Theoretical notes: pattern and process in the evolution of learning (Vol. 109, No. 1, 2002) 186-201; C Heyes, Four routes of cognitive evolution (*Psychological Review*, Vol. 110, No. 4, 2003) 713-727.
[cxcv] DF Sherry and DL Schacter, The evolution of multiple memory systems (*Psychological Review*: Vol. 94, No. 4, 1987) 438-454
[cxcvi] P Godfrey-Smith, Complexity and the Function of Mind in Nature (Cambridge University Press: New York, 1996) 22
[cxcvii] VV Pravosudov and NS Clayton, A test of the adaptive specialization hypothesis: population differences in caching, memory, and the hippocampus in black-capped chickadees (*Poecile atricapilla*) (*Behavioral Neuroscience*: Vol. 116, No. 4, 2002) 515-522
[cxcviii] Shettleworth 11, 12
[cxcix] Husserl 84
[cc] P Teilhard de Chardin, The Phenomenon of Man (Harper Perennial Modern Thought: New York, 1955/ 2008) 32
[cci] J Weiner; S Shettleworth; VP Bingman: K Cheng; S Healy; LF Jacobs; KJ Jeffrey; HA Mallot; R Menzel; and NS Newcombe, Animal navigation: a synthesis (in Animal Thinking: Contemporary Issues in Comparative Cognition; Menzel, R and Fischer J, Eds. The MIT Press: Cambridge, MA, 2011) 69-70
[ccii] D Zahavi, Husserl's Phenomenology (Stanford University Press 2003) 21-23
[cciii] HR Maturana, and FJ Varela, The Tree of Knowledge: The Biological Roots of Human Understanding Revised Edition (Shambhala Publications, Inc: Boston, Mass, 1987) 47
[cciv] AF Rossi; L Pessoa; R Desimone; and LG Ungerleider, The prefrontal cortex and the executive control of attention (*Exp Brain Res.* 192 (3) 2009) 489-497
[ccv] AM Triesman and G Gelade, A feature-integration theory of attention (*Cognitive Psychology* **12,** 1980) 97-136
[ccvi] Peirce 165

[ccvii] TM Hennessey; WB Rucker; and CG McDiarmid, Classical conditioning in paramecia (*Animal Learning & Behavior*, 7 (4), 1979) 417-423
[ccviii] DF Sherry and DL Schacter, The evolution of multiple memory systems (*Psychological Review* Vol. 94, No. 4, 1987) 438-454
[ccix] DB Polley; AR Hillock; C Spankovich; MV Popescu; DW Royal; and MT Wallace, Development and plasticity of intra- and intersensory information processing (J Am Acad Audio 19, Doi: 10.3766/jaa.19.10.6, 2008) 780-798.
[ccx] Polley et al 2008
[ccxi] LR Squire, Memory systems of the brain: A brief history and current perspective. (*Neurobiology of Learning and Memory* 82, 2004) 171-177
[ccxii] Sherry and Schacter 1987
[ccxiii] Squire 2004
[ccxiv] JR Stevens, Mechanisms for decisions about the future, in Animal Thinking: Contemporary Issues in Comparative Cognition; Menzel, R and Fischer J, Eds. (The MIT Press: Cambridge, MA, 2011) 96
JR Stevens; JN Wood; and MD Hauser, When quantity trumps number: discrimination experiments in cotton-top tamarins (*Saguinus Oedipus*) and common marmosets (*Callithrix jacchus*). (*Animal Cognition* 10, 2007) 429-437
[ccxv] TR Zentall, EA Wasserman, OF Lazareva, RKR Thompson; and MJ Rattermann, Concept learning in animals (*Comparative Cognition & Behavior Reviews.* Vol. 3, 2008) 13-45
[ccxvi] Hauser 524-5
RJ Herrnstein, 1991. Levels of categorization (In GM Edelman, WE Gall, and WM Cowan (Eds.), *Signals and Sense*, Somerset, NJ: Wiley-Liss, 1991) 385-413
[ccxvii] Shettleworth 162
[ccxviii] Hennessey et al 1979; HL Armus; AR Montgomery; and JL Jellison, Discrimination learning in paramecia (*P. caudatum*) (*The Psychological Record* 56, 2006) 489-498
[ccxix] Shettleworth 192
[ccxx] Shettleworth 222
[ccxxi] OF Lazareva; KL Freiburger; and EA Wasserman. Pigeons concurrently categorize photographs at both basic and superordinate levels (*Psychonomic Bulletin & Review* 11 (6), 2004) 1111-1117
[ccxxii] Hauser 553; Fodor 1994
[ccxxiii] Zentall et al 2008; Gentner and Christie from Penn et al 2008, 136
[ccxxiv] Shettleworth 109

MS Faneslow and AM Poulos, The neuroscience of mammalian associative learning (*Annu. Rev. Psychol.* 56, 2005) 207-34
[ccxxv] In Penn et al 2008
[ccxxvi] RA Rescorla, Pavlovian conditioning: it's not what you think it is (*American Psychologist,* 43 (3), 1988) 151-160
CR Gallistel, 2000. The replacement of general-purpose learning models with adaptively specialized modules (In M.S. Gazzaniga, ED. *The Cognitive Neurosciences. 2d ed.* MIT Press, Cambridge, MA 2000) 1179-1191
[ccxxvii] Rescorla 1988
[ccxxviii] Sherry and Schacter 1987; CM Coelho and H Purkis, The origins of specific phobias: influential theories and current perspectives (*Review of General Psychology* Vol 13, No.4, 2009) 335-348
[ccxxix] KL Hollis, The biological function of Pavlovian conditioning: the best defence is a good offence. (*Journal of Experimantal Psychology: Animal Behavior Processes* 10, 1984) 413-425
[ccxxx] G Hall, Learning about associatively activated stimulus representations: implications for acquired equivalence and perceptual learning (*Animal Learning & Behavior* 24 (3), 1996) 233-255
[ccxxxi] Rescorla 1988
[ccxxxii] PC Holland, Acquisition of representation-mediated conditioned food aversions (*Learning and Motivation, 12*(1), DOI: 10.1016/0023-9690(81)90022-9, 1981) 1-18
[ccxxxiii] Dickinson, A and BW Balleine, Causal cognition and goal-directed action (In C. Heyes & L. Huber (Eds.), *Vienna series in theoretical biology, The evolution of cognition*, Cambridge, MA, US: The MIT Press, 2000) 185-204
[ccxxxiv] Dickinson and Balleine 2012
[ccxxxv] Fodor 1983
[ccxxxvi] L Fogassi; PF Ferrari; B Gesierich; S Rozzi; F Chersi; and G Rizolatti, Parietal Lobe: From Action Organization to Intention Understanding (*Science.* Vol 308, 2005) 662-667
[ccxxxvii] Polley et al 2008
[ccxxxviii] Weiner et al 68
[ccxxxix] Polley et al 2008
[ccxl] Sheets-Johnstone 59
[ccxli] James 76
[ccxlii] G Gottlieb, The relevance of developmental-psychobiological metatheory to developmental neuropsychology (*Developmental Neuropsychology,* 19(1), 2001) 1-9
[ccxliii] Uexkull 181

[ccxliv] Shettleworth 550
[ccxlv] Shettleworth 13
[ccxlvi] G Gottlieb, On the epigenetic evolution of species-specific perception: the developmental manifold concept (*Cognitive Development* special issue, J. Langer and E. Turiel, 2002) 1-29; R Lickliter; DJ Lewkowicz; and RF Columbus, Intersensory experience and early perceptual development: the role of spatial contiguity in bobwhite chicks' responsiveness to multimodal maternal cues. (*Developmental Psychobiology* 29 (5), 1996) 403-416
[ccxlvii] Hauser 526
[ccxlviii] Gottlieb 2001
[ccxlix] J Wallman, A minimal visual restriction: preventing chicks from seeing their feet affects later responses to mealworms (*Developmental Psychobiology*, 12(4): 1979) 391-397
[ccl] Lickliter et al 1996
[ccli] JA Hogan, Structure and development of behavior systems (*Psychonomic Bulletin& Review* 1 (4), 1994) 439-450
[cclii] Gottlieb 2001
[ccliii] Polley et al 2008
[ccliv] Heyes 2003
[cclv] M Soler and JJ Soler, Innate versus learned recognition of conspecifics in greater spotted cuckoos *Clamator glandarius* (*Anim Cogn* 2: 1999) 97-102
[cclvi] Hauser 282
[cclvii] GCL Davey and AL Dixon, The expectancy bias model of selective associations: the relationship of judgements of CS dangerousness, CS-UCS similarity and prior fear to *a priori* and *a posteriori* covariation assessments (*Behav. Res. Ther.* Vol. 34, No.3, 1996) 235-252
[cclviii] Coehlo and Purkis 2009
[cclix] MEP Seligman, Phobias and preparedness (*Behavior Therapy* Vol. 2 (3), 1971) 307-320; Coehlo and Purkis 2009
[cclx] Kauffman quoted in Deacon 2012, 273; Gallistel 2002
[cclxi] Peirce 108
[cclxii] K Gotthard, and S Nylin, Adaptive plasticity as an adaptation: a selective review of plasticity in animal morphology and life history (OIKOS 74, 1995) 3-17
[cclxiii] W Cresswell; JL Quinn; MJ Whittingham; and S Butler, Good foragers can also be good at detecting predators (*Proceedings of The Royal Society of London B* 270: 2003)1069-1076
[cclxiv] Shettleworth 143
[cclxv] PM Groves and RF Thompson, Habituation: a dual-process theory (*Psychological Review* 77, 1970) 419-450

[cclxvi] CH Bailey and M Chen, Long-term memory in *Aplysia* modulates the total number of varicosities of single identified sensory neurons (*Proc. Natl. Acad. Sci. USA.* Vol. 85, 1988) 2373-2377
[cclxvii] G Tononi and GM Edelman, Consciousness and complexity (*Science,* Vol 282, 1998) 1846-1850
[cclxviii] Peirce 168
[cclxix] Peirce 226, 76, 168
[cclxx] Weiner et al 73-4
[cclxxi] VP Bingman, Making the case for intelligence in navigation (in Animal Thinking: Contemporary Issues in Comparative Cognition; Menzel, R and Fischer J, Eds. The MIT Press: Cambridge, MA, 2011) 48
[cclxxii] Stevens 2011, 98; A Dickson, Goal-directed behavior and future planning in animals (in Animal Thinking: Contemporary Issues in Comparative Cognition; Menzel, R and Fischer J, Eds. The MIT Press: Cambridge, MA, 2011) 79, 86; RR Hampton, Status of nonhuman memory monitoring and possible roles in planning and decision making (in Animal Thinking: Contemporary Issues in Comparative Cognition; Menzel, R and Fischer J, Eds. The MIT Press: Cambridge, MA, 2011) 112
[cclxxiii] Bridgeman in Penn et al 2008, 132
[cclxxiv] Uexkull 148; Juarrero 64
[cclxxv] Fogassi et al 2005
[cclxxvi] Deacon 1997
[cclxxvii] F Chersi; PF Ferrari; and L Fogassi, Neuronal chains for actions in the parietal lobe: a computational model (PLoS ONE 6(11): e27652. Doi: 10.1371/journal.Pone. 0027652, 2011)
[cclxxviii] Godfrey-Smith 1996, 163
[cclxxix] Godfrey-Smith 1996, 85
[cclxxx] Bradbury and Vehrencamp 4
[cclxxxi] SRX Dall; LA Giraldeau; O Olsson, JM McNamara; and DW Stephens, Information and its use by humans and animals in evolutionary ecology (*Trends in Ecology and Evolution* Vol. 20 No.4, 2005) 187-93
[cclxxxii] Bradbury and Vehrencamp 13; J Fischer, Where is the information in animal communication? (in Animal Thinking: Contemporary Issues in Comparative Cognition; Menzel, R and Fischer J, Eds. The MIT Press: Cambridge, MA, 2011) 157
[cclxxxiii] Bradbury and Vehrencamp 4
[cclxxxiv] Shettleworth 430
[cclxxxv] Husserl 30
[cclxxxvi] Bradbury and Vehrencamp 4, 369
[cclxxxvii] Shettleworth 72; Hauser 384

[cclxxxviii] L Rendell; R Boyd; D Cownden; M Enquist; K Eriksson; MW Feldman; L Fogarty; S Ghirlanda; T Lilicrap; and KN Laland, Why Copy Others? Insights from the Social Learning Strategies Tournament (*Science*, Vol 328, 2010) 208-213

[cclxxxix] Rendall et al 2009

[ccxc] Hauser 131
Ryan, MJ, Sexual Selection, Receiver Biases, and the Evolution of Sex Differences (*Science,* Vol. 281, 1987) 1999-2003

[ccxci] Hauser 604; Bradbury and Vehrencamp 321

[ccxcii] Bradbury and Vehrencamp 412

[ccxciii] A Nihat, and DC Krakauer, Geometric robustness theory and biological networks (*Theory Biosci* 125 (2), 200) 793-121

[ccxciv] Hauser 141, 510; Bradbury and Vehrencamp 16

[ccxcv] Nihat et al 2007

[ccxcvi] K Kleisner,. The semantic morphology of Adolf Portman: a starting point for the biosemiotics of organic form? (*Biosemiotics* 1, 2008) 207-219

[ccxcvii] Hauser 245; Kleisner 2008

[ccxcviii] Hauser 21; Deacon 1997, 415

[ccxcix] J Huxley, Ritualization of behavior in animals and man (*International Study on the main trends of Research in the Sciences of Man*. United Nations Educational Scientific and Cultural Organization, 1966)

[ccc] Bradbury and Vehrencamp 5, 550

[ccci] JS Scott; AY Kawahara; JH Skevington; SH Yen; A Sami; M Smith; and JE Yack, The evolutionary origins of ritualized acoustic signals in caterpillars. (*Nature Communications.* 1 (1) Doi: 10.1038/ncomms1002, 2010) 1-9

[cccii] Huxley 1966; Bradbury and Vehrencamp 421

[ccciii] Bradbury and Vehrencamp 446, 448

[ccciv] Scott et al 2010

[cccv] A Kosztolanyi; IC Cuthill; and T Szekely, Negotiation between parents over care: reversible compensation during incubation (*Behavioral Ecology* Vol 20 (2): https://doi.org/10.1093/beheco/arn140, 2009) 446–452

[cccvi] D Treer; IV Bocxlaer; S Matthijs; D Du Four; S Janssenswillen; B Willaert; and F Bossuyt, Love is blind: indiscriminate female mating responses to male courtship pheromones in newts (Salamandridae) (PLOS ONE Vol 8, (2) e565382013, 2013)

[cccvii] Husserl 27

Chapter 3: Intelligent Evolution

[cccviii] M Pigliucci and J Kaplan, Making Sense of Evolution: The Conceptual Foundations of Evolutionary Biology (The University of Chicago Press: Chicago, 2006) 29-33
[cccix] Bradbury and Vehrencamp, 400
[cccx] SJ Gould and RC Lewontin, The spandrels of San Marco and the Panglossian paradigm: A critique of the adaptationist programme (*Proceedings of the Royal Society of London* Series B, Biological Sciences, 205(1161), 1979) 581-598.
[cccxi] P Godfrey-Smith, Complexity and the Function of Mind in Nature (Cambridge University Press: NY, 1996) 207
[cccxii] Pigliucci and Kaplan, 18, 120
[cccxiii] S Kauffman, At Home in the Universe: The Search for the Laws of Self-Organization and Complexity (Oxford University Press: New York, 1995) 168-170
[cccxiv] Kauffman 1995, 173; S Gavrilets, A dynamical theory of speciation of holey adaptive landscapes (*Am. Nat.* 1999) 154: 1-22
[cccxv] Gavrilets 1999
[cccxvi] Pigliucci and Kaplan 2006, 42-3; M Pigliucci, Do we need an extended evolutionary synthesis? (*Evolution* 61-12, 2007) 2743-2749
[cccxvii] Bradbury and Vehrencamp, 334-336; Pigliucci and Kaplan, 119
[cccxviii] Bateson and Bateson 100
[cccxix] Pigliucci and Kaplan, 41-3, 90
[cccxx] SL Washburn, The evolution of man (*Scientific American.* Vol 239 (3), 1978) 194-208
[cccxxi] Pigliucci and Kaplan, 124,136
[cccxxii] G Gottlieb, On the epigenetic evolution of species-specific perception: the developmental manifold concept (*Cognitive Development* special issue, J. Langer and E. Turiel, 2002); SM Scheiner, Genetics and Evolutionary Plasticity (*Annu. Rev. Ecol. Syst.* 24, 1993) 35-68
[cccxxiii] K Gotthard and S Nylin,. Adaptive plasticity as an adaptation: a selective review of plasticity in animal morphology and life history (OIKOS 74: 1995) 3-17
K Sterelny, Evolvability reconsidered (In The Major Transitions in Evolution Revisited; B Calcott and K Sterelny, eds. The MIT Press: Cambridge, London, 2011) 87

[cccxxiv] M Wolf, G Sander van Doorn, and FJ Weissing, Evolutionary emergence of responsive and unresponsive personalities (PNAS, 105(41): 2008) 15825-15830
[cccxxv] MR Papini, Theoretical notes: pattern and process in the evolution of learning (109 (1): 2002) 186-201
[cccxxvi] Godfrey-Smith 1996, 147
[cccxxvii] Deacon 1997, 323
[cccxxviii] J von Uexkull, A Foray Into the Worlds of Animals And Humans with A Theory of Meaning (O'Neil, JD, trans University of Minnesota Press: 1934/2010) 174
[cccxxix] HR Maturana and FJ Varela, The Tree of Knowledge: The Biological Roots of Human Understanding Revised Edition (Shambala Publications, Inc. Boston, Mass: 1987) 102, 170
J Lovelock, The Ages of Gaia: A Biography of Our Living Earth (WW Norton & Company, NY, London: 1988) 12
[cccxxx] Maturana and Varela 232
[cccxxxi] Maturana and Varela 75; Lovelock 213
[cccxxxii] FJ Odling-Smee, KN Laland, and MW Feldman, Niche Construction: the Neglected Process in Evolution (Princeton University Press, Princeton and Oxford, 2003) 237
[cccxxxiii] Maturana and Varela 95
[cccxxxiv] Juarrero 142
[cccxxxv] Maturana and Varela 253
[cccxxxvi] R Lickliter, DJ Lewkowicz, and RF Columbus, Intersensory experience and early perceptual development: the role of spatial contiguity in bobwhite chicks' responsiveness to multimodal maternal cues (*Developmental Psychobiology* 29 (5), 1996) 403-416.
[cccxxxvii] Teihard de Chardin 150
[cccxxxviii] Hofstadter 27
[cccxxxix] G Gottlieb, Experiential canalization of behavioral development: results (*Developmental Psychology* 21 (1), 1991) 35-39
G Gottlieb, On the epigenetic evolution of species-specific perception: the developmental manifold concept. (*Cognitive Development* special issue, J. Langer and E. Turiel, eds 2002) 1287-1300
[cccxl] A Watanabe and K Aoki, The role of auditory feedback in the maintenance of song in adult male bengalese finches *Lonchura striata* var *domestica* (Zoological Science: **15**: 1998) 837-841
[cccxli] MF Cheng, Vocal self-stimulation: from the ring dove story to emotion-based vocal communication. (*Advances in the Study of Behavior,* Vol 33: 2003) 309-355

[cccxlii] JM Mateo. Self-referent phenotype matching and long-term maintenance of kin recognition. (*Animal Behavior*, doi 10.1016, 2010)
[cccxliii] Shettleworth 165
[cccxliv] Mateo 2010
[cccxlv] WG Holmes and PW Sherman, The ontogeny of kin recognition in two species of ground squirrels (*American Zoologist* 22: 1982) 491-517
[cccxlvi] Bradbury and Vehrencamp 347
[cccxlvii] Uexkull 52
[cccxlviii] SRX Dall, LA Giraldeau, O Olsson, JM McNamara, and DW Stephens, Information and its use by humans and animals in evolutionary ecology (*Trends in Ecology and Evolution* 20 (4), 2005) 187-93
[cccxlix] C Gruter, MS Balbuena, and WM Farina, Informational conflicts created by the waggle dance (*Proc. R. Soc. B* **275,** 2008) 1321-1327
[cccl] PO Gabriel, and JM Black, Behavioral syndromes, partner compatibility, and reproductive performance in Stellar's jays (*Ethology* **118,** 2012) 76-86
[cccli] BC Wheeler; WA Searcy, MH Christiansen, MC Corballis; J Fischer; C Gruter; D Margoliash; MJ Owen; T Price; R Seyfarth, and M Wild, Communication in Animal Thinking: Contemporary Issues in Comparative Cognition; Menzel, R and Fischer J, Eds. (The MIT Press: Cambridge, MA, 2011) 202
[ccclii] C Catmur, V Walsh, and C Heyes, Sensorimotor Learning Configures the Human Mirror System (Current Biology (17) 2007) 1527-1531
[cccliii] L Fogassi, PF Ferrari, B Gesierich, S Rozzi, F Chersi, and G Rizolatti, Parietal lobe: from action organization to intention understanding (*Science*, Vol 308, 2005) 662-667
[cccliv] Fogassi et al 2005
F Chersi, PF Ferrari, and L Fogassi, Neuronal chains for actions in the parietal lobe: a computational model (PLoS ONE 6(11): e27652. Doi: 10.1371/journal. Pone. 0027652, 2011)
[ccclv] Fogassi et al 2005; Catmur et al 2007
[ccclvi] Shettleworth 513
[ccclvii] JM Dally, NJ Emery, and NS Clayton, Food-caching western scrub-jays keep track of who was watching when (**SCIENCE** Vol. 312, 2006)1662-1665
[ccclviii] JM Dally, NS Clayton, and NJ Emery, The behavior and evolution of cache protection and pilferage (*Animal Behavior*, doi:10.1016/j.anbehav.2005.08.020, 2006)
[ccclix] Dally et al, 2006a; Shettleworth 446
NJ Emery and NS Clayton, Imaginative scrub jays, causal rooks, and a liberal application of Occam's aftershave in Penn et al 2008, 134

[ccclx] FBM De Waal, Putting the Altruism Back into Altruism: The Evolution of Empathy (*Annu. Rev. Psychol.* 59: 2008) 2790-300
[ccclxi] Cheng 2003
[ccclxii] Cheng 2003
[ccclxiii] De Waal 2008
[ccclxiv] A Seed; N Clayton; P Carruthers; A Dickinson; PW Glimcher; O Gunturkun; RR Hampton; A Kacelnik; M Shanahan; JR Stevens; and S Tebbich, Planning, Memory, and Decision Making, in Animal Thinking: Contemporary Issues in Comparative Cognition; Menzel, R and Fischer J, Eds. (The MIT Press: Cambridge, MA, 2011)
[ccclxv] P Carruthers, How we know our own minds: the relationship between mindreading and metacognition (*Behavioral and Brain Sciences* 32 (2), 2009) 121-138
[ccclxvi] Odling-Smee et al 181
[ccclxvii] Bradbury and Vehrencamp 375
[ccclxviii] Odling-Smee et al 3, 9-13, 113,123, 159
[ccclxix] Odling-Smee et al 34
[ccclxx] D Rendall, MJ Owren, and MJ Ryan, What do animal signals mean? (*Animal Behavior,* 78, 2009) 233-240
[ccclxxi] E Jablonka and MJ Lamb, The evolution of information in the major transitions (*Journal of Theoretical Biology*, 239, 2006) 236-246
[ccclxxii] MR Servedio, SA Saether, GP Saetre, Reinforcement and learning (*Evol Ecol* (2009)23:109-123. Doi 10.1007/s10682-007-9188-2)
[ccclxxiii] Sherry and Schacter 1987
[ccclxxiv] AE Houde and MA Hankes, Evolutionary mismatch of mating preference and male colour patterns in guppies (*Animal Behavior*, **53**, 1997) 343-351
MJ Ryan, Sexual selection, receiver biases, and the evolution of sex differences (**SCIENCE** Vol. 281, 1997) 1999-2003
G Arnqvist, Sensory exploitation and sexual conflict (*Philos Trans R Soc Lond B Biol Sci.* 361(1466):375 Published online 2006 Jan 4. Doi: 10.1098/rstb.2005.1790)
[ccclxxv] H Proctor, Sensory exploitation and the evolution of male mating behavior: a cladistics test using water mites (*Acari: Parasitengona*) (*Animal Behavior* (44):4, 1992) 745-752
[ccclxxvi] FH Rodd, KA Hughes, GF Grether, and CT Baril, A possible non-sexual origin of mate preference: are male guppies mimicking fruit? (*Proc. R. Soc. Lond.* **B, 269,** 2002) 475-481
[ccclxxvii] B Heinrich and SL Collins, Caterpillar leaf damage, and the game of hide-and-seek with birds (*Ecology,* 64(3), 1983) 592-602

[ccclxxviii] Peirce 222
[ccclxxix] BG Hall, On the specificity of adaptive mutations (*Genetics* 145: 1996) 39-44
J Cairns; J Overbaugh; and S Miller, The origin of mutants (*Nature*, 335 (6186), 1988) 142-5
[ccclxxx] CM Waters and BL Bassler, Quorum sensing: cell-to-cell communication in bacteria (*Annu. Rev. Cell Dev. Biol.* **21** : 2005)319-46
[ccclxxxi] JE Gonzalez-Pastor, Cannibalism: a social behavior in sporulating *Bacillus subtilis* (FEMS Microbial Rev **35,** 2011) 415-424
[ccclxxxii] M Ackermann, B Stecher, NE Freed, P Songhet, WD Hardt, and M Doebeli, Self-destructive cooperation mediated by phenotypic noise (*Nature* Vol 454, doi:1038/nature07067, 2008)
[ccclxxxiii] Gonzalez-Pastor 2011
[ccclxxxiv] JT Bonner, The Origins of Multicellularity (*Integrative Biology.* 1998) 27-36
[ccclxxxv] RE Michod, Evolutionary transitions in individuality: multicellularity and sex (In The Major Transitions in Evolution Revisited; B Calcott and K Sterelny, eds. The MIT Press: Cambridge, London, 2011) 169-98
[ccclxxxvi] RM Fisher, CK Cornwallis, and SA West, Group formation, relatedness, and the evolution of multicellularity (*Current Biology 23,* 2013)1120-1125
[ccclxxxvii] Bonner 1998; DW McShea and C Simpson, The miscellaneous transitions in evolution (In The Major Transitions in Evolution Revisited; B Calcott and K Sterelny, eds. The MIT Press: Cambridge, London, 2011) 19-34
[ccclxxxviii] C Simpson, How many levels are there? How insights from evolutionary transitions in individuality help measure the hierarchical complexity of life (In The Major Transitions in Evolution Revisited; B Calcott and K Sterelny, eds. The MIT Press: Cambridge, London, 2011) 199-226
[ccclxxxix] McShea and Simpson 2011
[cccxc] RM Fisher, CK Cornwallis, and SA West, Group formation, relatedness, and the evolution of multicellularity (*Current Biology 23,* 2013) 1120-1125
DC Queller, Relatedness and the fraternal major transitions (*Phil. Trans. R. Soc. Lond.* B **355,** 2000)1647-1655
[cccxci] RE Michod, and D Roze, Cooperation and conflict in the evolution of multicellularity (*Heredity* **86,** 2001)1-7
[cccxcii] Queller 2000
AH Knoll and D Hewitt, Phylogenetic, functional, and geological perspectives on complex multicellularity (In The Major Transitions in Evolution Revisited; B Calcott and K Sterelny, eds. The MIT Press: Cambridge, London, 2011) 251-70

[cccxciii] Jablonka and Lamb 2006
[cccxciv] B Calcott and K Sterelny, Introduction (In The Major Transitions in Evolution Revisited; B Calcott and K Sterelny, eds. The MIT Press: Cambridge, London, 2011) 1-14; McShea and Simpson 2011
[cccxcv] B Calcott, Alternative patterns of explanation for major transitions (In The Major Transitions in Evolution Revisited; B Calcott and K Sterelny, eds. The MIT Press: Cambridge, London, 2011) 35-52
[cccxcvi] RE Michod and MD Herron, Cooperation and conflict during evolutionary transitions in individuality (*Journal of Evolutionary Biology* 19, 2006) 1406-1409
[cccxcvii] Michod and Herron 2006; Calcott 2011
[cccxcviii] Queller 2000
[cccxcix] Michod and Roze 2001
[cd] Michod 2011
[cdi] Jantsch 242
[cdii] Queller 2000
[cdiii] Michod and Roze 2001
[cdiv] Deacon 1997, 194-197
[cdv] EJ Steele, RA Lindley, and RV Blanden, Lamarck's Signature: How Retrogenes are Changing Darwin's Natural Selection Paradigm (Perseus Books, Reading, MA: 1998) 147-148, 162
[cdvi] Kauffman 1995, 279
[cdvii] Michod and Herron 2006
[cdviii] E Swedenborg, Divine Love and Wisdom (George F. Dole, trans. Swedenborg Foundation, West Chester, PA: 2010) 9
[cdix] K Sterelny, Evolvability reconsidered (In The Major Transitions in Evolution Revisited; B Calcott and K Sterelny, eds. The MIT Press: Cambridge, London, 2011) 83-100
[cdx] Michod and Herron 2006
N Takeuchi and P Hogeweg, Multilevel selection in models of prebiotic evolution II: a direct comparison of compartmentalization and spatial self-organization (PLOS Computational Biology. Doi: 10.1371/journal.pcbi.1000542, 2009)
[cdxi] Takeuchi and Hogeweg 2009
[cdxii] FJ Dyson, Infinite in all directions (HarperCollins, NY: 1985) 69
[cdxiii] L Villarreal and G Witzany, Rethinking the quasispecies theory: from fittest type to cooperative consortia. (*World J Biol Chem* 4(4), 2013) 79-90
[cdxiv] Villareal and Witzany 2013; L Villareal, Viruses and host evolution: virus-mediated self- identity (In *Self and Nonself*, ed Carlos Lopez-Larrea, Landes Bioscience and Springer, 2012) 185-217

[cdxv] S Smit, M Yarus, and R Knight, Natural selection is not required to explain universal compositional patterns in RNA secondary structure categories (*RNA*, 12 (1), 2006)1-14
Villarreal and Witzany 2013
[cdxvi] Villareal 2012; Villareal and Witzany 2013
[cdxvii] Villareal and Witzany 2013
[cdxviii] Villareal and Witzany 2013
[cdxix] G Witzany, The agents of natural genome editing (*Journal of Molecular Cell Biology*, 3, 2011)181-189
[cdxx] Villareal and Witzany 2013
[cdxxi] Uexkull 144
[cdxxii] LP Villarreal, and G Witzany, The DNA habitat and its RNA inhabitants: at the dawn of RNA sociology (*Genomics Insights* 6, 2013) 1-12
[cdxxiii] Witzany 2011; Jablonka and Lamb 2006
[cdxxiv] CR Woese, On the evolution of cells (PNAS 99(13), 2002) 8742-8747
[cdxxv] Woese 2002
[cdxxvi] Witzany 2011; Villarreal and Witzany 2013b
[cdxxvii] Pierce 234

Chapter 4: Coming to Life

[cdxxviii] Teilhard de Chardin 302
[cdxxix] Kauffman 1995, 115
[cdxxx] Kauffman 1995, 43-48
[cdxxxi] SA Kauffman, Reinventing the Sacred: A New View of Science, Reason, and Religion (Basic Books: New York, 2008) 45-49
[cdxxxii] Juarrero 139
[cdxxxiii] Kauffman 1995, 24, 48, 69
[cdxxxiv] A Nihat and DC Krakauer, Geometric robustness theory and biological networks (Theory Biosci 125: 2, 2007) 93-121
SE Jorgensen and R Ulanowicz, Network calculations and ascendency based on eco-exergy (Ecological Modeling 220, 2009)1893-1896
[cdxxxv] DL Abel, Is Life Unique? (Life (Basel) (2) 1, 2012) 106-134: Juarrero 125
Simon 1962
[cdxxxvi] Juarrero 123
M Bickhard, The process dynamics of normative function (The Monist 85:1, 2002) 3-28

[cdxxxvii] T Deacon, Incomplete Nature: How Mind Emerged From Matter (W.W. Norton & Company, Inc: New York and London, 2012, 2013) 385, 503
[cdxxxviii] Kauffman 1995, 58
RE Ulanowicz; SJ Goerner; B Liettaer, and R Gomez, Quantifying sustainability: resilience, efficiency and the return of information theory (Ecological Complexity, **6**: 2009) 27-36
[cdxxxix] Deacon 2013, 470; Maturena and Varela 89
[cdxl] Deacon 2013, 243
HH Pattee, The Physics and Metaphysics of Biosemiotics (Journal of Biosemiotics: 1, 2005) 281-301.
[cdxli] J Campbell, Quantum Darwinism as a Darwinian Process (arXiv:1001.0745[physics.gen.ph] 2010)
[cdxlii] Deacon 2013, 251, 263
[cdxliii] Kauffman 2008, 80-84, 99
[cdxliv] J Campbell, Bayesian Methods and Universal Darwinism (arXiv: 1001.0068, 2009)
[cdxlv] Kauffman 2008, 131
[cdxlvi] Deacon 1997, 29
[cdxlvii] SN Salthe, Development (and Evolution) of the Universe (*Found Sci* 15: 2010) 357-367
[cdxlviii] Campbell 2009
[cdxlix] Deacon 2013, 318
[cdl] Ulanowicz et al 2009
[cdli] Thompson and Varela 2001
[cdlii] Jantsch 229
[cdliii] Maturena and Varela 242
[cdliv] Peirce 234
[cdlv] Bickhard 3-28
[cdlvi] Kauffman 2008, 84,114; Deacon 2013, 219
[cdlvii] Jantsch 41
[cdlviii] Bickhard 2002, 3-28
[cdlix] Jantsch 296
[cdlx] Juarrero 143
[cdlxi] Hoffmeyer 35-37
[cdlxii] E Jablonka and MJ Lamb, Epigenetic Inheritance and Evolution: The Lamarckian Dimension (Oxford University Press Inc, New York, 1995) 80-86
[cdlxiii] Hoffmeyer 133
[cdlxiv] Campbell 2009
[cdlxv] R Penrose, Shadows of the Mind: A Search for the Missing Science of Consciousness (Oxford University Press, 1994) 232

[cdlxvi] Juarrero 7
[cdlxvii] Kauffman 2008, 99
[cdlxviii] Simon 1962
[cdlxix] JH Holland, Signals and Boundaries: Building Blocks for Complex Adaptive Systems (MIT press, Cambridge, 2012) 81
[cdlxx] A Nihat; J Flack; and DC Krakauer, Robustness and complexity co-constructed in multimodal signaling networks (*Phil. Trans. R. Soc. B* **362**, 2007) 441-447
[cdlxxi] Holland 160
[cdlxxii] Jantsch 26
[cdlxxiii] Jantsch 296
[cdlxxiv] HH Pattee, Causation, control, and the evolution of complexity (In *Downward Causation: Minds, Bodies, Matter*. Edited by Peter B. Anderson, Claus Emmeche, Niels Ole Finnemann, Peder V. Christiansen, Aarhus University Press, 2000) 63-77
[cdlxxv] E Thompson and FJ Varela, Radical embodiment: neural dynamics and consciousness (*Trends in Cognitive Sciences*, Vol. 5. No. 10, 2001) 418-426
[cdlxxvi] Maturena and Varela 75
[cdlxxvii] RE Ulanowicz, A Phenomenology of evolving networks (*Systems Research* Vol. 6, No. 3, 1989) 209-217
[cdlxxviii] Simpson 2011
RE Ulanowicz and WF Wolff, Ecosystem flow networks: loaded dice? (*Mathematical Biosciences* 103: 1991) 45-68
[cdlxxix] Lovelock 97, 167, 213
[cdlxxx] Deacon 2013, 137
[cdlxxxi] Simon 1962
[cdlxxxii] Hoffmeyer xiv
[cdlxxxiii] Abel 2012
[cdlxxxiv] Abel 2012; P Lyon, To be or not to be: where is self-preservation in evolutionary theory? (In The Major Transitions in Evolution Revisited; B Calcott and K Sterelny, eds. The MIT Press: Cambridge, London, 2011) 105-126
[cdlxxxv] HH Pattee, The physics of symbols and the evolution of semiotic controls (*Workshop on Control Mechanisms for Complex Systems: Issues of Measurement and Semantic Analysis*,1996) 1-14
[cdlxxxvi] Hoffmeyer 2008, 5
[cdlxxxvii] Jantsch 255
[cdlxxxviii] Husserl 146
[cdlxxxix] Wallace 1996, 118

[cdxc] HH Pattee, The physics and metaphysics of biosemiotics (*Journal of Biosemiotics* (1), 2005) 281-301
[cdxci] J Ortega y Gasset, Meditations on Quixote (WW Norton and Company, Inc, NY: 1961) 143
[cdxcii] HH Pattee, Evolving self-reference: matter, symbols, and semantic closure (*Communication and Cognition—Artificial Intelligence,* (12): 1-2, 1995) 9-28
[cdxciii] Ortega y Gasset 87
[cdxciv] HH Pattee, How does a molecule become a message? (*Developmental Biology Supplement* (3), 1969)1-16.
[cdxcv] Pattee 1995
[cdxcvi] Pattee 2005
[cdxcvii] Pattee 2005
[cdxcviii] Pattee 1995
[cdxcix] Pattee 2006
[d] Salthe 2010; Hoffmeyer 2008, 286
[di] Pattee 1996
[dii] Pattee 2005
[diii] HH Pattee, The physics of symbols: bridging the epistemic cut (*Biosystems* (60), 2001) 5-21
[div] Pattee 2001
[dv] HH Pattee, Cell psychology: an evolutionary approach to the symbol-matter problem (*Cognition and Brain Theory,* **5(4)**, 1982)325-341
[dvi] Abel 2012
[dvii] Pattee 1996
[dviii] Pattee 2001
[dix] Wallace 118
[dx] Bateson and Bateson 17-19
[dxi] Bateson and Bateson 51
[dxii] Pattee 2006
[dxiii] Ortega y Gasset 87
[dxiv] Wilczek 1998

Chapter 5: Chaotic Evolution

[dxv] Kauffman 1995, 114

P Michelena, R Jeanson, JL Deneubourg, and AM Sibbald, Personality and collective decision-making in foraging herbivores (*Proc. R. Soc. B.* doi: 10.1098/rspb.2009.1926, 2009)

[dxvi] R Sole and B Goodwin, Signs of Life: How Complexity Pervades Biology (Basic Books, New York, 2000) 151

[dxvii] L Thomas, The Lives of a Cell: Notes of a Biology Watcher (Bantam: New York, 1979) 11

[dxviii] R Tonjes, N Masuda, and H Kori, Synchronization transition of identical phase oscillators in a directed small-world network (CHAOS **20,** 003108, 2010) 1-12

SN Dorogovtsev, AV Goltsev, and JFF Mendes, Critical phenomena in complex networks (arXiv:0705.0010v6, 2007)

HD Rozenfeld and HA Makse, Fractility and the percolation transition in complex networks (*Chemical Engineering Science* 64, 2009) 4572-4575

[dxix] Bradbury and Vehrencamp 637, 64; Tonjes et al 2010

[dxx] J Buhl, DJT Sumpter, ID Couzin, JJ Hale, E Despland, ER Miller, and SJ Simpson, From disorder to order in marching locusts (**SCIENCE** (312), 2006) 1402-1406

[dxxi] MEJ Newman, Mixing patterns in networks (arXiv: cond-mat/0209450[cond-mat.stat-mech] 2002)

[dxxii] C Song, S Havlin, and HA Makse, Origins of fractality in the growth of complex networks (*Nature Physics* **2**, 2006) 275-281

[dxxiii] Song et al2006; Rozenfeld and Makse 2009

LK Gallos, C Song, and HA Makse, A review of fractiliy and self-similarity in complex networks (*Physica A* (386), 2007) 686-691

[dxxiv] MD LaMar, and GD Smith, The effect of node-degree correlation on synchronization of identical pulse-coupled oscillators (*Phys. Rev. E* **81**, 2010) 046206

[dxxv] R Bshary and AS Grutter, Punishment and partner switching cause cooperative behavior in a cleaning mutualism (*Biol. Lett.***1**, 369-399 doi: 10.1098/rsbl.2005.0344, 2005)

[dxxvi] Bshary, R and D'Souza, AD Cooperation in communication networks: indirect reciprocity in interactions between cleaner fish and client reef fish (In *Animal Communication Networks,* ed. Peter K. McGregor. Cambridge University Press: 2005)521- 536

[dxxvii] Teilhard de Chardin 42

[dxxviii] Kauffman 1995, 26

[dxxix] Grossman and Thomae, quoted in GP Williams, Chaos Theory Tamed (Joseph Henry Press, Washington, DC: 1997) 229

[dxxx] D Ruelle, Chaotic Evolution and Strange Attractors (Cambridge University Press, Cambridge: 1989) 6, 7, 69
[dxxxi] Ruelle 7
[dxxxii] Ruelle 1989, pp 42, 46
[dxxxiii] Sole and Goodwin 5; Williams 227
[dxxxiv] Williams 231
[dxxxv] Williams 175
[dxxxvi] Pattee 2000
[dxxxvii] Kauffman 1995, 79, 100
S Wolfram, Cellular Automata and Complexity: Collected Papers (Westview Press, IL:1994) 241, 330
[dxxxviii] Ruelle 26
[dxxxix] Kauffman 1995, 90
[dxl] SN Salthe, The System of Interpretance, Naturalizing Meaning as Finality (*Biosemiotics* 1(3) 2008) 285-294
[dxli] Kauffman 1995, 188
[dxlii] Kauffman 1995, 224
[dxliii] Dyson 86
[dxliv] Dyson 93
[dxlv] Jantsch 50, 53
[dxlvi] Jantsch 224
[dxlvii] Sole and Goodwin 183
[dxlviii] Sole and Goodwin 43
[dxlix] Sole and Goodwin 18
[dl] Kauffman 2008, 140
[dli] Kauffman 2008, 223; Juarrero 21
[dlii] Juarrero 161
PL Luisi, The Emergence of Life: From Chemical Origins to Synthetic Biology (Cambridge University Press, Cambridge: 2006)108
[dliii] Juarrero 9; Luisi 55
[dliv] Ortega y Gasset 44
[dlv] GW Leibniz, Discourse on Metaphysics and Other Essays (Translated by D Garber and R, translators; Hackett Publishing Company, Indianapolis & Cambridge: 1991) 76
[dlvi] Peirce 226
[dlvii] Peirce 168
[dlviii] Peirce 228; James 14
[dlix] James 9
[dlx] Peirce 76

[dlxi] R Sheldrake, The Presence of the Past: the Memory of Nature (Park street Press, Rochester, VT: 1988/2012) 112
[dlxii] Kauffman 2008, 136
[dlxiii] James 9
[dlxiv] Sheldrake 2
[dlxv] Sheldrake 19
[dlxvi] Bohm 1980, 245
[dlxvii] Teilhard de Chardin 118
[dlxviii] Wolfram 322; Kauffman 1995, 11
[dlxix] Peirce 258
[dlxx] Husserl 49
[dlxxi] Kauffman 1995, 90
[dlxxii] L Rendell, R Boyd, D Cownden, M Enquist, K Eriksson, MW Feldman, L Fogarty, S Ghirlanda, T Lilicrap, and KN Laland, Why copy others? Insights from the social learning strategies tournament (**SCIENCE** (328) 5975, 2010) 208-213
[dlxxiii] W Weaver, Recent contributions to the mathematical theory of communication (*ETC: A Review of General Semantics* 10 (4), 1953) 261-281
[dlxxiv] Husserl 30
[dlxxv] Jantsch 51
[dlxxvi] Van Eenwyck 84
[dlxxvii] Maturana and Varela 222
[dlxxviii] Teilhard de Chardin 181
[dlxxix] Lakoff and Johnson 1980, 144
[dlxxx] K Danziger, Generative metaphor and the history of psychological discourse (In Leary, Ed. *Metaphors in the History of Psychology,* Cambridge University Press, Cambridge: 1990) 331-356
[dlxxxi] Simon 1962
[dlxxxii] DC Dennett, Real patterns (*The Journal of Philosophy* 88 (1), 1991) 27-51
[dlxxxiii] Peirce, quoted in Hoffmeyer 2008, 58
[dlxxxiv] Luisi 105
[dlxxxv] Juarrero 194
[dlxxxvi] Juarrero 180
[dlxxxvii] Husserl 39
[dlxxxviii] E Swedenborg, Divine Love and Wisdom (George F. Dole, translator, Swedenborg Foundation, West Chester, PA: 2010) 80
[dlxxxix] Swedenborg 65
[dxc] RE Ulanowicz, A phenomenology of evolving networks (*Systems Research* Vol. 6 (3), 1989) 209-217

[dxci] Gospel of Thomas, verse 18, in E Pagels, Beyond belief: the secret gospel of Thomas (Random House, Inc., New York, 2003) 230
[dxcii] Swedenborg 2
[dxciii] Nagel 67
[dxciv] Nagel 91
[dxcv] Nagel 92
[dxcvi] Teilhard de Chardin 56
[dxcvii] Dylan Thomas
[dxcviii] CJ Jung, The Archetypes and the Collective Unconscious (Bollingen Foundation Inc, New York: 1959) 31
[dxcix] Ortega y Gasset 89
[dc] Husserl 171
[dci] Husserl 173
[dcii] Ortega y Gasset 41

Chapter 6: Interface

[dciii] CJ Davia, Life, catalysis, and excitable media: a dynamics systems approach to metabolism and cognition (In J. Tuszynski, (Ed.), *The Emerging Physics of Consciousness*. Springer-Verlag, 2006) 255-292
[dciv] AN Mitra and G Mitra-Delmotte, Consciousness: a direct link with life's origin? arXiv: 1102.3158 [physics.hist-ph], 2011)
[dcv] VB Taranenko, G Slekys, and CO Weiss, Spatial resonance solitons (arXiv:nlin/0210073v1 [nlin.PS], 2002)
[dcvi] J McFadden, Quantum evolution: how physics' weirdest theory explains life's biggest mystery (W.W. Norton & Company Inc., New York: 2000) 120
[dcvii] Davia 2006
[dcviii] Davia 2006
[dcix] McFadden 176
[dcx] Davia 2006
[dcxi] A Goswami, The Self-Aware Universe: How Consciousness Creates the Material World (Jeremy P. Tarcher/Putnam, Penguin Putnam Inc, NY: 1993) 38
D Zohar, The Quantum Self: Human Nature and Consciousness Defined by the New Physics (HarperCollins, NY, 1990) 31
[dcxii] Davia 2006
L Brizhik, Biological role of pulsating magnetic fields: the role of solitons (arXiv:1141.6576v1 [physics.bio,ph], 2014)

[dcxiii] R Feynman, QED: the Strange Theory of Light and Matter (Penguin Books, London: 1985) 54, 123
Zohar 32
[dcxiv] WH Zurek, Quantum Darwninsm (arXiv: 0903.5082v1, 2009)
[dcxv] HH Pattee, Cell psychology: an evolutionary approach to the symbol-matter problem (*Cognition and Brain Theory*, **5(4)**, 1982) 325-341
[dcxvi] D Bohm, Wholeness and the Implicate Order (Routledge Classics, London and New York: 1980) 172
[dcxvii] Kauffman 2008, 228
[dcxviii] Leibniz 43
[dcxix] Zurek 2009
[dcxx] V Ogryzko, On two quantum approaches to adaptive mutations in bacteria (arXiv: 0805. 4316, 2008).
[dcxxi] Zurek 2009
[dcxxii] R Blume-Kohout and WH Zurek, Quantum Darwinism: entanglement, branches, and the emergent classicality of redundantly stored quantum information." (arXiv: quant-ph/0505031v2, 2005)
[dcxxiii] E Laszlo, The Self-Actualizing Cosmos: the Akasha Revolution in Science and Human Consciousness (Inner Traditions, Rochester, VT: 2007) 12
[dcxxiv] R Blume-Kohout and WH Zurek, Quantum Darwinism: entanglement, branches, and the emergent classicality of redundantly stored quantum information (arXiv: quant-ph/0505031v2, 2005)
[dcxxv] J Campbell, Quantum Darwinism as a Darwinian process (arXiv:1001.0745[physics.gen.ph], 2010)
[dcxxvi] Peirce 76
[dcxxvii] R Penrose, Shadows of the Mind: a Search for the Missing Science of Consciousness (Oxford University Press, 1994) 53-65
[dcxxviii] Peirce 229
[dcxxix] V Salari, J Tuszynski, R Rahnama, and G Bernroider, Plausibility of quantum coherent states in biological systems (arXiv: 1012.3879, 2010)
[dcxxx] Kauffman 2008, 210; McFadden 160
G Panitchayangkoon,;D Hayes, KA Fransted, JR Caram, E Harel, J Wen, RE Blankenship, and GS Engel, Long-lived quantum coherence in photosynthetic complexes at physiological temperature (*Proc Natl Acad Sci* (107) 29, 2010) 12766-12770
[dcxxxi] Laszlo 127; Salari et al 2010; Panitchayangkoon et al 2010
SM Dambrot, On a clear day: Noise-induced quantum coherence increases photosynthetic yield (Phys.org,2013)
[dcxxxii] McFadden 234; Pattee 2001

[dcxxxiii] J McFadden and J Al-Khalili, Life on the Edge: the Coming of Age of Quantum Biology (Crown Publishers, NY, 2014) 229
[dcxxxiv] McFadden and Al-Khalili 295
[dcxxxv] KB Clark, Bioreaction quantum computing without quantum diffusion (*NeuroQuantology* 10 (4), 2012) 646-654
[dcxxxvi] Ogryzko 2008
[dcxxxvii] McFadden 66,160
[dcxxxviii] McFadden and Al-Khalili 219, 224
[dcxxxix] Abel 2012
[dcxl] McFadden 252; Salari et al 2010
[dcxli] Ogryzko 2008; McFadden 251, 254
[dcxlii] KB Clark, Arrhenius-kinetics evidence for quantum tunneling in microbial 'social' decisions (*Communicative & Integrative Biology* 3(6), 2010)540-544
[dcxliii] Clark 2012
[dcxliv] Clark 2012
[dcxlv] Maturana and Varela 74
[dcxlvi] McFadden 231; Campbell 2010
[dcxlvii] McFadden 221-227
[dcxlviii] McFadden 28
[dcxlix] Kauffman 2008, 216
[dcl] Laszlo 6, 120
[dcli] Kauffman 2008, p 210
[dclii] AN Mitra and G Mitra-Delmotte, Consciousness: a direct link with life's origin? (arXiv: 1102.3158 [physics.hist-ph], 2011)
[dcliii] Zohar 84; Salari et al 2010
[dcliv] D Bohm, A new theory of the relationship of mind and matter (*Philosophical Psychology,* 3, (2) 1990)271-287
[dclv] AR Vasconcellos, FS Vannucchi, S Mascarenhas, and R Luzzi, Frohlich condensate: emergence of synergetic dissipative structures in information processing biological and condensed matter systems (*Information* (3), 2012) 601-620
[dclvi] M Jibu, S Hagan, SR Hameroff, KH Pribram, and K Yasue, Quantum optical coherence in cytoskeletal microtubules: implications for brain function (*BioSystems* 32, 1994) 195-209
[dclvii] GH Pollack, The Fourth Phase of Water: Beyond Solid, Liquid, Vapor. (Ebner & Sons Publishers, Seattle, WA: 2013)
[dclviii] Jibu et al 1994
[dclix] Jibu et al 1994
[dclx] Penrose 374
[dclxi] Penrose 65

[dclxii] Penrose 409-10
[dclxiii] S Hameroff and R Penrose, Consciousness in the universe: a review of the "Orch OR" theory. (*Physics of Life Reviews* 11, 2014) 39-78
[dclxiv] Zohar 85
[dclxv] M Tsodyks, T Kenet, A Grinvald, and A Arieli, Linking spontaneous activity of single cortical neurons and the underlying functional architecture (*Science* Vol 286 (5446), 1999) 1943-6
Sole and Goodwin 138
[dclxvi] McFadden 301
[dclxvii] Tononi and Edelman 1998
[dclxviii] JM Palva, S Palva, and K Kaila, Phase synchrony among neuronal oscillations in the human cortex (*The Journal of Neuro Science* 25 (15): 2005) 3962-3972;
McFadden and Al-Khalili 263
[dclxix] S Palva and JM Palva, New vistas for alpha-frequency band oscillation (TINS-503, 2007) 1-9
[dclxx] Deacon 2013, 501
[dclxxi] Davia 2006
[dclxxii] G Tononi, Phi: A Voyage From the Brain to the Soul (Pantheon Books: New York, 2012) 209
[dclxxiii] Ogryzko 2008; Kauffman 2008, 214
[dclxxiv] Goswami 97
[dclxxv] Sole and Goodwin 131
[dclxxvi] Davia 2006
[dclxxvii] Peirce 49
[dclxxviii] Bohm 1980, 73
[dclxxix] Bohm 1980, 68
[dclxxx] Peirce 12
[dclxxxi] Bateson and Bateson 90
[dclxxxii] A Cavagna,; A Cimarelli,; I Giardina,; G Parisi, and R Santagati, From empirical data to the inter-individual interactions: unveiling the rules of collective animal behavior (*Mathematical Models and Methods in Applied Sciences* Vol. 20, Suppl., 2010)1491-1510
[dclxxxiii] M Ballerini, N Cabibbo, R Candelier, A Cavagna, E Cisbani, I Giardina, V Lecomte, A Orlandi, G Parisi, A Procaccini, M Viale, and V Zdravkovic, Interaction ruling animal collective behavior depends on topological rather than metric distance: Evidence from a field study (*PNAS*, 105 (4), 2008) 1232-1237

[dclxxxiv] A Cavagna, A Cimarelli, I Giardina, G Parisi, R Santagati, F Stefanin, and M Viale, Scale-free correlations in starling flocks (*PNAS*, 107 (26), 2010) 11865-11870
[dclxxxv] Cavagna et al 2010a

Chapter 7: Universal Origins

[dclxxxvi] Peirce 228
[dclxxxvii] Leibniz 70
[dclxxxviii] Teilhard de Chardin 168
[dclxxxix] Jantsch 8
[dcxc] Leibniz 69
[dcxci] Husserl 145, 158
[dcxcii] Hoffmeyer 214
[dcxciii] Bohm 1980, 156
[dcxciv] B Greene, The Elegant Universe: Superstrings, Hidden Dimensions, and the Quest for the Ultimate Theory (Vintage Books, New York: 1999) 169
[dcxcv] B Greene, The Fabric of the Cosmos: Space, Time, and the Texture of Reality (Vintage Books, New York: 2004) 305-6
[dcxcvi] JR Gott, The Cosmic Web: Mysterious Architecture of the Universe (Princeton University Press, Princeton: 2016) 151
[dcxcvii] Greene 2004, 75
[dcxcviii] A Thomas, Hidden in Plain Sight: the Simple Link Between Relativity and Quantum Mechanics (CreateSpace Independent Publishing Platform, 2012) 131
[dcxcix] Maturana and Varela 95-99
[dcc] Thomas 125
[dcci] Maturana and Varela 75
[dccii] Penrose 220
[dcciii] Husserl 81
[dcciv] Penrose 219, 221
[dccv] Thomas 134-6, 154-5
[dccvi] St. Augustine 263
[dccvii] Bohm 1980, 248
[dccviii] Bohm 30, 237
[dccix] Bohm 257
[dccx] Bohm 1990
[dccxi] Bohm 1990; Jantsch 261
[dccxii] Bohm 1980, 248

[dccxiii] Leibniz 71
[dccxiv] Teilhard de Chardin 43
[dccxv] Bohm 1980, 110, 129, 242
[dccxvi] Bohm 1980, 111
[dccxvii] B Haisch, The God Theory: Universes, Zero-Point Fields, and What's Behind It All (Weiser Books, San Francisco, CA: 2006) 124
[dccxviii] Laszlo 11
[dccxix] Greene 1999, 155
[dccxx] Greene 1999, 236; Bohm 1980, 94
[dccxxi] XG Wen, From new states of matter to a unification of light and electrons (arXiv: cond-mat/0508020v2, 2007)
[dccxxii] XG Wen, Topological order: from long-range entangled quantum matter to unified origin of light and electrons (arXiv:1210.1281v2, 2012)
[dccxxiii] Quoted in Zabriskie, Introduction to Atom and Archetype: the Pauli/Jung Letters 1932-1958 (Meier, CA, Ed. Routledge, London and NY: 2001) xxxv
[dccxxiv] Bohm 1990
[dccxxv] Sheldrake 109
[dccxxvi] Zabriskie xxxv
[dccxxvii] PA LaViolette, Subquantum Kinetics: a Systems Approach to Physics and Cosmology (Starlane Publications, Niskayuna, NY: 1994) 29
[dccxxviii] LaViolette 1994, 25, 31
[dccxxix] LaViolette 1994, 58
PA LaViolette, Genesis of the Cosmos: the Ancient Science of Creation (Bear & Company, Rochester, VT, 2004) 116
[dccxxx] LaViolette 1994, 27, 29
[dccxxxi] Bohm 1980, 243
[dccxxxii] Thomas 59
[dccxxxiii] Bohm 1980, 184
[dccxxxiv] Greene 2004, 120
[dccxxxv] Bohm 1980, 251
[dccxxxvi] Greene 1999, 350
[dccxxxvii] Jantsch 84
[dccxxxviii] Greene 1999, 236
[dccxxxix] Greene 2004, 286
[dccxl] Greene 2004, 272
[dccxli] Bohm 1980, 244
[dccxlii] LaViolette 1994, 57
[dccxliii] LaViolette 2004, 39

[dccxliv] LaViolette 1994, 72, 77, 194
[dccxlv] LaViolette 2004, 57, 93
[dccxlvi] Teilhard de Chardin 49
[dccxlvii] Husserl 82
[dccxlviii] Leibniz 77
[dccxlix] Teilhard de Chardin 57
[dccl] Thomas 188
[dccli] Jantsch 32
[dcclii] Teilhard de Chardin 259
[dccliii] Teilhard 251
[dccliv] James 31
[dcclv] Salthe 2010
[dcclvi] Leibniz 17
[dcclvii] ML Von Franz, The process of individuation (In Jung, CJ (Ed), *Man and His Symbols*; Aldus Books, London: 1964) 226
[dcclviii] Bohm 1980, 67
[dcclix] Dyson 51
[dcclx] Penrose 8
[dcclxi] Bohm 1980, 223
[dcclxii] Thomas 26
[dcclxiii] Thomas 175-181
[dcclxiv] Goswami 215
[dcclxv] Greene 2004, 21
[dcclxvi] Teilhard de Chardin 265
[dcclxvii] Teilhard de Chardin 268

Chapter 8: The Conscious Cornerstone

[dcclxviii] Peirce 228
[dcclxix] Husserl 82
[dcclxx] Boehme 100
[dcclxxi] Boehme 64
[dcclxxii] Julian of Norwich, Revelations of Divine Love (Translated by Wolters, C. Penguin Books: London, 1966) 68
[dcclxxiii] KT Behanan, Yoga: Its Scientific Basis (Macmillan: New York, 1937) 87
[dcclxxiv] Wallace 8-9
[dcclxxv] Swedenborg 23
[dcclxxvi] Behanan 89

[dcclxxvii] Leibniz 78
[dcclxxviii] Paramahansa Yogananda, The Second Coming of Christ: The Resurrection of Christ Within You (Self-Realization Fellowship: USA, 2004) 13, 16
[dcclxxix] Col 1:15; John 1:3
[dcclxxx] Swedenborg 55
[dcclxxxi] Paramahansa Yogananda 13
[dcclxxxii] Swedenborg 30
[dcclxxxiii] SL MacGregor Mathers, translator, Kabbala Denudata: The Kabbala Unveiled (The Theosophical Publishing Company of New York: NY, 1912) 21, 44
[dcclxxxiv] MacGregor Mathers 16, 19
[dcclxxxv] MacGregor Mathers 15, 20
[dcclxxxvi] Boehme 38
[dcclxxxvii] Julian of Norwich 80
[dcclxxxviii] MacGregor Mathers 23-24
[dcclxxxix] Quoted in CJ Jung, The Archetypes and the Collective Unconscious (Bollingen Foundation Inc, New York, 1959) 338
[dccxc] Swedenborg 183
[dccxci] Swedenborg 190, 191
[dccxcii] Peirce 234
[dccxciii] Swedenborg 181
[dccxciv] Swedenborg 167
[dccxcv] LaViolette 2004, 12
[dccxcvi] Meier 126
[dccxcvii] Swedenborg 105
[dccxcviii] Meier 85
[dccxcix] St. Augustine 259
[dccc] St. Augustine 263, 198-199
[dccci] T Keating, The Contemplative Journey (Sounds True: Boulder, CO, 1997)
[dcccii] Rumi. Fountain of Fire (Nader Khalili, translator; Qalbi, recitation. Sura Charlier/ SoulGarden Music, 1999) track 6, poems 15-18
[dccciii] Swedenborg 20, 5
[dccciv] Boehme 60
[dcccv] Boehme 181
[dcccvi] CW Leadbeater, and A Besant, Occult Chemistry: Clairvoyant Observations on the Chemical Element (Zuubooks: San Bernadino, CA, 1919/2011) 11, 23
[dcccvii] Teilhard de Chardin 56

dcccviii TN Hahn, The Heart of Understanding: Commentaries on the Prajnaparamita Heart Sutra (Parallax Press: Berkeley1998) 1
dcccix Hahn 7
dcccx Leadbeater and Besant 23,122, 124
dcccxi M Sjoo, and B Mor, The Great Cosmic Mother: the Ancient Religion of the Goddess Rediscovered (Harper & Row Publishers, San Francisco: 1987) 63
dcccxii Gospel of Philip verse 8
dcccxiii Eliphaz Levi quoted in MacGregor Mathers 1912, p 36
dcccxiv John 1:5
dcccxv *Jung 1959,*178
dcccxvi Husserl 143
dcccxvii Leibniz 9
dcccxviii AC Bhaktivedanta Swami Prabhupada, KRSNA, The Supreme Personality of Godhead, Volume One (The Bhaktidevanta Book Trust: Los Angeles, 1984) 83
dcccxix Boehme 189
dcccxx James 64
dcccxxi Boehme 71
dcccxxii Teilhard de Chardin 262
dcccxxiii Hahn 17
dcccxxiv Boehme 186
dcccxxv Peirce 228
dcccxxvi Fr. T Merton, New Seeds of Contemplation (Abbey of Gethsemani, Inc., 1961) 40
dcccxxvii Quoted in Jakobson 1987, 427
dcccxxviii M LaFargue, The Tao of the Tao Te Ching: A Translation and Commentary (State University of New York Press: Albany, NY, 1992) Chapter 25, p 84
dcccxxix Boehme 64
dcccxxx Swedenborg 2
dcccxxxi Swedenborg 192
dcccxxxii Swedenborg 194
dcccxxxiii Teilhard de Chardin 268
dcccxxxiv Meister Eckhart and Thomas Aquinas, quoted in M Fox, One River, Many Wells: Wisdom Springing from Global Faiths (Jeremy P. Tarcher/ Putnam: New York, 2000) 31, 29
dcccxxxv Leibniz 269
dcccxxxvi Leibniz 36

dcccxxxvii Leibniz 35
dcccxxxviii Saint Augustine, Confessions (RS Pine-Coffin, translator. Penguin Books, London, 1961) 330
dcccxxxix K Wilber, Sex, Ecology, Spirituality: The Spirit of Evolution, Second Edition, revised (Shambala Publications, Inc. Boston, 2000) 28
dcccxl Teilhard de Chardin 71
dcccxli Teilhard de Chardin 170-171
dcccxlii Wilber 514
dcccxliii Thomas Aquinas, quoted in Fox 29
dcccxliv Ortega y Gasset 32
dcccxlv Orpheus quoted in Jung 1959, 326
dcccxlvi Teilhard de Chardin 251
dcccxlvii Teilhard de Chardin 251
dcccxlviii Teilhard de Chardin 259
dcccxlix Teilhard de Chardin 172
dcccl Teilhard de Chardin 302
dcccli Jantsch 300
dccclii Boehme 182
dcccliii W Binner, The Way of Life, According to Laotzu (Perigree Books: New York, 1944), Chapter 25, p 55
dcccliv Van Eenwyck 70
dccclv Merton 61
dccclvi Boehme 193
dccclvii Haisch 29, 31
dccclviii Swedenborg 132

Chapter 9: The Journey of Consciousness

dccclix Paramahansa Yogananda 2004, 13
dccclx Jung in Meier 101
dccclxi Boehme 186
dccclxii Julian of Norwich 81
dccclxiii Penrose 417
dccclxiv Teilhard de Chardin 166
dccclxv Lakoff and Johnson 1999, 11
dccclxvi Swedenborg 176
dccclxvii Meier 166-167
dccclxviii Meier 35
dccclxix Jung 1959, 313

[dccclxx] Jung in Meier 112
[dccclxxi] Jung 1964, 57
[dccclxxii] James 80
[dccclxxiii] Bateson and Bateson 94
[dccclxxiv] Jung 1959, 370
[dccclxxv] Jung 1964, 4
[dccclxxvi] Jung 1959, 281
[dccclxxvii] Jung 1959, 178
[dccclxxviii] Jung in Meier 100
[dccclxxix] Jung 1959, 214
[dccclxxx] Uexkull 161
[dccclxxxi] J Campbell, The Masks of God: Primitive Mythology (Viking Penguin Inc: New York, 1959) 6
[dccclxxxii] Jung in Meier, 70
[dccclxxxiii] Franz in Jung 1964, 220
[dccclxxxiv] Pauli in Meier 194
[dccclxxxv] Jung in Meier 7
[dccclxxxvi] James 9
[dccclxxxvii] Van Eenwyck, 23
[dccclxxxviii] ML von Franz, The Process of Individuation (In Man and His Symbols, CG Jung (Ed). Aldus Books: London, 1964) 209
[dccclxxxix] Jung in Meier, 69
[dcccxc] Van Eenwyck, 28
[dcccxci] Jung in Meier 211; Franz in Jung 1964, 22
[dcccxcii] Juarrero 37; M Conforti, Field, Form, and Fate: Patterns in Mind, Nature & Psyche, Revised Edition (Spring Journal, Inc., New Orleans: 2013) 17, 20
[dcccxciii] Jung 1964, 65
[dcccxciv] Teilhard de Chardin 171
[dcccxcv] Pauli in Meier 35
[dcccxcvi] Romans 7:15
[dcccxcvii] Jung 1959, 20
[dcccxcviii] Bohm 1980, 23
[dcccxcix] Jung 1959, 157
[cm] Jung 1964, 4
[cmi] Jung 1964, 73-83
[cmii] Jung 1964, 90
[cmiii] Van Eenwyck 28
[cmiv] Van Eenwyck 87
[cmv] KL King, The Gospel of Mary of Magdala: Jesus and the First Woman Apostle (Polebridge Press: Santa Rosa, 2003) 144-146

cmvi Quoted in Van Eenwyck 79
cmvii Campbell 1949, 10
cmviii Franz in Jung 1964, 215
cmix MacGregor Mathers 25
cmx LaViolette 2004, 151
cmxi Jung in Meier 69
cmxii Jung 1959, 18; Merton 38
cmxiii Merton 292-293
cmxiv J Campbell, The Hero with a Thousand Faces (Princeton University Press: Princeton, 1949) 41
cmxv Gen 1:2, 6,7
cmxvi Jung 1959, 239
cmxvii Husserl 69
cmxviii Merton 137
cmxix Ulanowicz 1989, referring to Salthe's hierarchy
cmxx Merton, 138
cmxxi Campbell 1959, 179
cmxxii Campbell 1949, 3
cmxxiii Jung 1959, 6
cmxxiv Jung 1964, 36
cmxxv Campbell 1959, 12
cmxxvi Campbell 1959, 109
cmxxvii Jung 1964, 32
cmxxviii Phil 62
cmxxix Fifth century Roman writer Macrobius writes, "Plain and naked exposition of herself is repugnant to nature. She wishes her secrets to be treated by myth. Thus the Mysteries themselves are hidden in the tunnels of figurative expression, so that…only an elite may know about the real secret, through the interpretation furnished by wisdom." Quoted in Smith 2005, p 62, note 88.
cmxxx Campbell 1949, 371
cmxxxi Wilber 275
cmxxxii Hoffmeyer xiii
cmxxxiii J Huizinga, quoted in Campbell 1959, 23
cmxxxiv Campbell 1959, 24
cmxxxv Campbell 1959, 28
cmxxxvi Sheets-Johnstone 153; J Diamond and AB Bond, A Comparative Analysis of Social Play in Birds (*Behavior* 140: 2003) 1091-1115
cmxxxvii Bateson and Bateson 31

[cmxxxviii] M Bekoff, Play signals as punctuation: the structure of social play in canids (*Behavior* **132**, 1995)419-429
[cmxxxix] Merton 259
[cmxl] Teilhard de Chardin 279
[cmxli] Quoted in MC Corballis, Language and episodic sharing (In Menzel, R and Fischer J, Eds. Animal Thinking: Contemporary Issues in Comparative Cognition, The MIT Press, Cambridge: MA, 2011) 181
[cmxlii] Merton 1
[cmxliii] Campbell 1949, 277
[cmxliv] Campbell 1949, 269
[cmxlv] Campbell 1949, 29, 35, 73
[cmxlvi] Campbell 1949, 91, 238
[cmxlvii] Teihard de Chardin 1955, p 262: "Each particular consciousness becoming still more itself and thus more clearly distinct from others the closer it gets to them in Omega."
[cmxlviii] Ortega y Gasset 149
[cmxlix] Jung 1959, 168; Campbell 1959, 71
[cml] B Zabiskie, Jung and Pauli: a Meeting of Rare Minds (Introduction to Meier 2001, 2001) xxxix; Jung 1964, 25
[cmli] John 1:10
[cmlii] Campbell 1949, 92
[cmliii] Campbell 1949, 17, 29
[cmliv] Campbell 1949, 40
[cmlv] Campbell 1949, 217
[cmlvi] King 122
[cmlvii] Campbell 1949, 308
[cmlviii] Ortega y Gasset 46
[cmlix] Jung 1959, 40
[cmlx] Kant quoted in Jung 1959, p 84
[cmlxi] Jung 1959, 93
[cmlxii] Bateson and Bateson 1987, p105: "If you try to model a phenomenon of a higher logical type at too low a level, you will get something that looks like pathology."
[cmlxiii] Pauli in Meier 12
[cmlxiv] Jung 1964, p 8
[cmlxv] Jung 1959, 351
[cmlxvi] Jung 1959, 157
[cmlxvii] Jung 1959, 84

cmlxviii F Turner, Beyond Geography: The Western Spirit Against the Wilderness (Rutgers University Press: New Brunswick, NJ, 1983/ 1994) 218, 256
cmlxix Swedenborg 180
cmlxx Jung 1959, 349
cmlxxi Quoted in LaViolette 2004, 127
cmlxxii K Pomorska, Poetics of Prose (in Roman Jakobson: Verbal Art, Verbal Sign, Verbal Time; K Pomorska and S Rudy, (Eds), University of Minnesotal, 1985)171
cmlxxiii William Irwin Thompson quoted in R Abrahams, Chaos, Gaia, and Eros: a Chaos Pioneer Uncovers the Three Great Streams of History (Epigraph Books: Rhinebeck, NY, 1994) 21: "Myth is the mirror-opposite of history. Myth is not the story of the ego of a civilization but the story of the soul."
cmlxxiv Campbell 1949, 249
cmlxxv Bateson and Bateson 34
cmlxxvi Hahn 2008, 101-2
cmlxxvii Abrahams 21

Chapter 10: The Road to Crucifixion

cmlxxviii Quoted in LaViolette 2004, 116
cmlxxix Jung 1959, 7
cmlxxx Campbell 1959, p 4: "An honest comparison [of sacraments from different religious traditions] immediately reveals that all have been built from one fund of mythological motifs—variously selected, organized, interpreted, and ritualized, according to local need, but revered by every people on earth."
cmlxxxi Campbell 1959, 112
cmlxxxii JL Henderson, Ancient Myths and Modern Man (In CJ Jung, Ed. Man and His Symbols, Aldus Books: London, 1964) 99; Campbell 1959, 143
cmlxxxiii St. Augustine 335
cmlxxxiv Boehme 179
cmlxxxv Franz in Jung 1964, 214
cmlxxxvi Julian of Norwich 144
cmlxxxvii Campbell 1949, 52
cmlxxxviii Behanan 54
cmlxxxix Paramahansa Yogananda, Autobiography of a Yogi (Self-Realization Fellowship: USA, 1946/ 1999) 196-98
cmxc Julian of Norwich 106
cmxci Julian of Norwich 153

[cmxcii] Campbell 1959, 18
[cmxciii] Paramahansa Yogananda 2004, 11-12
[cmxciv] Gen 3:15
[cmxcv] Ortega y Gasset 46
[cmxcvi] Swedenborg 87
[cmxcvii] Leadbeater and Besant 127
[cmxcviii] Wilber 348-49
[cmxcix] Franz in Jung 1964, 219
[m] Jung 1959, 170
[mi] Jung 1959, 168
[mii] Peirce 272
[miii] V Dinets; JC Brueggen; and JD Brueggen, Crocodilians use tools for hunting (*Ethology Ecology & Evolution* 27:1, 2015)74-78
[miv] Merton 225
[mv] Julian of Norwich 193
[mvi] Jung 1959, 35
[mvii] Jung 1959, 388
[mviii] The Gospel of Phillip, verse 82
[mix] Julian of Norwich 183
[mx] Jung 1959, 146
[mxi] Campbell 1949, 41, 43, 147
[mxii] Teilhard de Chardin 268
[mxiii] Campbell 1959, 128
[mxiv] Jung 1959, 109; Julian of Norwich 163
[mxv] Matt 10:34
[mxvi] Julian of Norwich 69
[mxvii] Merton 168
[mxviii] Jung 1959, 92
[mxix] Merton 171
[mxx] Merton 164
[mxxi] Jung 1959, 82
[mxxii] Campbell 1949, 114
[mxxiii] Campbell 1949, 382
[mxxiv] Jung 1964, 247-8
[mxxv] RI Pervo, The Acts of St. John (Poleridge Press, Salem, OR:2016) 95: 6,7
[mxxvi] Merton 163
[mxxvii] Julian of Norwich 100
[mxxviii] TN Hahn, Peaceful Action, Open Heart: Lessons from the Lotus Sutra (Parallax Press: Berkeley, 2008) 255

[mxxix] Gospel of Phillip verse 70
[mxxx] Jung 1959, 241
[mxxxi] Pagels 164-5
[mxxxii] Pagels 165
[mxxxiii] Ireneaus quoted in Pagels 2003, 164
[mxxxiv] The Acts of John 96: 33,34, 41
[mxxxv] 1 Corinthians 15:45-49
[mxxxvi] Franz in Jung 1964, 217
[mxxxvii] Campbell 1949, 288
[mxxxviii] Teilhard de Chardin 169
[mxxxix] In Meier 157
[mxl] Sjoo and Mor 80
[mxli] Jung 1959, 354
[mxlii] Gospel of Phillip verse 43
[mxliii] Gospel of Phillip verse 10
[mxliv] Romans 12:1
[mxlv] Paramahansa Yogananda 2004, 981
[mxlvi] Merton 283-284
[mxlvii] Campbell 1959, 18
[mxlviii] Luke 23:45
[mxlix] Gospel of Phillip verse 69
[ml] Gospel of Phillip verse 105
[mli] Campbell 1949, 260
[mlii] Campbell 1959, 180
[mliii] Merton 1961, 290
[mliv] Gospel of Phillip verse 46
[mlv] Merton 16
[mlvi] Campbell 1949, 8
[mlvii] Sjoo and Mor 80
[mlviii] Henderson in Jung 1964, 135
[mlix] Campbell 1949, 81-2, 319
[mlx] Kabbala Denudata, Chapter IV:6, "Because animals are included under the generic term man."
[mlxi] Pope Francis, Laudato Si': On Care for our Common Home (Encyclical, 2015) 171
[mlxii] Van Eenwyck 113

Chapter 11: Unfolding Evolution

[mlxiii] Halyoak and Thagard 1995, p 55: "The progression from reacting to physical similarity to performing relational mapping is based on a general strategy for deepening the abstraction of thinking, moving beyond direct sensory experience into the realm of concepts."
[mlxiv] Halyoak and Thagard 39, 42
[mlxv] Halyoak and Thagard 63
[mlxvi] Penn et al 2008, 121
[mlxvii] Halyoak and Thagard 54
[mlxviii] Bateson and Bateson p 28
[mlxix] Bateson and Bateson 193
[mlxx] As Ken Wilber (2000, p 275) explains: "At every stage of development...the next higher stage always appears to be a completely 'other world'...*Other worlds* become *this world* with increasing development and evolution."
[mlxxi] Hoffmeyer 2008, p 266: "Our magic and unquestioned belonging in the world was challenged and made fragile by the unavoidable separation of speech and what is spoken about."
[mlxxii] Peirce 165
[mlxxiii] Damasio 1996
[mlxxiv] Lakoff and Johnson 1999, 391-2
[mlxxv] P McReynolds, Motives and metaphors: a study in scientific creativity (In Leary, DE, Ed. *Metaphors in the History of Psychology*, Cambridge University Press: Cambridge, 1990) 141-143
[mlxxvi] Lakoff and Johnson 1999, 391-414
[mlxxvii] Wallace 208
[mlxxviii] Peirce 108
[mlxxix] R Hoffman, EL Cochran, and JM Nead, Cognitive metaphors in experimental psychology (In Leary, DE, Ed. *Metaphors in the History of Psychology*, Cambridge University Press: Cambridge, 1990) 214
[mlxxx] Leary 360
[mlxxxi] TS Kuhn, The Structure of Scientific Revolutions (The University of Chicago Press: Chicago, 1962) 200-201
[mlxxxii] Kuhn 135
[mlxxxiii] Kuhn, p 15: "In the absence of a paradigm or some candidate for a paradigm, all of the facts that could possibly pertain to the development of a given science are likely to seem equally relevant. As a result, early fact-

gathering is a far more nearly random activity than the one that subsequent scientific development makes familiar."
[mlxxxiv] Kuhn 11
[mlxxxv] Kuhn 7
[mlxxxvi] Bohm 11
[mlxxxvii] Kuhn 113
[mlxxxviii] Quoted in Leary 1990, 34
[mlxxxix] Kuhn 170
[mxc] KJ Gergen, Metaphor, metatheory, and the social world (In Leary, DE, Ed. *Metaphors in the History of Psychology*, Cambridge University Press: Cambridge, 1990) 286: "If people, including scientists, are "reality makers" and do not act simply as faithful recorders of—and responders to—the physical world, then the possibility of a completely objective basis for scientific knowledge is seriously jeopardized."
[mxci] Wallace 200
[mxcii] Deut 30:14, 15, 19
[mxciii] Jung 1959, 211
[mxciv] Jung 1959, 163-4
[mxcv] Guardini 85
[mxcvi] Merton 131
[mxcvii] Von Franz in Jung 1964, 182
[mxcviii] Jung 1964, 73
[mxcix] Guardini 90
[mc] Jung 1959, 349
[mci] Abrahams 151
[mcii] Jung 1964, 84
[mciii] Jung 1959, 211
[mciv] R Eisler, The Chalice & the Blade: Our History, Our Future (Harper & Row: San Francisco, 1987) 48
[mcv] Campbell 1949, 287
[mcvi] Jung 1964, 100
[mcvii] Jung 1959, 8
[mcviii] Jung 1959, 38
[mcix] Leary 3
[mcx] Jung 1959, 8
[mcxi] Campbell 1949, 236
[mcxii] Jung 1959, 145
[mcxiii] Jung 1959, 389
[mcxiv] Merton 21

[mcxv] Jung 1959, 104
[mcxvi] John 10:34
[mcxvii] Merton 61
[mcxviii] Merton 290-94
[mcxix] Pagels 167
[mcxx] Hahn 2008, 71
[mcxxi] Merton 292-3
[mcxxii] Julian of Norwich 114
[mcxxiii] Jung 1959, 337
[mcxxiv] Jung 1964, 36, 72
[mcxxv] Merton 71
[mcxxvi] Julian of Norwich 83
[mcxxvii] Julian of Norwich 91
[mcxxviii] Pope Francis 175
[mcxxix] Pope Francis 158
[mcxxx] Guardini 74
[mcxxxi] M Fox, The Coming of the Cosmic Christ: the Healing of Mother Earth and the Birth of a Global Renaissance (HarperSanFrancisco, 1988) 26
[mcxxxii] Rainer Maria Rilke, The Panther, (*New Poems,* JB Leishman, trans, New Directions: New York, 1964) 109
[mcxxxiii] Pope Francis 149
[mcxxxiv] Merton 163
[mcxxxv] Jung 1964, 36; Jung 1959, 174
[mcxxxvi] Jung 1964, 72
[mcxxxvii] Merton 72
[mcxxxviii] Jung 1959, 382
[mcxxxix] Jung 1959, 93,164-5
[mcxl] Teilhard de Chardin 264
[mcxli] Merton 75
[mcxlii] Teilhard de Chardin 267
[mcxliii] Ortega y Gasset 33
[mcxliv] Merton 72-76
[mcxlv] Guardini 160
[mcxlvi] Merton 291
[mcxlvii] A Jaffe, Symbolism in the Visual Arts (In Jung, CJ (Ed), *Man and His Symbols*; Aldus Books, London: 1964) 272
[mcxlviii] 0World Interview—Sacred Activism (7/7/13)
[mcxlix] Luke 23:34
[mcl] Teilhard de Chardin 260

[mcli] Swedenborg 63
[mclii] Swedenborg 63
[mcliii] Maturana and Varela 11
[mcliv] Merton 67
[mclv] Ortega y Gasset 35
[mclvi] Jung 1959, 102-103
[mclvii] Guardini 93
[mclviii] John 3:14
[mclix] S Kleinbaum, How to Live in the Wilderness (*Tikkun 21*(2), 2006) 63
[mclx] Paramahansa Yogananda 2004, 117
[mclxi] Hahn 2008, 142
[mclxii] Campbell 1959, 25
[mclxiii] Merton 171
[mclxiv] *The Tempest* 4.1
[mclxv] John 14:12
[mclxvi] Leibniz 72
[mclxvii] Campbell 1949, 89
[mclxviii] Paramahansa Yogananda, The Bhagavad Gita: Royal Science of God-Realization (Self-Realization Fellowship: USA, 1995/ 2010)
[mclxix] James 11, 14
[mclxx] Peirce 166
[mclxxi] Rumi. Fountain of Fire (Nader Khalili, translator; Qalbi, recitation. Sura Charlier/ SoulGarden Music, 1999) track 6, poems 15-18
[mclxxii] John 1:1
[mclxxiii] Rev 22:13
[mclxxiv] Merton 37
[mclxxv] Gospel of Phillip verse 22
[mclxxvi] Haisch 31
[mclxxvii] Phil 4:7
[mclxxviii] Wallace 302
[mclxxix] Maturana and Varela 234-5
[mclxxx] Acts of John 96: 29, 30

Bibliography

Abel, DL. 2012. Is Life Unique? *Life (Basel).* 2(1): 106-134

Abraham, R. 1994. *Chaos, Gaia, and Eros: A chaos Pioneer Uncovers the Three Great Streams of History.* Epigraph Books, Rhinebeck, NY

Ackermann, M; Stecher, B; Freed, NE; Songhet, P; Hardt, WD; and Doebeli, M. 2008. Self-destructive cooperation mediated by phenotypic noise. *Nature* Vol 454, doi:1038/nature07067

Armus, HL; Montgomery, AR; and Jellison, JL. 2006. Discrimination learning in paramecia (*P. caudatum*). *The Psychological Record* 56, 489-498

Arnqvist, G. 2006. Sensory exploitation and sexual conflict. *Philos Trans R Soc Lond B Biol Sci.* 361(1466):375. Published online 2006 Jan 4. Doi: 10.1098/rstb.2005.1790

Bailey, CH and Chen, M. 1988. Long-term memory in *Aplysia* modulates the total number of varicosities of single identified sensory neurons. *Proc. Natl. Acad. Sci. USA.* Vol.85, pp. 2373-2377

Ballerini, M; Cabibbo, N; Candelier, R; Cavagna, A; Cisbani, E; Giardina, I; Lecomte, V; Orlandi, A; Parisi, G; Procaccini, A; Viale, M; and Zdravkovic, V. 2008. Interaction ruling animal collective behavior depends on topological rather than metric distance: Evidence from a field study. *PNAS* vol. 105 no. 4, pp 1232-1237

Bass, AH; Gilland, EH; and Baker, R. 2008. Evolutionary Origins for Social Vocalization in a Vertebrate Hindbrain-Spinal Compartment. *Science* 321 (5887): 417-421

Bateson, G and Bateson, MC. 1987. *Angels Fear: Toward s an Epistemology of the Sacred.* MacMillan Publishing Co, NY

Behanan, KT. 1937. *Yoga: Its Scientific Basis.* Macmillan, New York.

Bekoff, M. 1995. Play signals as punctuation: the structure of social play in canids. *Behavior* 132 419-429

Bernard, GD and Remington, CL. 1991. Color Vision in *Lycaena* butterflies: Spectral tuning of receptor arrays in relation to behavioral ecology. *Proc. Natl. Acad. Sci. USA* Vol 88, pp 2783-2787

Bickhard, M. 2002. The process dynamics of normative function. *The Monist* 85: (1) 3-28

Binner, W. 1944. The Way of life, According to Laotzu. Perigree Books, New York

Blume-Kohout, R and Zurek, WH. 2005. Quantum Darwinism: Entanglement, Branches, and the Emergent Classicality of Redundantly Stored Quantum Information. arXiv: quant-ph/0505031v2

Boas, H. 2013. Cognitive Construction Grammar. In the Oxford Handbook of Construction Grammar. Oxford University Press

Boehme, J. 2001. *Jacob Boehme.* Ed. Robin Waterfield. North Atlantic Books, Berkeley, CA.

Bohm, D. 1980. *Wholeness and the Implicate Order.* Routledge Classics, London and New York.

Bohm, D. 1990. A new theory of the relationship of mind and matter. *Philosophical Psychology,* Vol. 3, No. 2 271-287

Bonner, JT. 1998. The Origins of Multicellularity. *Integrative Biology.* 27-36

Bradbury, JW and Vehrencamp, SL. 2011. *Principles of Animal Communication, Second Edition.* Sinauer Associates, Inc, MA

Brizhik, L. 2014. Biological role of pulsating magnetic fields: the role of solitons. arXiv:1141.6576v1[physics.bio,ph]

Bshary, R and D'Souza, AD. 2005. Cooperation in communication networks: indirect reciprocity in interactions between cleaner fish and client reef fish. In *Animal Communication Networks,* ed. Peter K. McGregor. 521- 536. Cambridge University Press

Bshary, R and Grutter, AS. 2005. Punishment and partner switching cause cooperative behavior in a cleaning mutualism. *Biol. Lett.*1, 369-399 doi: 10.1098/rsbl.2005.0344

Buhl, J; Sumpter, DJT; Couzin, ID; Hale, JJ, Despland, E; Miller, ER; and Simpson, SJ. 2006. From Disorder to Order in Marching Locusts. SCIENCE vol 312, pp 1402-1406

Bunge, SA; Wendelken, C; Badre, D; and Wagner, AD. 2005. Analogical Reasoning and Prefrontal Cortex: Evidence for Separable Retrieval and Integration Mechanisms. *Cerebral Cortex*; 15:239-249.

Buss, LW. 1983. Evolution, development, and the units of selection. *Proc. Natl. Acad. Sci. USA* Vol. 80, pp1387-1391

Bustamante, C; Liphardt, J, and Ritort, F. 2005. The Nonequilibrium Thermodynamics of small systems. *American Institute of Physics,* S-0031-9228-0507-020-1

Calcott, B and Sternly K, editors. 2011. The Major Transitions in Evolution Revisited. The MIT Press. Cambridge, MA.

Campbell, J. 1949. *The Hero with a Thousand Faces.* Princeton University Press, Princeton

Campbell, J. 1959. *The Masks of God: Primitive Mythology.* Viking Penguin Inc, New York

Campbell, J. 2009. Bayesian Methods and Universal Darwinism. arXiv: 1001.0068

Campbell, J. 2010. Quantum Darwinism as a Darwinian Process. arXiv:1001.0745[physics.gen.ph]

Carey S. 2000. The Origin of Concepts. Commentaries in *Journal of Cognition and Development*, 2000 (1), pp 37-41

Carey, S. 2004. Bootstrapping & the origin of concepts. *Daedalus.* Vol. 133 (1), pp 59-68

Carruthers, P. 2009. How we know our own minds: the relationship between mindreading and metacognition. *Behavioral and Brain Sciences,* 32 (2), 121-138

Catmur, C; Walsh, V; and Heyes, C. 2007. "Sensorimotor Learning Configures the Human Mirror System. *Current Biology* 17, 1527-1531.

Cavagna, A; Cimarelli, A; Giardina, I; Parisi, G; Santagati, R; Stefanin, F; and Viale, M. 2010. Scale-free correlations in starling flocks. *PNAS,* vol. 107, no. 26, pp11865-11870

Cavagna, A; Cimarelli, A; Giardina, I; Parisi, G and Santagati, R. 2010. From empirical data to the inter-individual interactions: unveiling the rules of collective animal behavior. *Mathematical Models and Methods in Applied Sciences* Vol. 20, Suppl. 1491-1510

Clark, KB. 2010. Arrhenius-kinetics evidence for quantum tunneling in microbial "social" decisions. *Communicative & Integrative Biology* 3:6, 540-544

Clark, KB. 2012. Bioreaction quantum computing without quantum diffusion. *NeuroQuantology* Vol 10, Issue 4, 646-654

Chalmers, DJ; French, RM; Hofstander, DR. 1991. High-Level Perception, Representation, and Analogy: A Critique of Artifical

Intelligence Methodology. *CRCC (Center for Research on Concepts and Cognition, Indiana U) Technical Report 49*

Cheng, MF. 2003. Vocal Self-Stimulation: From the Ring Dove Story to Emotion-Based Vocal Communication. *Advances in the Study of Behavior,* Vol 33, 309-355

Chersi, F; Ferrari, PF; and Fogassi, L. 2011. Neuronal Chains for Actions in the Parietal Lobe: A Computational Model. PLoS ONE 6(11): e27652. Doi: 10.1371/ journal. Pone. 0027652

Christensen, WD and Bickhard, MH. 2002. The Process Dynamics of Normative Function. *The Monist.* Vol. 85, Issue 1, pp 3-28

Coelho, CM and Purkis, H. 2009. The Origins of Specific Phobias: Influential Theories and Current Perspectives. Vol 13, No.4, 335-348

Conforti, M. 2013. *Field, Form, and Fate: Patterns in Mind, Nature & Psyche, Revised Edition.* Spring Journal, Inc., New Orleans

Cresswell, W; Quinn, JL; Whittingham, MJ; and Butler, S. 2003. Good foragers can also be good at detecting predators. *Proceedings of The Royal Society of London B* 270: 1069-1076

Croft, DP; James, R; Ward, AJW; Botham, MS; Mawdsley, D; and Krause, J. 2005. Assortative interactions and social networks in fish. *Oecologia,* 143: 211-219

Cronin, TW and Marshall, J. 2001. Parallel Processing and Image Analysis in the Eyes of Mantis Shrimps. *Biol. Bull.* 200: 177-183

Cristol, DA; Reynolds, EB; Lecrec, JE; Donner, AH; Farabaugh, CS; and Ziegenfus, CWS. 2003. Migratory dark-eyed juncos, *Junco hyemalis*, have better spatial memory and denser hippocampal neurons than nonmigratory conspecifics. *Animal Behavior*, 66, 317-328

Dally, JM; Clayton, NS; and Emery, NJ. 2006. The behavior and evolution of cache protection and pilferage. *Animal Behavior,* doi:10.1016/j.anbehav.2005.08.020

Dally, JM; Emery, NJ; and Clayton, NS. 2006. Food-Caching Western Scrub-Jays Keep Track of Who Was Watching When. SCIENCE 16 June 2006 Vol. 312, pp1662-1665

Dall, SRX; Giraldeau, LA; Olsson, O, McNamara, JM; and Stephens, DW. 2005. Information and its use by humans and animals in evolutionary ecology. *Trends in Ecology and Evolution* Vol. 20 No.4, 187-93

Dambrot, SM. 2013. On a clear day: Noise-induced quantum coherence increases photosynthetic yield. Phys.org

Damasio, AR. 1996. The somatic marker hypothesis and the possible functions of the prefrontal cortex. *Phil. Trans.R. Soc. Lond.* B 351, 1413-1420

Davey, GCL and Dixon AL. 1996. The expectancy bias model of selective associations: the relationship of judgements of CS dangerousness, CS-UCS similarity and prior fear to *a priori* and *a posteriori* covariation assessments. *Behav. Res. Ther.* Vol. 34, No.3, pp. 235-252

Davia, CJ. 2006. Life, catalysis, and excitable media: A dynamics systems approach to metabolism and cognition. In J. Tuszynski (Ed.). *The Emerging Physics of Consciousness.* Springer-Verlag, 255-929

Deacon, T. 1997. *The Symbolic Species: The Co-evolution of Language and the Brain.* W.W. Norton & Company, Inc. New York and London

Deacon, T. 2012. *Incomplete Nature: How Mind Emerged From Matter.* W.W. Norton & Company, Inc. New York and London

Demetrius, L and Tuszynski, JA. 2010. Quantum metabolism explains the allometric scaling of metabolic rates. *J.R. Soc. Interface* 7, 507-514

Denker, M; Timme, M; Diesmann, M; Wolf, F; and Geisel, T. 2004. Breaking Synchrony by Heterogeneity in Complex Networks. Physical Review Letters, vol 92, no 7

Dennett, DC. 1991. Real patterns. *The Journal of Philosophy.* Vol. 88, No.1, pp 27-51

De Waal, FBM. 2008. Putting the Altruism Back into Altruism: The Evolution of Empathy. *Annu. Rev. Psychol.* 59:2790-300

Diamond, J and Bond, AB. 2003. A Comparative Analysis of Social Play in Birds. *Behavior* 140, 1091-1115

Dickinson, A and Balleine, BW. 2012. Causal Cognition and Goal-Directed Action. In C. Heyes & L. Huber (Eds.), *Vienna series in theoretical biology, The evolution of cognition*, Cambridge, MA, US: The MIT Press, 185-204

Dinets, V; Brueggen, JC; and JD Brueggen. 2015. Crocodilians use tools for hunting. *Ethology Ecology & Evolution* 27:1, 74-78

Dorogovtsev, SN; Goltsev, AV; and Mendes, JFF. 2007. Critical Phenomena in complex networks. arXiv:0705.0010v6

Dunn, BD; Dalgleish, T; and Lawrence, AD. 2006. The somatic marker hypothesis: a critical evaluation. *Neuroscience and Biobehvioral Reviews* 30: 239-271

Dyson, FJ. 1985. *Infinite in all Directions.* HarperCollins, NY

Eisler, R. 1987. *The Chalice & The Blade: Our History, Our Future.* Harper & Row, San Francisco

Faneslow, MS and Poulos, AM. 2005. The Neuroscience of Mammalian Associative Learning. *Annu. Rev. Psychol.* 56:207-34

Feynman, R. 1985. *QED: The Strange Theory of Light and Matter.* Penguin Books, London

Fisher, RM, Cornwallis, CK, and West SA. 2013. Group Formation, Relatedness, and the Evolution of Multicellularity. *Current Biology 23,* 1120-1125

Flanagan, O. 1992. *Consciousness Reconsidered.* The MIT Press. Cambridge, Mass

Fodor, JA. 1983. *The Modularity of the Mind.* MIT press, Cambridge, MA

Fodor, J. 1994. Concepts: a potboiler. *Cognition* 95-113. 00100-0277/94 Elsevier Science B.V.

Fogassi, L; Ferrari, PF; Gesierich, B; Rozzi, S; Chersi, F; and Rizolatti, G. 2005. Parietal Lobe: From Action Organization to Intention Understanding. *Science.* Vol 308, 662-667

Fox, M. 1988. *The Coming of the Cosmic Christ: The Healing of mother Earth and the Birth of a Global Renaissance.* HarperSanFrancisco, CA

Fox, M. 2000. *One River, Many Wells: Wisdom Springing from Global Faiths.* Jeremy P. Tarcher/ Putnam, New York

Frenken, K; Marengo, L; and Valente, M. 1999. Interdependencies, nearly-decomposability, and adaptation. In: Brenner T. (eds) Computational Techniques for Modelling Learning in Economics. Advances in Computational Ecoomics, vol 11. Springer, Boston, MA

Friston, K. 2009. The free-energy principle: a rough guide to the brain? *Trends in Cognitive Sciences* Vol. 13 No. 7 293-300

Gabriel, PO and Black, JM. 2012. Behavioral Syndromes, Partner Compatibility, and Reproductive Performance in Stellar's Jays. *Ethology* 118, 76-86

Gallistel, CR. 2000. The Replacement of General-Purpose Learning Models with Adaptively Specialized Modules. In M.S. Gazzaniga, ED. *The Cognitive Nuerosciences. 2d ed.* (1179-1191) MIT Press, Cambridge, MA

Gallistel, CR. 2002. The Principle of Adaptive Specialization as it Applies to Learning and Memory. In R.H. Kluwe, G. Luer & F. Rosler (Eds.). *Principles of Human Learning and Memory.* Base: Birkenaeuser, pp 250-280

Gallos, LK; Song, C; and Makse, HA. 2007. A review of fractiliy and self-similarity in complex networks. *Physica A* 386 686-691

Gavrilets, S. 1999. A dynamical theory of speciation of holey adaptive landscapes. Am. Nat. 154: 1-22

Gentner, D. 2006. Psychology of Analogical Reasoning. *Encyclopedia of Cognitive Science,* 106-112.

Godfrey-Smith, P. 1996. *Complexity and the Function of Mind in Nature.* Cambridge University Press, NY

Godfrey-Smith, P. 2011. The Evolution of the Individual. The Lakatos Award Lecture, LSE

Gonzalez-Pastor, JE. 2011. Cannibalism: a social behavior in sporulating *Bacillus subtilis.* FEMS Microbial Rev 35, 415-424

Goswami, A. 1993. *The Self-Aware Universe: how consciousness creates the material world.* Jeremy P. Tarcher/Putnam, Penguin Putnam Inc, NY

Gotthard, K and Nylin, S. 1995. Adaptive plasticity as an adaptation: a selective review of plasticity in animal morphology and life history. OIKOS 74: 3-17

Gottlieb, G. 1991. Experiential Canalization of Behavioral Development: Results. *Developmental Psychology* Vol 21, No.1, 35-39

Gottlieb, G. 2001. The Relevance of Developmental-Psychobiological Metatheory to Developmental neuropsychology. *Developmental Neuropsychology,* 19(1), 1-9

Gottlieb, G. 2002. On the Epigenetic Evolution of Species-Specific Perception: The developmental Manifold Concept. *Cognitive Development* special issue, J. Langer and E. Turiel, 1287-1300

Gott, JR. 2016. *The Cosmic Web: Mysterious Architecture of the Universe.* Princeton University Press, Princeton

Gould, SJ. 1989. *Wonderful Life: The Burgess Shale and the Nature of History.* W. W. Norton & Company, New York

Gould, SJ, & Lewontin, RC. 1979. The Spandrels of San Marco and the Panglossian Paradigm: A Critique of the Adaptationist Programme. *Proceedings of the Royal Society of London. Series B, Biological Sciences, 205*(1161), 581-598.

Greene, B. 1999. *The Elegant Universe: Superstrings, Hidden Dimensions, and the Quest for the Ultimate Theory.* Vintage Books, New York

Greene, B. 2004. *The Fabric of the Cosmos: Space, Time, and the Texture of Reality.* Vintage Books, New York.

Griffin, DR. 1976. *The Question of Animal Awareness.* New York: Rockefeller Press

Griffin, DR and Speck, GB. (2004). "New Evidence of Animal Consciousness." *Animal Cognition* 7:5-18

Groves, PM and Thompson, RF. 1970. Habituation: a dual-process theory. *Psychological Review* 77: 419-450

Gruter, C; Balbuena, MS; and Farina, WM. (2008). "Informational conflicts created by the waggle dance." *Proc. R. Soc. B* (2008) 275, 1321-1327

Guardini, R. 1956/1998. *The End of the Modern World.* ISI Books. Wilmington, Delaware

Guckenheimer, J; Holmes, P. 1983, 2002. *Nonlinear Oscillations, Dynamical Systems, and Bifurcations of Vector Fields.* Springer-Verlag New York, Inc.

Hadden, LE. 1998. Naïve Preference and Filial Imprinting in the Domestic Chick: A Neural Network Model. In: Bower, JM (eds) Computational Neuroscience. Springer, Boston, MA

Hahn, TN. 1998. *The Heart of Understanding: Commentaries on the Prajnaparamita Heart Sutra.* Parallax Press, Berkeley

Hahn, TN. 2008. *Peaceful Action, Open Heart: Lessons from the Lotus Sutra.* Parallax Press, Berkeley.

Haisch, B. 2006. *The God Theory: Universes, Zero-Point Fields, and What's Behind it All.* Weiser Books, San Francisco, CA

Hall, B. 1996. On the specificity of adaptive mutations. *Genetics* 145: 39-44

Hall, G. 1996. Learning about associatively activated stimulus representations: Implications for acquired equivalence and perceptual learning. *Animal Learning & Behavior.* 24 (3), 233-255

Hauser, MD. 2011. *The Evolution of Communication.* The MIT Press. Cambridge, MA.

Hameroff, S and Penrose, R. 2014. Consciousness in the universe: a review of the "Orch OR" theory. *Physics of Life Reviews* 11: 39-78

Harcourt, JL; Biau, S; Johnstone, R; and Manica, A. 2010. Boldness and Information Use in Three-Spine Sticklebacks. *Ethology* 115 1-8

Heinrich, B and Collins, SL. 1983. Caterpillar leaf damage, and the game of hide-and-seek with birds. *Ecology,* 64(3), 592-602

Hemelrijk, CK and Hildenbrandt, H. 2012. Schools of fish and flocks of birds: their shape and internal structure by self-organization. *Interface Focus* 2, 726-737

Hemerijk, CK and Hildebrandt, H. 2008. Self-Organized Shape and Frontal Density of Fish School. *Ethology.* 254-254

Hennessey, TM; Rucker, WB; and McDiarmid, CG. 1979. Classical conditioning in paramecia. *Animal Learning & Behavior*, 7 (4), 417-423

Heyes, CM. 1993. Imitation, culture, and cognition. *Animal Behavior* 46, 999-1010.

Heyes, CM. 1998. Theory of Mind in nonhuman primates. *Behavioral and Brain Sciences* 21, 101-148

Heyes, C. 2003. Four Routes of Cognitive Evolution. *Psychological Review*, Vol. 110, No. 4, 713-727.

Hoffmeyer, J. 2008. *Biosemiotics: An Examination into the Signs of Life and Life Signs*. University of Scranton Press, Scranton and London

Hofstadter, DR. 1979. *Godel, Escher, Bach: an Eternal Golden Braid.* Basic Books, Inc.

Hogan, JA. 1994. Structure and development of behavior systems. *Psychonomic Bulletin& Review.* 1 (4), 439-450

Holland, JH. 2012. *Signals and Boundaries: Building Blocks for Complex Adaptive Systems.* MIT press, Cambridge

Holland, P. C. 1981. Acquisition of representation-mediated conditioned food aversions. *Learning and Motivation*, *12*(1), 1-18. DOI: 10.1016/0023-9690(81)90022-9

Hollis, KL. 1984. The biological function of Pavlovian conditioning: the best defence is a good offence. *Journal of*

Experimantal Psychology: Animal Behavior Processes 10: 413-425

Holmes, WG and Sherman, PW. 1982. The ontogeny of kin recognition in two species of ground squirrels. *American Zoologist* 22: 491-517

Holyoak, KJ and Thagard, P. 1995. *Mental Leaps: Analogy in Creative Thought*. The MIT Press. Cambridge, London

Houde, AE and Hankes, MA. 1997. Evolutionary mismatch of mating preference and male colour patterns in guppies. *Animal Behavior*, 1997, 53, 343-351

Husserl, E. 1999. *The Essential Husserl*. Welton, D, ed. Indiana University Press, Bloomington and Indianapolis.

Huxley, J. 1966. Ritualization of Behavior in Animals and Man. *International Study on the main trends of Research in the Sciences of Man.* United Nations Educational Scientific and Cultural Organization

Ishizaki, A and Fleming GR. 2012. Quantum Coherence in Photosynthetic Light Harvesting. *Annu. Rev. Condes. Matter Phys* 3: 333-61.

Jablonka, E and Lamb, MJ. 1995. *Epigenetic Inheritance and Evolution: The Lamarckian Dimension.* Oxford University Press Inc, New York

Jablonka, E and Lamb, MJ. 2006. The evolution of information in the major transitions. *Journal of Theoretical Biology*, 239, pp 236-246

Jacobs, LF. 1995. The Ecology of Spatial Cognition: Adaptive patterns of space use and hippocampal size in wild rodents. In E. Alleva et al (eds), *Behavioral Brain Research in Naturalistic and Semi-Naturalistic Settings.* 301-322. Kluwer Academic Publishers, Netherlands

Jakobson, R. 1985. *Verbal Art, Verbal Sign, Verbal Time.* University of Montana

Jakobson, R. 1987. *Language in Literature.* The Belknap Press of Harvard University Press. Cambridge, MA; London

James, W. 1978. *The Writings of William James: A comprehensive Edition.* McDermott, JJ; Ed. The University of Chicago Press, Chicago

Jantsch, E. 1980. *The Self-Organizing Universe: Scientific and Human Implications of the Emerging Paradigm of Evolution.* Pergamon Press

Jerison, HJ and Barlow, HB. 1985. Animal Intelligence as Encephalization. *Philosophical Transactions of the Royal Society of London. Series B, Biological Science,* Vol. 308, No 1135, Animal Intelligence, pp 21-35.

Jibu, M; Hagan, S; Hameroff, SR; Pribram, KH; and Yasue, K. 1994. Quantum optical coherence in cytoskeletal microtubules: implications for brain function. *BioSystems* 32:195-209

Jona-Lasinio, G. 2010. Analogies in Theoretical Physics. *Progress of Theoretical Physics Supplement* No. 184, 1-15

Jones, CM; Braithewaite, VA; and Healy, SD. 2003. The Evolution of Sex Differences in Spatial Ability. *Behavioral Neuroscience*, Vol 117, No. 3, 403-411

Jorgensen, SE and Ulanowicz, R. 2009. Network calculations and ascendency based on eco-exergy. *Ecological Modeling* 220: 1893-1896

Juarrero, A. 1999. *Dynamics in Action: Intentional Behavior as a Complex System.* Massachusetts Institute of Technology, Cambridge, MA

Julian of Norwich. 1966. *Revelations of Divine Love.* Translated by Wolters, C. Penguin Books, London

Jung, CJ. 1959. *The Archetypes and the Collective Unconscious.* Bollingen Foundation Inc, New York

Jung, CJ (Ed). 1964. *Man and His Symbols.* Aldus Books, London

Kant, E. 1781/ 2003. *The Critique of Pure Reason.* Translated by JMD Meiklejohn, Project Gutenburg E-book # 4280, 4

Kauffman, S. 1995. *At Home in the Universe: The Search for the Laws of Self-Organization and Complexity.* Oxford University Press, New York

Kauffman, SA. 2008. *Reinventing the Sacred: A New View of Science, Reason, and Religion.* Basic Books, New York

King, KL. 2003. *The Gospel of Mary of Magdala: Jesus and the First Woman Apostle.* Polebridge Press, Santa Rosa

Kleinlogel, S and White AG. 2008. The Secret World of Shrimps: PolarizationVision at Its Best. PLoS One 3(5): e2190. Doi: 10.1371/journal.pone.0002190

Kleisner, K. 2008. The Semantic Morphology of Adolf Portman: A Starting Point for the Biosemiotics of Organic Form? *Biosemiotics* 1: 207-219

Kosztolanyi, A; Cuthill, IC; and Szekely, T. 2008. Negotiation between parents over care: reversible compensation during incubation. *Behavioral Ecology* doi: 10.1093/beheco/arn140

Kuhn, TS. 1962. *The Structure of Scientific Revolutions*. The University of Chicago Press, Chicago

Krsiak, M. 2011. Tinbergen's four questions, biologically useless behavior and humanistic ethology. Act Nerv Super Redviva 2011; 53(3): 103-106

Lacy, S; Stilla, R; and Sathian, K. 2012. Metaphorically Feeling: Comprehending Textual Metaphors Activated Somatosensory Complex. *Brain & Language* March; 120(3): 416-421.

Lakoff, G and Johnson, M. 1980. *Metaphors We Live By*. The University of Chicago Press, Chicago

Lakoff, G and Johnson, M. 1999. *Philosophy in the Flesh: The Embodied Mind and its Challenge to Western Thought*. Basic Books, New York

LaMar, MD and Smith, GD. 2010. The effect of node-degree correlation on synchronization of identical pulse-coupled oscillators. *Phys. Rev. E* 81, 046206

Laszlo, E. 2007. *The Self-Actualizing Cosmos: The Akasha Revolution in Science and Human Consciousness.* Inner Traditions, Rochester, VT

LaViolette, PA. 1994. *Subquantum Kinetics: A Systems Approach to Physics and Cosmology.* Starlane Publications, Niskayuna, NY

LaViolette, PA. 2004. *Genesis of the Cosmos: The Ancient Science of Creation.* Bear & Company, Rochester, VT

Lazareve, OF; Freiburger, KL; and Wasserman EA. 2004. Pigeons concurrently categorize photographs at both basic and superordinate levels. *Psychonomic Bulletin & Review* 11 (6), 1111-1117

Leadbeater, CW and Besant, A. 1919/2011. *Occult Chemistry: Clairvoyant Observations on the Chemical Elements.* Zuubooks, San Bernadino, CA

Leary, DE, Ed. 1990. *Metaphors in the History of Psychology.* Cambridge University Press, Cambridge

Leaver, LA; Hopewell, L; Caldwell, C; and Mallarky, L. 2007. Audience effects on food caching in grey squirrels (*Sciurus carolensis*): evidence for pilferage avoidance strategies. *Anim Cogn* 10:23-27 DOI 10.1007/s10071-006-0026-7

LaFargue, M. 1992. *The Tao of the Tao Te Ching: A Translation and Commentary.* State University of New York Press: Albany, NY

Lehmann, L; Keller, L; West, S; and Roze, D. 2007. Group selection and kin selection: two concepts but one process. *PNAS*, vol. 104, no. 16, pp 6736-6739

Leibniz, GW. 1991. *Discourse on Metaphysics and Other Essays*. Translated by Garber, D and Ariew, R. Hackett Publishing Compamy. Indianapolis & Cambridge

Levine, SC and Carey, S. 1982. Up Front: the acquisition of a concept and a word. *J. Child Lang*. 9, 645-657

Lickliter, R; Lewkowicz, DJ; and Columbus, RF. 1996. Intersensory Experience and Early Perceptual Development: The Role of Spatial Contiguity in Bobwhite Chicks' Responsiveness to Multimodal Maternal Cues. *Developmental Psychobiology* 29 (5): 403-416

Lipton, BH and Bhaerrman, S. 2009. *Spontaneous Evolution: Our Positive Future (and a way to get there from here)*. Hay House, Inc, US

Luisi, PL. 2006. *The Emergence of Life: From Chemical Origins to Synthetic Biology*. Cambridge University Press, Cambridge

LoLordo, VM; Jacobs, WJ; and Foree, DD. 1982. Failure to block control by a relevant stimulus. *Animal Learning& Behavior*. 10 (2), 183-193

Lovelock, J. 1988. *The Ages of Gaia: A Biography of Our Living Earth*. WW Norton & Company, NY, London

MacGregor Mathers, SL, translator. 1912. *Kabbala Denudata: The Kabbala Unveiled.* The Theosophical Publishing Company of New York, NY

Magnhagen, C and Bunnefeld, N. 2009. Express your personality or go along with the group: what determines the behavior of shoaling perch? *Proc. R. Soc. B* 276, 3369-3375

Marino, L. 2004. Cetacean Brain Evolution: Multiplication Generates Complexity. *International Journal of Comparative Psychology,* 17, 1-16

Mateo, JM. 2010. Self-referent phenotype matching and long-term maintenance of kin recognition. *Animal Behavior*, doi 10.1016

Maturana, HR and Varela, FJ. 1987. *The Tree of Knowledge: The Biological Roots of Human Understanding Revised Edition.* Shambala Publications, Inc. Boston, Mass

McDonald, MJ; Gehrig, SM; Maintjes, PL; Zhang, XX; and Rainey, PB. 2009. Adaptive Divergence in Experimental Populations of *Pseudomonas.* IV. Genetic constraints Guide Evolutionary Trajectories in a Parallele Adaptive Radiation. Genetics 183: 1041-1053

McFadden, J and Al-Khalili, J. 2014. *Life on the Edge: The Coming of Age of Quantum Biology.* Crown Publishers, NY

McFadden, J. 2000. *Quantum Evolution: How Physics' Weirdest Theory Explains Life's Biggest Mystery.* W.W. Norton &Company Inc., New York.

Meier, CA, Ed. 2001. *Atom and Archetype: The Pauli/ Jung Letters 1932-1958.* Routledge, London and NY.

Merali, Z. 2007. The universe is a string-net liquid. *New scientist.* Updated by Xiao-Gang Wen

Merleau-Ponty, M. 1964. Eye and Mind. In. Northwest University Press

Menzel, R and Fischer J, Eds. 2011. *Animal Thinking: Contemporary Issues in Comparative Cognition.* The MIT Press, Cambridge, MA

Merton, T. 1961. *New Seeds of Contemplation.* Abbey of Gethsemani, Inc.

Michelena, P; Jeanson, R; Deneubourg, JL; and Sibbald, AM. 2009. Personality and collective decision-making in foraging herbivores. *Proc. R. Soc. B.* doi: 10.1098/rspb.2009.1926

Michelena, P; Sibbald, AM; Erhard, HW; and McLeod, JE. 2008. Effects of group size and personality on social foraging: the distribution of sheep across patches. *Behavioral Ecology* doi: 10.1093/beheco/arn126 145-152

Michod, RE and Herron, MD. 2006. Cooperation and conflict during evolutionary transitions in individuality. *Journal of Evolutionary Biology* 19: 1406-1409

Michod, RE and Roze, D. 2001. Cooperation and conflict in the evolution of multicellularity. *Heredity* 86 1-7

Mitra, AN and Mitra-Delmotte, G. 2011. Consciousness: A direct link with life's origin? arXiv: 1102.3158 [physics.hist-ph]

Nagel, T. 2012. *Mind & Cosmos: Why the Materialist Neo-Darwinian Conception of Nature is Almost Certainly False.* Oxford University Press

Nanay, B. 2005. Can Cumulative Selection Explain Adaptation? *Philosophy of Science*, 72 pp. 1099-1112

Newman, MEJ. 2002. Mixing patterns in networks. arXiv: cond-mat/0209450[cond-mat.stat-mech]

Newman, MEJ and Watts, DJ. 1999. Scaling and percolation in the small-world network model. arXiv: cond-mat/9904419 [cond-mat.stat-mech]

Nihat, A; Flack, J; and Krakauer, DC. 2007. Robustness and complexity co-constructed in multimodal signaling networks. *Phil. Trans. R. Soc. B* 362, 441-447

Nihat, A and Krakauer, DC. 2007. Geometric robustness theory and biological networks. *Theory Biosci* 125 (2): 93-121

Nowak, MA and May RM. 1992. Evolutionary games and spatial chaos. Nature Vol. 359 826-829

Nowak, MA. 2000. Evolutionary Biology of Language. *Phil. Trans. R. Soc. Lond.* B 355, 1615-1622

Nowak, MA; Tarnita, CE; and Antal, T. 2010. Evolutionary dynamics in structured populations. *Phi. Trans. R. soc. B* 365, 19-30

Odling-Smee, FJ; Laland, KN; and Feldman, MW. 2003. *Niche Construction: the Neglected Process in Evolution.* Princeton University Press, Princeton and Oxford

Ogryzko, V. 2008. On two quantum approaches to adaptive mutations in bacteria. arXiv: 0805. 4316

Oosten, JE; Magnhagen, C; and Hemelrijk, CK. 2010. Boldness by habituation and social interactions: a model. *Behav Ecol Sociobiol* 64: 793-802

O'Regan, JK. 1992. Solving the "Real" Mysteries of Visual Perception: The World as an Outside Memory. *Canadian Journal of Psychology* 46: 3, 461-488

Ortega y Gasset, J. 1961. *Meditations on Quixote.* WW Norton and Company, Inc, NY

Pagels, E. 2003. *Beyond Belief: The Secret Gospel of Thomas.* Random House, Inc., New York.

Palagi, E. 2007. Sharing the motivation to play: the use of signals in adult bonobos. *Animal Behavior* 75, 887-896

Palva, JM; Palva, S; and Kaila K. 2005. Phase Synchrony Among Neuronal Oscillations in the Human Cortex. *The Journal of Neuro Science* 25 (15): 3962-3972

Palva S and Palva JM. 2007. New vistas for alpha-frequency band oscillation. TINS-503, 1-9

Panitchayangkoon, G; Hayes, D; Fransted, KA; Caram, JR; Harel E; Wen, J; Blankenship, RE; and Engel, GS. 2010. Long-lived quantum coherence in photosynthetic complexes at physiological temperature. *Proc Natl Acad Sci* (107) 29: 12766-12770

Papini, MR. 2002. Theoretical Notes: Pattern and Process in the Evolution of Learning. Vol. 109, No. 1, 186-201

Paramahansa Yogananda. 1995/ 2010. *The Bhagavad Gita: Royal Science of God-Realization.* Self-Realization Fellowship, USA

Paramahansa Yogananda. 2004. *The Second Coming of Christ: The Resurrection of Christ Within You.* Self-Realization Fellowship, USA

Pattee, HH. 1969. How Does a Molecule Become a Message? *Developmental Biology Supplement 3*, 1-16.

Pattee, HH. 1982. Cell Psychology: An Evolutionary Approach to the Symbol-Matter Problem. *Cognition and Brain Theory,* 5(4), 325-341

Pattee, HH. 1995. Evolving Self-Reference: Matter, Symbols, and Semantic Closure. *Communication and Cognition—Artificial Intelligence,* vol 12, nos 1-2, pp 9-28

Pattee, HH. 1996. The Physics of Symbols and the Evolution of Semiotic Controls. *Workshop on Control Mechanisms for Complex Systems: Issues of Measurement and Semantic Analysis*

Pattee, HH. 2000. Causation, Control, and the Evolution of Complexity. In *Downward Causation: Minds, Bodies, Matter.*

Edited by Peter B. Anderson, Claus Emmeche, Niels Ole Finnemann, Peder V. Christiansen, Aarhus University Press, 2000, pp 63-77

Pattee, HH. 2001. The Physics of Symbols: Bridging the Epistemic Cut. *Biosystems.* Vol. 60, pp 5-21

Pattee, HH. 2005. The Physics and Metaphysics of Biosemiotics. *Journal of Biosemiotics* 1, 281-301.

Pattee, HH. 2006. The Physics of Autonomous Biological Information. *Biological Theory*, Summer 2006, Vol 1, No 3:224-226.

Pattee, H and Kull, K. 2009. A biosemiotics conversation: Between physics and semiotics. *Sign System Studies* 37 (1-2) 311-331 (Tartu University Press, Estonia).

Peirce, CS. 1991. *Pierce on Signs: Writings on Semiotic by Charles Sanders Pierce*. Hoopes, J; Ed. The University of North Carolina Press, Chapel Hill and London

Pervo, RI. 2016. *The Acts of John.* Polebridge Press, Salem, OR

Penn, DC; Holyoak, KJ; and Povinelli, DJ. 2008. Darwin's mistake: Explaining the discontinuity between human and nonhuman minds. *Behavioral and Brain Sciences* 31, 109-178

Penrose, R. 1994. *Shadows of the Mind: A Search for the Missing Science of Consciousness.* Oxford University Press

Penrose, R. 1998. Quantum computation, entanglement, and state reduction. *Phil. Trans. R. Soc. Lond.* A 356, 1927-1939

Pigliucci, M and Kaplan, J. 2006. *Making Sense of Evolution: The Conceptual Foundations of Evolutionary Biology*. The University of Chicago Press, Chicago

Pigliucci, M. 2007. Do we need an extended evolutionary synthesis?. *Evolution 61-12:* 2743-2749

Pollack, GH. 2013. *The Fourth Phase of Water: Beyond Solid Liquid Vapor.* Ebner & Sons Publishers, Seattle, WA

Polley, DB; Hillock, AR; Spankovich, C; Popescu, MV; Royal, DW; and Wallace, MT. 2008. Development and Plasticity of Intra- and Intersensory Information Processing. J Am Acad Audiol 19:780-798. Doi: 10.3766/jaa.19.10.6

Pope Francis. 2015. *Laudato Si': On Care for our Common Home* [Encyclical].

Pradeu, T. 2010. The Organism in Developmental Systems Theory. *Biological Theory* 5(3): 216-222

Pravosudov, VV and Clayton, NS. 2002. A Test of the Adaptive Specialization Hypothesis: Population Differences in Caching, Memory, and the hippocampus in Black-Capped Chickadees (*Poecile atricapilla*). *Behavioral Neuroscience,* Vol. 116, No. 4, 515-522

Proctor, H. 1992. Sensory exploitation and the evolution of male mating behavior: a cladistics test using water mites (Acari: Parasitengona). *Animal Behavior*: Vol 44, Issue 4, pp 745-752

Queller, DC. 2000. Relatedness and the fraternal major transitions. *Phil. Trans. R. Soc. Lond.* B 355, 1647-1655

Rendall, L; Boyd, R; Cownden, D; Enquist, M; Eriksson, K; Feldman, MW; Fogarty, L; Ghirlanda, S; Lilicrap,T; and Laland, KN. 2010. Why Copy Others? Insights from the Social Learning Strategies Tournament. SCIENCE (328) 5975, 208-213

Rendall, D; Owren, MJ; and Ryan, MJ. 2009. What do animal signals mean? *Animal Behavior,* 78, pp 233-240

Rescorla, RA. 1988. Pavlovian Conditioning: It's Not What You Think It Is. *American Psychologist,* 43 (3), 151-160

Rilke, RM. The Panther, in *New Poems.* JB Leishman, trans. New Directions: New York, 109

Rodd, FH; Hughes, KA; Grether, GF, and Baril, CT. 2002. A possible non-sexual origin of mate preference: are male guppies mimicking fruit? *Proc. R. Soc. Lond.* B,269, 475-481

Rossi, AF; Pessoa, L; Desimone, R; and Ungerleider, LG. 2009. The prefrontal cortex and the executive control of attention. *Exp Brain Res.* 192 (3) 489-497

Ruelle, D. 1989. *Chaotic Evolution and Strange Attractors.* Cambridge University Press, Cambridge.

Ruggeri, M; Major, JC Jr; McKeown, C; Knighton, RW; Puliafito, CA; and Jiao, S. 2010. Retinal structure of birds of prey revealed by ultra-high resolution spectral-domain optical coherence tomography. *Invest Opthalmol Vis Sci,* 51 (11) 5789-5795

Rumi. 1999. *Fountain of Fire*. Nader Khalili, translator; Qalbi, recitation. Sura Charlier/ SoulGarden Music

Ryan, MJ. 1987. Sexual Selection, Receiver Biases, and the Evolution of Sex Differences. *Science*, Vol. 281, pp 1999-2003

Rozenfeld, HD and Makse, HA. 2009. Fractility and the percolation transition in complex networks. *Chemical Engineering Science* 64, 4572-4575

Rozenfeld, HD; Song, C; and Makse, HA. (2010). "Small World-Fractal Transition in Complex Networks: Renormalization Group Approach.) *Phys. Rev. Lett.* 104, 025701. arXiv: 0909.4832 [cond-mat.ds-nn]

Saint Augustine. 1961. *Confessions*. RS Pine-Coffin, translator. Penguin Books, London

Salari, V; Tuszynski, J; Rahnama, R; and Bernroider, G. 2010. Plausibility of quantum coherent states in biological systems. arXiv: 1012.3879

Salthe, SN. 2008. The System of Interpretance, Naturalizing Meaning as Finality. *Biosemiotics* Vol. 1, Issue 3, 285-294

Salthe, SN. 2010. Development (and Evolution) of the Universe. *Found Sci* 15: 357-367

Scheiner, SM and Lyman, RF. 1989. The genetics of phenotypic plasticity: I. Heritability. *J. Evol. Biol.* 2:95-107

Scheiner, SM. 1993. Genetics and Evolutionary Plasticity. *Annu. Rev. Ecol. Syst.* 24: 35-68

Schumm, BA. 2004. *Deep Down Things: The Breathtaking Beauty of Particle Physics.* The Johns Hopkins University Press. Baltimore, MD

Scott, JS; Kawahara, AY; Skevington, JH; Yen, SH; Sami, A; Smith, M; and Yack JE. 2010. The evolutionary origins of ritualized acoustic signals in caterpillars. *Nature Communications.* Doi: 10.1038/ncomms1002

Servedio, MR; Saether, SA; Saetre, GP. 2009. Reinforcement and Learning. *Evol Ecol* 23:109-123. Doi 10.1007/s10682-007-9188-2

Shannon, CE. 1948. A Mathematical Theory of Communication. *The Bell System Technical Journal,* Vol. 27, pp 379-423, 623-656

Shea, N. 2011. Developmental Systems Theory Formulated as a Claim about Inherited Representations. *Philos Sci.* 78(1):60-82 doi: 10.1086/658110

Sheets-Johnstone, M. 1990. *The Roots of Thinking.* Temple University Press, Philadelphia

Sheldrake, R. 1988/2012. *The Presence of the Past: The Memory of Nature.* Park street Press, Rochester, VT

Sherry, DF and Schacter, DL. 1987. The Evolution of Multiple Memory Systems. *Psychological Review* Vol. 94, No. 4, 438-454

Shettleworth, SJ. 2010. *Cognition, Evolution, and Behavior, Second Edition.* Oxford University Press, New York

Simon, HA. 1962. The Architecture of Complexity. *Proceedings of the American Philosophical Society,* Vol. 106, No. 6, pp. 467-482

Sjoo, M and Mor, B. 1987. *The Great Cosmic Mother: the Ancient Religion of the Goddess Rediscovered.* Harper & Row Publishers, San Francisco

Smith, AP (Translated and Annotated). 2005. *The Gospel of Phillip: Annotated & Explained.* SkyLight Paths Publishing, Woodstock, VT

Smith, LD. 1982. Purpose and Cognition: The Limits of Neorealist Influence on Tolman's Psychology. *Behaviorism.* Vol. 10, No. 2, pp 151-163

Smit, S; Yarus, M; and Knight, R. 2006. Natural selection is not required to explain universal compositional patterns in RNA secondary structure categories. *RNA,* Vol. 12, No. 1, 1-14

Soler, M and Soler, JJ. 1999. Innate versus learned recognition of conspecifics in greater spotted cuckoos *Clamator glandarius.* Anim Cogn 2: 97-102

Sole, R and Goodwin, B. 2000. *Signs of Life: How Complexity Pervades Biology.* Basic Books, New York.

Song, C; Havlin, S; and Makse, HA. 2006. Origins of fractality in the growth of complex networks. *Nature Physics* 2, pp 275-281

Spellman, BA and Holyoak, KJ. 1996. Pragmatics in Analogical Mapping. *Cognitive Psychology* 31, 307-346

Squire, LR. 2004. Memory systems of the brain: A brief history and current perspective. *Neurobiology of Learning and Memory* 82 (2004) 171-177

Steele, EJ, Lindley, RA, and Blanden RV. 1998. *Lamarck's signature: How Retrogenes are Changing Darwin's Natural Selection Paradigm.* Perseus Books. Reading, MA

Stevens, JR; Wood, JN; and Hauser, MD. 2007. When Quantity trumps number: Discrimination Experiments in Cotton-Top Tamarins (*Saguinus Oedipus*) and Common Marmosets (*Callithrix jacchus*). *Animal Cognition* 10, 429-437

Swedenborg, E. 2010. *Divine Love and Wisdom.* George F. Dole, *translator.* Swedenborg Foundation, West Chester, PA

Szathmary, E. 2005. In search of the simplest cell. *Nature* vol 433 469-470

Takeuchi, N and Hogeweg, P. 2009. Multilevel Selection in Models of Prebiotic Evolution II: A Direct Comparison of Compartmentalization and Spatial Self-Organization. PLOS Computational Biology. Doi: 10.1371/ journal.pcbi.1000542

Talbot, M. 1991. *The Holographic Universe.* HarperCollins Publishers, New York

Taranenko, VB; Slekys, G; and Weiss, CO. 2002. Spatial resonance solitons. arXiv:nlin/0210073v1 [nlin.PS]

Teilhard de Chardin, P. 1955/ 2008. *The Phenomenon of Man.* Harper Perennial Modern Thought, New York

Thomas, A. 2012. *Hidden in Plain Sight: The Simple Link Between Relativity and Quantum Mechanics.* CreateSpace Independent Publishing Platform

Thomas, L. 1979. The Lives of a Cell: Notes of a Biology Watcher. Bantam, New York

Thompson, E and Varela, FJ. 2001. Radical embodiment: neural dynamics and consciousness. *Trends in Cognitive Sciences* Vol. 5. No. 10 418-426

Thorne, KS. 1994. *Black Holes & Time Warps: Einstein's Outrageous Legacy.* WW Norton & Company, New York

Tonjes, R; Masuda, N; and Kori, H. 2010. Synchronization transition of identical phase oscillators in a directed small-world network. CHAOS 20, 003108, pp 1-12

Tononi, G and Edelman, GM. 1998. Consciousness and Complexity. *Science.* Vol 282, 1846-1850

Tononi, G. 2012. *Phi: A Journey from the Brain to the Soul.* Pantheon Books, New York

Treer, D; Bocxlaer, IV; Matthijs, S; Du Four, D; Janssenswillen, S; Willaert, B; and Bossuyt, F. 2013. Love Is Blind: Indiscriminate Female Mating Responses to Male Courtship Pheromones in Newts (Salamandridae). PLOS ONE Volume 8, Issue 2, e56538

Triesman, AM and Gelade G. 1980. A Feature-Integration Theory of Attention. *Cognitive Psychology* 12, 97-136

Treisman, A. 1998. Feature Binding, attention, and object perception. *Phil. Trans. R. Lond.* B, 353, 1295-1306

Tsodyks, M; Kenet, T; Grinvald, A, and Arieli, A. 1999. Linking Spontaneous Activity of Single Cortical Neurons and the Underlying Functional Architecture. *Science* Vol 286 (5446), 1943-6

Turner, F. 1983/ 1994. *Beyond Geography: The Western Spirit Against the Wilderness."* Rutgers University Press, New Brunswick, NJ

Ulanowicz, RE; Goerner, SJ; Liettaer, B; and Gomez, R. 2009. Quantifying sustainability: Resilience, efficiency and the return of information theory. *Ecological Complexity* 6: 27-36

Ulanowicz, RE. 1989. A Phenomenology of Evolving Networks. *Systems Research* Vol. 6, No. 3, pp 209-217

Ulanowicz, RE and Wolff, WF. 1991. Ecosystem Flow Networks: Loaded Dice? *Mathematical Biosciences* 103:45-68

Van Eenwyck, JR. 1997. *Archetypes & Strange Attractors: The Chaotic World of Symbols.* Inner City Books, Toronto.

Vasconcellos, Ar; Vannucchi, FS; Mascarenhas, S; and Luzzi, R. 2012. Frohlich condensate: Emergence of synergetic dissipative structures in information processing biological and condensed matter systems. *Information* (3): 601-620

Villarreal, LP and Witzany, G. 2013. Rethinking the quasispecies theory: From fittest type to cooperative consortia. *World J Biol Chem* 4(4):79-90

Villarreal, LP and Witzany, G. 2013. The DNA Habitat and its RNA Inhabitants: At the Dawn of RNA Sociology. *Genomics Insights* 6:1-12

Villareal, LP. 2012. Viruses and Host Evolution: Virus-Mediated Self Identity. In *Self and Nonself,* ed Carlos Lopez-Larrea. Landes Bioscience and Springer, 185-217

Von Uexkull, J. 1934/2010. *A Foray Into the Worlds of Animals And Humans* with *A Theory of Meaning.* O'Neil, JD, trans University of Minnesota Press

Wallace, WA. 1996. *The Modeling of Nature: Philosophy of Science and Philosophy in Synthesis.* The Catholic University of America Press, Washington, DC

Wallman, J. 1979. A Minimal Visual Restriction: Preventing Chicks from Seeing their Feet Affects Later Responses to Mealworms. *Developmental Psychobiology,* 12(4): 391-397

Washburn, SL. 1978. The Evolution of Man. *Scientific American.* Vol 239 (3), pp

Watanabe, A and Aoki, K. 1998. The Role of Auditory Feedback in the Maintenance of Song in Adult Male Bengalese Finches *Lonchura striata* var *domestica.* Zoological Science: 15: 837-841

Waters, CM and Bassler, BL. 2005. Quorum Sensing: Cell-to-Cell Communication in Bacteria. *Annu. Rev. Cell Dev. Biol.* 21:319-46

Weaver, W. 1953. Recent Contributions to the Mathematical Theory of Communication. *ETC: A Review of General Semantics.* Vol. 10, No. 4, pp 261-281

Wen, XG. 2007. From new states of matter to a unification of light and electrons. arXiv: cond-mat/0508020v2

Wen, XG. 2012. Topological order: from long-range entangled quantum matter to unified origin of light and electrons. arXiv:1210.1281v2

Wilber, K. 2000. *Sex, Ecology, Spirituality: The Spirit of Evolution, Second Edition, revised.* Shambala Publications, Inc. Boston

Wilczek, F. 1998. Why are there Analogies between Condensed Matter and Particle Theory? *Physics Today,* 11-13

Williams, GP. 1997. *Chaos Theory Tamed.* Joseph Henry Press, Washington, DC

Witzany, G. 2011. The agents of natural genome editing. *Journal of Molecular Cell Biology,* 3, 181-189

Woese, CR. 2002. On the evolution of cells. PNAS vol. 99 no. 13, 8742-8747

Wolfram, S. 1994. *Cellular Automata and Complexity: Collected Papers.* Westview Press, IL

Wolf, M; Sander van Doorn, G; and Weissing, FJ. 2008. Evolutionary emergence of responsive and unresponsive personalities. PNAS, vol. 105, no. 41 15825-15830

Wolters, C (Translator). 1966. *Julian of Norwich: Revelations of Divine Love.* Penguin Books Ltd, London.

Yang, LC; Li, MH; Wilson, FA; Hu, XT; Ma, YY. 2013. Prefrontal attention and multiple reference frames during working memory in primates. *Chin Sci Bull*, 58: 449-455, doi: 10.1007/s11143-012-5462-y

Zahar, E. 2001. *Poincare's Philosophy: From Conventions to Phenomenology.* Open Court Publishing, Chicago and La Salle

Zahavi, D. 2003. Husserl's Phenomenology. Stanford University Press.

Zentall, TR; Wasserman, EA; Lazareva, OF; Thompson RKR; and Rattermann, MJ. 2008. Concept Learning in Animals. *Comparative Cognition & Behavior Reviews.* Vol. 3, 13-45

Zohar, D. 1990. *The Quantum Self: Human Nature and Consciousness Defined by the New Physics.* HarperCollins, NY

Zurek, WH. 2009. Quantum Darwninsm. arXiv: 0903.5082v1

Zyga, L. 2009. Study rules out Frohlich condensates in quantum consciousness model. PhysOrg.com

Made in the USA
Monee, IL
15 July 2020